MW01277201

Feathered Entanglements

Edited by Scott E. Simon
and Frédéric Laugrand

Feathered Entanglements

Human-Bird Relations in
the Anthropocene

UBCPress · Vancouver

Printed in Canada on FSC-certified ancient-forest-free paper (100% post-consumer recycled) that is processed chlorine- and acid-free.

UBC Press is a Benetech Global Certified Accessible™ publisher. The epub version of this book meets stringent accessibility standards, ensuring it is available to people with diverse needs.

Library and Archives Canada Cataloguing in Publication

Title: Feathered entanglements : human-bird relations in the anthropocene / edited by Scott E. Simon and Frédéric Laugrand.

Names: Simon, Scott, editor | Laugrand, Frédéric, editor

Description: Includes bibliographical references and index.

Identifiers: Canadiana (print) 20240422813 | Canadiana (ebook) 2024042283X | ISBN 9780774870009 (hardcover) | ISBN 9780774870023 (PDF) | ISBN 9780774870030 (EPUB)

Subjects: LCSH: Birds – Effect of human beings on – Indo-Pacific Region. | LCSH: Birds – Indo-Pacific Region. | LCSH: Human-animal relationships – Indo-Pacific Region.

Classification: LCC QL676.57.I67 F43 2024 | DDC 598.0959—dc23

UBC Press gratefully acknowledges the financial support for our publishing program of the Government of Canada and the British Columbia Arts Council.

UBC Press is situated on the traditional, ancestral, and unceded territory of the xʷməθkʷəy̓əm (Musqueam) people. This land has always been a place of learning for the xʷməθkʷəy̓əm, who have passed on their culture, history, and traditions for millennia, from one generation to the next.

UBC Press
The University of British Columbia
www.ubcpress.ca

Contents

Figures and Tables

Figures

Tables

Preface and Acknowledgments

THIS BOOK EMERGED from conversations between Scott E. Simon, Frédéric Laugrand, and various contributors that occurred as a result of our SSHRC-funded research project "Austronesian Worlds: Human-Animal Entanglements in the Pacific Anthropocene," a multi-country interdisciplinary endeavour. One poetic way of understanding how our various paths merged is the Chinese concept of *yuanfen*, often translated as "destiny" but which definitely has connotations of entanglement. The basic notion is that, even across differing lifetimes, relations of cause and effect bring people together who ultimately belong together, for reasons that we can only guess at. Perhaps the authors of this book were, in past lifetimes, members of a flock of migratory birds making their way south from Siberia, along the archipelago of islands that form Japan, Taiwan, and the Philippines, to winter near the equator. Less poetically, we are all united by our curiosity about both the worlds of non-human animals, especially the birds that fly over us every day, and the cultural diversity of the human groups who relate to those birds in different ways. For example, the Black-faced Spoonbills that breed off the coast of Korea in the summer and spend their winters from Taiwan to Vietnam encounter diverse human cultures during their voyages and, we can hypothesize, thus get entangled in those societies in very different ways. We all share an interest in the human societies of the Indo-Pacific, a broad arc of humanity from the Indian to the Pacific Ocean. We have finally brought together the various members of our flock to write this book.

The initial intellectual work of this volume was shaped by the "Austronesian Worlds" project, with Scott E. Simon as principal investigator and Frédéric Laugrand as co-investigator, but also by collaborators Atsushi Nobayashi at the National Museum of Ethnology (Minpaku) in Osaka and Yi-tze Lee at National Dong Hwa University in Taiwan. Scott Simon taught at National Dong Hwa University before returning to Canada in 2001, and he visits there every year, thus exploring the avian worlds of eastern Taiwan and exchanging observations and ideas over the years with Lee. He first met Nobayashi at the International Union of Anthropological and Ethnological Sciences in Chiba, Japan, in 2014. Their collaboration, and this project, began when Nobayashi invited Simon to spend a year at Minpaku, where he could extend his research, previously focused on Indigenous peoples in Taiwan, to Japan.

For his part, Frédéric Laugrand had started collecting oral testimonies from four Indigenous groups in the Philippines – the Alangan Mangyan, the Ibaloy, the Blaan, and the Ayta. With his son Antoine Laugrand, they set up various events (such as interviews and workshops) on the topic of knowledge transfer. This work resulted in the publication of twenty-two books in a series entitled Verbatim. Laugrand completed these activities while he was moving from Laval University in Canada to the University of Louvain (UCLouvain) in Belgium. He began to collaborate with Scott Simon, and the idea of a book on birds in South Asia gradually emerged as a joint project. Their collaboration now continues through "Biodiversity, Local Knowledge and Zoonoses in Austronesia: Ethnography of Bats and Related Interspecific Communities," a project funded by a grant from the European Research Council. The other contributors to this book were encountered – due to yuanfen – at both anthropological and ornithological conferences in Canada, the United States, Europe, and Japan.

We formally shared the results of our various research projects at two conferences. The first was "Ecological and Cultural Approaches to Taiwan and Neighbouring Islands," an international symposium held at Minpaku in July 2018. The second was a panel entitled "Human-Bird Entanglements in the Pacific Anthropocene" at the joint meeting of the American Anthropological Association and Canadian Anthropology Society in Vancouver in November 2019. These panels brought together Simon's collaborators in Asia with Laugrand's collaborators from Europe but also permitted them to reach out to other scholars working on human-bird relations across the Indo-Pacific. We have all endeavoured in our own ways to understand the entwined worlds of both humans and birds. Nonetheless, only Andrew Gosler, who is an anthropologist and an ornithologist, manages to incorporate both disciplines in his work. By working together, at conferences and then virtually during the COVID-19 pandemic, we were able to produce this book. Finally, with its publication, the threads of our shared destinies have come together.

This book was made possible by funding from the Social Sciences and Humanities Research Council of Canada for the project "Austronesian Worlds: Human-Animal Entanglements in the Pacific Anthropocene." Funding for certain publication costs was provided by the University of Ottawa Collabzium "Always Be Closing" Grant.

Feathered Entanglements

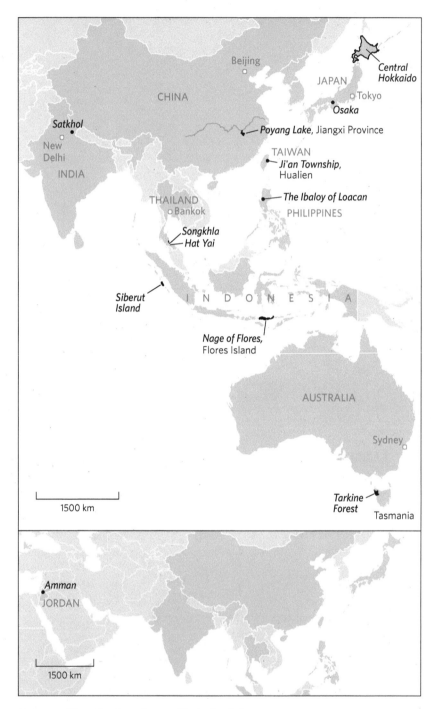

Beijing

CHINA

JAPAN

Central
Hokkaido

Tokyo

Osaka

Satkhol

New
Delhi

INDIA

Poyang Lake, Jiangxi Province

TAIWAN
Ji'an Township,
Hualien

THAILAND
Bankok

The Ibaloy of Loacan
PHILIPPINES

Songkhla
Hat Yai

Siberut
Island

I N D O N E S I A

Nage of Flores,
Flores Island

AUSTRALIA

Sydney

1500 km

Tarkine
Forest

Tasmania

Amman
JORDAN

1500 km

Figure 0.1 Map of regions discussed in the book. | Cartography by Eric Leinberger

Introduction
Humans and Birds in the Anthropocene
Frédéric Laugrand and Scott E. Simon

I would have liked, once in my life, to communicate fully with an animal. This goal is unattainable. It is almost painful for me to know that I will never be able to know the matter and structure from which the universe was composed. That would have meant: being able to speak with a bird. But this is a frontier that we cannot pass. Crossing this border would be a great pleasure for me. If you could find me a good fairy to grant me a wish, this is what I would choose.

– Claude Lévi-Strauss, "Entre Marx et Rousseau"[1]

HUMANS HAVE ALWAYS been fascinated by birds, like Claude Lévi-Strauss, who dreamt of being able to communicate with them. They are omnipresent in mythology, particularly in the Americas. Before resigning himself to the impossibility of his dream, Lévi-Strauss wrote this conclusion to *The Naked Man* ([1971] 1981, 690–91):

When, in *La Pensée sauvage* [*The Savage Mind,* 270–72], I interpreted the names we give to birds as indicating that their various species, taken as a whole, appear to us as a sort of metaphorical counterpart of human society, I did not realize that an objective relation of the same type exists between their brains and ours. It would seem that mammals and birds, in evolving from their common source, the reptiles, followed two divergent paths as regards the development of the brain and arrived at complementary solutions.[2]

Here, the anthropologist evokes the neurological structure of human and avian brains. His prudence contrasts with the audacity of some ornithologists, such as Noah Strycker (2018), who seems to think that he can understand, as the title of his book *Ce que les oiseaux disent des hommes* suggests, "what birds say about humans." Humans and birds have often collaborated, such as in hunting and aerial surveillance with falcons and eagles, during war, in games with pigeons, breeding fowl and other birds, sharing daily life with parrots and parakeets, and feeding corpses to vultures in traditional Tibetan funerals (Satheesan 1998; MaMing et al. 2016). Humans control these various situations, but the birds are sentient beings who are receptive to them. For their own reasons, birds fly across the entire geography of human societies, in ways paralleled by no other living beings. It is thus fascinating to think about the social and cultural entanglements that occur among the intersections of human and bird migration and movement.

At this hour of the sixth extinction, many humans feel the tragedy of having failed to communicate with birds, even as our knowledge of them has developed throughout history. Shepard Krech (2005, 718) notes that about 150 avian species have vanished since 1800; as of 2005, another 1,100 were threatened (see also Krech 2009). David Steadman (1997, 51, 77) observes that such a loss must be "recognized as one of the major environmental consequences of the human colonization of Oceania," where birds are not only eaten but also kept as pets. Today, philosopher Thom van Dooren (2014, 2019) links the destiny of humans with that of birds. Contemporary anthropology is now taking stock of these intersubjective relations with avian fauna and the ties that link humans to them as our fellow living beings.

The History of Ornithology and the Study of Birds

Birds have long fascinated humans. Ancient petroglyphs and cave paintings attest to this interest. Recently, from a study of over a thousand eggshells, anthropologists and archaeologists discovered that the cassowary may have been one of the first birds raised by humans, in Papua New Guinea over eighteen thousand years ago. Hunters may have collected the unhatched eggs of this dangerous but flightless bird and raised the chicks to adulthood (Douglass et al. 2021). Falconry also emerged early among hunting peoples in the Orient, appearing later in the West. Without a doubt, these practices were among the first configurations in which humans and birds worked together in a kind of entanglement of their relations. As Shuhei Uda discusses in Chapter 1, fishing with cormorants has a long pedigree in China. Pierre Gourou (1972, 125) describes it as well, noting that fishers sometimes share a bit of opium with the birds to ensure their loyalty. In short, the knowledge and interest that humans have for birds are very much a part of ancient traditions. In the West, the Etruscans created a divinatory science that the Romans elaborated by inventing the term "auspice" (from *auspicum*, omen, and from *specere*, to look). The Greeks christened it ornithomancy: the study of bird flight as an omen of the future. Aristotle and Pliny devoted lengthy reflections to birds, trying to identify and categorize them.

Bird symbolism took off in Abrahamic traditions and Romanesque art (Davy 1992). In a text written by Persian poet Farîd-Ud-Dîn 'Attar (1996), thirty birds under the leadership of the hoopoe, the wisest bird from the Qur'an, search for the Simorgh, who will be their king. Christian imagery often refers to birds, such as the dove and the swallow, or the Caladrius, a legendary snow-white bird said to live in the king's house and able to take sickness into itself and fly away, thereby healing the person. In the Middle Ages, the most interesting works on birds are illustrated falconry manuals imported from Mesopotamia and other regions of the Orient. European scholars spread this knowledge. A good example is *De arte venandi cum avibus (On the Art of Hunting with Birds)* by Emperor Frederick II (1194–1250). At that time, chicken raising also flourished across Europe. In the same manner, the chicken probably came to Europe from Asia around the seventh century, as China and Papua New Guinea practised poultry raising.

With all these developments, knowledge about birds increased. In the sixteenth century, several studies, such as those by Guillaume Rondelet, William Turner, and Conrad Gessner, described multiple species of birds. In his 1555 book *Histoire de la nature des oyseaux (The History of the Nature of Birds)*, Pierre Belon was one of the first to propose a classification system for all birds. Ulisse Aldrovandi published the first naturalist encyclopedia, of which three volumes were dedicated to birds, divided into land birds, water birds, and songbirds. Centred on the description and classification of these animals, these works multiplied in the seventeenth and eighteenth centuries, with a considerable number of achievements that cannot all be cited here. Scholars soon studied exotic species and the anatomy and morphology of birds. At the time, taxidermy techniques were deficient, preventing the constitution of sustainable collections. In the mid-seventeenth century, the first great ornithologists emerged, mostly in England. Francis Willughby and John Ray's work *Ornithologiae libri tres* (1676) was the first scientific treatise on birds in Europe. In 1758, Carl Linnaeus refined this knowledge by proposing that birds be classified according to the morphology of their beaks and feet. Again, this knowledge developed mostly in England, with *Historiae avium* by Jacob Theodor Klein (1750) and contributions by Thomas Pennant, John William Lewin, and John Latham. In France, George-Louis Leclerc de Buffon, Louis Jean Pierre Vieillot, and several others proposed various classifications. In 1817, Georges Cuvier identified six orders: birds of prey, passerines, climbers, Gallinaceans, waders, and web-footed birds. Henri Marie Ducrotay de Blainville added three new groups: parrots, pigeons, and ostriches.

The first ornithology associations were founded in the mid-eighteenth century in the Anglo-Saxon world. Humans who were passionate about birds sought to understand their distribution and phylogeny – and soon, the evolution of their species. Paradoxically, many species disappeared during this period because of hunting and the overexploitation of resources. Some scientists, such as Richard Bowdler Sharpe, proposed new classifications, whereas others, thanks to the banding technique developed in 1899, researched migratory birds. In the twentieth century, James Lee Peters created his classification system, which evolved with the addition of DNA technology, especially in terms of phylogeny.

This short overview of ornithology is incomplete, as each country has its own naturalists and bird specialists. As just one example, France boasts Léon Olphe-Galliard, René d'Abadie, Jacques Delemain, Noël Mayaud, Jean Dorst, and Laurent Yeatman. We cannot forget the work of ethologists such as Konrad Lorenz or Amotz Zahavi, who, among others, allowed us to understand bird behaviours. John James Audubon, Robert Bateman, and others created art that revealed a strong intimacy between humans and birds. Philipp Franz Siebold worked with Japanese naturalists and illustrators during the isolationist Tokugawa period and amassed a large number of bird specimens and knowledge of birds that he published in volume 4 of *Fauna Japonica* in 1839 (Siebold et. al. [1839] 1975). The worldwide existence of various ornithological associations made it possible to collect considerable data about birds and gave rise to further entanglements.

In Europe, birds have long featured in folklore and literature. For example, in his monumental book on French folklore, Paul Sébillot ([1904–07] 2018) devoted two chapters to wild and domestic birds. In this book, he provides a substantial number of proverbs, sayings, stories, beliefs, and practices. In

1914, as the Great War broke out, famous French sociologist Robert Hertz ([1928] 1970) collected numerous testimonies, proverbs, and reproductions of bird cries from French peasants who were gathered in the trenches. Again, this wealth of information shows the richness of European traditions regarding birdlore. Nonetheless, a great deal of knowledge has disappeared, even as many regions are reviving some old practices.

An example is Hunt the Wren, an old custom that still lingers across Europe, particularly in Ireland and on the Isle of Man, though many of its features have changed. It is unclear whether the hunt retains its sacrificial dimension, but it has lost much of its meaning. In the old variants of the ritual, the captured wren – then considered the king of birds – was set on a ceremonial pole. On the Isle of Man, the ritual now takes place on December 26 (St. Stephen's Day) and consists of singing and dancing a traditional song around a decorated pole. In the eighteenth century, the bird was hunted and killed after prayers on December 24 or 25, then laid on a bier "with the utmost Solemnity" and buried in the churchyard (Miller 2018, ii). In Normandy, the wren was so important that it was named Bertault's God or the Ox of God. In the south of France, wrens were hunted in December; once a bird was captured, it was suspended inside two wooden hoops and shown to the public in the street, with people declaring, "Herewith the king of the birds" (Baudry 1861, 383). In Carcassonne, the wren was attached to a stick decorated with a garland made of leaves of olive, oak, and mistletoe. An English proverb keeps track of all these beliefs, showing that they also existed in England: "A robin and a wren are God Almighty's cock and hen" (Baudry 1861, 383). Edward A. Armstrong (1955, 1958) studied the historical and symbolic meaning of the wren and later traced the rich magico-religious beliefs concerning birds in a distant past, connecting biology, folklore, and paleontology.

Much of this knowledge has been lost or become the prerogative of passionate amateurs or specialists. Professional ornithologists are far less numerous than the amateurs and birders. Among the countless publications in ornithology, the *Handbook of the Birds of the World* is the newest encyclopedia covering the near totality of the living species of birds.[3] The inventory remains incomplete because new species are still being discovered to this day.

In the non-Western tradition, knowledge about birds followed a different path, as non-Western peoples have shown little interest in phylogeny and classification projects. They prefer understanding the interactions of birds with other animals and their environs, concentrating on their nutritive and

healing properties, using their knowledge as needed for hunting or for understanding future events. Birds also feature in myths, rituals, hunting activities,
and divinatory systems. As anthropologists have shown, they often indicate
rhythms or deliver messages. For example, Lévi-Strauss ([1991] 1995, 88)
observes,

> All of North American mythology associates Owls with periodic phenom-
> ena: the alternance of day and night, on the one hand, the measured
> duration of human life on the other. There is a close relationship between
> these phenomena since souls, reincarnated into nocturnal birds of prey,
> inhabit the world of the dead during the day and come back at night to
> the world of the living.

The first anthropologists explored birds in detail and tried to understand
local classifications (Bulmer 1967, 1989; Berlin 1990; Healey 1993), hoping
to find links between Indigenous taxonomies and those of Western societies
(Boster, Berlin, and O'Neill 1986; Van den Broek 1988; Hamil, Sidky, and
Subedi 2002). In a rich vein of scholarship, many documented and discussed
bird names and categories (such as Hohn 1973; Kane 2015). The work of
Nicole Revel (1975) with the Palawan and of Gregory Forth (1996, 2004,
2006b, 2009, 2010) with the Nagé of Indonesia are particularly rigorous
and exemplary in this respect. The authors were able, among other things,
to show that Indigenous names for birds are often onomatopoetic, mimicking the calls, cries, and songs that birds produce.

The works mentioned above demonstrate the extent of the problem of
categorization and symbolic knowledge. A good example of this conundrum is the cassowary, which the Karam of Papua New Guinea do not
define as a bird (Bulmer 1967). By contrast, they see bats and fruit bats as
birds or as beings connected to them (Laugrand and Laugrand 2023;
Laugrand, Laugrand, and Simon 2023). Since the 1970s, anthropologists
have widened their interests and studied the place and role of birds in shamanism, divinatory systems, popular imagery, and symbolic universes
(Metcalf 1976; Dove 1993, 1996; Cauquelin 2006; Forth 2006a, 2007, 2016,
2017; Le Roux and Sellato 2006; Hutter 2008; Régnier 2008; Low 2011;
Simon 2015, 2018; Laugrand, Laugrand, and Tremblay 2019).

Of course, what sets birds apart for the most part is their ability to fly.
Rita H. Régnier (2007, 7) reminds us that nearly everywhere on the planet,
bird flight "has for a long-time suggested ideas of freedom, independence,

weightlessness, and speed. This results in the role of a messenger attributed to the bird as intermediary between the world below and the world above, which is the residence of the divine." Most parts of the bird possess meaning, especially the wings. For example, virtually all dragons and many other mythical beings are winged, recalling the link between reptiles and things that fly, first by revealing their common origins and secondly by enabling movement and migration (for an example opposing the python to the swan, see Geinaert-Martin 1992). Bird flight has given rise to various studies, especially in societies that observe birds to make predictions and that associate them with their ancestors or deceased souls. Feathers and feet are also meaningful, as in Papua New Guinea, where much of human dance reproduces or adapts bird behaviours.

The example of the Inuit and the raven is interesting since shamans are inspired by the bird's behaviour to define that of two officiants who reunite human couples in winter ceremonies, thus renewing society. The beak of the raven inspired many societies on the northwest coast of Canada, especially the Haida and the Kwakwaka'wakw (Mauzé 2011), who use it in their masks for ceremonial transformation. The literature on ravens is also considerable, as the bird is widely distributed in the West and the Arctic (Charrin 1983; Oosten and Laugrand 2006; Fienup-Riordan 2017; Krupnik 2017; Kondo 2021) and largely in all paleo-Asiatic societies (Meletinsky 1973, 1980; Matthieu 1984). Raven is a creator and a trickster. Many Indigenous societies credit it with creating the sexes, introducing light, and bringing technology or tattooing; elsewhere, however, it is an unreliable being, a scavenger who consumes carrion and is associated with death. Ambivalent by nature, it resembles what makes society possible and what must remain outside it (Oosten and Laugrand 2006). In China and Japan, the raven is associated with the sun; and Japan has the Yatagarasu, a giant three-legged crow deity (Erkes 1925). Like other corvids, ravens can use tools, a technological skill that has particularly intrigued Westerners.

In anthropology, we are still learning about birdsongs. The pioneering scholarship of Steven Feld (2012) is now followed by many other ethnomusicologists. As in Christian traditions, where birdsongs correspond to human voices, those voices evoke the presence of the ancestors. Various ethnic groups in Siberia and Central Asia also pay great attention to the melody of bird sounds, considering some birds as messengers and connecting them to human souls. As in the old European tradition about the wren mentioned above, most of these groups believe that birds have a king or a lord. This figure is often represented by an eagle who also played – with the raven – a key role in local shamanic traditions. Many birds are also eaten. Yet, the practices involving birds vary, as illustrated by the Buryats of southeastern Siberia. One group of Siberian Buryats, the Khongodors, considered the swan as their totem animal and thus did not hunt it. They performed a ritual of sprinkling flying swans with milk. But some Buryat groups killed the bird for ceremonial purposes (Badmaev 2020, 108–9).

Studies on birds have become even more important with the ontological turn (Feld 2012; Kockelman 2016) and the ecological turn (Smith 2010; Jerolmack 2013; Jernigan 2016; Franco and Minggu 2019). Researchers have expanded their spectrum, analyzing the birds and their human observers (Keck 2015, 2020; Manceron 2015, 2022; Simon, Chapter 5, this volume), bringing out a multitude of relations. Recently, two other currents have emerged. The first is related to the idea of developing a science for everyone and highlighting ethno-ornithologies rather than confining the approach to a singular ornithological knowledge, which permits the recognition of multiple ways of doing science and studying birds, including folklore (Tidemann and Gosler 2010; Gosler 2017; Despret 2019). Sonia Tidemann and Andrew Gosler (2010) crossed an important threshold by publishing the first volume that places not only professional ornithologists and anthropologists on the same level, but also Indigenous elders and others from various backgrounds. The second current is an interest in interspecies or multispecies relations (Rose 2009; Kohn 2013; van Dooren 2014; Chandler 2017; Rudge 2019), emphasizing the inextricable links between humans and birds, especially in regard to their destiny. These works vary by author, but they show an overarching shift: birds are no longer examined solely in terms of their representations and images, but from the perspective of relations and perceptions that consider their sensitivity, "wisdom" (Birkhead 2008, 2012, 2014), "intelligence" (Emery 2017), and "genius" (Ackerman 2016), as they are capable of deceiving, simulating, and manipulating.

This approach has proved enticing for ornithologists and philosophers, though it seems classic for many anthropologists who have long understood it in multiple field sites and in various contexts, thanks to revelations provided by the people with whom they work. For example, the Inuit monitor birdsong to predict the weather and seasonal change, observe ravens and loons to spot game in the distance, or take inspiration from the leadership techniques of geese. Inuit hunters all simultaneously admire, respect, hunt, and consume these animals, with which communication is possible in certain contexts, notably shamanic ones. By contrast, the Sediq and Truku of Taiwan no longer use the *sisil (Alcippe morrisonia)*, a songbird that is endemic to their country, to identify the presence of prey. Instead, the bird now symbolizes both the systems of ornithomancy that they once practised and the affirmation of identity in the Taiwanese indigenist movements. The sisil is still thought to bring good fortune, and it recalls the importance of the forest for the Indigenous peoples of Taiwan (Simon 2018, 152). Another key Taiwanese bird is the *qadis*, or Mountain Hawk-eagle *(Nisaetus nipalensis)*, which is central to the Paiwan people (Huang et al. 2021). Its feathers are used on a headdress symbolizing the status of a tribal chief, a hero, or a high-ranked person. In the Philippines, eagles and hornbills are also seen as important birds (Gonzalez 2011).

More generally, close relations between humans and birds appear most particularly at the level of myth, to the extent that numerous tales use birds to think through big problems that can affect humans, such as impossible marriages, incest, violence, and cannibalism. However, though humans have greatly progressed in their knowledge of birds and bird communication, species barriers, hierarchies, and other important distinctions remain. In overcoming these obstacles, totemic systems have gone the farthest in integrating certain things that fly, such as bats, into the very heart of human kinship systems (see Rose 2009). Animist systems also establish equivalencies between humans and things that fly, but though these considerations are grounded in respect for non-human species, they in no way exclude hunting them. We should recall that, as Lévi-Strauss demonstrates, Western societies themselves conceive of the world of birds as a metaphorical human society or a parallel world. This appears not only in European mythology and folklore but also in the naming of birds, which tends to be metonymic rather than metaphorical. As Lévi-Strauss (1966, 205) explains, "When species of birds are christened 'Pierrot,' 'Margot' or 'Jacquot,' these names are drawn from a portion which is the preserve of human beings and the relation of bird names to human names is thus that of part to whole." Significantly, the situation is the opposite for dogs, who do not form a distinct society but are part of human society and are usually given metaphorical names (such as Medor or Fido). Thus, Lévi-Strauss (1966, 205) formulates a general rule: "When the relation between (human and animal) species is socially conceived as metaphorical, the relation between the respective systems of naming takes on a metonymic character; and when the relation between species is conceived as metonymic, the system of naming assumes a metaphorical character."

The Bird: A Constant Model for Humans?

Ever since the first works on birds done on the basis of the major texts of Abrahamic religions and Eastern philosophies, historians have described birds as models who can deliver invaluable secrets, such as those regarding detachment, liberty, love, and beauty (Davy 1992). Marie-Madeleine Davy (1992, 9), a well-known historian of flying things, emphasizes several symbolic aspects of birds:

> Nothing is more fascinating than the symbol of the bird for the reason of the diversity of domains in which he participates: flight, song, feathers and colours. An intermediary between the low and the high, the earth and the sky, not only does the bird offer a teaching, but he also possesses the rare privilege of constituting a model for humans.

In many civilizations, birds are often presented as heroes, major actors as the protagonists in numerous legends. The opinions of specialists of Asia and Europe about heroic birds converge, with birds appearing at once as heroes and divinities, to repeat the title of the rich collective work – *Oiseaux: Héros et devins* – edited by Régnier (2007). Another edited volume about Southeast Asian birds emphasizes their aesthetic and symbolic aspects, describing them as "divine messengers" (Le Roux and Sellato 2006).

In 2021, at the hour of the Anthropocene and the sixth extinction, the universe of birds has certainly not revealed all its secrets. The idea of the bird as a model and source of inspiration nonetheless remains intact. In a book dedicated to how to think about the living, the ethologist and philosopher Vinciane Despret (2021, 89) writes,

> In the case of birds, the investigation resulted in a conclusion in the form of a happy ending: the constitution of a territory permits each person to co-inhabit with the others, parade around, and show his life force. If a bird whistles at the top of its lungs, it is for attracting attention as much as for materializing a boundary. Like words for humans, song permits the bird to weave a web around himself, to create relations, to exchange. Little by little, the original melody changes, fusions with that of the neighbours, and becomes a choir. It has even been found that birds pass the baton and organize "speaking tours."

Neither aggression nor dominance are the basis of bird social life, a true model for inhabiting territory and playing with borders. The implication is crystal clear: humans, who have never stopped squabbling over territory, should learn a lesson from birds. Raphaël Mathevet and Arnaud Béchet (2020) provide a relevant example with their case study about the Camargue flamingo.

These lessons are not just about territory or governance. Biomimetism shows that humans have been inspired by birds for a long time. A nice example is the clockwork duck invented in the eighteenth century by Jacques de Vaucanson. A complex automaton made of hundreds of tiny parts, it ate and drank, appearing to digest the food and defecate like a real duck. De Vaucanson hoped to reconstitute the gastro-intestinal tract of the bird to determine whether it used a mechanical or a chemical process to digest food. But that is not all. Ducks inspired the Wright brothers and the engineer Alberto Santos-Dumont in their creation of airplanes with small wings in the front. Small wings near the front – or even the whole plane or missile using such a configuration – are still called "canards," because they look like ducks with their necks stretched out. Aviators copied the curved wings of storks, as was the case of Otto and Gustav Lilienthal, who wrote the German original of *Birdflight as the Basis of Aviation* in 1889 (Lilienthal and Lilienthal 1911). Nowadays, the anti-glare vision of the Black Stork *(Ciconia nigra),* a fishing bird, is of interest to automotive engineers. As for the condor, it stimulated Paul MacCready in the construction of his *Gossamer Condor,* an airplane powered by pedals. Even in modern jets, winglets – tiny wings situated on the tips of the larger wings – reduce turbulence. Humans have also learned from the owl, making trains and planes less noisy by adapting the principle of the jagged feathers that give it silent flight. Many other human technologies came from observing birds, such as the aerodynamic biomechanics of the penguin, the form of the kingfisher used for high-speed trains such as the *shinkansen,* and the woodpecker's beak for ice axes and jackhammers.

Birds are regularly honoured in many fields. The present text is no exception, as its objective is to explore the complex entanglements between humans and birds. The images, representations, and the place of birds vary considerably not only from group to group and culture to culture, but also according to the birds referenced. Thus, many hunting societies are fascinated by migratory birds. The Cree and the Inuit, for example, wait impatiently for the arrival of the flocks that herald the spring and good meat but also their own summer dispersion, a more individual life after the restricted social life of Arctic winters. Birds announce the months and the seasons, as Robert Hertz ([1928] 1970) demonstrated by gathering information from the many French peasants who knew their songs and habits. Studying oral literature and the works of many writers, Daniel Fabre (1986) shows that birds have long been associated with expressions of love, but this use has begun to decline with modernity.

We also underline that though humans typically admire the beauty, qualities, and skills of birds, they can also be a source of dread, as illustrated in *The Birds* (1963), a well-known film by Alfred Hitchcock that was based on the eponymous short story by Daphne du Maurier. Set in a beach community in California, the film revolves around increasingly violent incidents in which birds attack humans. The director chose not to reveal why the attacks were occurring, hoping to bring out the primitive fear of being targeted without reason by furtive, rapid, and powerful beings. The shoot required many special effects, but the organizers were quickly overwhelmed by multiple incidents. The birds, including crows, sparrows, bullfinches, buntings, ravens, and gulls, did not always respond as expected by their trainers, even snapping at and harassing certain actors. In the West especially, fear of birds, or ornithophobia, affects many people, who cannot stand the sight of feathers and beaks. More broadly speaking, birds sometimes find themselves at the centre of major disagreements. An example is the Canada Goose, which finds itself in the midst of conflicts between conservation biologists, Indigenous hunters, and sports hunters (Roué 2009). In France, gulls have grown increasingly aggressive in markets, having become accustomed to receiving handouts of food from well-meaning people (Gramaglia 2010). And a flock of starlings can decimate a newly planted field in less than thirty minutes.

In many traditions, the flying bird is closely linked to the crawling reptile that has also stirred up fear since time immemorial. Davy (1992, 19) notes this opposition and that these animals have often been messengers, carriers of a secret language that must be deciphered. According to Genesis 1:20, the bird was created on the same day as the fish, and the reptiles appeared the next day. Davy writes that scientific knowledge has inverted this chronology – snakes and dinosaurs preceded birds, who are their descendants. But Psalm 148:10, Davy (1992, 20) adds, groups them together: "Praise the Lord, reptiles and winged birds." She points out that for the Greeks, such as Aristophanes, birds preceded the gods, and snakes originally had wings. Becoming winged, she underlines, is thus "both an acquisition and a return to the original condition, from whence comes the extent of the symbolism of the bird" (Davy 1992, 25).

According to paleontological tradition, the ancestor of the bird appeared some 160 million years ago, with *Archaeopteryx,* whose fossils were unearthed in Germany. Nonetheless, important vagueness remains. Recently, the place of *Archaeopteryx* as the forerunner of all birds has been contested, with the identification in China of *Xiaotingia zhengi,* which predates it (Kaplan 2011). Fossil remains indicate that *Xiaotingia zhengi* had feathers, claws, and teeth. The extant avian fauna go back 60 million years, with the appearance of the first cormorants and waders.

Regardless, this long history of birds and their contact with humans explains in part why they occupy such an important place in our myths. Asia abounds with traditions regarding serpent dragons – "mythic" birds without wings – many of which are featured on historical monuments. In China, India, Cambodia, and Indonesia, for example, these figures remain alive in iconography and stories, with perhaps the most ancient being the Chinese bestiary *Shan Hai Jing (Classic of Mountains and Seas),* portions of which were published as early as the fourth century BCE. The Abrahamic traditions are not to be outdone, and birds are present in their bestiaries as well. Thus, the dove is associated with light; its presence on many baptismal fonts evokes the Virgin and metaphysical purity, but also intelligence and chastity (Davy 1992, 71). Other birds, such as the swallow, the tit, or the peacock, convey positive connotations, but some species are unloved, which gives rise to many beliefs that are qualified as superstitious. So it is for the magpie, the raven, the owl, and the stork. Finally, many birds that are called the bird-of-paradise or the *simorgh* in Iran are of great value and evoke divinity or the Holy Spirit (Davy 1992). Literature, poetry, and the arts echo so many of these conceptions that it is not possible to go into detail here.

Associated simultaneously with the earthly world because of their reptilian origins and with the aerial, luminous world, as uncontested masters of the skies, birds can announce a death or deliver other messages by their presence or their flight. This capacity to link contrasting universes created ancient practices of ornithomancy but may also explain the fascination that birds still exercise over human communities. Such a fascination is rooted in a long past, as was brilliantly shown by Edward A. Armstrong (1958, 114) in his book on the folklore of birds:

Our enquiry into the origin of the English goose feast and the custom of breaking the wishbone has led us to some of the earliest magico-religious ideas known to have been cherished by man. As we proceed, we shall find further evidence that modern folklore is derived from ancient fertility conceptions which were once widespread throughout Europe and Asia, and even further afield.

This may explain why birdlore varies so extensively today and, at the same time, may reveal intriguing similarities.

From Cockfights to Extinction

Allow us to present two authors whose works on birds highlight their involvement with humans: Clifford Geertz, who founded interpretive anthropology, and Thom van Dooren, who originated what is called "environmental humanities."

In the 1970s, American anthropologist Clifford Geertz (1973) published a pioneering study on the cockfight. He concentrated on Bali, though the practice exists in most Southeast Asian countries, in island nations of the Indian Ocean, and in northern France. Geertz was one of the first anthropologists to show that the cockfight ritual represented more than one might imagine and that it could be understood as a total social fact, to which one could add a reference to Marcel Mauss (1872–1950). On the basis of his work in Bali, Geertz founded a new research program that formed the underpinnings of interpretive anthropology. As he wrote, cockfighting was prohibited in Bali, except for a few special occasions. One day, as he attended an illegal match, the police arrived unexpectedly, the spectators scattered in panic, and he himself took refuge in a courtyard to avoid being arrested. Cockfighting may be banned in Bali, but it still engenders passion in the men who spend years raising and training the birds until the fateful day. The spectacle of the fight is brief compared to the months of preparation, and Geertz suggests that what is at stake has far more to do with the status of the owners than with a simple game in which bets are laid and money changes hands. Owners identify strongly with their birds, who fight for their lives in the ring, and bouts are preceded by an informal session in which owners choose which birds will be matched against each other. Often reserved for men of different families or clans, Balinese cockfights occur in strict intimacy. Esteem, honour, dignity, and respect are all at play (Geertz

1973). The matches divide or unite the groups of people involved in the cock fight, contributing sometimes to the tensions inherent in hierarchical societies and producing strong emotions, where vitality meets death. Thus, a major part of Balinese culture is represented in these cockfights. They are true contexts from which an observer can describe in depth the density of the culture that he discovers and can translate it or objectify it in texts that are the basis of his interpretation. With cockfighting, a whole series of entanglements comes to light.

Half a century later, other entanglements emerged in the work of Thom van Dooren. Positioning himself as a field philosopher, van Dooren connected several disciplines, from cultural studies to philosophy and from human and social sciences to science and technology to environmental studies. It was he who, following the work of Deborah Bird Rose, founded the journal *Environmental Humanities* in 2012, whose purpose was to animate a new field of the same name. Like many others in philosophy and anthropology, van Dooren was deeply concerned by the massive extinction and the degradation of biodiversity that characterizes this new era called the Anthropocene, in which human activity is devastating the environment. Combining biology, anthropology, and philosophy, he became interested in the disappearance of species, particularly of birds, seeking to understand how it affected humans. In *Flight Ways: Life and Loss at the Edge of Extinction*, van Dooren (2014) dedicates several chapters to birds that are on the path to disappearance. Referring to bird and animal species as "more-than-human others," he emphasizes that entire sections of knowledge, wisdom, practices, histories, worlds, and existences will vanish if a species is eradicated. However, non-modern societies that are also preoccupied with the preservation of birds, though often by other means than just conservation, do not use this language. The Inuit do not advocate stopping the hunt of animals at risk of extinction, convinced that the lack of interest by humans is part of the problem. Two qualities of van Dooren's work are his suggestion that human exceptionalism should be ended and his examples of the great tragedy now unfolding.

"Anthropocene," "capitalocene," and "pathocene" all designate the major impact that humans have had on the planet for the past several centuries, which is marked by total exploitation, both brutal and disproportionate, of what we agree to call "natural resources." Everywhere on the earth, in the seas, and in the air, the human species is a predator, displaying little respect for other forms of life or for its own co-specifics. And as urbanization spreads across the globe, the situation is becoming increasingly dire. Andrew Gosler and Caroline Jackson-Houlston (2012) describe the sad effects of this trend, pointing to a widespread disengagement from nature and an ignorance about it. One must admit that – like the Dodo on the island of Mauritius, the Great Auk, the Passenger Pigeon, and many others – birds have paid a heavy price for our folly. Measuring the catastrophe, van Dooren invites us to rethink our lives with the birds that surround us and to imagine solutions to stop their disappearance. He demonstrates great empathy for avian fauna and all the living things that are related to them. His monograph on vultures (van Dooren 2011) shows that these birds are not mere scavengers that devour carrion, but creators of worlds and incredible mothers. In *The Wake of Crows*, van Dooren (2019) continues to explore the question of how humans can live with crows in a world in full transformation due to processes of globalization, colonization, urbanization, and climate change. He answers the question based on observations he made with crows and imagines what could be multi-species ethics, taking for granted that we live in interspecies and interconnected communities.

So, how can we, standing on the shoulders of Lévi-Strauss, Geertz, and van Dooren, understand the tie between humans and birds?

Contents of this Book

In this volume, considering the era of the Anthropocene and working with new ethnographic contexts, we reflect on the links between the lives of humans and birds. We are interested in the Indo-Pacific, a broad geographical area that spans the countries near, adjacent to, and in the Indian and Pacific Oceans. Except for two chapters, most of the book is about human-bird relations along the East Asian–Australasian Flyway, a route followed by migratory birds as they shuttle from Siberia in the north, along the Western Pacific lateral, to Australia and New Zealand. The Indo-Pacific region, which is home to 60 percent of the human population, is marked by great cultural and biological diversity, including in the avian world. We are indebted to earlier works in anthropology, including ethno-biology and comparative studies of taxonomy, as well as to more recent intellectual currents such as the ontological turn and multi-species ethnography. Our goal is to learn from all these approaches as we seek to understand the various intersections between very real human and avian lives. The book is divided into three parts, named to evoke Lévi-Strauss's ([1962] 1991, 89) oft-cited dictum (about totemism) that "animals are good to think." We aim for a great diversity in writing style and perspectives on human-bird relations across this geographical space, with the result that the chapters are an eclectic mix of traditional ethnography, poetics, and even art.

In Part 1, "Birds Are Good to Be With," the authors take an innovative approach, looking at birds in their relations with humans. In Chapter 1, Shuhei Uda uses the concept of multiple joining methods, or mutual joint commitment, to show how humans and cormorants have together created fishing practices that benefit both. He also compares cormorant fishing in China and Japan. Etienne Dalemans, author of Chapter 2, conducted his ethnographic fieldwork in the Thai city of Hat Yai, focusing on singing contests between Red-whiskered Bulbuls. In a sonorous ethnography, he shows how humans and birds enter an acoustic community. In Chapter 3, Perrine Lachenal takes us to the rooftops of Amman, Jordan, to explore how working-class men affirm their masculinity through pigeon keeping, a passion that is shared across the Indo-Pacific. Her sensorial ethnography provides new insights into a very intimate human-bird relationship. Anthropologist Aïko Cappe and artist Colin Schildhauer join forces in Chapter 4 to understand the birds of the Tarkine rainforest in Tasmania. Theirs is a non-traditional ethnography, more about birds than humans, with the result being a poignant, or what some might call a romantic, piece of nature writing. In Chapter 5, Scott E. Simon, inspired by the phenomenology of Maurice Merleau-Ponty and drawing from a year of fieldwork in Osaka, explores birding as a constant dance of fleeting encounters. These five chapters demonstrate that the characteristics of various birds shape the human-bird relationship at least as much as differences between human groups. There is much to be learned through observation of all the partners involved, non-human as well as human.

In Part 2, "Birds Are Good to Think With," the authors examine how birds become integrated into human symbolic systems, engaging with the work of Lévi-Strauss and making new contributions to cognitive anthropology. In Chapter 6, John Leavitt, who has conducted field research in the Indian Himalayas since the early 1980s, discusses Kumaoni ways of living with birds and hearing emotion in bird sounds. Through stories from the field, and Kumaoni songs and literary traditions, birds are good to think with but also good to feel emotion with. Chapter 7, a collaborative ethnography by Frédéric Laugrand, Antoine Laugrand, Jazil Tamang, and Gliseria Magapin, explores bird knowledge among the Ibaloy on the island of Luzon in the Philippines. Because birds can indicate the passage of seasons and changes in weather, their wisdom is relevant to us, as we learn to live with the changes in climate and weather that are part of the Anthropocene. In Chapter 8, Gregory Forth examines how birds are used as metaphors among the Nage of Flores Island, Indonesia. These chapters show that human-bird entanglements bring birds into human symbolic systems. The birds can thus help us to think in new ways about the world that we share with them and about our own lives.

Part 3, "Birds Are Good to Craft With," examines bird symbolism in craft and ritual. In Chapter 9, Atsushi Nobayashi delves into archaeology and the bird-shaped artifacts produced during the Jomon and Yayoi periods of Japan. Speculating on their possible uses, he suggests that the Jomon period defined birds largely as good to eat, whereas the Yayoi period also saw them as good to make. In another collaborative ethnography, Chapter 10, Lionel Simon and Syarul Sakaliou of Madobag village explore how the Mentawaians of Indonesia represent birds in decorative artifacts that are placed inside their houses. The objects bring well-being to the household while expressing Mentawai cosmology. In Chapter 11, Yi-tze Lee, who does research with the Nanshi Amis people in the Eastern Rift Valley of Taiwan, shows how birds and feathers are used in rituals, which are subject to radical transformation due to the pressures of modernization. In the epilogue, Andrew G. Gosler discusses the importance of ethno-ornithology in an era in which humans everywhere seem increasingly alienated from birds and the rest of the natural world. Despite these changes, humans and birds are still involved in a relational ecology in the era of the Anthropocene. These chapters show various ways in which humans incorporate birds and bird symbolism into the material culture that, in turn, also shapes how humans perceive the social world.

These studies, ranging geographically from Jordan to Tasmania and across the major civilizations of India, China, Japan, and Austronesia, demonstrate a great diversity in human-bird entanglements. Birds are important in themselves, of course, but they also become incorporated into human so-cieties as working partners, as parts of symbolic systems, and as material culture. Humans and birds can and do learn from one another. They are partners in worlding, in ways often overlooked in Western ontologies that usually imagine nature and culture as entirely separate realms, thus reducing birds to beings who are somehow "out there" in the forest, but who have little to teach us. Perhaps the human species would not have caused so much ecological damage if it had imagined the world as full of other lives, including birds, who have a right to exist and to enjoy suitable, stable habitats. Attention to entanglements shows us that we need each other. As we collectively face the challenges of climate change and other negative impacts of the Anthropocene, it would behoove us to learn from birds and the wisdom of Indigenous and other peoples around the world.

NOTES

1 The French original reads, "J'aurais aimé, une fois dans ma vie, pleinement communiquer avec un animal. C'est un but inaccessible. Il m'est presque douloureux de savoir que je ne pourrai jamais trouver de quoi est composée la matière et la structure de l'univers. Cela eût signifié: être capable de parler avec un oiseau. Mais là est la frontière qu'on ne peut franchir. Traverser cette frontière serait un grand bonheur pour moi. Si vous pouviez me procurer une bonne fée qui exaucerait un de mes vœux, c'est celui-là que je choisirais." C. Lévi-Strauss, "Entre Marx et Rousseau," interview with F. Raddatz, *Die Zeit*, September 2, 1983, quoted in M. Lévi-Strauss and Loyer (2021, 123–24). Unless otherwise indicated, all translations in this introduction are by the authors.
2 The French original reads, "Quand dans *La Pensée sauvage* (p. 270–272), j'interprétais les noms que nous donnons aux oiseaux comme l'indice que l'ensemble de leurs espèces évoque pour nous une sorte de contrepartie métaphorique de la société humaine, je ne me doutais pas qu'une relation de même type existât objectivement entre leur cerveau et le nôtre. Il semble, en effet, qu'à partir des reptiles où ils ont leur commune origine, l'évolution cérébrale des mammifères et celle des oiseaux aient suivi des lignes divergentes, mais conduisant à des solutions complémentaires."
3 Between 1992 and 2013, seventeen volumes of the handbook, edited under the direction of Josep del Hoyo, Andrew Elliot, Jordi Sargatal, and David Christie, et al., were published in Barcelona (del Hoyo et al. 1992–2013).

WORKS CITED

Ackerman, Jennifer. 2016. *The Genius of Birds.* New York: Penguin Books.
Armstrong, Edward A. 1955. *The Wren.* London: Collins.
–. 1958. *The Folklore of Birds: An Enquiry into the Origin and Distribution of Some Magico-Religious Traditions.* London: Collins.
'Attar, Farîd-Ud-Dîn. 1996. *Le langage des oiseaux.* Paris: Éditions Albin Michel.
Badmaev, A.A. 2020. "Traditional Buryat Beliefs about Birds." *Archaeology, Ethnology and Anthropology of Eurasia* 48, 2: 106–13.
Baudry, F. 1861. "Les mythes du feu et breuvage céleste chez les nations européennes." *Revue Germanique* 14: 353–87.
Berlin, Brent. 1990. "The Chicken and the Egg-Head Revisited: Further Evidence for the Intellectualist Bases of Ethnobiological Classification." In *Ethnobiology: Implications and Applications,* ed. Darrell A. Posey and William L. Overal, 1: 19–33. Belém, Brazil: Museu Paraense Emilio Goeldi.

Birkhead, Tim. 2008. *The Wisdom of Birds: An Illustrated History of Ornithology.* London: Bloomsbury.

—. 2012. *Bird Sense: What Is It Like to Be a Bird?* New York: Walker.

—. 2014. *Ten Thousand Birds: Ornithology since Darwin.* Princeton: Princeton University Press.

Boster, James, Brent Berlin, and John O'Neill. 1986. "The Correspondence of Jivaroan to Scientific Ornithology." *American Anthropologist* 88, 3: 569–83.

Bulmer, Ralph. 1967. "Why Is the Cassowary Not a Bird? A Problem of Zoological Taxonomy among the Karam of the New Guinea Highlands." *Man* 2, 1: 5–25.

—. 1989. "The Uncleanness of the Birds of Leviticus and Deuteronomy." *Man* 24, 2: 304–21.

Cauquelin, Josiane. 2006. "Paroles d'oiseaux à Puyuma (Taïwan)." In *Les messagers divins: Aspects esthétiques et symboliques des oiseaux en Asie du Sud-Est,* ed. Pierre Le Roux and Bernard Sellato, 191–209. Paris: Éditions connaissances et savoirs.

Chandler, Murray, ed. 2017. *The Winged: An Upper Missouri River Ethno-Ornithology.* Tucson: University of Arizona Press.

Charrin, Anne-Victoire. 1983. *Le petit monde du Grand Corbeau, récit du Grand Nord sibérien.* Paris: Presses Universitaires de France.

Davy, Marie-Madeleine. 1992. *L'oiseau et sa symbolique.* Paris: Albin Michel.

Despret, Vinciane. 2019. *Habiter en oiseau.* Paris: Actes Sud.

—. 2021. "À l'écoute des oiseaux." In *Penser le vivant,* ed. Laurence Dahan-Gaida, Christine Maillard, Gisèle Séginger, and Laurence Talairach-Vielmas, 84–96. Paris: Éditions de la Maison des sciences de l'homme.

Douglass, Kristina, Dylan Gaffney, Teresa J. Feo, Priyangi Bulathsinhala, Andrew L. Mack, Megan Spitzer, and Glenn R. Summerhayes. 2021. "Late Pleistocene/Early Holocene Sites in the Montane Forests of New Guinea Yield Early Record of Cassowary Hunting and Egg Harvesting." *Proceedings of the National Academy of Sciences* 118, 40. https://doi.org/10.1073/pnas.2100117118.

Dove, Michael R. 1993. "Humility, and Adaptation in the Tropical Forest: The Agricultural Augury of 'the Kantu.'" *Ethnology* 32, 2: 145–67.

—. 1996. "Process versus Product in Bornean Augury: A Traditional Knowledge System's Solution to the Problem of Knowing." In *Redefining Nature: Ecology, Culture and Domestication,* ed. R.F. Ellen and Katsuyoshi Fukui, 557–96. Oxford: Berg.

Emery, Nathan. 2017. *L'étonnante intelligence des oiseaux.* Paris: Éditions Quae.

Erkes, Eduard. 1925. "Chinesisch-Amerikanische Mythenparallelen." *T'oung Pao,* 2nd ser., 24, 1: 32–53. http://www.jstor.org/stable/4526775.

Fabre, Daniel. 1986. "La voie des oiseaux: Sur quelques récits d'apprentissage." *L'Homme* 26, 99: 7–40.

Feld, Steven. 2012. *Sound and Sentiment: Birds, Weeping, Poetics, and Song in Kaluli Expression.* 3rd ed. Durham: Duke University Press.

Fienup-Riordan, Ann. 2017. "How Raven Marked the Land When the Earth Was New." *Études Inuit Studies* 41, 1–2: 215–42.

Forth, Gregory. 1996. "Nage Birds: Issues in Ethnoornithological Classification." *Anthropos* 91: 89–109.

—. 2004. *Nage Birds: Classification and Symbolism among an Eastern Indonesian People.* London: Routledge.

—. 2006a. "Sounds, Spirits, Symbols and Signs: Birds in Nage Cosmology." In *Les messagers divins: aspects esthétiques et symboliques des oiseaux en Asie du Sud-Est,* ed. Pierre Le Roux and Bernard Sellato, 579–614. Paris: Éditions connaissances et savoirs.

—. 2006b. "Words for 'Bird' in Eastern Indonesia." *Journal of Ethnobiology* 26: 177–207.

–. 2007. "Pigeon and Friarbird Revisited: A Further Analysis of an Eastern Indonesian Mythicoornithological Contrast." *Anthropos* 102: 495–513.

–. 2009. "Symbolic Birds and Ironic Bats: Varieties of Classification in Nage Folk Ornithology." *Ethnology* 48, 2: 139–59.

–. 2010. "What's in a Bird's Name: Relationships among Ethno-Ornithological Terms in Nage and Other Malayo-Polynesian Languages." In *Ethno-Ornithology: Birds, Indigenous Peoples, Culture, and Society*, ed. Sonia Tidemann and Andrew Gosler, 223–37. London: Earthscan.

–. 2016. *Why the Porcupine Is Not a Bird: Explorations in the Folk Zoology of an Eastern Indonesian People*. Toronto: University of Toronto Press.

–. 2017. "What a Little Bird Tells Us about Symbolic Thought: The Russet-Capped Stubtail (Tesia everetti) in Nage Augury, Myth, and Metaphor." *Journal of Ethnobiology* 37: 682–99.

Franco, Merlin F., and Misa Juliana Minggu. 2019. "When the Seeds Sprout, the Hornbills Hatch: Understanding the Traditional Ecological Knowledge of the Ibans of Brunei Darussalam on Hornbills." *Journal of Ethnobiology and Ethnomedicine* 15, 46. https://doi.org/10.1186/s13002-019-0325-0.

Geertz, Clifford. 1973. *The Interpretation of Cultures*. New York: Basic Books.

Geinaert-Martin, Danielle. 1992. *The Woven Land of Laboya: Socio-Cosmic Ideas and Values in West Sumba, Eastern Indonesia*. Leiden: CNWS.

Gonzalez, J.C.T. 2011. "Enumerating the Ethno-Ornithological Importance of Philippine Hornbills." *Raffles Bulletin of Zoology* 24: 149–61.

Gosler, Andrew G. 2017. "The Human Factor: Ecological Salience in Ornithology and Ethno-Ornithology." *Journal of Ethnobiology* 37: 637–62.

Gosler, A.G., and C.M. Jackson-Houlston. 2012. "A Nightingale by Any Other Name? Relations Between Scientific and Vernacular Bird Naming." British Ornithologists' Union Proceedings – Ecosystem Services: Do We Need Birds? https://bou.org.uk/wp-content/uploads/2020/06/2012-ecosystem-services-goslerjackson-houlston.pdf.

Gourou, Pierre. 1972. *La Terre et l'homme en Extrême-Orient*. Paris: Flammarion.

Gramaglia, Christelle. 2010. "Les goélands leucophée sont-ils trop nombreux? L'émergence d'un problème public." *Études Rurales* 185: 133–48.

Hamil, James, H. Sidky, and Janardan Subedi. 2002. "Structure and Function in a Tibeto-Burman Folk Taxonomy." *Anthropological Linguistics* 44, 1: 65–84.

Healey, Christopher. 1993. "Folk Taxonomy and Mythology of Birds of Paradise in the New Guinea Highlands." *Ethnology* 32, 1: 19–34.

Hertz, Robert. (1928) 1970. *Sociologie religieuse et folklore*. Paris: Presses universitaires de France. http://classiques.uqac.ca/classiques/hertz_robert/socio_religieuse_folklore/hertz_socio_rel_folklore.pdf.

Hohn, E.O. 1973. "*Mammal and Bird Names in the Indian Languages of the Lake Athabasca Area.*" *Arctic* 26: 163–71.

Hoyo, Josep del., Andrew Elliott, Sargatal Jordi, José Cabot, N.J. Collar, David A. Christie, Richard Allen, Hilary Burn, and Norman Arlott, eds. 1992–2013. *Handbook of the Birds of the World*. Barcelona: Lynx Edicions.

Huang, Yung-Kun, Agathe Lemaitre, Hsin-Ju Wu, and Yuan-Hsun Sun. 2021. "A Sacred Bird at the Crossroads of Destiny: Ethno-Ornithology of the Mountain Hawk-Eagle (Qadis) for the Paiwan People in Taiwan." *Journal of Ethnobiology* 41, 4: 535–52.

Hutter, M. 2008. *Oiseaux, héros et devins*. Paris: Éditions L'Harmattan.

Jernigan, Kevin. 2016. "Beings of a Feather: Learning about the Lives of Birds with Amazonian Peoples." *Ethnobiology Letters* 7, 2: 41–47.

Jerolmack, Colin. 2013. *The Global Pigeon*. Chicago: University of Chicago Press.

Kane, Stephanie C. 2015. "Names and Folklore from the Embera (Choco) in Darien, Panama." *Ethnobiology Letters* 6, 1: 32–62.

Kaplan, Matt. 2011. "*Archaeopteryx* No Longer First Bird." *Nature*. https://doi.org/10.1038/news.2011.443.

Keck, Frédéric. 2015. "Sentinels for the Environment: Birdwatchers in Taiwan and Hong Kong." *China Perspectives* 2, 102: 43–52.

—. 2020. *Avian Reservoirs: Virus Hunters and Birdwatchers in Chinese Sentinels Posts*. Durham: Duke University Press.

Klein, Jacob Theodor. 1750. *Historiae avium prodromus, cum praefatione de ordine animalum in genere*. Lubecae: Schmidt.

Kockelman, Paul. 2016. *The Chicken and the Quetzal: Incommensurate Ontologies and Portable Values in Guatemala's Cloud Forest*. Durham: Duke University Press.

Kohn, Eduardo. 2013. *How Forests Think: Toward an Anthropology beyond the Human*. Berkeley: University of California Press.

Kondo, Shiaki. 2021. "Dog and Human from Raven's Perspective: An Interpretation of Raven Myths of Alaskan Athabascans." *Polar Science* 28: 1–8. https://doi.org/10.1016/j.polar.2020.100633.

Krech, Shepard. 2005. "Telling Stories about Extinct Birds." *Environmental History* 10, 4: 718–20.

—. 2009. *Spirits of the Air: Birds and American Indians in the South*. Athens: University of Georgia Press.

Krupnik, Igor. 2017. "Siberian Yupik Names for Birds: What Can Bird Names Tell Us about Language and Knowledge Transitions?" *Études Inuit Studies* 41, 1–2: 179–214.

Laugrand, Frédéric, and Antoine Laugrand. 2023. *Les voies de l'ombre: comment les chauves-souris sèment le trouble*. Paris: Museum national d'histoire naturelle, collection nature et sociétés.

Laugrand, Frédéric, Antoine Laugrand, and Lionel Simon. 2023. "Sources of Ambivalence, Contagion, or Sympathy: Bats and What They Tell Anthropology." *Current Anthropology* 64, 3: 321–51.

Laugrand, Frédéric, Antoine Laugrand, and Guy Tremblay. 2019. "Lorsque les oiseaux donnent le rythme: Chants et présages chez les Blaans de Mindanao (Philippines)." *Anthropologie et Sociétés* 42, 2–3: 171–98.

Le Roux, Pierre, and Bernard Sellato, eds. 2006. *Les messagers divins: Aspects esthétiques des oiseaux en Asie du Sud-Est* (Divine messengers: Bird symbolism and aesthetics in Southeast Asia). Paris: Éditions connaissances et savoirs.

Lévi-Strauss, Claude. (1962) 1991. *Totemism*. Translated by Rodney Needham. London: Merlin Press.

—. (1962) 1996. *The Savage Mind*. Translated by anonymous. London: Weidenfeld and Nicolson.

—. (1971) 1981. *The Naked Man*. Translated by Jonathan Cape. New York: Harper and Row.

—. (1991) 1995. *The Story of Lynx*. Translated by Catherine Tihanyi. Chicago: University of Chicago Press.

Lévi-Strauss, Monique, and Emmanuelle Loyer, eds. 2021. *L'Abécédaire de Claude Lévi-Strauss*. Paris: Éditions de l'Observatoire.

Lilienthal, Otto, and Gustav Lilienthal. 1911. *Birdflight as the Basis of Aviation: A Contribution towards a System of Aviation Compiled from the Results of Numerous Experiments Made by O. and G. Lilienthal*. London: Longmans, Green.

Low, Chris. 2011. "Birds and Khoesan: Linking Spirits and Healing with Day-to-Day Life." *Africa: Journal of the International African Institute* 81, 2: 295–313.

MaMing, Roller, Li Lee, Xiaomin Yang, and Paul Buzzard. 2016. "Vultures and Sky Burials on the Qinghai-Tibet Plateau." *Vulture News* 71 (November): 22–35. http://dx.doi.org/10.4314/vulnew.v71i1.2.

Manceron, V. 2015. "What Is It Like to Be a Bird? Imagination zoologique et proximité à distance chez les amateurs d'oiseaux en Angleterre." In *Bêtes à pensées: Visions des mondes animaux*, ed. Michèle Cros, Julien Bondaz, and Frédéric Laugrand, 117–40. Paris: Éditions des Archives contemporaines.

–. 2022. *Les veilleurs du vivant. Avec les naturalistes amateurs.* Paris: La Découverte.

Mathevet, Raphaël, and Arnaud Béchet. 2020. *Politiques du flamand rose.* Marseille: Wildproject.

Matthieu, Rémi. 1984. "Le corbeau dans la mythologie de l'ancienne Chine." *Revue d'histoire des religions* 201, 3: 281–309.

Mauzé, Marie. 2011. "Corbeau et le destin des hommes." *Lizières:* 55–61.

Meletinsky, E.M. 1973. "Typological Analysis of the Palaeo-Asiatic Raven Myths." *Acta Ethnographica Academiae Scientiarum Hungaricae* 22, 1–2: 107–55.

–. 1980. "L'épique du corbeau chez les Paléoasiates." *Diogène* 110: 120–35.

Metcalf, Peter. 1976. "Birds and Deities in Borneo." *Bijdragen tot de Taal-, Land- en Volkenkunde* 18: 96–123.

Miller, Stephen. 2018. *Hunt the Wren: The Early Descriptions, 1731–1845.* Onchan: Chiollagh Books for Culture Vannin.

Oosten, Jarich, and Frédéric Laugrand. 2006. "The Bringer of Light: The Raven in Inuit Tradition." *Polar Record* 42, 222: 187–204.

Régnier, Rita H., ed. 2008. *Oiseaux: Héros et devins.* Paris: L'Harmattan.

Revel, Nicole. 1975. "Le vocabulaire des oiseaux en Palawan: quelques réflexions sur le problème des taxonomies indigènes." In *L'homme et l'animal: Premier colloque d'ethnozoologie,* ed. Raymond Pujol, 317–33. Paris: Institut international d'ethnosciences.

Rose, Deborah Bird. 2009. *Vers des humanités écologiques.* Marseille: Wildproject.

Roué, Marie. 2009. "Une oie qui traverse les frontières: La bernache du Canada." *Ethnologie française* 1, 39: 23–34.

Rudge, Alice. 2019. "The Sounds of People and Birds: Music, Memory and Longing among the Batek of Peninsular Malaysia." *Hunter Gatherer Research* 4, 1: 3–23.

Satheesan, S.M. 1998. "The Role of Vultures in the Disposal of Human Corpses in India and Tibet." *Vulture News* 39: 32–33.

Sébillot, Paul. (1904–07) 2018. *Le Folklore de France: La faune.* Cressé, France: PRNG éditions.

Siebold, Philipp Franz von, C.J. Temminck, H. Schlegel, and W. de Haan. (1839) 1975. *Fauna Japonica: Aves.* Tokyo: Kodansha.

Simon, Scott. 2015. "Émissaires des ancêtres: Les oiseaux dans la vie et la cosmologie des Sadyaq de Taiwan." *Anthropologie et Sociétés* 39, 1–2: 179–99.

–. 2018. "Penser avec des oiseaux: L'ornithomancie et l'autochtonie à Taiwan." *Anthropologie et Sociétés* 42, 2–3: 151–69.

Smith, Derek A. 2010. "The Harvest of Rain-Forest Birds by Indigenous Communities in Panama." *Geographical Review* 100, 2: 187–203.

Steadman, David W. 1997. "Extinctions of Polynesian Birds: Reciprocal Impacts of Birds and People." In *Historical Ecology in the Pacific Islands: Prehistoric Environmental and Landscape Change,* ed. Patrick V. Kirch and Terry L. Hunt, 51–79. New Haven: Yale University Press.

Strycker, Noah. 2018. *Ce que les oiseaux disent des hommes.* Paris: Flammarion.

Tidemann, Sonia, and Andrew Gosler. 2010. *Ethno-Ornithology: Birds, Indigenous Peoples, Culture and Society.* London: Earthscan.

Van den Broek, Gerard J. 1988. "A Structural Analysis of Dutch Bird Nomenclature." *Anthropologica* 30, 1: 61–73.

Van Dooren, Thom. 2011. *Vulture.* London: Reaktion Books.

–. 2014. *Flight Ways: Life and Loss at the Edge of Extinction.* New York: Columbia University Press.

–. 2019. *The Wake of Crows: Living and Dying in Shared Worlds.* New York: Columbia University Press.

Willughby, Francis, and John Ray. 1676. *Ornithologiæ libri tres.* London: Joannis Martyn.

Part One

Birds Are Good to Be With
(Birds as Partners)

1

Multiple Joining Methods among Fish, Birds, and Fishers
A Regional Case Study of Chinese Cormorant Fishing

Shuhei Uda

A TYPICAL CORMORANT-FISHING day begins when fishers release around twenty cormorants into a lake from their perches on the boats. They shout several times, using their paddles to splash the birds, and hit the water with bamboo sticks to signal that fishing should start. In response, the cormorants, who have been clustering around the boats, begin to dive. When they catch a fish, they bob to the surface, and the fishers take them onboard where they disgorge it. If they catch a large fish, they receive a small one as a reward and are then returned to the water. Many fish by following the moving boats. When the session ends, the birds are given five hundred grams of fish and are allowed to settle on their perches.

Fishing with cormorants has a long history in many parts of the world, and fully understanding this practice necessitates observing multiple joining methods among fishers, birds, and their prey. Individuals use cormorants for subsistence fishing by intervening in their behaviour and ecology. When the birds are in the water, they make no attempt to escape, but follow the boats and dive for fish nearby. Thus, the activity requires a "joint commitment" between human and bird based on an interaction in which the former influences the behaviour and ecology of the latter. Changes on the animal side exert an influence on human actions, which in turn influence animal behaviour. Interactions between fishers and birds vary depending on the fishing environment, the gear used, and the fish caught. This chapter clarifies the relationship between fishers and cormorants in China, examining the interactions between fish, birds, and fishers as a way of coping with the geographic context and environmental conditions. It provides an important theoretical contribution to studies of human-animal relations.

In recent years, anthropological studies have reconsidered the human-animal relationship to provide a new perspective on the traditional Euro-American dichotomy in which it is assumed that humans should control animals and keep them captive. Conducting ethnographic surveys, researchers have identified several important concepts for understanding human-animal relations, such as joint commitment, hybrid community, multi-species ethnography, more-than-human society, and post-domesticity (see, for example, Bulliet 2005; Haraway 2008; Kirksey and Helmreich 2010; Stépanoff 2012; Ingold 2013; Tsing 2013). In academic trends after the ontological turn, some ethnographies that challenge the traditional perspective have decentred the role of humans in the ecological relationship, emphasizing the autonomy and agency of animals (Swanson, Lien, and Ween 2018; Schroer 2019, 2). These studies deny that human-animal relations fall into stark dichotomies in which humans are active and animals are passive (Ingold 2013, 14–17; Anderson et al. 2017, 412). Cormorant fishing requires that the birds act autonomously and collaborate with humans. After all, they, not the fishers, are the ones who search for and catch the fish every day.

Animals used for food-related purposes can be divided into three categories: hunted animals, animals bred for consumption, and animals that help humans in subsistence and production activities. Animals in the first category provide food and materials to sustain human life. Those in the second – pigs, cattle, goats, chickens, and sheep – supply meat, milk and leather, eggs, feathers, and wool. The third category aids in searching for and capturing target animals or plants, pulls ploughs or sleds, or furnishes transport. A species can occupy multiple categories, and the category may vary by period or region. Cormorants that are used in fishing fall into the third category, of subsistence animals. This category turns on collaboration between humans and animals. In cormorant fishing, the animals become extensions of human action. Thus, the fishers must work with the birds' behaviour and ecology and must not attempt to distort their nature. In China and Japan, fishers and cormorants are partners, based on their combination of technique and experience.

Although cormorant fishing methods may seem homogeneous, practices in China differ from those of Japan. In China, the birds are bred in captivity and are tamed for fishing; thus, they are domesticated. The fishers prefer to use domesticated birds rather than those caught in the wild (Uda 2019). In Japan, fishers catch wild cormorants and tame them, as has been the practice for over 1,500 years. They value the "wildness" of the birds, which they leverage for fishing, and refuse to domesticate them, despite being able to do so (Uda 2017). Furthermore, they do not name their birds, believing that bestowing a name on an animal fosters emotional attachment. In this, they avoid becoming attached to the birds they use for fishing. This factor of domestication is the main difference between Chinese and Japanese cormorant fishing.

It is difficult to apply new technologies to cormorant fishing for the simple reason that the birds cannot be mechanized. This form of fishing cannot support the high cost of modern fishing technologies. Therefore, fishers depend on the autonomy and collaboration of the birds. Agustin Fuentes (2007, 140) proposes five patterns of relationships between humans and animals: integrated, engaged, penalized, and idealized or demonized. The relationship in cormorant fishing falls into the first category, integration, because the fishers must integrate their goal with the natural behaviour of the birds, who must search for and catch fish without attempting to escape. Examining this relationship in detail, one can see that cormorant fishing consists of three dimensions: fish, birds, and fishers (Figure 1.1). Multiple joining methods connect the three. This chapter clarifies the reasons for the similarities and differences in the numerous connections between humans, birds, and fishing materials in China.

Fish   Cormorants   Fishers

Figure 1.1 Cormorant fishing consists of three dimensions: fish, birds, and humans.

The Subject and Methods

Cormorant fishing is practised in Europe, Japan, and China. It was introduced to Europe from China between the sixteenth and seventeenth centuries. Royalty and the aristocracy enjoyed it as a pleasure or sport, like falconry, from the seventeenth to the nineteenth centuries (Freeman and Salvin 1859; Laufer 1931; Beike 2012). In Japan, where it is called *ukai,* it has been practised for 1,500 years. During the 1950s, it took place in over a hundred locations around the country, but this has dwindled to only ten spots. During a period of strong economic growth in the 1960s and 1970s, Japan's rivers and lakes became polluted, with the result that both freshwater fish populations and fishing declined. Cormorant fishing as a subsistence practice followed suit; today, it is exclusively offered as a tourist attraction.

In a study of Japanese cormorant fishing, Hiroaki Kani (1966) uses historical documents, such as photographs, poems, and magazines, to examine the distribution and historical development of fishing techniques. Toru Shinohara (1990) documents the methods and knowledge of taming techniques and the acclimation of the birds. Other studies focus on regional subsistence techniques, such as the capture of wild cormorants, taming skills, and the structure of fishing boats (Mogami 1958; Takuno 1990; Uda 2016, 2017). Thanks to these studies, we possess a detailed understanding of the lives and methods of Japanese fishers. They work with wild-caught birds, do not breed them in captivity, use ropes to control the diving birds, and engage in night fishing. They construct burial mounds or stone monuments and hold memorial services for cormorants that have died. No instance of a Chinese memorial service for a dead cormorant has been reported.

However, few studies have examined cormorant fishing in China. Although it occurs at sightseeing locations, most of it is undertaken as a livelihood. Despite its significance, little information is available (Manzi and Coomes 2002). The author studied the incubation techniques used in Shandong and Yunnan Provinces, and found that domesticated cormorants laid more eggs and had a higher hatching rate than their wild counterparts (Uda 2008, 2019). He also observed the subsistence strategy of fishers at Poyang Lake, Jiangxi Province, and discovered that, before the founding of the People's Republic of China, they had adapted their methods and rules to accommodate historical changes in the social and natural environments (Uda 2011).

Nevertheless, these studies focused mostly on a single area. Although adjacent villages can use similar methods, they differ throughout China. For example, those of central China, including those at Poyang Lake, differ geographically and ecologically from those of the eastern and western regions of the country and the coastal and mountain villages. The distribution, characteristics, and regional variation in Chinese cormorant fishing remain unclear, and thus a comparative study is necessary.

Aiming to fill this gap, the present study proceeded over three phases performed from 2005 to 2015: it collected qualitative data in fishing villages, examined regional similarities and differences, and evaluated fishing based on these results. Via interviews and observations, it gathered data from 139 villages in which cormorant fishing was practised. To obtain background characteristics for each village, the author interviewed fishers about their methods, rules, and breeding techniques, as well as historical changes in fishing and current fishery conditions. The author also used a participant-observer approach to gather information about techniques. The following sections describe fishing methods, the birds themselves, the boats, and other fishing skills.

Multiple Joining Methods of Cormorant Fishing

The Use of Cormorants

Data collected during the study revealed that fishing methods can be divided into six types, according to the use of birds and gear (Figure 1.2).

M1 is practised primarily in Weishan Lake of Shandong Province, where fishers own a boat and twenty to twenty-five cormorants. They fish for one hour in locations where rocks, snags, and sunken ships are present on the lake bottom, because fish tend to congregate there. Before moving on, they sort their catch according to market value and bring the birds back to the boat. They commonly fish alone but sometimes together. From spring to autumn, when the lake is high and the fishing area is large, they act alone. When the water level drops during the winter and the area decreases, five to six people may use 100 to 120 birds to fish together. However, they do not change their method.

M2 is used in fifty-five places – such as Baoding City of Hebei Province, Chaohu City and Huangshan City of Anhui Province, and Yiyang City of Hunan Province – where one or perhaps two boats move along the river or

	Aerial view	Cross section
Fishers allow cormorants to catch fish freely — M1		
M2		
M3		
Fishers drive fish into gill nets using cormorants — M4		
M5		
M6		

🐦 : Cormorant　　🛶 :Fishing boat　　┊ : Gill net

⬆ : Direction　　◁ :The flow of River

Figure 1.2 Types of cormorant fishing in China. In M1 to M3, cormorants fish without the aid of a net: in M1, boats remain in place for about an hour; in M2, the boat moves along a river or a lakeshore, accompanied by fishing birds; in M3, three boats work cooperatively. M4 to M6 involve the use of nets: in M4, the birds drive fish into a net that is placed upstream from the boat; in M5, two nets are used, one upstream and one downstream; in M6, a W-shaped net is used.

the lakeshore. For example, in Yiyang City, individuals own about fifteen cormorants, which perch on the edge of the boat as it moves to a fishing location on the lakeshore. Upon reaching the spot, the cormorants fish while the boat continues to move along the shore. In Jintang City of Sichuan Province, each person owns about six birds. They fish while moving along the riverbank in search of locations with the best and most rapidly obtained yields.

M3 is practised at Poyang Lake of Jiangxi Province and Dongting Lake of Hunan Province, where two or three boats move along the river or the lakeshore. This method involves pairs of family members: these can be parent and child, husband and wife, or brothers. Two types of boats are used. The first, a large boat, leads the way, dragging an iron wire behind it, which stirs up bottom dwellers such as carp and catfish, making them easier to catch. One or two small boats follow it. When a bird captures a fish, it rises to the surface and clambers onto a bamboo pole that the fisher uses to bring it into the boat.

Methods M4 to M6 all involve the use of nets. M4 occurs in sixty-four places – such as Taizhou City of Zhejiang Province, Nanping City of Fujian Province, and Suining City of Sichuan Province. In this method, a gill net is positioned upstream (sometimes downstream) from the boat. Once it is set, the fisher retreats downstream, beats the water with a bamboo pole to disturb the fish, and signals to the cormorants that they should begin diving by shouting "wo, wo, wo," or "ya, ya, ya." The boat moves slowly upstream, accompanied by the birds, and the fleeing fish become entangled in the net, which spans the river. At the end of the session, they are removed from the net and the birds are returned to the boat. One cycle lasts fifteen to twenty minutes and is repeated many times a day.

M5 is used in sixty-three places – such as Tongnan County of Chongqing Province, Shaoxing City of Zhejiang Province, and Tongren District of Guizhou Province. It is similar to M4, but it involves the use of two gill nets, one upstream and one downstream, to create an enclosed area in the river, and two to three fishers, who work together. Here too, the nets span the river, and fish are driven into them by the birds. Once the session is over, the nets are brought into the boats and the fish are removed, after which the cormorants are returned to the boats. This cycle takes forty to fifty minutes.

M5, which is favoured for the wider rivers, is more time consuming than M4, the method of choice for narrow rivers that are less than 30 metres wide. For example, Xiaomeng River in Zizhong, Sichuan Province, is about 25 metres wide; Xiaoan River in the Tongliang area of Chongqing City is 20 metres wide; and Xiaguan River in Xinghua City, Jiangsu Province, is 30 metres wide. In contrast, M5 is used in rivers that are wider than 100 metres. For instance, the Fu River in the Tongnan area near Chongqing is 250 metres wide; the Jialing River in the Hechuan district of Chongqing is 200 metres wide; and the Yongan River in Xianju, Zhejiang Province, is 150 metres wide. In these wide rivers, placing the two nets and driving the fish takes longer than in a narrow river. Relying on just one upstream net would be ineffective because the fish would have ample room to reverse course and escape downstream. Penning them in with two nets prevents them from doing so, though setting up and applying the system requires extra time.

M6, where cormorants drive fish into a W-shaped gill net, is used in the rivers of Jiangsu Province. In this method, four to five fishers work together. One boat heads upstream to put the net in place. Once it is set, two to three boats follow it, and the fishers beat the water with bamboo poles, enabling eighty to a hundred cormorants to drive fish into the net. More fishers bring up the rear, gathering up the net and removing the fish. Each net is 100 metres long and 200 centimetres high.

Acquiring Cormorants

All cormorant fishers in China own Great Cormorants *(Phalacrocorax carbo)*, which can be bred in captivity. Chicks are incubated at home, often by a hen, and the young birds are trained to fish. Some individuals breed and train their own birds; others purchase young cormorants. Since all are born in captivity, all are domesticated.

Fishers who breed cormorants live primarily in Shandong and Jiangsu Provinces, as well as several other locations – such as Wuhu City of Anhui Province, Jingshou City of Hebei Province, and Dali City of Yunnan Province. The nesting season is from March through May. Breeding techniques in Shandong and Jiangsu Provinces are similar in many ways but with some slight variations.

The first commonality between the two provinces is the selection of young male and female birds with good body shapes and high reproductive capacities. One man in Shandong Province said, "If I raise cormorants with good body shapes, I can sell them at a high price to other fishermen. So, I select cormorants with good body shapes." Another in Jiangsu Province said, "There are few unfertilized eggs when I use young cormorants with high reproductive capacities." Male cormorants used for breeding are three to eight years old, and females are three to five years old. It is understood that female birds of older than six often lay unfertilized eggs or produce no clutches at all.

The second common attribute is the use of hens to sit on the eggs (Figure 1.3). One hen can brood five to eight cormorant eggs. When newly laid eggs are removed from the nest of a cormorant, the female is encouraged to lay more. One fisher in Shandong Province said, "Female cormorants are quite lazy about sitting on their eggs patiently. On other hand, hens sit on cormorant eggs devotedly." All fishers thus use hens for this purpose.

The third commonality is the use of specially manufactured incubators for newly hatched chicks. Lined with straw and cloth, they are kept inside at a fixed temperature of 25 degrees Celsius. The lining helps to regulate the body temperatures of the featherless hatchlings.

When it comes to feeding nestlings, techniques differ in the two provinces. In Jiangsu Province, they are given eel that is purchased at local markets during the first ten days after hatching (Figure 1.4). Wielding a

Figure 1.3 A hen incubates cormorant eggs.

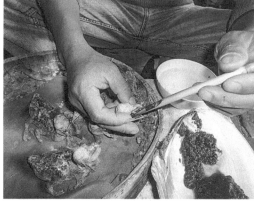

Figure 1.4 Feeding minced eel to nestlings.

carving knife, a fisher reduces the meat to a fine mince and uses a bamboo chopstick to insert tiny pieces into the beaks of the baby birds. Eel meat is soft and nutritious, making it suitable for them. After ten days, they are given crushed Silver Carp and Crucian Carp. In contrast, hatchlings in Shandong Province receive only Crucian Carp, which is crushed after the meat is separated from the bones with a knife.

Many fishers in Shandong and Jiangsu Provinces breed and raise cormorants for their own use only, but some sell young birds to other fishers. Once the cormorants weigh over 1.5 kilograms, they are moved into the house. Transported in bamboo baskets, they are sold in Jiangxi, Hunan, Hubei, Sichuan, and Guangdong Provinces.

Most Chinese fishers purchase young birds as needed. They may buy new ones to replace those lost to disease or to such accidents as being struck by the propeller of the boat. They inform the breeders of Shandong and Jiangsu Provinces of the number of birds they require each spring. The breeders then travel to each fishing village to sell the birds. In areas near Shandong and Jiangsu Provinces, a male cormorant costs 400–600 yuan and a female costs 200–300 yuan; in more distant areas, males cost 600–1,000 yuan and females cost 400–500 yuan (100 Chinese yuan is about US$14). In Yangzhou City of Hunan Province, Hechuan City of Chongqing Province, and Jinhua City of Zhejiang Province, fishers typically own no female cormorants. In these areas, they possess three to six birds and use a gill net method to fish. They prefer male birds because they are better than the females at catching fish.

People who do not own female cormorants, who lack knowledge of breeding techniques, or who do not breed their birds must replenish their stock by purchasing new birds when the need arises. This occurs in Chengde City of Hunan and Shangrao City of Jiangxi. In these areas, nets are not used for fishing. Both males and the less-expensive females are purchased. For example, forty fishers in W village south of Poyang Lake in Jiangxi Province kept 962 cormorants (683 males, 279 females; Figure 1.5). If a bird happens to produce eggs, the fisher will bring the clutch home in hopes of getting it to hatch. However, without the use of a hen or a purchased incubator, hatching and survival rates are low.

In Shandong and Jiangsu Provinces, cormorant breeding is a time-consuming and labour-intensive process: Hens sit on the eggs, which fishers turn twice a day to promote healthy development of the embryo. They carefully monitor incubator temperatures, feed nestlings with fresh fish

Figure 1.5 Pairs of cormorants perch on a boat.

three times a day, and keep a young bird at home for about fifty days. Some take a break from fishing during the breeding season to concentrate on this task. Fishers at Dongting and Poyang Lakes, however, use hens to sit on the eggs but do not refrain from fishing. Because the eggs receive less human attention, hatching and survival rates are lower, requiring these fishers to purchase new cormorants when needed.

Boats

In China, two types of boats are used for cormorant fishing (Figure 1.6): large boats that can carry at least twelve birds (B1–B3) and small boats that take from two to six (B4–B6).

B1-type boats, which are fitted with perches, are used in Shandong, Hunan, and Jiangsu Provinces. Constructed by ships' carpenters, they can last for ten years. They are 4.0 to 4.2 metres long, and they range from 70–80 to 130–140 centimetres wide. Two water tanks at the front hold the fish, and a wooden box contains food and fishing gear. Perches, 60–70 centimetres in length and projecting 20–30 centimetres above both gunwales, are designed to accommodate two birds each.

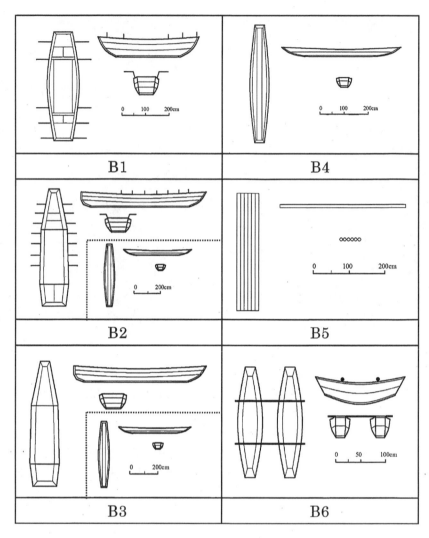

Figure 1.6 Types of Chinese cormorant-fishing boats.

B2 boats are used in Poyang Lake. They come in two sizes – large and small. The larger ones, which are furnished with screw propellers, are 9.2 to 9.3 metres long and range from 70–80 to 190–200 centimetres wide. The small ones, which are rowboats, are 5.2 to 5.3 metres long and range from 40–50 to 120–130 centimetres wide. Employing method M3, the large boats drag an iron wire in front of the others to rouse bottom-dwelling fish, which are then caught by the cormorants. In this method, a large and a small boat cooperate, working in rivers and along lakefronts. Some large boats are outfitted with gas-ring cookers, bedding, cookware, and tableware, enabling people to live aboard. Like the B1 version, B2 boats include perches for the birds.

B3 boats, large and lacking perches, are used in Hunan Province. They are 9.4 to 9.5 metres long and range from 60–70 to 190–200 centimetres wide. The small rowboats in this category are 5.0 to 5.1 metres long and range from 38–40 to 110–120 centimetres wide. Fishers who employ B3 boats typically own about twenty-five birds, which perch directly on the gunwales when they are not fishing. B3 boats also use the iron-wire method to fish in rivers and along lakefronts.

Unlike the craft already mentioned, the B4, the B5, and the B6 employ nets to catch fish. B4s, which are short and narrow, are used in Chongqing, Jiangsu, Hunan, Sichuan, and Fujian Provinces. They are 4.3 to 4.4 metres long and range from 40–50 to 70–80 centimetres wide. They carry two to six cormorants, gill nets, and baskets to take the fish. The fishers push them along with a bamboo pole and place nets that span the river, into which the cormorants drive the fish. In this method, fishers release and retrieve the birds, and cast and retrieve the nets. They opt for short and narrow boats because they can make tight turns and move rapidly.

Observed in Zhejiang, Fujian, and Guangxi Provinces, B5 boats are actually rafts consisting of six bamboo poles and are built by the fishers themselves. They are 4.3 to 4.4 metres long and 70 to 80 centimetres wide. They last for just one year, so fishers must purchase bamboo and make new rafts each spring. They carry gill nets, cormorants, and fish baskets, and are propelled with four-metre-long bamboo poles.

B6 boats are small catamarans used in Hubei Province. They are made of two small boats, each 1.8 metres long, 20–30 centimetres wide, and 30 centimetres deep (Figure 1.7). Lashed together with bamboo, the two sections are 40 centimetres apart. Constructed by ships' carpenters, they last for ten years and cost 500 yuan. They are transported to fishing locations on rivers or lakes via a bicycle or motorcycle. Individuals who own B6 boats typically keep four cormorants, which perch on the gunwales and drive fish into gill nets. The fishers place one foot on each side of the boat and propel it with a bamboo pole.

The B6 has the virtue of portability, so it is used in areas of Hubei Province where fishers visit a number of locations each day. In these regions, several rivers flow in parallel, and moving from one to another requires overland travel. The fishers understand that excessive fishing in a narrow river will

Figure 1.7 Cormorant fishing from catamarans.

diminish the long-term production capacity of the fish. Large boats would be difficult to transport from river to river, whereas the B6 can be carried on a bicycle, making it the preferred model for fishers who frequently move overland.

Throat Binding and Wing Clipping

Once they arrive at a fishing location, fishers tie a cord around the base of their birds' throats. This prevents them from swallowing larger fish, which they hold in their gullets, but allows them to swallow smaller ones. The birds are then released into the water to fish while their owners watch from the boat.

Various binding materials are employed: rice and wheat straw, reed and corn stems, and cloth rope. Rice straw is one of the most frequently used. Fishers obtain bundles of rice stems from farmhouses and store them in dehydrated form. When a bundle is to be used, it is soaked in water and crumpled until it becomes soft. When fishing is over for the day, the collar is cut to allow the birds to fish for themselves. In Shandong Province, where wheat is widely cultivated, wheat straw is used in the same way.

In Yangzhou City, Jiangsu Province, stems of the wild reeds that colonize riverbanks are used. This material breaks less readily than rice or wheat straw. Fishers cut the reeds and use them after they have dried. In Sichuan Province, some individuals opt for strips of cloth rope because they are as effective as reed stems and can be reused.

The collar is tightened to various degrees, though generally until one finger can be inserted between it and the bird's throat. However, some people prefer a tight binding because the birds will stop fishing after they have eaten enough small fish. Others always choose a looser binding so that the birds can swallow small fish, believing that they will be motivated to catch more if they are capable of eating. In some instances, the throats of fractious cormorants are bound loosely, whereas those of docile ones are bound more tightly, in recognition of their differing characters.

In every bird, the primary feathers of one wing are clipped to impair its ability to fly. When only one wing is clipped, a bird will fly in circles and cannot manage long distances. In the spring, when birds are transitioning into their breeding plumage, many fishers will clip the winter plumage. They cut four to eight primary feathers of the right or left wing. Several methods are used. In many areas, four to seven feathers are cut, but one to two feathers on the leading edge of the wing are left untouched (Figure 1.8).

Figure 1.8 Clipping the flight feathers of a cormorant.

This method is easy and widely used. Other fishers leave the shafts and a few leading-edge feathers in place, clipping several feathers. In both these methods, the birds retain their ability to dive and swim because the feathers on the leading edge of the wing remain intact.

Types of Cormorant Fishing in China

In focusing on cormorants, gear, and fishers, the previous discussion has clarified the single joining methods between each aspect of the human-animal relationship. Working with data from the author's study, this section examines regional similarities and differences in fishing methods to reveal the multiple joining methods among fish, birds, and humans, taking each characteristic into account.

Cormorant fishing in China can be compared on the basis of two attributes: method (with or without a net) and acquisition of the birds (home breeding versus purchasing). These can be divided into four types:

- Type A: Home-bred cormorants fish without a net.
- Type B: Purchased cormorants fish without a net.
- Type C: Home-bred cormorants drive fish into gill nets.
- Type D: Purchased cormorants drive fish into gill nets.

Table 1.1 shows the locales, season, gear, number of birds, and form of acquisition for each type. Figure 1.9 shows the locations of the villages and regions where the types are practised.

Table 1.1 Types and characteristics of cormorant fishing in China

	Fishing method			
	Cormorants fish without a net		Cormorants drive fish into gill nets	
Locale	Lake, river, creek, marsh		River, creek	
Season	All year		Mainly winter	
Gear	Bamboo pole		Bamboo pole and gill net	
Cormorants	Fifteen to twenty-five birds		Four to six birds	
	Cormorant acquisition			
	Home-bred	Purchased	Home-bred	Purchased
Type	A	B	C	D

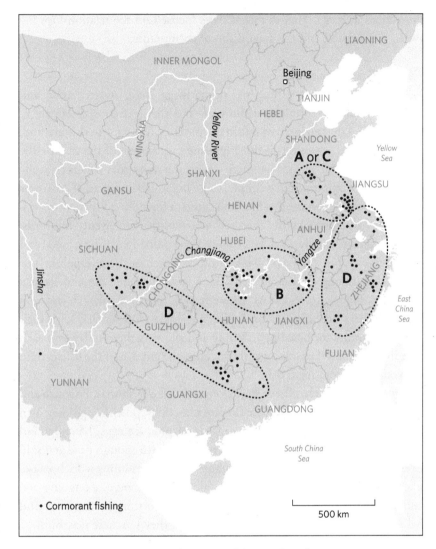

Figure 1.9 Distribution and types of cormorant fishing in China. | Cartography by Eric Leinberger

This classification system allows for the comparison of the 139 villages researched by the author. Type A is practised in 19 villages, type B in 26, type C in 23, and type D in 71, with some overlap. Although differences between fishing methods and boats could ostensibly be used as a comparator, those who fish without a net own large boats, whereas those who use nets own small boats. Therefore, differences in method are mirrored by differences in boats. Hence, this analysis focused on the relationships between the method and the acquisition of cormorants.

Fishing Types A and B

Fishing without a net is practised primarily in lakes, rivers, creeks, and marshes. It occurs throughout the year, and the gear consists largely of bamboo poles that are used to return the birds to the boats. In this method, the number of cormorants is directly related to the size of the catch – the more the birds, the greater the catch – with the result that fishers typically own many cormorants. For example, those in Hunan and Jiangxi Provinces have about twenty to twenty-five, and those in Shandong Province possess about twenty. Most who use this method own fifteen to twenty-five birds.

The acquisition of birds differs among these individuals. Some breed and raise their own birds (type A), whereas others purchase them (type B). Type A fishers were observed in eastern China (e.g., in Shandong and Jiangsu Provinces, Figure 1.9, circle A), where fishing occurs in lakes, rivers, and creeks. Fishers breed cormorants, selecting males and females with high predation ability for breeding in spring and allowing them to lay eggs each breeding season. Hens take over the incubation duties, and the fishers train the young cormorants to fish.

Type B fishers were observed at Dongting Lake in Hunan Province and Poyang Lake in Jiangxi Province (Figure 1.9, circle B). Although they own both male and female birds, some of whom produce eggs, hatching and survival rates are low because the fishers do not have enough time and skill to engage in breeding. Raising cormorants is time-consuming work because, like virtually all baby birds, the vulnerable hatchlings require ongoing care and attention. Type B fishers prefer to spend their time on the water and believe that breeding is not worthwhile. Thus, they purchase new birds.

Fishing Types C and D

Using cormorants to drive fish into gill nets is practised in rivers and creeks. Some of the individuals who employ this method are agricultural workers fishing during the off-season. For example, in Yancheng City, Jiangsu Province, they cultivate rice paddies from spring to autumn and begin fishing after the harvest. Other people fish during the winter and travel to Shanghai, Hangzhou, or Guangdong to find work during the summer. In these areas, cormorant fishing forms a portion of the subsistence calendar.

These fishers possess only a few birds. For example, each fisher in the Tongnan region of Chongqing owns about three, and those in the cities of Shaoxing, Zhejiang Province, and Wuhu, Anhui Province, have about four each. The numbers are small because using cormorants in combination with nets provides a sufficient catch. Many of these fishers are busy with agriculture for six months of the year when they also breed cormorants at home. During this season, they must purchase fish daily in local markets. Each cormorant requires five hundred grams of fish per day, a great expense for anyone who does not fish during the summer. The decision of how many birds to keep always includes a consideration of the cost of feed.

The type C and D methods differ according to acquisition of birds. Type C fishers breed and raise their own, whereas type D purchase them. Type C fishing occurs in Jiangsu Province (Figure 1.9, circle C), an area with a lattice-like pattern of creeks used for drainage, irrigation, and waterborne traffic. Gill nets are employed in these creeks, and cormorants are bred in the spring.

Type D fishing takes place in the upper reaches of the Yangtze River and its branches and in southern Hunan and Guangxi, Guandong, Guizhou, Chongqing, Sichuan, Zhejiang, and Fujian Provinces (Figure 1.9, circles D). Fishers typically purchase male cormorants with high predation ability, but no females. Each owns four to six male birds and, of course, cannot breed them. They must purchase new ones as needed.

Cormorant Fishing in China and Japan: A Comparison

Cormorant fishing in China and Japan displays two major differences: in China, unlike in Japan, birds are bred in captivity, and Chinese fishers do not use ropes to attach their birds to the boat.

The differences in attitude toward breeding may be explained by the relative ease of capturing wild cormorants in the two countries (see Uda 2019 for more on the reasons to breed cormorants). China is an enormous country, and the population of cormorants per square kilometre is small. Under these conditions, catching wild birds is difficult. Therefore, releasing wild-caught cormorants once the fishing season ends would simply mean that fishers must go through the inconvenience of catching and taming replacements every year, not to mention the possibility of failing to acquire any. Thus, despite the time and effort involved, keeping and breeding birds is an attractive and practical solution. If these individuals did not intervene in cormorant reproduction, they would not be able to obtain birds.

Japanese fishers mainly use the Japanese Cormorant *(Phalacrocorax capillatus)*, which is a migratory bird. They can capture new birds during the annual spring and autumn migrations. As a result, they have no need to breed them, which takes time and effort (Uda 2017). Newly captured wild cormorants, particularly young birds, become accustomed to human contact fairly easily and thus can be tamed for fishing in a short period (Uda 2008). Furthermore, they eat various types of fish, as well as pork and tofu. Because they will accept such a wide range of foods, deciding on their supper menu is not a problem. Wild animals are difficult to keep if they are aggressive, overly timid, or hard to feed. Wild cormorants present no challenge in this regard. These conditions allow mutual commitments between birds and fishers, and differences in the ease with which wild cormorants can be caught lead to different attitudes regarding domestication.

In Japan, each cormorant is leashed to the boat during fishing, which is not the case in China. Japanese cormorant fishing is commonly practised in fast-running mountain streams, where the boisterous current can carry boats away from birds that are resting on the bank. Employing a rope to connect them to the boat prevents this from happening.

When considering why Chinese fishers do not use ropes in this way, one must contemplate the relationships between the fishing area, the method used, and the nature of breeding. In China, cormorant fishing often takes place in lakes, marshes, and wide, slow-moving rivers where there is little danger that the placid current will separate boats from birds. The birds fish freely in these areas, and the practice continues throughout the entire year. As mentioned above, the number of cormorants has a direct impact on the size of the catch. However, using ropes would limit the number of birds to six to eight, with the unwelcome result of a diminished catch.

In China, cormorants often drive fish from widespread locations into a net. The areas involved can be over a hundred metres wide, and the birds must be able to swim unencumbered if they are to succeed in their task. Indeed, fishers beat the water with bamboo poles to disperse them. In this situation, tethering the birds to the boats would simply be counterproductive. Thus, fishers who use nets in rivers do not employ rope.

And lastly, many Chinese fishers breed their cormorants and raise them from hatchlings to fledglings. The cormorant is an altricial species – chicks are born blind and naked, and are unable to obtain food on their own.

Thus, they must be cared for by humans. Their eyes open six to seven days after hatching, at which point the fisher ensures that they become imprinted on him or her. As they mature, they repeatedly see manmade objects and grow accustomed to being handled. Through this regular contact, specific behavioural patterns are established. Consequently, they make no attempt to escape, even when they are touched or loaded onto a boat. Because they are imprinted on the fisher and will naturally stay close, there is no need for a rope.

Conclusion

In China, cormorant fishing can be categorized into four types: (A) home-bred birds fish without a net, (B) purchased birds fish without a net, (C) home-bred birds drive fish into nets, and (D) purchased birds drive fish into nets. Types A and C occur mainly in Shandong and Jiangsu Provinces in eastern China. Type B is favoured at Poyang Lake, Jiangxi Province, and Dongting Lake, Hunan Province, in the middle reaches of the Changjiang River. Type D is practised in the upper reaches of the Changjiang River in northeastern Guangxi Province, southern Hunan Province, and Zhejiang and Fujian Provinces.

In the past, some scholars have focused on innovations in fishing tools or the mechanization of fish boats in China. They explained that many people had not abandoned fishing but had introduced modern technology such as GPS and fish finders. These researchers regarded the introduction and creation of new methods as local adaptations whose purpose was to maintain subsistence and enhance people's ability to cope with their particular circumstances (Yohe and Tol 2002, 27–32). However, in cormorant fishing, which has typically not embraced modern technology, the present study shows that local adaptations involve various arrangements of the relations among birds, gear, and humans. Geographic conditions have prompted fishers to generate certain joining methods and to rely on the autonomy of the birds.

Of course, because China is so vast, this study could not possibly examine all instances of its cormorant fishing. Instead, it recorded current practices in many villages to identify regional differences. Thus, it did not fully consider the presence and distribution of historical changes in cormorant fishing. Future research should focus on changes, continuities, reorganizations, and innovations and should conduct regional comparisons over various periods.

The goal of cormorant fishing never varies, but the human-bird relationship does, not only between China and Japan but also among communities in each country. In both cases, cormorants represent a means of subsistence, but they are not necessarily domesticated in the sense of being bred by humans. Yet, whether they are domesticated or tamed – defining characteristics of what Descola (2013, 232–44) classifies as "naturalist" or "animist" ontologies – is not a choice made exclusively by humans. The birds possess some agency and can enter into relationships of joint commitment with humans in some circumstances. In human-animal entanglements, consideration of the animal is always important.

WORKS CITED

Anderson, David G., Jan Peter Laurens Loovers, Sara Asu Schroer, and Robert P. Wishar. 2017. "Architectures of Domestication: On Emplacing Human-Animal Relations in the North." *Journal of the Royal Anthropological Institute* 23, 2: 398–418.

Beike, Marcus. 2012. "The History of Cormorant Fishing in Europe." *Vogelwelt* 133: 1–21.

Bulliet, Richard W. 2005. *Hunters, Herders, and Hamburgers: The Past and Future of Human-Animal Relationships.* New York: Columbia University Press.

Descola, Philippe. 2013. *Beyond Nature and Culture.* Translated by Janet Lloyd. Chicago: University of Chicago Press.

Freeman, Gage E., and Francis H. Salvin. 1859. *Falconry: Its Claims, History and Practice.* London: Longman, Green, Longman, and Roberts.

Fuentes, Agustin. 2007. "Monkey and Human Interconnections: The Wild, the Captive, and the In-Between." In *Where the Wild Things Are Now: Domestication Reconsidered,* ed. Rebecca Cassidy and Molly Mullin, 123–45. New York: Routledge.

Haraway, Donna J. 2008. *When Species Meet.* Minneapolis: University of Minnesota Press.

Ingold, Tim. 2013. "Anthropology beyond Humanity." *Suomen Antropologi: Journal of the Finnish Anthropological Society* 38, 3: 5–23

Kani, Hiroaki 可児弘明. 1966. 鵜飼 [Cormorant fishing]. Tokyo: Chūokōronsha 東京：中央公論社.

Kirksey, S. Eben, and Stefan Helmreich. 2010. "The Emergence of Multispecies Ethnography." *Cultural Anthropology* 25, 4: 545–76.

Laufer, Berthold. 1931. *The Domestication of the Cormorant in China and Japan.* Chicago: Field Museum of Natural History.

Manzi, Maya, and Oliver T. Coomes. 2002. "Cormorant Fishing in Southwestern China: A Traditional Fishery under Siege." *Geographical Review* 92, 4: 597–603.

Mogami, Takanori 最上孝敬. 1958. "鵜飼の伝承" [Transmission of cormorant fishing]. *Bulletin of the Folklore Society of Japan* 日本民俗学 13: 1–37.

Schroer, Sara Asu. 2019. "Jakob von Uexküll: The Concept of *Umwelt* and Its Potentials for an Anthropology beyond the Human." *Ethos* 86, 3: 1–21.

Shinohara, Toru. 1990. 自然と民俗―心意のなかの動植物 *(Shizen to Minzoku: Shini no Nakano Doshokubutu).* Tokyo: Nihon Editor School Press 日本エディタースクール出版部.

Stépanoff, Charles. 2012. "Human-Animal 'Joint Commitment' in a Reindeer Herding System." *HAU: Journal of Ethnographic Theory* 2, 2: 287–312.

Swanson, Heather Anne, Marianne Elisabeth Lien, and Gro B. Ween. 2018. *Domestication Gone Wild: Politics and Practices of Multispecies Relations*. Durham: Duke University Press.

Takuno, Yukinori 宅野幸徳. 1990. "高津川の放し鵜飼" [Cormorant fishing in the Takatsu River]. *Mingu Kenkyū* 民具研究 86: 1–14.

Tsing, Anna. 2013. "More-than-Human Sociality: A Call for Critical Description." In *Anthropology and Nature*, ed. Kirsten Hastrup, 27–42. New York: Routledge.

Uda, Shuhei 卯田宗平. 2008. "ウを飼い馴らす技法——中国・鵜飼い漁におけるウの馴化の事例から" [Why acclimatize a cormorant? Case study on the acclimatization technique in fishing with cormorants in China]. *Bulletin of the Folklore Society of Japan* 日本民俗学 254: 86–113.

—. 2011. "The Local Adaptation of Cormorant Fishers: A Case Study of Poyang Lake, China." *Japanese Review of Cultural Anthropology* 12: 101–22.

—. 2016. "鵜飼い漁誕生の初期条件——野生ウミウを飼い馴らす技術の事例から" [Preliminary conditions behind the birth of cormorant fishing: A study of taming techniques for training wild cormorants]. *Bulletin of the Folklore Society of Japan* 日本民俗学 286: 35–65.

—. 2017. "なぜ宇治川の鵜飼においてウミウは産卵したのか——ウミウの捕獲作業および飼育方法をめぐる地域間比較研究" [Why did a Japanese cormorant lay eggs during cormorant fishing of the Uji River? A comparative study of capture techniques and breeding methods]. *Bulletin of the National Museum of Ethnology* 国立民族学博物館研究報告 42, 2: 125–211.

—. 2019. "カワウの人工繁殖をめぐる漁師の技法と生殖介入の動機——中国雲南省洱海における鵜飼い漁師たちの繁殖技術の事例から" [Cormorant fisher breeding techniques and motivation for reproductive intervention: A case study of artificial breeding techniques maintained by cormorant fishers on Erhai Lake, Yunnan Province, China]. *Bulletin of the National Museum of Ethnology* 43, 4: 555–668.

Yohe, Gary, and Richard S.J. Tol. 2002. "Indicators for Social and Economic Coping Capacity: Moving toward a Working Definition of Adaptive Capacity." *Global Environmental Change* 12, 1: 25–40.

2

Bird-Singing Contests Rules and Communication Frames for Animals and Men

Sonorous Ethnography with the Bulbul Breeders of Southern Thailand

Etienne Dalemans

IN HIS BOOK ABOUT how we use our ears – our ability and codes to listen – to share the sonorous space with our peers, Peter Szendy (2001, 22, emphasis in original) asks a fundamental question: "Can one *make a listening listened to*? Can I convey *my* listening, so singular? It seems very unlikely and yet so desirable, so necessary too."[1] I am afraid I will not be able to answer this question, and nor is doing so the purpose of this chapter, but I will try to bring as much sensory detail as possible to make apparent the harmonies that can occur between humans and animals.

This chapter is based on my four-month ethnographic observation of the breeders of Red-whiskered Bulbuls in Hat Yai, a large city in southern Thailand. My observations are conditioned by my approach to the field of research, through the path I constructed to understand the local society. From a sensory point of view, transmitting my impressions is a rather complicated task, especially because I am writing about things that should be heard rather than read about (hence Szendy's introductory question). This is why I have included a lot of Thai-language renditions of birdsongs throughout the chapter. I truly hope that readers will be able to immerse themselves into the ambient sounds of the singing competitions between bulbuls. I understand this might be a complete failure since most of the experiments I conducted are not covered in the literature outside of Thailand.

I introduce this chapter with an approach grounded on oral callings and names since this will lead us to the entanglement (call and answer) between the bird and its master. In everyday interactions, Thai societies cast a vast nebula of names to indicate the relative social status of individuals. Mostly, they refer to the age and gender (and sometimes ethnicity or physical characteristics) of one's interlocutor (for examples, see the appendix). For instance, if I address a man who seems to be a little older than myself, I will call him *pee* (older brother). He would respond by calling me *nong* (younger brother). If he seems to be at least fifty years old, I would address him as *lung* (old uncle). This system is widespread throughout the community of the *pee-nong* (brothers and sisters) of the "great Thai nation-family" and within the home. Titles can be adjusted according to the relationships of the people involved (for instance, "mother" and "father," "aunt" and "uncle," and "grandfather" and "grandmother" are not restricted to one's blood kin). Here, animals also deserve a title when they nurture a relationship, as in the bulbul-breeding world. In that case, the birds are typically called "nong" and will be taken care of as family members.

In the case of bird breeding, the Red-whiskered Bulbuls and their breeders communicate especially – but not exclusively – through the sonorous environment, with codes and songs. This participates in building an acoustic community, as Raymond Murray Schafer (2010, 308) notes. This community is attentive to the discussions between bird and master. "Breaking the silence" therefore achieves a new meaning, an audacious act of empathy.

My Thai name is Ayaraa, from the legendary and holy elephant figure of the Ramayana. Commonly, I am called Chaang – which means "elephant" – preceded by nong, pee, or whichever title is suitable to my interlocutor. During my ethnographic inquiry, I frequented the *sanaam kaeng nok* (bird contest fields) in the mornings, usually in the company of Pee Stuart. He was among my first informants, and he remained an important one until the end of my stay. A retired banker around sixty years old (I would have called him Lung Stuart, but he would not let me), he had bred birds since the age of twelve. I met him on my first visit to a bird contest field called Sanaam Norah, where he was introduced to me – in a slightly humorous way – as a "specialist." He took me under his wing and conveyed me to various places to meet people (bird-farmers, cage-builders, and bird-catchers and -sellers), including Chang Pot, who was the second of my main informants. He was one of the best birdcage makers in Hat Yai and had been for over ten years. Although he was about the same age as Stuart, he addressed him as Pee Stuart. I called him Adjaan Pot, Professor Pot, and he spent almost three months teaching me how to craft birdcages. I was therefore called Nong Chaang Luugsit Chang Pot (young Chaang, the apprentice of Chang Pot). Spending my days watching birds compete on the sanaam and discussing in Chang Pot's workshop inspired me to consider the intricate aspects of human-bird relationships.

An Animal-Friendly Society

In southern Thailand, including in urban areas, animals are a part of daily life, and living spaces are arranged accordingly. On the ceilings of residential front porches, birdcages often hang from a metal rod (Figure 2.1) or can be positioned close to the *salaa,* an open palm-roofed pavilion, which is sometimes equipped with a table and benches. In the suburbs, in the case of a more rural dwelling, the clay court at the front of the house accommodates cattle and fighting bulls, which are tied to a pole near a manger.

The whole of the pee-nong comes together outside during the fresh periods of the day to share the meal and talk about each other's lives. Pee Stuart took me to Songkhla three times to visit with Bang Moot and some of his other friends. During these trips, he liked to drop by the shop of an old friend. While he discussed business with the shopkeeper, I sat with the men who came to hang their birdcages from the rods provided for the purpose.

Most bird breeders and breeders of other competition animals (*ua chon,* bullfight; *gai chon,* cockfight; and *nok kao,* Zebra Dove) will tell you that

Figure 2.1 Birdcages hang on a house in the village of Baan Kao Kiao, Songkhla Lake.

Figure 2.2 Pao (on the right) meeting my neighbour's bulbul in the area of Plak Tong, Hat Yai.

the young animal, nong, must be taken out as often as possible to socialize it, familiarize it with the greater world, keep it fit (especially bulls, which are taken out "for a run"), and have it meet potential future adversaries, if possible. The male Red-whiskered Bulbul sings in the presence of other males to show off his superiority and chase away his rivals. In this respect, he becomes a champion through a precisely defined form of singing. The frequent or daily meeting of male bulbuls is perceived as the main rule of bird training, especially since it reinforces the bond between the breeder and the bird. In time, the two develop a deep understanding of each other's emotions (Bowman n.d., 25, 32). Thus, when I went to my neighbour's place in the evening, I took my five-month-old bulbul named Pao with me and hung his cage with the others. Beyond these moments, it is also important for the fledgling to become familiar with every type of environment. A bird breeder and competitor will frequent several contest fields.

Memories of Bird Breeding

Bird breeding is said to be an ancient and traditional discipline of southern Thailand. Therefore, we must try to clarify what is correct and what isn't. What emanates from the practice itself is that the breeders are united by a strong feeling of a shared tradition.

Here, it is useful to quote a passage from Alexander Horstmann (2012, 118): "[This] underlines the dialectical relationship with past and present, or tradition and modernity, and thus allows modernity to 'spiritualize' itself." However, I would change the penultimate word to "traditionalize," as the relationship between past and present, or tradition and modernity, allows modernity to traditionalize itself. In this chapter, I make the following assumption: as globalization affected southern Thailand during the second half of the twentieth century, the economy and agro-industry developed (particularly in the rubber industry), inequalities worsened, and *farang* tourism increased (farang means "foreigner" but mostly "white occidental foreigner"), some local populations turned to shared interests, specifically Red-whiskered Bulbul contests. I will do my best to expose the clues that led me to this assumption.

The origin of private bird breeding in Asia is unknown to me, but it seems ancient. According to my informants, it is obscured by the mists of time. The oldest record of breeding Red-whiskered Bulbuls would be in China in 1867 (Siilaama Busyaderm 1999, 1). The presence of singing caged bulbuls seems to engender a form of sonorous well-being in tea salons, stimulating conversation among clients (Sapsin 2009, 64). Written records note that the practice of breeding Zebra Doves began about ninety years earlier. Malikka Khunanurak (1987) suggests that the trapping and farming of these doves started in Siam during the reign of the Rattanakosin family, especially under Rama II around 1782 (Ammapan 1998, 111). Observation and breeding manuals have been circulating since then. Zebra Dove farming developed in the southern region before 1887, particularly in Nakhon Sri Thammarat, where the practice quickly spread to the central region and this commerce developed exponentially (Ammapan 1998, 112). Zebra Dove contests probably began before 1936 in Pattani, in rural and disadvantaged areas where birdsong breaks the monotony of life. From the start, Buddhists and Muslims participated in the competitions (Khunanurak 1987, 25–26). Contests built up throughout the area, quickly becoming a major trade in "southern culture" – according to Abdulladeef Karee (2016, 1), hanging a birdcage on the front porch affirms that the resident is a part of local culture, in addition to beautifying the house. Because of the increasing demand for the resources required to obtain and nurture the Zebra Dove, Red-whiskered Bulbul breeding began to develop more than twenty years ago (Karee 2016, 41).

Known as the "red-bearded masked passerine" *(nok bprood hua khôn krao daeng)*, the Red-whiskered Bulbul has also typically been called the "comma-headed cage bird" *(nok grong hua djuk)* since 1998 (Siilaama Busyaderm 1999, 57) or more commonly *nok grong* (cage bird) or even *nok hua djuk* (comma-headed bird). It currently seems to be the favoured contest bird in Hat Yai. Although my informants stated that the domestic breeding of passerines had been pretty common "since antique times," the written sources indicate that contests developed during the 1960s and 1970s. The first of these took place in Satun around 1961 (Siilaama Busyaderm 1999, 1; Sapsin 2009, 64; Karee 2016, 46) and spread to the provinces of Satun, Songkhla, and Nakhon Sri Thammarat throughout the 1960s (Ritthaisong 1994, 11). At first, they consisted of physical combat between two male bulbuls in a cage, seemingly inspired by cockfights (gai chon), but this format did not persist. Because the bulbul is not sturdy enough to withstand shocks and flesh wounds, people looked for less harmful ways to evaluate its combativeness. Inspired by the then-popular Zebra Dove cooing contests from the extreme southern part of Thailand, the idea of a bulbul singing contest emerged in 1972. This idea is attributed to a governor of Songkhla, though exactly which one remains unknown (Siilaama Busyaderm 1999, 2; Sapsin 2009, 64), with the support of local political institutions. Sources agree on the date and place of the first official match: on the field "behind the train station" of Hat Yai (now inactive) in 1976 (Karee 2016, 46; Ritthaisong 1994, 63; Siilaama Busyaderm 1999, 2).

Bird-singing competitions rapidly spread to Bangkok and other regions of the country. In 1981, the first contest at Djatu Djak, a popular area of the capital, included only sixteen birds (Ritthaisong 1994, 12; Siilaama Busyaderm 1999; Karee 2016). Nowadays, bird breeders are scattered throughout Southeast Asia, coming together for annual or biannual international contests.

Flowers and Whistles

During my four-month ethnographic investigation in Hat Yai, I went to the sanaam kaeng nok (bird contest field) every day to observe the contests and training sessions and to teach Pao to sing in the proper manner, which allowed me to understand the details and difficulties of the discipline.

Hat Yai is filled with these jousting spots, all of which attract local breeders, lifelong friends, and field addicts. To give an idea of the vastness and frequency of the competitions, I have included a detailed schedule for one week of contests in Hat Yai (Table 2.1). I have assigned a letter grade to each field, a classification that is based on the frequency of matches, the number of players, and the quality of judging; in short, it conveys the reputation of the various fields. This classification is not immutable, and my informants expressed some doubts about its accuracy. The fact remains, however, that some fields have greater renown than others.

Table 2.1 charts competition days and three game types (known as *see yog, saa gon,* and *marathon*). Empty cells designate normal training days during which no competitions occur, whereas shaded ones indicate that no birds or breeders are on the field. "THB," which refers to Thai bahts, specifies the size of the winning purse. Text enclosed in parentheses spells out the rules for each contest. For example, in many see yog matches, birds must sing "8 rwm." In other words, they must sing a *doog,* a five-to-six-syllable sentence that begins with a call followed by four or five syllables, and must do so eight times (discussed more fully below). Numbers followed by an asterisk indicate monthly registration fees. The *sieng toong* competition is absent from the chart because it is confined to provincial and national contests that occur once a year or so.

Technical Considerations and the Rules of the Game

People usually meet on the field *dton chao* (in the morning), as early as 8:00 a.m. In Hat Yai, singing contests mostly begin between 10:30 and 10:45 a.m., and the field is usually empty by about noon, though the length of the event depends on the number of contestants. As Table 2.1 shows, the Bao and Khlong Wa fields set aside certain days when no games are played and breeders do not come to the field. Except on one Sunday every month, Khlong Wa is used as a pasture for fighting bulls. These two fields do not have porch roofs or restaurants, which are useful for discussion and exchange. Interestingly, participating in the Sunday meet at Khlong Wa is expensive – its see yog is *bat paeng* (expensive ticket). Its registration fee usually varies between 1,000 and 10,000 bahts per bird, which means that the winnings are also significant. Fields that are used for purposes other than singing contests can also schedule their events in the late afternoon, around 5:00 or 6:00 p.m. The schedule in rural fields is often tied to that of the rubber industry, with contests held around 7:00 or 8:00 a.m., before employees go to work.

The contest field is a large grassy area (around 100–400 square metres) with a central framework of four rows 2.3 metres high and as long as the

Table 2.1 Hat Yai bird contest schedule

Field	Division	Monday	Tuesday	Wednesday	Thursday	Friday	Saturday	Sunday
						Schedule, game, and registration fee		
Bao	C					*See yog* THB 100		*See yog* THB 120
Chokesamaan	D		*See yog* (8 rwm) THB 100		*See yog* (8 rwm) THB 100		*See yog* (8 rwm) THB 100	
Djan Wi Rôt	C	*See yog* THB 100			*See yog* THB 120			*See yog* THB 150
Khlong Wa	A+							***See yog bat paeng***
Kiao	C			*See yog* (8 rwm) THB 100		*See yog* (8 rwm) THB 100		*See yog* (8 rwm) THB 100
Norah	A			*See yog* (8 rwm) THB 100			***Saa gon*** **THB 200**	*See yog* (8 rwm) THB 150
Parinyaa	B		*See yog* (8 rwm) THB 100		*See yog* (8 rwm) THB 100	*See yog* (8 rwm) THB 100		*See yog* (9 rwm) THB 200
Pasawaang	D		*See yog* THB 80		*See yog* THB 60		***Marathon*** **THB 100**	*See yog* THB 80
Plaa Khem	D			*See yog* (8 rwm) THB 100				*See yog* (8 rwm) THB 100

▼ **Table 2.1**

Schedule, game, and registration fee

Field	Division	Monday	Tuesday	Wednesday	Thursday	Friday	Saturday	Sunday
Pra Chad Cheun Djai	B	*See yog* (8 rwm) THB 100		*See yog* (8 rwm) THB 120 (200*)			*See yog* (8 rwm) THB 100	
Rao Nok Nay Air	C		*See yog* THB 100			*See yog* THB 200		*See yog* THB 100
Sapaan Damm	C	*See yog* THB 100		*See yog* THB 100	*See yog* THB 200		*See yog* THB 100	*See yog* THB 100
Soi Yip Soong	C	*See yog* (8 rwm) THB 100				*See yog* (8 rwm) THB 100	*See yog* (8 rwm) THB 100	*See yog* (8 rwm) THB 100
Tesa Pattana	C	*See yog* (8 rwm) THB 100			*See yog* (8 rwm) THB 100		*See yog* (8 rwm) THB 100	
Tung Ree	B		*See yog* (8 rwm) THB 100		*See yog* (8 rwm) THB 100		*See yog* (8 rwm) THB 100	*See yog* (8 rwm) THB 250
Tung Ree 2	C					*See yog* (8 rwm) THB 100	*See yog* (8 rwm) THB 100	*See yog* (8 rwm) THB 100

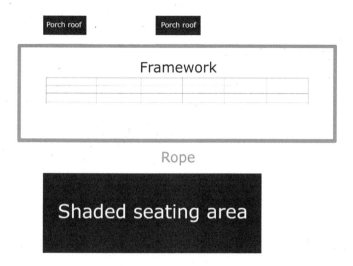

Framework

Porch roof   Porch roof

Rope

Shaded seating area

Figure 2.3 Aerial view of a typical bird contest field.

field allows. Both sides of the field have benches and porch roofs, including a main shaded seating area with a small food stall that sells tea, coffee, and steamed food. Here, common conversation and arbitral talks are held (about the distribution of the referees on the field, the arrangement and sale of breeders' tickets, and the details of the time mastery component).

Saa Gon

The main idea behind bulbul contests is to establish which bird has the best combativeness. When a male bulbul encounters another, it will attempt to steal that bird's food, drive it off, or peck at it. These attacks are generally preceded by a ritual display: leaping, flying around, crying, and singing in a demonstration of power known as the *lilaa*. During the lilaa, a bird lifts its wings, puffs out its chest, opens its beak as wide as possible, and fans its tail. In doing so, it presents "a threat display to an invader by moving its body sideways, jerking its head up and down, and raising the two wings" (Sotthibandhu 2003, 556).

The saa gon (universal, Haas 1964, 534, or more correctly "classical") highlights this aspect of the bird's behaviour. Now largely confined to more official events, it is the oldest gameplay in the competition repertoire. In it, the combativeness of the bird is evaluated out of a possible score of 100: tone (25 points), eloquence (referring to the phrasing, selection, and order of the syllables, 30 points), attentiveness throughout the singing (20 points), lilaa (10 points), and calls (5 points) (Somwang 2012, 334).[2]

These criteria are evaluated for each bird, one after another, for forty-five seconds. The time is measured with the use of a pierced bowl laid in a clear glass jar of water: once the bowl fills with water and sinks, the forty-five seconds have elapsed. The judges alternately stand in pairs in front of a bird to observe and evaluate it. The competition is long and slow. The first round takes about an hour. The cheering, shouting, and clapping are intermittent and relatively smooth. The birds who compete in this game are champions. They must distinguish themselves in several ways, unlike in the briefer competitions of sieng toong or see yog.

Saa gon contests are neither frequent nor popular. Now that the see yog form has become prevalent, most breeders do not train their birds for the physical exertion of the lilaa. The few who compete in the saa gon usually do so for its prestige. Their birdcages are large, comfortable, and highly decorated. In short, this is an expensive competition. A bird that is capable of holding its own at a saa gon meet will be multi-talented and unusual. Showing it off and providing it with suitably magnificent housing is therefore important.

Judging begins when a judge engages in *khum* (cover), in which he swipes his fingers along the sides of the cage to stimulate the bird to perform. At this point, the particular details of the cage may inform him of who owns the bird. He often takes a quick peek at the audience to see the breeder cheering. If the breeder is a friend, the temptation to inflate the bird's score can be strong, and biased judging is easy to conceal due to the complicated evaluation criteria in saa gon events. Apart from the lilaa and the number of times the bird sings during the allotted period, assessing the criteria is often a subjective process. Nowadays, considering the small number of saa gon contests and, consequently, the impartial quality of judging, there are few conflicts about defeats and victories, which were frequent in the past. On the other hand, no matter the type of gameplay, a judge who cheats can discourage breeders from continuing with the sport or may diminish their attendance at events and will darken the reputation of the organizer (Karee 2016, 43).

Sieng Toong

Sieng toong means "golden sound." This type of game was created to remedy the conflicts due to unfair judging in saa gon contests, particularly in connection with the bird's physical behaviour. The sieng toong emphasizes the

Figure 2.4 Made of gleaming mabolo wood and inlaid with iridescent mother-of-pearl, bulbul cages hang on Sanaam Norah during a saa gon competition, December 1, 2018. Featuring easily discernible styles and details, cages signify social standing.

beauty of the song, which is assessed through the criteria of tone and eloquence, each of which has a possible score of twenty-five points. The golden sound occurs in bulbul songs that can be written as *djok kwik go ri li yoo*. I find it rather interesting that professional players consider the syllables and the sentence enunciation as "Arabic" or "Yawee" (Ammapan 1998, 127).[3] From region to region, birds sing differing versions of the golden sound. As Allison Doupe and Patricia Kuhl (1999, 575) point out, "Many songbirds have song 'dialects,' particular constellations of acoustic features that are well defined and restricted to local geographic areas. Just as with human dialects, these song dialects are culturally transmitted (Marler and Tamura 1962)." Hence, the golden sound can also be expressed as *fok fik go ri kwai yoo, yog rik fo fik li yoo*, and so on. Here too, birds sing a doog, a five-to-six-syllable sentence that starts with a call followed by four or five syllables. The doog (flower) consists of the following:

1   A call: *djok, fok,* or *yog*.
2   A development of three to four syllables, in which the third and fourth are almost identical: *kwik go ri li, kwik go fik li,* or *kwik go li li*.
3   A final, long fading-out syllable: *yoo*.

Before a sieng toong competition begins, its organizers decide in advance what the acceptable golden sound will be. In Hat Yai, it typically consists of "djok kwik go ri li yoo." During a one-minute round, a judge evaluates the tone and eloquence of the golden sound alone, for a possible total score of fifty points.

See Yog (and Marathon)

Although the sieng toong is popular in the central regions and Bangkok, it has been increasingly abandoned in the southern provinces of Thailand, where the profitable see yog (four rounds) has taken precedence. This type of gameplay leaves even fewer occasions for biased judging since its phases are simpler and quicker than those of the sieng toong. Its rules were devised to leave little space for contesting the validity of awarded points. The see yog is also the recognized game in the world of bird-singing contests, calibrating most of the exchanges and principles ruling the sonorous environment of this acoustic community (Schafer 2010, 308) outside of the contest field as well.

For its part, see yog concentrates on the number of times a bird sings a doog within a certain period. This criterion is evaluated simply and effectively. During a single round (yog) of between fifteen and eighteen seconds (Karee 2016, 48), the judge counts the number of doog executed by the bird. As mentioned above, one doog is a sung sentence in which a call is followed by a certain number of syllables. Occasionally, a bird will omit the call, launching immediately into the rest of the sentence. On the other hand, bulbuls frequently sing a series of djok calls but never move on to conclude the song. In the case of such subsongs (Marler 1970, 670), the doog is not achieved.

The game begins with a series of four yog in which each bird participates. Every yog proceeds as follows: after running his fingers along the bars of the bird's cage, the judge retreats to a distance of three metres. The "time catcher," usually sitting at the front of the shaded seating area, blows his whistle as he places the time-keeping bowl on the water, and (if all goes well) the bird will begin to sing. Once the bowl sinks to the bottom, which takes about fifteen seconds, the catcher blows his whistle. The judge writes the number of doog performed by the bird on the scorecard hanging under the cage (or sometimes on a rope). He goes around the framework four times, evaluating each bird, one after another. During the four rounds, a bird can potentially score between zero and eight doog. However, if it is to progress in the game,

Table 2.2 Examples of success or failure to reach the minimum qualification threshold (m.q.t.)

Competitor	Yog 1	Yog 2	Yog 3	Yog 4	Total	M.q.t.	Qualified
A	1	5	0	2	1+5+0+2=8		Yes
B	0	0	2	4	0+0+2+4=6	8	No

it must sing eight, as indicated by the title of the contest: *see yog eight doog.* In matches where the eight doog are *ruam* (gathered, indicated by "rwm" in Table 2.1), a bird must only complete the eight before the end of the fourth yog, no matter their distribution over each yog. For example, in Table 2.2, competitor B sang only six doog, failing to reach the minimum threshold of eight, and therefore lost the match.

In games where the four yog are not ruam, the bird must sing a minimum of two doog per yog, which is difficult and restrictive. For example, as shown in Table 2.3, although competitor B produced a total of twelve doog during the four rounds, it did not sing at least two of them in every round, and thus it failed to reach the minimum doog threshold per yog (the m.d.y.). By contrast, though competitor A produced slightly fewer doog, it sang at least two in each yog, thus satisfying the requirements of the game. Unlike competitor B, it moved on to the next phase of the contest.

As mentioned above, I assigned a letter grade to the various fields in Hat Yai, indicating the quality of each one. For example, games at Pasawaang, which scored a D, require only six gathered doog. The three provinces of the deep south (Pattani, Yala, and Narathiwat) are renowned for their competitions of ten to twelve doog, even "ungathered" (some bouts demand a minimum of four doog per yog).

The rigour of the judges is a fundamental criterion for assigning letter grades to each field. For instance, during the contest on Sanaam

Table 2.3 Examples of success or failure to reach the minimum doog threshold per yog (m.d.y.)

Competitor	M.d.y.	Yog 1	Yog 2	Yog 3	Yog 4	Total	M.q.t.	Qualified
A		2	3	2	4	2+3+2+4=11		Yes
B	2	2	1	4	5	2+1+4+5=12	8	No

Chokesamaan on November 29, 2018, 79 percent of the birds moved on to the second round, which could tend to indicate that the judge was lenient on the number of doog, perhaps for social reasons (such as friendship with the breeder), and that the field was of a low division, where achieving victory was easy. A success rate of 50 percent, such as the one on Sanaam Tung Ree during a contest of 288 birds, suggests a higher-division field. Fields renowned for their judging – such as Sanaam Pra Chad Cheun Djai and Sanaam Soi 22 – have a success rate of approximately 30 percent.

Back on the contest field, the first round is followed by a short break during which the breeders attend to their birds. Competitors are fewer now, as birds that failed to perform properly have been removed, and many breeders leave the pitch. This is when the first comments about judging are heard. The game moves into an elimination phase of a single fifteen-second yog per bird. The bird that sings the most doog wins the game. Surprisingly, the winner sometimes performs only two doog at this point. Often, a third round is necessary to settle the results (some contests have prizes for the first ten or fifteen birds in the ranking). During a game on Sanaam Pra Chad Cheun Djai on December 5, 2018, seven rounds were required before the winner emerged (including the first round).

Marathon is a variation of the see yog. It is played in a single tour of six yog. The doog can be shorter, as scores are awarded for every three-syllable sentence (such as *pig kuay jiaew*), which means that the calls count as well (Karee 2016, 47–48). This leads to higher scores of nearly twenty doog for the winner. Imported from Malaysia (Karee 2016, 14), marathon is older than the see yog, but it failed to become popular because it was seen as too easy. Every bulbul is perfectly capable of producing calls (such as *pip pip pip, kuay jiaew*, or *djok djok*) and therefore of doing well in marathon, whereas the other contests are more demanding, requiring a speedier performance or simply better singing.

The prizes are usually cups, home appliances, or, rarely, vehicles. Daily prizes are monetary and of varying amounts, from 500 bahts for small contests, as in Sanaam Pasawaang, to 18,000 for the Sanaam Khlong Wa victory of December 1, 2018. In national competitions, prizes can range from 200,000 to 1,600,000 bahts (Techachoochert and Round 2013, 49). Breeders who possess winning birds can earn the equivalent of a standard monthly salary: from 15,000 to 30,000 bahts (Karee 2016, 44). The small daily gains are immediately reinjected into the field's structures: the winner treats his friends or his team to a drink.

Breeders frequently establish teams to share costs and prizes or to book spots during major contests (Karee 2016, 50) but also to work in solidarity. The captain of team Rak Nok regularly came to pick up one bird or another from Chang Pot to take it to a contest or to train it on the nearby field of Parinyaa. Chang Pot had founded the team over ten years earlier but no longer went to the field due to lasting conflicts around the judging. Teams put pressure on the judges by standing around the field and displaying their colours on the cage covers. During my inquiry, the big winner was team Hero. Every day, its members participated in contests on most fields in Hat Yai. You could see their colours everywhere.

According to my informants from outside the world of bird-singing contests, gambling on bulbul competitions is a financial drain for many people. From my point of view, this was not at all what occurred during the meets. In any case, Thailand is a place of widespread animal gaming (ua chon, bullfight; gai chon, cockfight; *plaa gat,* fish fight). Another popular misconception focuses on the "barbaric" nature of the sport, which originated with Muslim farmers who locked birds into small prisons for their own amusement. If caging a bird goes against the natural order of things, the breeders with whom I spoke pointed out that it was not as ugly as bull- and cockfights, where violence is the name of the game. For me, as for the breeders, nothing savage occurs in the bulbul contests. It is all a question of measure, balance, and harmony.

Most bulbul breeders are men. During my study, I met only three women who participated in competitions. When I tried to determine why their numbers were so small, I was told that women did not have the necessary sensitivity to rear a bulbul. However, more women took part in bird-singing contests during the 1980s and 1990s, especially those involving Zebra Doves (see Khunanurak 1987; Rungrut 2017).

The Tale of Tewadaa

A research report written by Abdulladeef Karee (2016, 2–3) tells us that bulbul competitions are places for betting, with the kind of gambling that is permitted in Islam. They are a game of luck "à la musulmane." However, I did not perceive that luck was particularly important. It may occasionally play a role: Red-whiskered Bulbuls prefer to sing on warm, sunny days, so breeders who compete during fine weather could consider themselves fortunate. And if a female bulbul should chance to fly over the field, the males will react with a vigorous display of courtship song, another lucky happenstance. But on the whole, birds win contests through their own efforts. They are trained champions who experience defeats and pile up victories, making a prize list for themselves and building a reputation. Because of this, they are sold at prices that reflect their value. Some of them even become legendary, as is the case of Tewadaa.

Sitting on Plaa Khem field on the morning of December 20, 2018, Bang Korok invited me to his table and poured me a cup of tea. He called upon Nong and told him to hang Pao on the framework. He asked me if I intended to take Pao to Sanaam Sapaan Damm for the contest of that day. I said no and explained that Pao was still too soft to compete. Bang Korok went on: "What type of cage are you crafting at the moment, Chaang?" As I showed him a picture of my next cage, I added, "sip haa see plawaan Songkhla" (fifteen bars Songkhla whale). Every birdcage is assembled according to a model, either regional or particular to a craftsman. In this case, the Songkhla whale is the generic classical model of the Songkhla region, which is close to Hat Yai. "Fifteen bars" refers to the number of bars on each side of the cage, which indicates its dimensions.

Bang Korok reacted with surprise: "Ah, a Tewadaa cage!" Confused, I repeated the name of the style and said that I had never heard of a Tewadaa cage. The imam, who was listening to our conversation, joined us at the table and asked Bang Korok to tell me about a bird named Ai Plaap Tewadaa, or Tewadaa for short. In reply, Bang Korok explained that about thirty years ago, a breeder named Pee Jiew had owned this bird, which he often took to the field near the station (Sanaam Sattani Rot Fai) in a cage of the plawaan Songkhla style. The bird did so well in competitions that it became famous throughout the city, and people often referred to the cage "of Tewadaa," which quickly turned into the "Tewadaa cage." Bang Korok saw him at times.

Ai Plaap Tewadaa was successful not only for his victories on the field but also because of his excellent relationship with his master. One day, Bang Korok saw Pee Jiew hang Tewadaa's cage on the framework, after which he told the crowd that he would leave it covered – which blocks out the sunlight and causes the bird to stay silent – but that he would get Tewadaa to reply to his call. He then stepped back and called to the bird; Tewadaa answered. The breeder-bird exchange was a success outside of the normal game rules. This harmony in the exchange is at the heart of the bird-singing discipline.

Discussing with Nong: Breaking the Silence

The bulbul and its master build a bond that comes close to what Ian Hacking describes as a "sympathetic resonance." That is, not only is the breeder "in touch with the entire range of animal emotions" (cited in Bowman n.d., 24–25), but also he communicates with and even guides the animal. The duo "musicates" – this is my own translation of Marie Baltazar and Laurent Legrain's (2020, 181) expression "musiquer," which I find relevant in the sense of "manipulating the sonorous environment." Thus, the pair achieves a form of resonance with each other. This resonance can be reached only through training and empathy between the two. Knowledgeable onlookers recognize the tight bond between bird and breeder, often saluting it after the competition.

Commonly spanning only fifteen seconds, a yog is a short and intense experience for the duo, during which the master will try to bond with the bulbul and make it sing as much as possible. Therefore, breeders develop

Table 2.4 Scenarios of sonorous sequences during a yog

Phase	Actor	Action	Sound
1	Judge	Moves toward the cage	
2	Time catcher	Blows whistle and lays the bowl in the water	*Triiit!*
3	Master	Calls to the bird	*Nam nam nam nam nam! / Laew laew laew laew!*
4a	Bird	Answers correctly	*Djok kwik go ri li yoo*
4b	Bird	Does not react	
4c	Bird	Answers incorrectly	*Djok / Kwik go ri li / Pip pip pip*
5a	Audience	Reacts	*Mmmmh! / Öööööh!*
5b	Audience	Does not react	
5c	Audience	Partially reacts	*Mmmmh! / Öööööh!*
6	Repeat phases 3 and 4a as much as possible		
7	Time catcher	Blows whistle when the bowl is submerged	*Triiit!*
8	Judge	Moves on to the next cage	

languages and formulas to call to the bird and signal that it must sing. Whether they succeed is grounded in the bond built through training and in everyday life, just as with Pee Jiew and Tewadaa. When a judge moves toward a cage, the owner can choose whether to position himself at the rope and cheer on the bird. This choice depends on his motivation to win and desire to show off his bond with the bird. Consider, for example, the sonorous sequence outlined in Table 2.4.

A successful sequence would therefore sound like the one laid out in Table 2.5. Phase 3 is not mandatory. The master is not required to rise and stand at the rope to cheer on the bird. His choice relies on his willingness to break the silence and become involved in the sonorous scene. However, if he decides to do so, he must be sure that it is worth it. A master who takes this step puts himself on the line – in public. A scenario like that given in Table 2.6 would be embarrassing for him.

Phases 4 and 5 usually occur when young and/or inexperienced birds participate in a competition.

Writing about the sisil hunters in Taiwan, who must process waves of information as they stalk the bird, Scott Simon (2020, 81) notes that they must "be able to react quickly to this information around them, in ways that may appear almost supernatural but that are based on years of experience

Table 2.5 Scenario for a successful yog

Phase	Actor	Action	Sound
3	Master	Calls to the bird	*Nam nam nam nam nam! / Laew laew laew laew!*
4	Bird	Answers	*Djok kwik go ri li yoo*
5	Audience	Reacts	*Mmmmh! / Öööööh!*

Table 2.6 Scenario for an unsuccessful yog

Phase	Actor	Action	Sound
3	Master	Calls to the bird	*Nam nam nam nam nam! / Laew laew laew laew!*
4	Bird	Does not react	
5	Audience	Does not react	

Figure 2.5 A see yog game on Sanaam Soi Yip Song, November 30, 2018. A group of spectators stands at the left, looking toward the bird, as the master urges it to sing. The judge is at the right, counting the number of doog on his fingers.

(Descola 2013, 100)." This is equally true of the bulbul breeders and competitors in southern Thailand, especially during a fifteen-second yog where the stakes are high. Raymond Murray Schafer (1994, 152) tells us this:

> In the visual figure-ground perception test, the figure and ground may be reversed but they cannot both be perceived simultaneously ... If we are to pursue the figure-ground issue in terms of aural perception, we will want to fix the points when an acoustic figure is dropped to become an unperceived ground or when a ground suddenly flips up as a figure.

To me, this plays out through the judging at a singing contest. Seize the moment when the bulbul's song becomes an acoustic figure: the doog.

As Alain Corbin (RTBF 2020) points out, "Knowing to listen means to master the art of hushing." This comment can be linked with the silence that falls on the field during moments of high tension, when most spectators stop cheering as they concentrate on counting the number of doog. Their silence tends to throw the dialogue between bird and breeder into high relief. For the brief instant of the yog, it is centre stage. Schafer (1994, 257) makes a similar observation regarding the relationship between silence and sound: "When silence precedes sound, nervous anticipation makes it more vibrant. When it interrupts or follows the sound, it reverberates with the tissue of that which sounded, and this state continues as long as the memory holds it. Ergo, however dimly, silence sounds."

I argue that the sequence cumulating in phases 3, 4a, and 5a represents a successful demonstration of sympathetic resonance (Table 2.3). This moment seems to be the essence of the game itself. As the tale of Tewadaa confirms, the duo's ability to communicate and bond is the source of awe and success in this discipline. From the point of view of long-time breeders such as those whom I met during my inquiry, nothing can compare to the bond between master and bird. Whenever it is publicly seen and recognized, the feeling of accomplishment reaches its climax.

Conclusion

Dealing with harmonies in Thai society is the focus of this research. Placing a sensitive approach at the heart of my methodology is important to me. What is at stake goes beyond sight or speech. The roots of this essay's reflections are, of course, my close informants, who graciously shared their world with me and taught me about the body and the senses. I will forever stay connected to Chang Pot through listening and respect: the sonic environment of his workshop, singing shamas and bulbul progressively made sense according to the sonorous space and its dynamics. The daily welcoming of the breeders on the sanaam kaeng nok, shared meals, and moments of teaching all generate a profound respect for silence and the importance of speech. All these elements combine in the construction of meaningful vectors.

The relationships I witnessed between the bulbuls and their breeders or, in more general terms, in the surroundings of the sanaam kaeng nok, are initiated in sensitivity: "moral imagination – imaginative efforts, cultivation of sensibilities, emotional resonance, etc. – [is] crucial to understanding animals' lives" (Bowman n.d., 25). This relationship is epiphanic to me in the way the pee-nong "musicate" (Baltazar and Legrain 2020) together.

This society of southern Thailand has, for many decades, developed and entertained a way of "musicating" beyond what occidental objectivism calls "species." Scott Simon (2020, 81) tells us about his Taiwanese experience: "When they are in the forest, birds appear as persons." I understand and support this point of view along with the "ecology of selves" such as described by Eduardo Kohn (2013), except that, from the experiments I conducted in Hat Yai, birds do not appear as people because they exist and interact in a certain place, but according to the dynamics in which they are entangled. They are truly a part of the pee-nong community, without needing to be animated by the spirit of a (human) close one (Kohn 2013, 112).

The pee-nong community builds a rich, sonorous environment that lets its members express their relative positions. The space-time capsule of the bird game opens the possibility of redefining these positions. In the Red-whiskered Bulbul competitions, this human-bird relationship is continuously being redefined.

Appendix: Glossary of Thai Words

Family and brotherhood

Masculine		Feminine	
Older brother	Pee	Older sister	Pee
Younger brother	Nong	Younger sister	Nong
Father	Po	Mother	Mae
Child/son	Luug	Child/daughter	Luug
Young uncle	Na	Young aunt	Na
Old uncle	Lung	Old aunt	Pa
Paternal grandfather	Puu	Paternal grandmother	Yai
Maternal grandfather	Dta	Maternal grandmother	Ya

Formal titles (regardless of gender)

You/Miss/Mr. (polite)	Khun
Mr. (very polite, only for men)	Nay
Apprentice/disciple	Luugsit
Craftsman	Chang
Teacher	Kruu
Professor/Master	Adjaan
Doctor	Mo
President	Nayog

Titles referring to ethno-cultural and/or physical characteristics

Muslim brother	Bang
Older Chinese brother	Gô
The Chinese one	Djaek
The black one	Damm
The fat one	Uan

NOTE

1. Unless otherwise indicated, all translations are my own.
2. Somwang doesn't account for the remaining ten points.
3. The Yawee are a southern cultural group often mistakenly considered by southerners to be Arabic because of their religion (Islam).

WORKS CITED

Ammapan, Somprach รศ.อัมมะพันธุ์, สมปราชญ์ท. 1998. *กีฬาพื้นเมืองภาคใต้* [Sports of the southern regions]. Pattani: Prince of Songkhla University ปัตตานี: มหาวิทยาลัยสงขลานครินทร์. Thai calendar year of publication 2541.

Baltazar, Marie, and Laurent Legrain. 2020. "Acoustémologie et empreinte sonore: Faire avec et faire par les sons. Être avec et être par les sons." *Cahiers de littérature orale* 87: 175–94.

Bowman, Chellie. n.d. "Essay 1 towards an Anthropology of Birds: A Critical Review." Unpublished manuscript.

Descola, Philippe. 2013. *Beyond Nature and Culture.* Translated by Janet Lloyd. Chicago: University of Chicago Press.

Doupe, Allison J., and Patricia K. Kuhl. 1999. "Birdsong and Human Speech: Common Themes and Mechanisms." *Annual Review of Neuroscience* 22: 567–631.

Haas, Mary R. 1964. *Thai-English Student's Dictionary.* Stanford: Stanford University Press.

Horstmann, Alexander. 2012. "Échanges de gestuelles religieuses dans l'espace rituel: performance des traditions rituelles et négociation des frontières entre les communautés dans le bassin du lac Songkhla." *Anthropologie et Sociétés* 36, 3: 117–36.

Karee, Abdulladeef การี, อับดุลลาตีฝ. 2016. *รายงานวิจัยฉบับสมบูรณ์: นกกรงหัวจุก: ผนันพื้นบ้านในสังคมมุสลิมสามจังหวัดชายแดนภาคใต้* [Accomplished research report: Red-whiskered Bulbul: Bets within Muslim type village communities in the three southern provinces]. Bangkok: Center for Gambling Studies กรุงเทพมหานคร: ศูนย์ศึกษาปัญหาการพนัน. Thai year 2559.

Khunanurak, Malikka รศ. คณานรักษ์, มัลลิกา. 1987. *การเลี้ยงและการเล่นนกเขาชวาเสียง* [Breeding and game for singing Zebra Dove]. Pattani: Prince of Songkhla University ปัตตานี: มหาวิทยาลัยสงขลานครินทร์. Thai year 2530.

Kohn, Eduardo. 2013. *How Forests Think: Toward an Anthropology beyond the Human.* Berkeley: University of California Press.

Marler, Peter. 1970. "Birdsong and Speech Development: Could There Be Parallels? There May Be Basic Rules Governing Vocal Learning to Which Many Species Conform, Including Man." *American Scientist* 58, 6: 669–73.

Marler, Peter, and M. Tamura. 1962. "Song 'Dialects' in Three Populations of White-crowned Sparrows." *The Condor* 64, 5: 368–77.

Ritthaisong, Thanakorn ฤทธิ์ใธสง, ธนากร. 1994. *คู่มือการเพาะพันธุ์นกปรอดหนวดแดงมืออาชีพ* [Professional Pycnonotus Red-whiskered Bulbul breeding guide]. Suphanburi สุพรรณบุรี. Thai year 2537.

RTBF (Radio-télévision belge de la Communauté française). 2020. "Éloge du silence, avec Alain Corbin." Brussels. https://www.rtbf.be/lapremiere/article/detail_alain-corbin-eloge-du-silence?id=9659530&fbclid=IwAR0FUXkıRELohvSEO__2D7Fbhskb_7wpNJDJaCI2TZcxs4pGEdRjVbjmi-Q.

Rungrut, Suppatra รุ่งรัตน์, สุพัตรา. 2017. "ต้นกำเนิดนกเขาชวา เงินล้านของประเทศไทย" [The origin of million Thai bahts Zebra Dove in Thailand]. *วารสารมหาวิทยาลัยราชภัฏยะลา* [Journal of Yala Rajabat University] 12, 2: 153–66. Thai year 2560.

Sapsin, Watee ทรัพย์สิน, วาที. 2009. "กรงเจ๊ะอาแม: ใครๆก็อยากได้" [Jae Amer cages: Everyone wants one]. มหาวิทยาลัยสงขลานครินทร์ [Prince of Songkhla University] 30, 3: 62–66. Thai year 2552.

Schafer, Raymond Murray. 1994. *The Soundscape. Our Sonic Environment and the Tuning of the World.* Rochester: Destiny Books.

—. 2010. *Le paysage sonore. Le monde comme musique.* Clamecy: Wildprojects Editions

Siilaama Busyaderm, Songkrand สีลามะ บุษยาเดิม, สงกรานต์. 1999. *ตำนานเขียน: นกปรอดหนวดแดงของประเทศไทย* [Written legend: Thailand's Red-whiskered Bulbul]. Bangkok: K. Pl. Bangkok กรุงเทพมหานคร: บริษัท เค.พี.กรุงเทพ. Thai year 2542.

Simon, Scott. 2020. "A Little Bird Told Me: Changing Human-Bird Relations on a Formosan Indigenous Territory." *Anthropologica* 62, 1: 70–84.

Somwang, Buyrod สมหวัง, บุริรอด. 2012. *นกปรอดหนวดแดง: ผสมพันธุ์ตามวิธีนายหัว* [Red-whiskered Bulbul: Breeding according to the "Mr. Hua" method]. Surat Thani: Tabee Takhsin Red-whiskered Bulbul Club สุราษฎร์ธานี: ชมรมปรอดหนวดแดง ตะปี ตากสิน. Thai year 2555.

Sotthibandhu, Sunthorn. 2003. "Territorial Defense of the Red-Whiskered Bulbul, Pycnonotus Jocosus (Pycnonotidae), in a Semi-Wild Habitat of the Bird." *Songkhlanakarin Journal of Science and Technology* 25, 5: 553–63.

Szendy, Peter. 2001. *Écoute. Une histoire de nos oreilles.* Paris: Les Éditions de Minuit.

Techachoochert, Supatchaya, and Philip D. Round. 2013. "Red-Whiskered Bulbul: Are Trapping and Unregulated Avicultural Practices Pushing This Species towards Extinction in Thailand?" *Birding Asia* 20: 49–52.

3

The Rooftop of the City

Pigeon-Keeping Practices and the Construction of Masculinities in Amman, Jordan

Perrine Lachenal

CLIMB THE STAIRS. This is how every meeting with a pigeon-breeder begins – a flight of stairs that leads to a roof. We don't stop at any floor as we continue our ascent. We can hear coos, the flapping of wings, and the sound of little bells before we arrive at the top. The smell grows stronger as we approach the birds. The odour is overwhelming. With time, you get used to it and start recognizing it throughout the winding streets of Amman, a pungent reminder of the popularity of pigeon keeping in the city. It is only upon reaching the rooftop that my eyes confirm what my ears and nose already know: the pigeons are here. Some of them, perched, seem to be admiring the view, while others are busy drinking, pecking at the concrete, or fighting over seeds that have just been tossed on the ground. A neophyte to pigeon breeding, I don't yet know the names of the different types of pigeons here. Still, I can't help but notice the diversity of sizes, colours, beaks, and feathers in the flock of birds. I'm invited to take a tour of the cages, meet the keeper's favourites, contemplate the promise of eggs soon to hatch, and then take my seat on a plastic chair. Coffee is served – impossible to refuse – and, finally, the interview can begin.

The ethnographic investigation that is the basis for this chapter on pigeon keeping in the Jordanian capital was carried out high above the city. This spatial characteristic is not a simple detail but rather the point of departure for my reflections. Urban anthropology has yet to explore the rooftops of Middle Eastern cities, which, through the breeding activities carried out there, represent singular territories for examination. Here is a space where we look at humans' relationships with animals, thereby attesting to the multi-species dimension of urban life and addressing contemporary reconfigurations of gender and class. Pigeon keeping, a popular hobby among men in Amman's working-class neighbourhoods, is a good illustration of this point. In this chapter, I show that pigeons, as well as the relationships and games in which they are involved in Jordan, constitute a unique ethnographic lens through which to examine the construction of masculinities. Assuming that gender is also based beyond the human experience, I present an analysis of the relationships between humans and birds. In this sense, pigeons are not only mediums of gendered socialization but also actors who contribute to reconfigurations of gender.

Looking for Pigeons

In working-class neighbourhoods of Middle Eastern cities, the relationships between humans and domesticated birds occur mainly on rooftops. The importance of pigeon-keeping activities – breeding, training, and competition – illustrates the upward movement of subaltern experiences and uses of urban space, drawing observation toward a locale that has been minimally explored by urban anthropology: the sky (Frembgen and Rollier 2014).[1]

High Up: Spaces and Objects of Urban Subalternity in the Middle East

Urban anthropology that does not consider the vertical dimension of city space fails to observe the diverse ways of inhabiting a city – "faire ville" as Michel Agier (2015) writes – and their gendered dimension, as I have shown in previous work (Lachenal 2012, 2018). It was, for instance, from balconies, windows, and rooftops that many women experienced – and, in some cases, strategically participated in – Egypt's revolutionary process in 2011. Assef Bayat (2000) mentions the spatial dimension of tensions opposing "subalterns" of the state in the Middle East. He explores street vendors' strategies of occupying sidewalks, alleyways, and other corners of the city as forms of action impinging on the government's prerogative to control space and practise urban governance. Bayat (2000, 547) suggests considering the "multidirectional" nature of this impingement movement, noting that subaltern practices also make their way into high-up spaces, along walls

Figure 3.1 Dovecote on rooftop, Amman, October 2019.

perforated with improvised windows, on expanded balconies, added floors, and rooftops that have been renovated and transformed into living spaces, utility rooms, or barns. Focusing the analysis on rooftops and the activities that occur there enables us to take a closer look at popular ways of inhabiting cities in the Middle East (Abd Elrahman and Mahmoud 2014) and to scrutinize "the urbanity of the marginalized," as described by Kamel Doraï and Nicolas Puig (2012). Adopting this bird's-eye view also means assuming a link between individuals' relationships to spaces and the processes of political subjectification (Bayart 2004).

An investigation carried out by geographer Marie Piessat (2018) reveals differing uses for rooftop terraces in Cairo. In working-class neighbourhoods, they are mostly used for breeding animals – cows, goats, chickens, and pigs in Christian areas – which provide the family with meat, milk, and eggs. In these spaces, it is also common to find dovecotes and large wooden or concrete structures housing birds that will ultimately be sold in the market. Figure 3.1 shows an example from Jordan. It is taken in Tabarbour, a district in the northeast of Amman, at Abu Shadi's home. Abu Shadi is proud of his flock, accommodating nearly a hundred birds.

Pigeon trade in the Middle East – whether in Egypt, Lebanon, Syria, or Jordan – is a widespread activity that is an economically attractive investment. However, most pigeons living on rooftops in Cairo, Beirut, Damascus, and Amman are not destined for trade. Instead, they are bred to participate in competitions that can be qualified, depending on the context, as "game," "war," or "sport." The principle is simple: each breeder makes his pigeons fly from the rooftop, hoping to entice birds from the flocks of other breeders who will permanently join them, with the result that he will ultimately be recognized as possessing the most loyal pigeons who command the greatest territory of influence. These bird games, which take up a significant amount of time in the daily life of breeders, are organized neither in the public space (Geertz 1973) nor under the eye of any authority whose prerogative would be to determine a ranking. In the suburbs of Beirut, Amman, Cairo, or Damascus, pigeon competitions are organized far from the government's gaze, in spaces that are inaccessible to it. In this context, it is noteworthy that during the 2006 avian flu and 2010 pig flu epidemics, sanitation inspectors infiltrated alleyways and courtyards in Egypt but were unable to access the rooftops where most breeding activities happen (*Le Monde* 2008).

Pigeon Keeping: A Hobby for Bad Boys?

The *kashshāsh*, who breeds and trains his pigeons for competitions, is a central masculine figure in Middle Eastern societies. The stigmatizing way in which he is represented and the efforts to discipline him reveal the mechanisms through which people are relegated to inferior ranks, as well as how social power relationships form in cities across the Arab world.

With their obvious aesthetic dimension, pigeon-keeping practices have piqued the interest of journalists over the past several years. News articles portray a controversial activity practised by young unemployed men (*Al-Akhbar* 2015; *Middle East Eye* 2015; *Al-Jazeera* 2017). Pigeon keeping is presented as a suspect hobby that has regained popularity in Lebanon and Jordan following the massive influx of Syrian refugees. In cities – and this is true beyond the Middle East (Digard 2003; Jerolmack 2013) – pigeon-breeders have a bad reputation. They are portrayed as working-class thugs with a propensity for lying, stealing, betting, and using the rooftops of their dovecotes to spy on neighbours, observe surrounding apartments, and catch glimpses of naked women (Barbosa 2013). It is even said that the testimony of a kashshāsh cannot be accepted in a law court, as the suspicion of dishonesty is too great (*Independent* 2000). In Middle Eastern cities, pigeon breeding and competitions are organized illicitly, often defying disciplinary measures that try to regulate them. The problems that arise from competitions between keepers, especially the fights and settling of scores that sometimes ensue, seem to justify the authorities' numerous attempts to prohibit them. The authorities use various arguments, such as the threat to public health or the proximity of an airport, to clip the birds' wings – often literally. Gustavo Barbosa (2013) repeatedly mentions conflicts relating to pigeon breeding and competitions in Shatila, a refugee camp in Lebanon, where he carried out fieldwork. The camp's security committee was determined to see pigeon-keepers disappear as quickly as possible, ostensibly for reasons of "public order." Ultimately, it used the argument of the camp's proximity to the Beirut airport, where a stray pigeon had allegedly gotten into the jet engine of an airplane and risked causing a crash. Camp authorities decided to ban pigeon keeping and required breeders to kill their birds or reduce the length of their feathers so that they could not fly. They threatened to arrest anyone who did not respect the new measures. Aladin Goushegir (1997) and Jean-Pierre Digard (2003) write about similar strategies in Iran, where authorities also saw pigeon keeping as an undesirable activity. In 1998, they used the same argument of airport proximity to ban pigeon breeding in the city of Mashhad and set up a toll-free number for denouncing pigeon-keepers.

Pigeon breeding is associated with problematic and suspicious models of masculinity. In contrast to Bali, where prominent locals devote themselves to bird domestication and competition (Geertz 1973), in Cairo, Beirut, and Amman, mostly men of low social standing who live on the fringes of the cities practise these activities (Barbosa 2013; Alshawawreh 2018; Aubin-Boltanski 2021). Whereas cockfights shed light on Bali's system of prominence, pigeon competitions offer insight into urban marginality. In this context, it is worth confronting common representations of pigeon-breeders by meeting the men themselves. What is it like to be a kashshāsh? What does it mean to care for pigeons? And how do breeders cope with the negative depiction of this passion? These were the questions I had in mind when I left for Amman for my first ethnographic study in the fall of 2019.

Investigating Amman's Rooftops: A High-Perched Ethnography

My fieldwork was conducted with the support of Shakk, a research group investigating the social and political reconfigurations following the 2011

Syrian uprising and the subsequent war.[2] Thanks to it, I could spend two weeks in Amman – a very expensive city – and rely on the institutional and scientific support of the French research institute there. Given the brevity of my stay, I tried to anticipate as much as I could before travelling. I knew that the pigeon-keeping world is exclusively masculine, in Jordan and around the globe (Goushegir 1997; Digard 2003; Jerolmack 2013; Frembgen and Rollier 2014). Concealing the fact that I am not a Jordanian man was impossible, especially as I was six months pregnant at the time, and I was afraid that I would encounter difficulties. I needed a guide, and Ali, a Jordanian freelance journalist, was perfect. On a friend's recommendation, I contacted him a few days before travelling. Ali showed immediate enthusiasm for my research project and agreed to assist me, seizing the opportunity to prepare on his own a journalistic article on pigeon keeping in Amman. Without his help, I would not have managed to spend so many hours in the alleys of the Friday pigeon market or whole evenings at pigeon cafes. I was the only woman there. If my pregnancy excluded me from seduction games, it was still not easy to present myself as a legitimate interlocutor with whom to open up about a passion for pigeons. With Ali by my side, it was much simpler. He was the icebreaker, introducing me to sellers and breeders as a French researcher investigating the social representations of the kashshāsh in Jordanian society. Since I could not blend into the background, Ali made me very visible: for instance, he made me sit in the front row during auctions, with the result that I received special attention and loud dedications at the microphone. This visibility is a determinant aspect of my fieldwork: People knew I was there and why I was there. They also knew that I was assisted by a journalist. The manner in which the breeders talked to us was influenced by their perception of our work. That is how I understood their efforts to defend their status and the reputation of their passion: through us, their spokespersons, they were talking to those outside their neighbourhoods and even outside Jordan. It is worth mentioning that Ali sat beside me during most of my interviews. He aided me with the Jordanian dialect and helped transcribe the interviews later. He is still a treasured interlocutor as I write this essay.

Thus began my ethnographic investigation in Amman, seeking to analyze, in terms of masculinities, the social practices and narratives associated with pigeons in Jordanian society. Taking place on the rooftops of the city, it explores the spatial and gendered dimension of a socially depreciated pastime rooted in the love of birds.

Figure 3.2 An interview taking place on Abu-Shadi's rooftop

Caring for Birds

It is difficult not to notice the hundreds of pigeons that fly above Jordan's capital at the end of each day. One can sometimes guess, by studying their circular trajectories, where their breeders are located. Sometimes, it is even possible to catch a glimpse of the keeper's silhouette on his rooftop. He usually holds a stick or sheet that helps him to direct any pigeons heading for an early landing. He decides the right moment to call his birds back: once they have flown well enough – or when he notices that other lost birds have joined them – he raises his voice to beckon them back, throws seeds on the ground, or brandishes a female bird flapping her wings. My interviews often took place as the pigeons returned to the roof before nightfall. And so – before hundreds of birds pecking at the ground – the men tell me about their initiation into pigeon keeping. Figure 3.2, taken on Abu Shadi's roof, shows the setting of my interviews: on a small plastic table, one can see glasses of tea and packs of cigarettes. A few young men, from neighbouring families, came to attend the interview. In front of us, the birds are busy eating.

The Love of Birds: Interspecies Relationship

The profile of each keeper is unique, and yet all of them described a common passion initially transmitted to them by other men, often older. This is what Abu Shadi, a man in his fifties who works in public administration, told me:

> When I was little, I played with my brothers' and father's pigeons. At that time, I didn't understand the point of pigeon breeding. I began to understand later on. At first, I just did like others, I imitated other breeders. It's like cigarettes: most people start smoking because they see others smoking. They don't know what it means to smoke, but they do it. It's the same for me, I didn't know why I was interested in pigeons, I was doing what others did.

The comparison between pigeon keeping and smoking, recurrent in the stories told by my informants – all of whom were smokers – sheds light on the addictive nature of the activity. I am told that once a neophyte pigeon-keeper has installed a few cages on his roof, observed the eggs hatch, and made his birds fly, it is difficult for him to stop. His hobby becomes costly and time consuming, even if selling his birds can earn him a bit of money. Over time, the pigeons occupy a significant place in the lives of their owners. Their growing fascination can give rise to tensions. For instance, marriage is commonly seen as incompatible with pigeon keeping. Married breeders recalled that they were often forced to stop the activity for a time during the beginning of their marriage as their new bride and her family disapproved of the hobby. Some chose to carry on in secret, temporarily displacing their flock to a friend or relative's rooftop. Others, like Abu Shadi, had to make special arrangements: "I try to share my time between my pigeons and my family, to find a balance so that there aren't any tensions. I wake up every morning at 6:30 to spend an hour with my pigeons and feed them before going down to have breakfast with my daughters and wife."

A breeder's attachment to his birds, perceived as undermining his commitment to his family, was nevertheless described in parenting terms. Breeders repeatedly said that the pigeons were "like my children," evoking sleepless nights spent watching over them and the sacrifices made for them. The keepers expressed a sense of having many responsibilities, some of which were non-negotiable. Abu Abdullah, who worked in a small business in Jabal Amman in the city centre, explained that "my pigeons are part of my family, and I treat them like my children. Every afternoon from 3 to 5, I'm not around. That's it. I'm with them. Even if my father came back from his grave, I would tell him that between the hours of 3 and 5, I'm busy."

In Chapter 2 of this book, Etienne Dalemans reports the use of a similar rhetorical register regarding bird-singing contests in southern Thailand: birds are named as if they were part of the breeder's family. But in this case, they are seen as "younger brothers/sisters," not as children. One could assume that the collaborative performances in which they are involved are understood through a more horizontal perspective.

What makes the connection between a breeder and his pigeons unique is the collective quality of the relationship: the kashshāsh often interacts with a large group of birds. Interestingly, it is very rare that the pigeons are named, except for one or two birds that show salient characteristics. This does not prevent breeders from recognizing their birds, being attached to them, and even projecting mutual sentiments onto them. One of my interviewees was Bilal, a twenty-something breeder with no professional activity who lived in Jabal Hussein, a Palestinian refugee camp that has become a "city" over the past decades (Destremeau 1996). He told me, "My pigeons know me. Most of the time, we understand each other without speaking because they know me very well ... They obey only me. Even if someone imitated my movements and voice, they wouldn't come."

Hamdi, a driver in his thirties, sadly recalled having had to stop pigeon keeping overnight due to an unmanageable flea infestation: "It broke my heart to abandon them like that. I loved my pigeons, but more importantly, I know the pigeons knew I loved them. They felt how I took good care of them when I came to see them two or three times a day."

Strikingly, my interviewees unanimously expressed their attachment to their birds and their love for them (Laugrand, Cros, and Bondaz 2015; Dalemans, Chapter 2 this volume). For these men, the topic of pigeons seemed to offer a preferred discursive frame to show affection. When Seham Boutata (2020) investigated goldfinch keeping in Algeria, she discovered a similar phenomenon: according to her, the sensible and poetic way in which bird lovers – men only – express their attachment to goldfinches should be understood in light of the social and gendered rules that prevent them from openly expressing romantic love. Poetry, as Lila Abu-Lughod's (1986) classic in anthropology revealed decades ago, can be a strategic site in which to voice affection and commitment. In the case of Algerian goldfinches, relationships with animals seem to provide a socially acceptable way of showing feelings that, if between humans, would have to be kept silent. It will be interesting to carry on with this hypothesis during future fieldwork in Amman, investigating the ways that sentiments toward pigeons contribute to coping with, challenging, or strengthening (Krawietz 2014) social and gendered norms.

Viagra and Pearls: Techniques and Accessories of Care

Taking care of pigeons involves more than just feeding them, making them fly, and cleaning their coops. It is also about keeping them healthy and beautiful. Indeed, care occupies a large portion of a breeder's time. Health is a recurring topic, and many treatments are used to "strengthen" birds and prevent infections and epidemics. A wide variety of veterinary products are sold at diverse prices depending on their country of origin. Breeders shop at specialized stores where they find various disinfectants, medications, and vitamins to strengthen the birds' immune defence and combat pests, to which they are sensitive.

Many of these products – some of which are called "Viagra" – aim to develop "sexual ardour." Possessing fertile birds is crucial, ensuring both the growth of the flock and the chance that the kashshāsh can sell some of his birds at the market and make some money out of it. Besides this rational argument, more symbolic readings are possible: Many researchers insist on the link between birds and masculine sexualities, paying attention to terminologies, art, and food (Geertz 1973; Grieco 2010; Barbosa 2013).[3] In differing times and spaces, they explain, the names of birds often designate penises, and their meat and eggs are believed to increase men's sexual power. Conducting fieldwork in a Lebanese refugee camp, Emma Aubin-Boltanski (2021) analyzes the pigeon competitions there in terms of "sexual honour," considering the loss of a bird as a loss of virility.

Pigeon care also includes an aesthetic dimension, as indicated by the accessories – beads, rings, and bells of various sizes – that breeders use to decorate their birds. These adornments are sold by the handful in stands throughout the pigeon market held each Friday in downtown Amman. Figure 3.3 shows the rings, plastic or metal, that can be slipped onto the legs of the birds. Some accessories are worn on the leg, others on the wing. Every colour is available. Abu Abdallah, for example, chose beads in shades of blue, the colours of his favourite soccer team.

Figure 3.3 Adornments for pigeons at the Amman bird market, October 2019.

One vendor in the market showed me rings handcrafted by his wife, made in the colours of the Palestinian flag. Sometimes engraved, the rings can also identify birds during competitions. However, I was told that any self-respecting breeder always recognized his own birds, even from a distance and while they were in motion, and had no need of an identifying ring.

Looking after pigeons is a commitment since they are fragile and need daily attention. Speaking of their passion, the kashshāsh whom I met evoked a love story, drawing outlines of particular models of masculinities structured around care practices and interspecies relationships. If not for the love of birds, they argued, why choose a hobby that consumed time, cost money, and damaged your reputation?

Masculinities under Pressure
One day, I joined a research assistant named Monia for coffee in downtown Amman. When I told her about my project, she said, "It's pretty funny that men choose to love these animals to assert themselves. Pigeons aren't dinosaurs ... They're so small and weak!" The pigeon is neither rooster nor falcon,

nor any other bird that serves as a vector for projections of victorious virility (Geertz 1973; Calvet et al. 2007; Barbosa 2013; Koch 2015). In competitions between keepers, the winner is the one whose birds demonstrate not speed, aggression, or power, but loyalty. Their return is proof of the attachment that bonds them to their breeder.

Attachment and Loyalty: Birds Have Qualities

Projecting human qualities onto the birds, my interlocutors boasted the virtues of their pigeons, including the endurance and perseverance required for them to return to their home rooftop. "Pigeons never give up," explained Abu Abdallah in a martial tone as he introduced me to one of his favourite birds: "Even if he were exhausted, this one here would continue: he would sleep on the roof for a few hours and resume his journey right away. He would never give up. He would rather die than surrender."

The loyalty of the birds is tested every day from the moment they take flight above the city. Once in the sky, they encounter birds from other rooftops. At this moment, when the flocks mingle, the risk of losing birds is greatest for the breeders. And because the pigeons are free to land wherever they choose, their return to the owner is meaningful. The birds, said Abu Abdallah, "know who is in charge": they are linked to him. Chapters 1 and 2 of this book – dealing with cormorant fishing in China and bulbul-singing contests in Thailand – report comparable connections between birds and their breeders. Shuhei Uda evokes a true "collaboration" between cormorants and fishers based on a "joint commitment," and Etienne Dalemans describes an emotional attachment between the bird and its breeder, performed through constant communication between both of them.

A good breeder is not supposed to lose his pigeons. If he is good, they will come back to him. And if they do, their return may also be motivated by loyalty to their female and offspring. Because of this unconditional attachment to the "couple" and the "family," keepers wave a female in the air as they call the birds back. Beyond being loyal and faithful, pigeons, I was told, are peaceful and loving creatures that never make any problems. In this sense, Abu Shadi explained, they are "better than humans":

> Pigeons don't hate, they have only love to give. They are not like humans; they don't cause problems. Me, on the other hand, sometimes when I go

out with my friends, I run into trouble. But when I return to my birds, everything is okay. That's why I love my pigeons so much, because of the peace they bring me.

Bilal voiced a similar opinion: "People lie, but not pigeons. With people, you always run into problems. In the neighbourhood and the city, people make problems for you. With pigeons, it's different."

The anthropomorphic discourse used to characterize pigeons is revelatory about the social representations of their observers (Despret 2009; Haraway 2019). In the present case, these depictions turn on faithfulness in intimate relationships, family responsibility, and masculine loyalty. This point is particularly interesting because, as noted above, it is precisely these three domains that are challenged by the practice of pigeon keeping. Its poor reputation stems from the perception that it removes men from their wives and children, plunging them into rivalries with other men. The birds thus appear to constitute a metaphorical society from which breeders draw to counterbalance the negative social portrayals associated with their hobby.

Dismissing Stigmas: The Others Are the Thugs

Distinguishing themselves from (undesirable) others seemed particularly important to my interviewees considering that the passion for pigeons seems much more socially widespread than is known.

Upon arriving in Amman, I set out in search of pigeon-keepers, asking around for tips and contacts. The responses to my requests were so consistent that they are worth analyzing. Initially, those whom I asked expressed surprise about my topic, then warned me about the bad company I would inevitably encounter. Finally, they provided contact information for a respectable friend or relative who was devoted to the hobby. It was also common that the breeders whom I met – some through shared acquaintances, others at the bird market – deplored the fact that "thugs" were keen on pigeon keeping. They urged me to avoid spending time with certain pigeon-keepers and told me how to contact those who had a good reputation. It seems that, in pigeon keeping, each man is the exception that proves the rule.

My interviews enabled me to understand that powerful challenges relating to distinction influenced the speech and actions of keepers. The hobby was so freighted with negative portrayals that any occasion was ripe for attempting to contradict them. And although my interlocutors described themselves as bird lovers, they always made a point of asserting that they "were not like the others." Although the passion for birds was a way of asserting their masculinity, it also carried another set of stakes that were just as important: social and territorial distinction. In this respect, we can recall what Daniel Fabre argues in "La voie des oiseaux" (1986). He describes French rituals of manhood that not only enable the "production of boys" but that also trace a dividing line between rural and urban masculinities. For Jordanian pigeon-keepers, the distinction seems to be between social classes, distinguishing "bad" lower-class breeders who are looking for trouble from respectable "good" ones. Scientific jargon, used to convey the knowledge necessary for breeding pigeons, is a preferred tool in their efforts to make this social and moral distinction. As Abu Shadi explained, there were those who "really" knew pigeons, and then there were the "others." If a breeder of the second type was asked anything about his birds,

> he won't know how to answer. He doesn't know anything about the animals he breeds, whereas we [Abu Shadi's entourage] know everything. For each bird, we know the number of rows of feathers on his wings, how much time and how he flies. The others ... don't know anything about them. It's not a passion. If you are passionate about pigeons, you want to know everything about them in the smallest detail. These young men of the new generation are not very educated. They are amateurs.

The divide between "us" and "them" was often expressed in terms of generations, the assumption being, as is the case here, that things were better in the past. According to Abu Abdallah, "My father, may God preserve him, taught me everything about pigeons. So I learned everything from the previous generation. The new generation doesn't know anything about pigeons, the only thing they care about is business."

Some breeders, similarly careful to assert that they were not like the "others," opted nonetheless for the opposite interpretation: whereas pigeon keeping was once a hobby for thugs, this was no longer the case. Here again, they used the science argument: the questionable and approximate beliefs of the past had been replaced by scientific techniques and real veterinary knowledge.

My interlocutors also brought up the sanitation issue associated with bird breeding, emphasizing the amount of time they devoted to cleaning cages and the products they used to do so. My meeting with Nasser al-Hindi, a "first-class" breeder, was paradigmatic in this regard. Nasser is well known in the pigeon-keeping world. Googling for his name will bring up his photo – dark suit, impeccably trimmed beard, rings on his fingers – often accompanied by the details of how much money this collector has spent in recent years on buying pigeons. Even ignoring this notoriety, a few steps in his sumptuous aviary in the Al-Zohour district of Amman is enough to make it clear that we are far from the improvised dovecotes on the roofs of underprivileged districts. My visit to Nasser's rooftop was revealing about the stigmatizing representations associated with pigeon keeping, so visible – or more precisely, pungent – were the devices used to neutralize them. As I climbed the stairs to the roof, a strong floral scent invaded my nostrils, evidence of a recent and intensive application of deodorizing spray to mask the bird smell. At the top, the walls of the dovecote were decorated with hand-sanitizer dispensers, white scrubs, and several contraptions contributing to the scientific appearance of Nasser's endeavour. Indeed, he explained that he was not like "other" breeders since his objective was to create, through cunning cross-breeding experiments, a new race of birds. He insisted that he paid great attention to sanitation and stressed that his birds were "clean" (Keck 2014). His social milieu seemed incompatible with his passion. In this regard, he recalled his "clandestine" initiation into pigeon keeping:

> My father loved animals. We had birds at home, mainly canaries. But he was against pigeons because the reputation of the pigeon-breeders was so bad back then ... I was a teenager. I was walking to school at that time. I remember one morning when I was walking, I looked at the sky and noticed a flock of pigeons ... With the morning light, they were so beautiful. I was fascinated. After school, I went to find the breeder and bought a couple from him ... I kept them at home, I just wanted to watch them. I didn't know what to do with them! I put them on our roof and kept them secret from my father. He was a pharmacist; he was very strict. He would never have accepted. I didn't want him to get angry with me, but I didn't want to give up my passion either. My mother knew, but she never said anything. Fortunately! I finally raised them for three years on the roof.

After completing his military service, Nasser opened a pet store, a sort of disguise that allowed him to get closer to pigeons and to obtain increasing numbers over time. He closed the store after several years to focus exclusively on breeding and selling pigeons. At the end of our interview, he insisted once more that he had never made his birds fly.

The defaming representations of Jordanian pigeon-keepers could lead one to conclude that they are a homogeneous group, a collective incarnation of problematic masculinity. My fieldwork suggests that, far from constituting a coherent social entity, pigeon-keepers in Amman are divided by gender and class relations. During our interviews, they defended pigeon keeping and their practices while projecting the stigma of bad boys onto other breeders. The latter were always described as "less" – less passionate, educated, civilized, and clean – than the men with whom I spoke. We thus encounter in Jordan what has also been observed with those involved in pigeon competitions in Great Britain, the United States, and India (Johnes 2007; Jerolmack 2013; Kavesh 2019).

From Pigeons to Doves: An Ambivalent Kind of Bird

The pigeon-keepers I met – whether through interviews, at the bird market, or in auction rooms – were tireless in defending their hobby against its poor reputation. Individual demonstrations accompanied more general arguments aiming to redeem the practice. As the following remark illustrates, this sort of rehabilitation can take place through a reinterpretation of common negative perceptions. Abu Shadi, a man in his fifties who oversaw the pigeon auctions I attended, explained it to me in this way:

> It is said that men who breed pigeons cannot testify in a court of justice because they are bad people who lie and steal. But no one knows the real meaning of this story. If breeders can't testify, it's not because they lie but because their gaze is always turned towards the sky. It's as simple as that. They cannot testify to anything because they aren't watching what happens on the earth. They are facing the sky.

Here, the keeper is described as a man enamoured with freedom, a dreamer and a poet. A similar ambivalence occurs in media reports concerning the Arab world. In contrast with articles deploring the social and health disasters caused by the revival of pigeon keeping in Cairo, Amman, and Beirut, some reports portray pigeons in a positive light. During the war in Syria, they were providential messengers connecting one bombarded neighbourhood to another when there was no internet, or they were valuable commodities packed into suitcases and used as currency at the border (*AFP* 2012; *BBC News* 2016).[4] The United Nations High Commissioner for Refugees (UNHCR 2015, 2017) even published online information panels regarding the breeding of these "birds of peace" – depicted in their white form – which had developed in Syrian refugee camps in Beirut and Athens. These positive accounts depict the pigeons, which men make fly above their heads, as embodying a fluidity of movement distinctly opposed to the impossibilities, including in their spatial dimension (Suerbaum 2017), that shape the lives of their breeders: limited mobility, never-ending queues at administrative buildings, frequent police controls, inaccessible visas, and an uncertain future. Through their birds, owners challenge their daily experiences of life in the city and the relationships of subordination that restrict their existence (*Washington Post* 2017). It is a hobby that brings peace, I was also told in interviews. Aubin-Boltanski (2021) confirms that, in the Lebanese refugee camp she investigated, Syrian men found this pastime a rare occasion to dream and exert their own agency, though they felt neglected and diminished by their exile and the humanitarian system on which they depended.

Each description of pigeons, therefore, corresponds with a specific model of masculinity, and the adjectives used to qualify the birds – dirty and threatening or intelligent and romantic – seem to extend automatically to the humans who interact with them. Depending on the context, breeders can simultaneously embody young thugs and respectable refugees. In this sense, pigeon-keeping practices present a unique opportunity for understanding the processes of distinction and social marginalization in the Middle East, as well as the processes of subjectivation associated with them.

Conclusion

For Jivajos and Sécoyas in the Amazon, the Kaluli in Papua New Guinea, and the Yorubas in Nigeria (Feld 1982; Lévi-Strauss 1985; Descola 2005; Anthony 2007), the calls and feathers of birds inspire human songs and dances and, in turn, are the foundation of our aesthetic, emotional, and gendered experience of the world.[5] In their own way, in the urban terrain and concrete rooftops of Amman, pigeons – through the relationships in which they are involved – contribute to shaping their breeders' connection to the world and their representations of social order.

City rooftops are heuristic spaces that can be used to understand some of urban anthropology's central questions in a new way. The study of breeding activities in these spaces across Arab societies enables us to address, as I show in this chapter, the interspecies dimension of "inhabiting" – to borrow from the title of Vinciane Despret's (2019) latest book – and power relations in cities. The case of pigeon keeping in the Jordanian capital, where the pastime is particularly widespread in working-class neighbourhoods, shows that it is worth examining in terms of gender. In particular, pigeon-keeping practices challenge varying representations of masculinity and inform us about the relationship of working-class men to the world by enabling analysis of their situations of domination and their ways of coping with them daily.

This chapter, based on preliminary fieldwork, focuses on models of socially differentiated masculinities that express themselves through a fascination with pigeons. What remains to be seen, and could be the subject of a subsequent ethnographic study, is the place of Jordanian women in bird-related activities. Although they did not attend my rooftop interviews, they were not absent from the world of pigeon keeping and were often mentioned as playing an important role. They might encourage it – as in the case of Nasser al-Hindi's mother, who concealed his passion for birds from her husband. Or they might limit it – as in the case of Abu Shadi's wife, who resented the time he spent on his birds. It is women who cook the pigeons that are no longer wanted, who help clean the cages, and who bring coffee up flights of stairs to the men, ever focused on the skies. Rather than highlighting the gendered segregation that seems to organize pigeon-keeping activities, we should shed light on the connections and holes that exist between worlds perceived as opposites (Meneley 1996; Abbou, Hammou, and Lachenal 2022). Moving forward, it is therefore the interspecies, gender, social, and spatial borders that must all be considered in their depth and hybridity.

NOTES

1 Carried out in Pakistan, the ethnographic investigations of Jurgen Frembgen and Paul Rollier (2014) also reveal the similarities between kite competitions and pigeon racing, popular practices that organize and structure, from the sky, competition between models of subaltern masculinities.

2 "Shakk. From Revolt to War in Syria: Conflict, Displacements, Uncertainties," https://shakk. hypotheses.org/abstract. SHAKK is a collective research project led by the Centre d'études en Sciences sociales du religieux, l'Institut français du Proche-Orient, the audiovisual department of the Bibliothèque Nationale de France, and the Institute of Research and Study on the Arab and Muslim Worlds.

3 Additionally, writing about European languages, Allen Grieco (2010) highlights the semantic proximity of the names for little birds and the penis. It is noteworthy that, in Arabic, the word "pigeon" – *hamâm* – also refers to little boys' penises. In this sense, it is remarkably close to the English word "cock."
4 Pigeon messengers were also used during the Second World War (*Telegraph* 2018).
5 There's no need to travel as far as the Amazon or New Guinea to see the use of feathers in mechanisms of social and gendered distinction. Discussing furs and feathers in European fashion, Anne Monjaret (2008) explains that in Paris at the beginning of the twentieth century, there was a veritable frenzy among upper-class women for access to ostrich feathers imported from Sudan.

WORKS CITED

Abbou, Julie, Karim Hammou, and Perrine Lachenal, eds. 2022. *Dans l'épaisseur d'une ligne: explorer les frontières du genre.* Aix-en-Provence: Presses universitaires de Provence.
Abd Elrahman, Ahmed, and Randa Mahmoud. 2014. "La planification *controversée* du Grand Caire avant/après 2011." *Égypte/Monde arabe* 11: 177–201.
Abu-Lughod, Lila. 1986. *Veiled Sentiments: Honor and Poetry in a Bedouin Society.* Berkeley: University of California Press.
AFP. 2012. "Syrie: des pigeons voyageurs contre le siège de Homs." *AFP,* 15 February. https://www.youtube.com/watch?v=PzL8uKqHqOc.
Agier, Michel. 2015. *Anthropologie de la ville.* Paris: Presses universitaires de France.
Al-Akhbar. 2015. "kashshāsh al-hamām: lîsa kul al-kashshāsh rashāsh." *Al-Akhbar,* March 25. https://al-akhbar.com/Baladi/14811.
Al-Jazeera. 2017. "Pigeon Battles of Cairo." *Al-Jazeera,* September 17. https://www.aljazeera.com/program/witness/2017/9/17/pigeon-battles-of-cairo-egypts-high-flying-sport/.
Alshawawreh, Lara. 2018. "Sheltering Animals in Refugee Camps." *Forced Migration Review* 58: 8–10.
Anthony, Ming. 2007. "La pintade et la plume rouge de perroquet dans la tradition afro-brésilienne." In *Le symbolisme des animaux,* ed. Edmond Dounias, Elisabeth Motte-Florac, and Margaret Dunham, 809–25. Paris: IRD.
Aubin-Boltanski, Emma. 2021. "Des oiseaux pour se raconter et rêver: ethnographie d'une passion colombophile (Liban)." *Ethnologie française* 51, 2: 347–61.
Barbosa, Gustavo. 2013. "Non-Cockfights: On Doing/Undoing Gender in Shatila, Lebanon." PhD diss., London School of Economics. https://etheses.lse.ac.uk/898.
Bayart, Jean-François. 2004. *Le gouvernement du monde.* Paris: Fayard.
Bayat, Assef. 2000. "From 'Dangerous Classes' to 'Quiet Rebels': Politics of the Urban Sub-altern in the Global South." *International Sociology* 15: 533–57.
BBC News. 2016. "In Search of Syria's Pigeon Smugglers." *BBC News,* March 16. https://www.bbc.com/news/magazine-35813468.
Boutata, Seham. 2020. *La mélancolie du maknine.* Paris: Le Seuil.
Calvet, Florence, Jean-Paul Demonchaux, Régis Lamand, and Gilles Bornert. 2007. "Une brève histoire de la colombophilie." *Revue historique des armées* 248: 93–105.
Descola, Philippe. 2005. *Par-delà nature et culture.* Paris: Gallimard.
Despret, Vinciane. 2009. "Quand les mâles dominaient: Controverses autour des hiérarchies chez les primates." *Ethnologie française* 39, 1: 45–55.
–. 2019. *Habiter en oiseaux.* Paris: Actes Sud.
Destremeau, Blandine. 1996. "Les camps de réfugiés palestiniens et la ville: entre enclave et quartier." In *Amman, Ville et société,* ed. Jean Hannoyer and Seteney Shami, 527–52. Beirut: Presses de l'IFPO.

Digard Jean-Pierre. 2003. "Les animaux révélateurs des tensions politiques en République islamique d'Iran." *Études rurales* 165–66: 123–31.

Doraï, Kamel, and Nicolas Puig. 2012. *L'urbanité des marges: Migrants et réfugiés dans les villes du Proche-Orient*. Paris: Téraèdre.

Fabre, Daniel. 1986. "La voie des oiseaux: Sur quelques récits d'apprentissage." *L'Homme* 26, 99: 7–40.

Feld, Steven. 1982. *Sound and Sentiment: Birds, Weeping, Poetics, and Song in Kaluli Expression*. Philadelphia: University of Pennsylvania Press.

Frembgen, Jurgen, and Paul Rollier. 2014. *Wrestlers, Pigeon Fanciers, and Kite Flyers: Traditional Sports and Pastimes in Lahore*. Karachi: Oxford University Press.

Geertz, Clifford. 1973. "Deep Play: Notes on the Balinese Cockfight." In Clifford Geertz, *The Interpretation of Cultures*, 412–53. New York: Basic Books.

Goushegir, Aladin. 1997. *Le combat du colombophile: Jeu aux pigeons et stigmatisation sociale*. Tehran: Institut français de recherche d'Iran.

Grieco, Allen. 2010. "From Roosters to Cocks: Italian Renaissance Fowl and Sexuality." In *Erotic Cultures of Renaissance Italy*, ed. Sarah F. Matthews-Grieco, 89–140. London: Routledge.

Haraway, Donna. 2019. *Manifeste des espèces compagnes*. Paris: Flammarion.

Independent. 2000. "In Jordan the Gentle Art of Keeping Pigeons Is Seen as Dangerously Sexy." *Independent*, December 17. https://www.independent.co.uk/news/world/middle-east/in-jordan-the-gentle-art-of-keeping-pigeons-is-seen-as-dangerously-sexy-627544.html.

Jerolmack, Colin. 2013. *The Global Pigeon*. Chicago: University of Chicago Press.

Johnes, Martin. 2007. "Pigeon Racing and Working-Class Culture in Britain, 1850–1950." *Cultural and Social History* 4, 3: 361–83.

Kavesh, Muhammad. 2019. "From the Passions of Kings to the Pastimes of the People: Pigeon Flying, Cockfighting, and Dogfighting in South Asia." *Pakistan Journal of Historical Studies* 3, 1: 61–83.

Keck, Frédéric. 2014. "From Purgatory to Sentinel: 'Forms/Events' in the Field of Zoonoses." *Cambridge Anthropology* 32: 47–61.

Koch, Natalie. 2015. "Gulf Nationalism and the Geopolitics of Constructing Falconry as a Heritage Sport." *Studies in Ethnicity and Nationalism* 15, 3: 522–39.

Krawietz, Birgit. 2014. "Falconry as a Cultural Icon of the Arab Gulf Region." *In Under Construction: Logics of Urbanism in the Gulf Region*, ed. Katrin Bromber, Birgit Krawietz, and Steffen Wippel, 131–46. London: Routledge.

Lachenal, Perrine. 2012. "Le Caire, 2011: Plongée ethnographique au cœur des lajân sha'abeya [comités populaires]." *Année du Maghreb* 8: 193–206.

–. 2018. "Des 'mises en martyr' contestées: Enjeux sociaux et sexués de l'iconographie de la révolution égyptienne." *Archives de sciences sociales des religions* 181: 69–93.

Laugrand, Frédéric, Michèle Cros, and Julien Bondaz. 2015. "Présentation: les questions d'affects dans les liaisons animales." *Anthropologie et Sociétés* 39, 1–2: 15–35.

Lévi-Strauss, Claude. 1985. "D'un Oiseau l'autre: Un exemple de transformation mythique." *L'Homme* 93, 25: 5–12.

Meneley, Anne. 1996. *Tournaments of Value: Sociability and Hierarchy in a Yemen Town*. Toronto: University of Toronto Press.

Middle East Eye. 2015. "The Pigeon-Trainers of Beirut." *Middle East Eye*, June 20. https://www.middleeasteye.net/features/video-pigeon-trainers-beirut.

Le Monde. 2008. "Au Caire, l'Égypte d'en bas survit en haut." *Le Monde*, April 21. https://www.lemonde.fr/afrique/article/2008/04/21/au-caire-l-egypte-d-en-bas-survit-en-haut_1036513_3212.html.

Monjaret, Anne. 2008. "Plume et mode à la Belle Epoque: les plumassiers parisiens face à la question animale." *Techniques et cultures* 50: 228–55.

Piessat, Marie. 2018. "Urbanités africaines/Portfolio: Les toits du Caire, des espaces ressource?" Urbanités, October 22. https://www.revue-urbanites.fr/urbanites-africaines-piessat.

Suerbaum, Magdalena. 2017. "What Does It Mean to Be Young for Syrian Men Living as Refugees in Cairo?" *Middle East Topics and Arguments* 9: 122–31.

Telegraph. 2018. "WW2 Squad Shot Down 'Nazi' Falcons Who Were Eating Our Carrier Pigeons." *Telegraph,* May 31. https://www.telegraph.co.uk/news/2018/05/31/mi5s-unit -daily-licence-kill-ww2-squad-shot-nazi-falcons-eating.

UNHCR (United Nations High Commissioner for Refugees). 2015. "The Birds of Peace." UNHCR, August 6. https://www.unhcr.org/news/stories/birds-peace.

–. 2017. "Syrians in Greece: The Syrian Pigeon Whisperer." UNHCR, July 20. youtube. com/watch?v=h7gvNuTwFN4.

Washington Post. 2017. "'The Pigeons Make Me Feel Free': An Old Pastime Thrives in a Palestinian Refugee Camp." *Washington Post,* August 14. https://www.washingtonpost.com/ news/in-sight/wp/2017/08/14/the-pigeons-make-me-feel-free-an-old-pastime-thrives -in-a-palestinian-refugee-camp/.

4

From the Ground to the Canopy

An Introduction to the Tarkine Forest through Its Birds

Aïko Cappe and Colin Schildhauer

ONE OF THE LARGEST primordial temperate rainforests left in the world is located in northwestern Tasmania – the Tarkine or *takayna* (in Palawa Kani, a local Aboriginal language). With over 400,000 hectares of wilderness dating back to Gondwanaland, the Tarkine supports a unique yet fragile ecosystem inhabited by hundreds of endemic species, sixty of which are threatened or endangered due to deforestation and mining. Most of its large mammals are nocturnal, making them difficult to spot during the day. For this reason, birds are a primary wildlife presence in any exploration of the forest. The Tarkine is home to more than 130 bird species, including 11 of Tasmania's 12 endemic species. It is also an important migratory staging site for two endangered species of parrot that breed only in Tasmania: the Swift Parrot and the Orange-bellied Parrot. The latter is critically endangered, with only about 140 birds remaining. These numbers are predicted to decline over the next decade, and with the continuation of global warming and deforestation this parrot could become extinct.

Forests have enchanted and intrigued humans for ages. The Tarkine embodies this allure, delighting visitors from all over the world with its dense foliage and the myriad species in its dank undergrowth. In this chapter we explore its overwhelming presence of beauty and microcosmic complexities to gain a better understanding of its dynamism and singularity, in an attempt to portray the understory ambiance with a focus on its endemic bird species. We will become immersed beneath the canopy, listening to and observing the various bird species in a melodic song of revelatory interconnectedness.

Through the lens of an anthropologist (Cappe) and a visual artist (Schildhauer), let's delve into the colours and sounds of Tarkine ornithology. As Steven Feld (1990) notes in his inspiring *Sound and Sentiment,* the rainforest melody invites us into a story in which birds, through their songs and knowledge, poetically introduce us to a universe. A way to apprehend a world from an acoustic introduction, it also echoes Chapter 2 in this volume and its notion of acoustic community.

In this chapter, we propose a multi-perspective reflection on the four layers of takayna (emergent, canopy, understory, forest floor) and the birds that populate them. As a passionate artist and bird enthusiast, Colin Schildhauer received a master's degree in fine arts at the University of Tasmania, where he conceived a project focused on the deforestation of the Tarkine. Between 2018 and 2020 Colin made over a dozen trips into the Tarkine, using his brushes and paint to document the aesthetic contrast between clearcut areas and pristine habitat. He recalls the experience as an ascension to an elevated sensory stimulus and remoteness, synthesizing a newfound relationship with the birds that surrounded him. For her part, Aïko Cappe started fieldwork for a PhD in anthropology about the Tarkine. For her master's degree, working on a concept of sensory animal ethnography, she had conducted nine months of fieldwork in the Yukon, following wolf tracks. She realized that she needed to consider a larger ecosystem entanglement, one that would be characterized by greater unexpected yet exciting collaborations and tensions. During her first three months in the Tarkine, birds became her prominent companions, offering an inspiring entrance into the rhythms of forest life.

We will discuss the manner in which birds invited themselves into our respective research as influencers and will set up a dialogue between two perspectives and two approaches in two distinct mediums. Paintings are in dialogue with text, and an artistic approach is complemented by an anthropological one, both working from subjective and empirical experiences.

Meet the Tarkine

From the Idea of Wilderness to Reality

For Australians, Tasmania is often symbolically synonymous with wilderness, just as Alaska is for Americans or the Yukon is for Canadians. Yet for over a century, mining and logging have degraded the pristine landscape of the Tarkine. As pastoral borders widen and commercial growth expands, wildlife is increasingly pushed deeper into the heart of the Tarkine, an area so dense and remote that it is difficult for humans to penetrate.

From the gloom of the undergrowth to the sunny expanses of the canopy, the Tarkine universe is filled with complexity and richness. As you hike deep into the trees, with their austere shades of green and red, the sounds of cars, people, and machinery fade away, and the voice of the forest begins to grow. Birds call in harmony, and the wind whispers through the canopy. The sunlight is slowly replaced by a dark humidity you can feel, and rustles from above draw your gaze to the mosaic of colour formed by the canopy and the sky.

Colin Schildhauer painted Figure 4.1 in the Tarkine, where he spent countless hours bushwalking and painting *en plein air*. From canopy to forest floor, the various layers of a functioning forest tell their story of ancient times and changing weather. The upper area of the painting, with its shades of blue and green, offers the poetic light and colours that come with the canopy and sky. The three Swift Parrots camouflage with the greens of the trees and contrast with the reds and dark umbers of the forest floor. Bird speciation lends a sense of bio-dynamism to the forest layers, linking the canopy with the darker ground below. An overlapping relationship along the forest boundaries seems to organize the trees in accord with the beat of the parrots' wings. You can almost hear the birds singing and flapping their wings, structuring the forest life, pace, and activity.

To hear various bird calls in such a way prompts us to wonder what call belongs to what bird and what they signify. Who is their intended recipient? Perhaps the birds are transferring information to other Swift Parrots, communicating far and wide through a network of sound. Would their message be intelligible to birds of another species? Would mammals or insects make sense of the calls, and for that matter, do the trees? For an observer on the ground, calls are often the only indication that a bird is nearby, and memorizing them can enable identification of the species while also giving an idea of how many individual birds are present at a particular location. As humans, we can listen to the calls and try to make sense of them.

> I can hear bird wings flapping. Those birds seem to be flying pretty low.
> Some of those birds are singing in a way I never could have imagined. Some
> have little melodic acute songs while others are more curious noises, not very
> melodic ... I realize how much I will have to change my perception of the
> forest. Open my ears and not focus so much on my eyes anymore.
>
> – Aïko Cappe

Figure 4.1 *Swift Parrots in Flight* 112×103cm (oil on canvas). This painting was inspired by a small flock of Swift Parrots that zoomed over Colin's head while he was painting decaying tree stumps near the Julius River. The forest was particularly warm and still that afternoon. He was in the middle of a painting when the silence was cut by the rhythmic beating of ten or so wings approaching from behind. He spotted them only once they had flown over him, disappearing into the understory's mosaic of greens, reds, and blues, the same three colours that this parrot has acquired as plumage over millions of years of evolution.

Paying attention to bird calls and trying to understand them is also a starting point for connecting what is happening in the treetops with what we experience on the forest floor. Together, the shadows and colours, the canopy and ground, endangered Swift Parrots and common pademelons (small members of the macropod family) make up the components of the Tarkine's ecological singularity of place.

Why are birds such an important part of our experience in the Tarkine? Because many are active during the daylight hours, they are the first and most obvious type of beings that we encounter there. If you stay for many weeks, the more elusive ground-dwelling species begin to reveal themselves: not only various types of birds that live lower in the forest, but also marsupials such as pademelons, wallabies, and quolls. Are humans and birds somewhat at ease with each other because they are separated by a vertical space? Are birds more curious than other forms of life? If you sit on the ground for too long, red spiders with a blue spot on their back will often take an inquisitive stroll over your anatomy. And we must not ignore the insects, which are omnipresent in the forest. Insects are a major food item for birds, and their buzzing harmonizes with the calling of birds. We can hear all the flying creatures but sometimes catch only a glimpse of them. Often, we never see them.

Birds can also help to push our senses in a new direction. Common expressions such as "point of view" or "having a vision of something" emphasize that sight takes precedence over our other senses, but birds can help us to "see" differently. If you concentrate only on what your eyes tell you during a visit to the Tarkine, you will certainly miss most of it. The undergrowth is so thick that seeing more than fifty metres in any direction is a challenge, and the dense canopy blocks the sunlight from reaching the forest floor, shrouding it in deep shadow and providing excellent concealment for ground-dwelling species. The birds that frequent the canopy are quite colourful, while the terrestrial mammals are darker, with grey or black fur, helping them to blend into their environment. Beyond our deep reliance on sight, the Tarkine invites us to listen. Listen to the birds. Listen to the wind. Listen to the trees. Listen to the forest. Listen in the most literal way but also in a figurative way, which will teach us to learn from the forest.

Listen to the Birds and Imagine the Forest

I can hear some birds. They seem to be high in the canopy. One is pretty close and keeps repeating the same sound again and again. Sometimes he would change the end of his song, adding an intermediate tone while his singing deepens. It is hard to know for sure if I keep hearing the same bird or if there are a few of them hanging together, but the rhythm of the song makes me think that it could be just one bird.

Further away, I can hear a different song. The tone is more monotone and the bird is quieter. He would only sing sporadically. Despite a tone similar to the one singing close by, they have different voices that make them easy to distinguish. The further one's singing sometimes sounds like a goose call.

The closer one stopped singing, but a new one started far away with a very metallic song.

– Aïko Cappe

How can we represent a world that we can hear but not see? During her immersion in the forest, Aïko Cappe noticed that what she could hear but not see was always subject to doubt, as if our mind could invent sounds but not images, as if the other senses were only complements rather than essential. For her, becoming in tune with the Tarkine meant forgetting the way her senses have been conditioned and the apprehension of what is real and what is not. When it is purely auditory, does the Tarkine become an imaginary world? Shifting our emphasis from visual stimuli enables us to engage with the forest not only as something to observe and describe, but also and significantly as something we must feel, understand, and be connected to not only to translate, but to share (Abram 2013; Tassin 2020).

When Aïko jots down her impressions of these sounds in her field notes, is she writing fiction? Is Colin Schildhauer painting an imaginary Tarkine? Maybe. But what is the real thing? Who has the authority to decide, more than the forest itself? And why should its reality be static? As a very dynamic and complex world, the Tarkine can never be fully perceived. So, everyone has his or her own experience of it, and by extension a unique definition of what/who the Tarkine is. There's nothing new about researcher reflexivity (Ghasarian 2002), but one's reactions also depend on personal interests, sensibility, ability, and in regards to art, interpretation. What you perceive and understand about the Tarkine may differ quite markedly from what you are able to convey about it, which is why sharing and comparing expressions of the Tarkine are so relevant.

In his artwork, Colin decided to represent birds ontologically, as accessible validations of the various species of beings that humans may or may not notice on a daily basis. Throughout history, birds have symbolized a multitude of anthropomorphic values. For instance, the owl symbolized wisdom in ancient Greece, and a dove represents divinity in Judaism and Christianity. In 1949, Pablo Picasso used a dove in his design for the World Peace Congress, making it a universal symbol of peace. The ability to fly has always astounded humans, and because of this, birds have been greatly admired and respected, linking the terrestrial to the heavens. Colin chose to represent them in a way that aims to raise awareness of the bounties of life. By depicting birds purely through observation, he begins to understand more about their characteristics, habits, and movements. Then, by highlighting key features and embellishing special characteristics, he hopes to create a universal spiritual symbolism that encourages viewers to reconnect the commonalities of life with nature and its biome. Through a reconnection with nature, the human ego can dissolve the anthropic division it has created, recognizing the role that humanity plays in the interconnected web of life.

You must let yourself go with what the forest has to propose and be able to figure out things from their sounds. Birdsongs give rhythm to the Tarkine. They become your main companion. Once you are in sync with the rhythm, you are in tune with the place. Ironically, in the daytime it seems much quieter when birds are singing than when they remain silent.

I arrived at Julius River a couple of hours before dusk and brought my gouache paints out for a bush walk into the old-growth myrtle sinkholes. The forest lay quiet. Sunshine illuminated the forest floor through beams of light from the canopy above. Once I set up my paints, the act of creating a painting is a relatively quiet process. I feel this allows for the forest to accept my presence and fall back into its steady vibration. The quietness is engulfing with breath. The breath of transcendence into the cosmos. New sounds arise, the footsteps of a small skink treading across a moss-covered log, the reverberations of beating wings from a passing flock of Swift Parrots, and the sprinkles of rain falling from the clouds to the babble of the rivulet. Today is a national holiday, and all is quiet in the forest except for life. The canopy hosts a symphony of bird calls, trilling and squawking through the myrtle leaves. Tomorrow, logging will be back in operation, and the ripping and roaring of machinery and saws will grow louder.

– Colin Schildhauer

I have been in the forest for about 10 days listening to all kinds of sounds. I'm still having a hard time linking bird calls with their species, although there is one metallic song that I'm able to recognize. A loud one. It can have various song patterns but always emanates with a metallic tone. One day I was walking deeper into the forest on an ancient path. A young myrtle with brushy branches had fallen down across the path. It has been there since before I came, but the tree is still green and the smell strong. It was a very windy day. No birds singing.

No insects buzzing. Only the melody of the wind across the leaves in the canopy. It must be very windy up above the canopy because I could feel the wind's touch even down on the ground. I walk slowly, trying to be as quiet as possible, trying not to scare any animals. A couple of meters before the fallen myrtle I stop to look at some tufts of moss. When I look up, an imposing green and blue bird is standing on the myrtle trunk looking at me. Surprised, I freeze up. Look at the bird. We stare at each other for a couple of minutes, which seemed much longer. Then it flew away. As I step over the fallen myrtle trunk a second one comes out of the brushy branches, then another, and another. There were five of them in total, flying away singing that metallic tone I recognized. Later, I asked an expert about the forest, describing the bird and the singing. Seems like I met a group of Green Rosellas.

– Aïko Cappe

Such encounters remind us that encounters between humans and non-humans must be reciprocal. In the forest, we are not the only ones who are watching and trying to figure things out. Its inhabitants are doing just the same as us, and it's quite apparent that we're the ones under scrutiny, as they often tread unnoticed. It's during such encounters that we can begin to comprehend each other (Agier 2015). Indeed, we are learning a lot from forest residents, but at some point they learn from us as well. The learning becomes mutual.

The Tarkine Is Always Watching You

The moment you step into the trees, you're under close observation by the forest beings. No matter how quiet you try to be, your presence is always noticed. In any ethnographic fieldwork, the first weeks are always about adapting to the environment, training your body and your senses to see, to listen, to smell, and to feel differently. To adapt, you must surrender your senses to comply with the perceptions of all the life around you.

My integration in the forest is not only about me being able to understand it, but also about the forest accepting me. I must deconstruct myself in order to let the forest reshape me, and when the forest opens doors, I enter and explore them with curiosity and respect.

– Aïko Cappe

This process is often reciprocal. Surrendering to the pace of the forest can be quite challenging, as it is very different from what we are used to, and somehow it affects you beyond the forest immersion. Being watched also means that you must act with caution as you are still learning what is appropriate and respectful for this place, in this world, what you should or shouldn't do. It invites you to pay close attention to how this environment and the actors react to your presence, to your actions. Discipline becomes key, and to tread lightly is to become in sync with the forest. You must learn from empirical intersubjective experience (Goulet 1994, 1998, 2011). To feel the pace of the forest and to understand its reality is the goal that Aïko and Colin share. Through their observations, they strive to describe not only what they see, smell, hear, and touch, but also how it feels to be watched by the forest. Colin's painting *Wedge-tail Vigil* depicts two Wedge-tailed Eagles soaring through a smoky sky backlit by the afternoon sun. The sunlight glows with saturated yellows while the plumes of smoke from the burn-off are muted with suffocating greens. The eagles' eyes are glued to piles of slashed trees in search of prey while bordering old-growth trees watch powerlessly over the smoky haze of their fallen ancestors. (Figure 4.2). Colin recalls that the dark silhouette of an eagle often appeared in breaks in the canopy, sharp-cut against the sky, as the bird scanned the forest for unwelcome visitors and fearful prey.

Colin began to paint under the supervision of a Wedge-tailed Eagle perched high on the border between what had been cut and what remained. It watched him diligently as he began contrasting the foliage of the lone tree to the orange stumps below. Brushing away the splinters on the stumps enabled him to count the tree rings and calculate the ages of the fallen trees. Soon a burn-off would ensue, and shortly after, new eucalypt saplings would be planted. After a bare minimum of thirty years, they too would be felled once again as a "working forest."

The next time Colin visited this spot, the giant eucalypt he had painted was gone and where it once stood now rose thin plumes of smoke while off in the distance the silhouette of a Wedge-tailed Eagle circled through the sky above.

The Tasmanian Wedge-tailed Eagle is a keystone species in Tasmania's biome. It's very similar to its mainland Australian cousin but is slightly larger. After the extinction of the thylacine (Tasmanian tiger) in 1936, the eagle became Tasmania's apex predator, helping to keep the ecosystem in balance by feeding on marsupials and rodents. Because it mainly inhabits

Figure 4.2 *Wedge-tail Vigil* 55×55cm (oil on canvas). One day, Colin set up his easel in a clearcut. It had rained that morning, and the poignant smell of moist eucalypt heartwood steamed through the splintered wreckage. In the centre of the clearing, touching the heavens, stood a *Eucalyptus obliqua*. They can grow up to a hundred metres in height and are some of the tallest flowering plants in the world. At some point, possibly due to a lightning strike or heavy winds, the trunk had lost its upper portion, as indicated by the much slimmer new growth that sprang from the break. It had recovered, and undoubtedly continued its watch over the forest.

the canopy and the upper and emergent layers of the forest, it can be difficult to see. With its acute eyesight, it surveys the forest floor and patches of grassland until it launches into a silent dive to scoop up terrestrial prey with fierce talons. This bird is an outlying example of an endemic species that seems to be adapting to deforestation by using clearcut areas for hunting. As the trees fall and prey species scramble to find new shelter, they are exposed and become easy pickings. The problem here is that they will diminish in tandem with their habitat, decreasing the food supply for the eagle. Everything is interconnected. Aïko Cappe once observed a couple of Wedge-tailed Eagles circling a dead pademelon in open grassland. Crows hung around, waiting to approach the carcass but only after the eagles had left. The eagles were silent while the crows were very noisy. Catching a glimpse of a Wedge-tailed Eagle is to experience overlap of the forest layers, from their acute gaze from the canopies above to their talon-led dive to the forest floor below. Aside from eagles, there are other birds that introduce us to the Tarkine.

Encounter Birds, Encounter the Forest

Spending time in the forest eventually involves meeting birds. Some live on the ground; others inhabit the understory just below the canopy. These species are the most common and in constant awareness of your presence as visitors. Sometimes, they seem merely to tolerate you, whereas others are more interactive.

> I was walking at the end of the day when I ended up in the middle of a "Yellow-tailed Black Cockatoo party." These black parrots are adorned with barred pale-yellow tail feathers that complement yellow spots on their cheeks. There were about 20 of them spread between three to four trees. They were flying very low, and being extremely social emitting their noisy squawks. I couldn't tell how they were receiving me. I stood there for a few minutes watching them, and listening. Some would fly by very low. Some would just stare at me from a higher branch. I observed their singing had changed after I left. We were so close. They were so noisy. Even if they didn't stop singing, I felt like they were getting quieter while I was walking away. That was an interesting encounter. They didn't seem afraid of me, but not very comfortable having me around for so long either.
>
> – Aïko Cappe

How do these birds introduce us to the forest? As biologist Marc Bekoff points out, every animal is a way to know the world (Despret 2020, 15). In our case, each bird is a way to know the Tarkine and its nature. Linnaean taxonomy of birds is quite inappropriate since it is hard to believe that a Bassian Thrush and a Wedge-tailed Eagle would have the same knowledge/experience of the Tarkine. Given this, we propose to appreciate and understand the forest through microhabitats or zones. Here, we are inspired by the work of Florence Brunois (2005, 2007) in Papua New Guinea, where she designed what she referred to as an ethno-ethology (Lestel, Brunois, and Burgat 2006). The Kasua people of Papua New Guinea invited Brunois to experience their world beyond purely human interaction by introducing her to the way they interacted with their environment. This included encounters with wildlife, plants, and various microcosms that the Kasua used to navigate life on a daily basis. Through the lens of the Kasua, Brunois learned about their symbiotic relationship with their surroundings. She conducted further research in understanding the forest zones from floor to canopy, including all the entities that inhabited them, whether visible or not (Brunois 2015).

In our case, we wished to understand how birds invited us to comprehend the Tarkine, and this may be where the work of Steven Feld (1990) inspired us. By listening to birds, we hope to learn more about the organization of the forest's vertical layers. Considering that each bird offers a unique way of understanding a distinct zone, its knowledge raises new questions on how to understand the Tarkine. The more we are able to connect with the differing perspectives on the Tarkine, the more we can hope to gain a complex understanding of it. This organization is indicative of specialized behaviours, yet it doesn't mean that an eagle will never venture down to the ground or that a Bassian Thrush digging in detritus on the forest floor in search of insects (as seen in Figure 4.3) will not visit the treetop canopies. These outlying behaviours are often very interesting, prompting new questions that delve even deeper into the subject. They can challenge our assumptions about what we see as common singularities in the ecosystem and can reveal potential dynamics that are less apparent in our local methods of observation, whether this means events existing in unrecognized timeframes or triggered by alternative phenomena.

Each bird presents knowledge of the particular forest area in which it is designed to thrive. Of course, the territory of a Wedge-tailed Eagle will be much larger than that of a Bassian Thrush, yet territory can be defined in numerous ways (Despret 2020). There seem to be many ways to entangle it, vertically as well as horizontally, and like the forest itself, the interests of birds are so variable (what they eat, the kind of habitat they need, reproduction methods, their priority in territoriality) that they allow for many entanglements. This is another reason that they make such good mediators between us and the Tarkine.

Figure 4.3 *Digging through Detritus for Insects, Bassian Thrush*, 25x36cm (oil on board). Whenever a flock of Yellow-tailed Black Cockatoos, Swift Parrots, or Green Rosellas flew by Colin noticed they would intentionally buzz his painting setup, conducting an investigation into his presence as a guest in the forest. He also had multiple encounters with Bassian Thrush, a terrestrial bird that hops along the forest floor rummaging through leaves and dirt in search of insects. These birds seemed to be the most curious, often flitting around his feet and making intermittent bits of eye contact that reflected a mutual confirmation of each other's presence.

Conveying the Tarkine

Now that we've introduced the Tarkine and its birds, we will discuss the challenges we encountered in our respective processes. How did the Tarkine challenge our projects? How did we have to adapt our methodologies and our tools? How did we decide to translate the Tarkine world?

Translating the Tarkine

Ethnographic description involves not only writing about what you see, but also making it seen or felt by a reader. This process, often implicit, can seem quite obvious, yet it is a practice of incredible complexity (Laplantine 1998). You must translate what you see, smell, feel, and taste into language, sometimes creating descriptions for ineffable sensations or inexplicable experiences.

Might that be where art can play a role as an interesting alternative or complement? Unlike artists, anthropologists are stuck with words, interrogating the relationship between what they can experience and what they can put into words. Aïko detailed some of the challenges that arose during her fieldwork.

Despite some knowledge of musical terms, she ran out of words to describe what she could hear in the forest. Birds singing, forest sounds. Trees cracking in so many different ways. So many subtleties that struggle to be reduced to a single word. She realized how poor her language (French) is to describe sounds and all the auditory world. She often found herself using a metaphorical description, or trying to draw the melody in a symbolic way. She guesses it helped her understand why music has its own language, its own expression, and maybe why there are just some things words cannot accurately describe.

A literal description is much harder than it seems. During her first attempt of description on a very small patch of forest, she was tempted to follow a lead that would bind the different elements of her descriptions together. She started to describe the river, then birds singing, then the moss. Sometimes she would go from birds singing to a tree, to the sound of wood creaking, then to another bird singing. We can never describe one element to the point of exhaustion as everything is in a constant state of flux. Every description can always be more precise, be more accurate. The perspective can change. But does she need to describe absolutely everything? Everything she can see? hear? smell? feel? Plus, all those elements are alive and dynamic, which make the description even harder at the moment, but only reliable for this particular moment.

This interrogates the "objective" side of a description. But can a description really be objective (Agier 2015)? Is a photograph any more objective than a painting? Is an Impressionistic painting more objective than an abstract one? This is precisely the challenge of ethnographic description, to connect things that we typically consider separately.

Every description involves a translation and consequently an interpretation. As we say in French, "translation is betrayal." In our case, the task of description was particularly complex because we were attempting to translate our embodied experience of a non-verbal world, an effort that raised the issue of our relationship with our subject matter. Whether in anthropology or in art, both cases must create representations of things that have been taken out of their original context. We seek to find a way to express sensations as symbols.

Below, we use a dialogue between anthropological and artistic approaches, sharing our experiences in the Tarkine through a question-answer format. We make no claim to speak for all artists or all anthropologists, so the discussion will be between the discipline that trained us and our own sensibilities.

How is an artist interacting with objective/subjective forms of expression?

When I create a painting, I immerse myself in my surroundings. I tune my senses to fuller awareness. Through meditated observation, I experience light, colour, sound – the weather, sea, sky, and land. Through elevated sensory stimulation, I interpret what I feel and see in paint. Utilizing the freedom to explore and create, my paintings seek to share a new understanding of what they depict, where objectivity provides identity and subjectivity offers curiosity and reflection.

When you paint a landscape, do you consider it as a description? An interpretation? What do you express? And how do you choose what you express?

I try to explore the various textures and colours. I believe that everything contains a specific rhythm and flow that is unique to its existence. It could be the way a Bassian Thrush picks apart the forest floor as it forages for food or the quiet wing beats of a flock of Swift Parrots flying above. When I paint a land- or seascape I look for rhythms as well – for instance fractaling tree branches swaying in the wind or the bending and folding of geologic strata that has occurred over long periods of time.

How do you translate physical and emotional sensations into shapes and colours?

I feel that the blueprint for a universal code is ingrained in everything. What art can do is allow people to study this code and express it through a lens unique to them. When I approach a landscape with my paints, I'm thinking about what makes it different from any other locale – for example, tuning into the physiognomic qualities that differentiate a wetland from a riparian habitat or a forest's canopy from its understory. All have evolved over millions of years to support certain forms of life. When I observe these qualities, my consciousness is evoked with emotional connections to the environment, including the sounds, smells, colours, textures, and patterns. I take these qualities and begin expressing them through colour and form to create a visual interpretation.

When they embark on their fieldwork, anthropologists are strangers who question everything in the society they study. As they describe its most common events, their alterity invites them to question the most obvious behaviour and practices. They notice the way that people walk, eat, talk, move their bodies, and so on. During this part of the ethnographical process, descriptive language plays a key role (Laplantine 1998). Yet, many details can't be discerned at first, revealing themselves only after long periods of immersion (Despret 2020). This is equally true of a Gondwana rainforest such as the Tarkine, which has flourished for 200 million years even as it has been subject to constant change. As we mentioned earlier, the reciprocity of the encounter means that the forest is also evolving in its nascent perception of us.

After her first month in the Tarkine, Aïko Cappe

started to encounter more and more animals. I started to notice different mushrooms, new colours, and many subtleties in the smells. For instance, after a few weeks some neighbouring possums seemed to forgive my intruding presence. On sunny days, there was even a snake that began hanging around. It's not that they weren't there before, just that we probably weren't yet ready to reveal ourselves to each other.

Colin, in your experience, how does familiarity with a place affect your perception of it, and by extension how does it affect your creative process?

I feel that familiarity with a location is a precious relationship, one from which I can never stop learning. The more I spend time building a relationship with a location, the more it reveals itself to me. The Greek philosopher Heraclitus once said that "change is the only constant." Variables that lie outside the location, such as weather events or seasonal change, are in constant flux and will alter or transform it, but becoming familiar with a location entails becoming familiar with these changes. It's ephemeral solidarity, just as our bodies and mind are under constant change, yet we maintain our ego, our identity.

How do your paintings evolve when you paint the same place many times over the years?

When I depict a familiar location, I find that my paintings become more metaphorical for my emotional connection to that place. I try to extract and convey qualities beyond the visual field and to dig deeper into the essence of its existence.

Those discussions invite us to raise the question of the differences in knowledge that an artist versus an anthropologist can gather about a place.

The ethnographic description is a phase where observation skills, sensitivities, intelligence, and scientific imagination work together (Laplantine 1998). These are also parameters in Colin's work, but the Tarkine experience cannot be reduced to its visual aspect, and we both had to find a way to translate our embodied experience (Turner 2001). To achieve this, Colin turned to his easel, brushes, and paint, whereas Aïko attempted to refer to her sensing experience of the place, using her whole body as ethnographic data (Laplantine 2018; Pink 2009).

Sharing the Tarkine

The next challenge is to find a way through paintings and words to let you, the reader, experience the Tarkine for yourself, to see and to be seen. This is how the collaboration of painting and text can become even more relevant. We were both challenged by how to translate our experiences, the only difference now being how we share them.

Why would an artist choose to share his work? Is there a "disciplinary" agreement on the purpose for doing so? How do you make the decision? What expectations/considerations/obligations do you have when you share your paintings of the Tarkine?

I share my work in hopes of stimulating curiosity and deepening the viewer's connection to the natural environment. I believe that over the past two centuries, we have become blind to our dependence on nature. We continually widen the gap between ourselves and the natural world, seeing ourselves as superior to the environments that gave us life. Seeking to remedy this division, my paintings encourage viewers to reconsider both the interconnected web of life and our need to coexist with nature.

Although anthropology typically concentrates on human societies, Aïko decided to apply an anthropological approach to the Tarkine because of its relevance in apprehending alterity. Part of this means studying the relationship between humans and the Tarkine, a place that is foreign to her but rich in the history of human presence. She observes the forest, the social interaction of wildlife within it, tensions and collaborations, and communications. Through this, she will learn to evolve in a world that is very different from her own, one that involves heightened awareness and sensitivities not only about what she can experience, but also about the way in which she will experience it (Laplantine 1998, 2017). Through this lens, anthropology suddenly becomes a brilliant catalyst to a structured approach for studying human relationships with birds in a forest.

Putting Experiences into Perspective

We mentioned how the "bird" category doesn't mean a great deal in the Tarkine or to our approaches and perspective, since grouping a Bassian Thrush and a Wedge-tailed Eagle into the same category doesn't make much sense. The taxonomic system could be questioned, and exploring this further in connection with the Tarkine would be interesting. And within this "bird" category, of what relevance is assigning its various creatures to one species or another? Attempting to adopt a Tarkine perspective, we wonder how the concept of species would actually apply. This doesn't mean that the species categorization is never relevant in anthropology, and Chapters 1, 2, and 3 in this book all deal with specific species of birds. But despite the choice of a particular type of bird, more singular relationships (between individual humans and birds) can also be apprehended, especially in Chapter 2, where Dalemans looks at individual birds rather than particular species in the context of bird-singing contests. And that's where all the chapters in this first part offer an interesting point of comparison as to the types of relationships each author has encountered in their own fieldwork. Our purpose isn't to support an anti-specist perspective (Singer 1975) and claim that species taxonomy isn't relevant, since we don't agree that all beings are interchangeable and that all share a common perspective.

Despite the vivacity of political concerns around the Tarkine rainforest, and that whole species discussion, our experiences of the Tarkine affected us on an ontological rather than political level (Kohn 2015). We both felt a deep alterity, which characterizes in many ways our relationship to the Tarkine. It is precisely that feeling of alterity that raised our interest in mobilizing anthropological questions. Using anthropological questions on subjects of nature isn't new. Many anthropologists have tried to theorize those relationships between humans and nature. We can think of Philippe Descola's work (2005), or Eduardo Viveiros de Castro, and more recently Eduardo Kohn, as we are focusing on a forest subject. The perspectivist approach (Viveiros de Castro 2009) doesn't apply so well in our case, and despite our focus on bird songs, a semiotic approach (Kohn 2007) doesn't quite fit either. Kohn's delineation of an anthropology that extends beyond the human and the potential of tools like Von Uexküll's ([1940] 1982) *Umwelt*[1] help us deconstruct a certain ethnocentrism for sure, but at some point they too get in the way of the "Tarkine perspective."

When we are in the forest, we meet singular beings. When Colin encountered a curious Bassian Thrush while painting or Aïko met the Green Rosellas, the experience was never about a human and birds. It was more about beings interacting with each other among the entanglements of life webs in the forest. The way we make sense with them doesn't demand categorization, and species names aren't required. At most, these are useful only for transcribing and interpreting the Tarkine for the reader.

Somehow, by inhabiting the forest (Ingold 2004, 2008; Despret 2020), we must learn new ways of thinking about forests to make sense not of them, but with them. Ethnographic experiments must be done before this ambition can be realized, but the premises we established supported our intuitions and remain promising.

Conclusion

From the ground to the sky, through darkness and colours, birds give rhythmic poetry and enlightenment to the Tarkine experience. They are significant to us (as humans) in our experiences because of our diurnal way of life, because of our abilities to see and listen. Can we talk about a human-bird couple? Would birds be as relevant if another type of being were discovering the Tarkine? Though we ourselves came from elsewhere, with differing backgrounds and affinities, we were both amazed by these birds.

Through our respective cultural, personal, and disciplinarian differences, we coalesced over analogous sensibilities, and our experiences dovetailed in the beauty of the Tarkine. Our projects are open-ended, and the fusion of an artist-anthropologist partnership seems boundless. Similar purposes can be expressed in such different ways, which makes this interdisciplinary dialogue so rich and relevant.

NOTE

1 With the *Umwelt* theory, Von Uexküll ([1940] 1982) expresses a simple observation: different animals in the same ecosystem pick up on different environmental signals.

WORKS CITED

Abram, David. 2013. *Comment la terre s'est tue. Pour une écologie des sens.* Paris: Éditions la Découverte.

Agier, Michel. 2015. "Le dire-vrai de l'anthropologue. Réflexions sur l'enquête ethnographique du point de vue de la rencontre, des subjectivités et du savoir." Ethnographiques.org 30. https://www.ethnographiques.org/2015/Agier.

Brunois, Florence. 2005. "Pour une approche interactive des savoirs locaux: l'ethno-éthologie." *Le Journal de la Société des océanistes* 120–21: 32–40.

–. 2007. *Le jardin du casoar, la forêt des Kasua. Savoir-être et savoir-faire écologiques.* Paris: Éditions de la maison des sciences de l'Homme, CNRS Éditions.

–. 2015. "L'animal dans une société sans miroir. Les Kasua de Nouvelle-Guinée." *Anthropologie et Sociétés* 39, 1–2: 85–101.

Descola, Philippe. 2005. *Par-delà nature et culture.* Paris: Éditions Gallimard.

Despret, Vinciane. 2020. *Habiter en oiseaux.* Paris: Éditions Actes Sud.

Feld, Steven. 1990. *Sound and Sentiment: Birds, Weeping, Poetics and Song in Kaluli Expression.* Philadelphia: University of Pennsylvania Press.

Ghasarian, Christian, ed. 2002. *De l'ethnographie à l'anthropologie réflexive: Nouveaux terrains, nouvelles pratiques, nouveaux enjeux.* Paris: Armand Colin.

Goulet, Jean-Guy. 1994. "Dreams and Vision in Other Lifeworlds." In *Being Changed by Cross-Cultural Encounters: The Anthropology of Extraordinary Experience,* ed. David E. Young and Jean-Guy Goulet, 16–38. Peterborough: Broadview Press.

–. 1998. *Ways of Knowing: Experience, Knowledge and Power among the Dene Tha.* Vancouver: UBC Press.

–. 2011. "Trois manières d'être sur le terrain. Une brève histoire des conceptions de l'inter-subjectivités." *Anthropologie et Sociétés* 35, 3: 107–25.

Ingold, Tim. 2004. "Beyond Biology and Culture: The Meaning of Evolution in a Relational World." *Social Anthropology* 12, 2: 209–21.

–. 2008. "Binding against Boundaries: Entanglement of Life in an Open World." *Environment and Planning A* 40, 8: 1806–10.

Kohn, Eduardo. 2007. *How Forests Think: Toward an Anthropology beyond the Human.* Berkeley: University of California Press.

–. 2015. "Anthropology of Ontologies." *Annual Review of Anthropology* 44: 311–27.

Laplantine, François. 1998. *La description ethnographique.* Paris: Éditions Nathan.

–. 2017. *Le social et le sensible: Introduction à une anthropologie modale.* Paris: Téraèdre.

–. 2018. *Penser le sensible.* Paris: Éditions Pocket.

Lestel, Dominique, Florence Brunois, and Florence Burgat. 2006. "Etho-ethnology and ethno-ethology." *Social Science Information* 45 (2): 155–77.

Pink, Sarah. 2009. *Doing Sensory Ethnography.* London: Sage.

Singer, Peter. 1975. *Animal Liberation: A New Ethics for Our Treatments of Animals.* New York: Random House.

Tassin, Jacques. 2020. *Pour une écologie du sensible.* Paris: Éditions Odile Jacob.

Turner, Aaron. 2001. "Embodied Ethnography: Doing Culture." *Social Anthropology* 8, 1: 51–60.

Viveiros de Castro, Eduardo. 2009. *Métaphysiques cannibales.* Paris: Presses universitaires de France.

Von Uexküll, Jakob. (1940) 1982. "The Theory of Meaning." *Semiotica* 42: 25–82.

5

Entangled Lives
Toward a Phenomenology of Amateur Birding in Modern Japan
Scott E. Simon

True philosophy entails learning to see the world anew.

– Maurice Merleau-Ponty, *Phenomenology of Perception*

To see is to enter into a universe of beings that show themselves.

– Maurice Merleau-Ponty, *Phenomenology of Perception*

DURING THE YEAR that I lived in Osaka, my days began early, just as the crows made their first caws, as if they were tasked to announce the rising of the sun. If I'd scheduled a birding trip for that day, I would marvel briefly at the Brown-eared Bulbuls in the trees next to my balcony before collecting my binoculars and camera and setting off on my bicycle to the train station. Google maps helped me negotiate public transport from Minoh, an Osaka suburb in the foothills north of the city, to the train or subway station where I would meet up with a birding group organized by the Osaka branch of the Wild Bird Society of Japan (WBSJ).

Once, as I changed from the Hankyū suburban rail to the subway at Umeda Station, I stopped for breakfast in a cafe up the stairs at the end of the platform. As I ate, I watched the scene below, where ten bay platforms served nine tracks. When a train arrived, the doors opened along one side, releasing hundreds of people, who began streaming toward the exits. Then the doors opened on the other side, and passengers stepped aboard. As each train pulled out, it was quickly replaced with another. I enjoyed watching the people, judging from their clothing if they were salarymen and office ladies going to work, uniformed schoolchildren heading for class, or people in more casual dress on their way to some other destination. On an average day, some 2.4 million people pass through this station, one of the busiest in the world. I video-recorded the action as a way of remembering and showing my students the type of human movement that is most typical of a day in urban Japan. Amazing to me, but probably invisible to most commuters, tiny sparrows dove between the crowds, capable of finding even small bread crumbs dropped on the platform. Crows watched from the wires above. Even Umeda Station is a node of multi-species entanglements.

I was especially amused because during that year I was myself immersed in a very different kind of movement – the study of birds and people who study birds. Just a few days previously, I had stood on the plains of Izumi in Kyushu, watching thousands of migratory cranes as they flew into the fields around the crane conservation area where they would be fed. Looking at the trains and thinking of the cranes, I reflected on the meaning of human and avian movement. A big difference is that most human commuters travel alone, whereas cranes tend to fly and feed with their family groups. Running a train network involves a degree of planning and coordination of movement, even between people who will never encounter each other, so this type of movement is exclusively human. Perhaps because of the weaknesses of our bodies or perhaps because birds have sparked in us a desire to fly faster and farther than our physical limits permit, we alone rely on technology for our movements through the world. But, in the age of phenomenological anthropology, popularized by Tim Ingold, all of this opens up to new questions for reflection. What does it mean, for humans and non-humans, to move through the world? Are human and avian worlds entangled or completely incommensurable? How do human interactions with birds enable the enactment of a specific Japanese ontology, or a culturally grounded way of being-with other living creatures?

Theoretical Context

There is a copious literature on "the Japanese sense of nature," much of which is based on a careful reading of geographer and philosopher Augustin Berque (1986), anthropologist and primatologist Pamela Asquith (2019), or biologist Kinji Imanishi (2002). John Knight (2006) wrote a detailed ethnography of human-wildlife relations on the Kii Peninsula, focusing on large mammals. Barbara Ambros (2012) explored the place of animals in Japanese religion, with an emphasis on pet funerals and memorials. Using Asquith's readings of Japanese primatologists Imanishi and Masao Kawai, philosopher Donna Haraway (1989) tried to understand "the" Japanese view of non-human primates. She argued that Japanese primatology has four special characteristics: "provisionization" (providing wild animals with food); the ability to identify individuals amid large numbers of animals and to sense their personality; long-term research on primate groups in ways that resemble ethnography; and a philosophic synthesis of the meaning of these three characteristics. Haraway (1989, 252) sums this up in a discussion by Japanese primatologist Masao Kawai of *kyōkan*, a sense of being-with, in which the researcher becomes "fused with the monkeys' lives" as the foundation of reliable scientific knowledge.[1] Using Japan as a rhetorical foil, Haraway makes the philosophical point that "science" in the West is a product of a particular hegemonic history. In anthropology at least, there is broad consensus that, as philosopher Maurice Merleau-Ponty ([1945] 2012, 411) points out, scientific parole is a cultural artifact that purports to translate truths found in nature.

Japan is widely depicted as radically different from the West, usually as more group-oriented, holistic, and in tune with nature.[2] This corresponds with common assumptions held by the Japanese – that their mentality differs fundamentally from that of everyone else and that their "nature" is unique, as Japan has four distinct seasons and a propensity for natural disasters (Martinez 2005, 186). This discourse is often inspired by interpretations of Tetsurō Watsuji's *Climate and Culture* (1989), originally published as *Fūdo* in 1935, in which he argued that Japan's culture was shaped by its monsoon climate. In her deconstruction of this narrative, Dolores P. Martinez (2005) makes the case that the Japanese may not have traditionally used the Western discourse of conquest, but that they nonetheless saw nature as something that needed to be worked on and appeased to become acceptable. Most importantly, "the experience of nature for urban dwellers in Japan has more in common with the experiences of urban dwellers throughout the industrialized, developed world than it does with ... the experience of fishermen" (Martinez 2005, 188). Anthropologist Harumi Befu (2001, 9) characterizes the homogenizing discourse of *nihonjinron* (theory of Japanese) as a kind of civil religion that distinguishes the Japanese from their wartime victors while avoiding national symbols, including the national flag and anthem, that are tainted by association with a now dishonoured war effort. Looking at birds with humans in Japan, I hope to better understand the tortuous path that leads from humans interacting with non-humans to anthropological understandings of culture and even nationalist imaginations of nihonjinron.

As I think and write about birds, I find inspiration in new anthropological approaches of phenomenology and ontology, as ways of exploring human-animal relations and how specific humans in specific contexts relate to specific non-human others. Phenomenology, with a focus on embodiment, makes it possible to imagine culture, not as national mentality or explanatory force, but as continually emergent and improvised within the flux of lived experience (Laplante and Sacrini 2016, 12). Tim Ingold, the most prominent advocate of this approach, is especially influenced by philosophers Martin Heidegger and Maurice Merleau-Ponty. He draws upon the concept of the meshwork, the web of life of "entangled lines of life, growth and movement" (Ingold 2011, 63). In his studies of how human and non-human lives meet along paths of movement, Ingold (2011, 63) refers to a kind of "animic ontology" in which some people (usually called animists) are continually alive and open to a "world in continuous birth," which they embrace as a source of astonishment. Phenomenology goes beyond both empiricism (the notion that a world full of objects exists objectively) and intellectualism or idealism (the notion that the mind orders the world before it can be perceived) to focus instead on how the body in motion perceives the world. This approach encourages us to become aware of the phenomenal layer of reality, which is intrinsically and eternally pre-logical (Merleau-Ponty [1945] 2012, 287). This form of attention provides new insights into both human-animal interactions and human cultures.

Anthropologist Philippe Descola ([2005] 2013) proposes a theory to understand how ontologies created by humans to organize what they observe in the world are based on innate cognitive integrating schemas, shaped by the experiences of moving and acquiring skills in the world, and shared in communal life. For Descola, the number of possible ontologies is limited to four, based on whether the physicalities and interiorities of humans and animals are similar or dissimilar. These are *naturalism,* the ontology of modernity, in which humans and animals share continuity in anatomy (physicality) but are radically different in terms of mind (interiority); *animism,* in which humans and animals may have very different bodies but share continuity of interiority; *totemism,* in which humans and animals share similarities in both interiority and physicality; and *analogism*, in which humans and animals are dissimilar in both interiority and physicality (Descola [2005] 2013, 122). For Descola ([2005] 2013, 111), the very heart of anthropology is to understand "the logic of this work of composition, by lending an ear to the themes and harmonies that stand out from the great hum of the world and concentrating on emerging orders whose regularity is detectable behind the proliferation of different customs." Descola ([2005] 2013, 30) has very little to say about Japan, though, following Berque (1986), he does assert that in Japanese thought there is "no place for a conscious objectification of nature or for such a withdrawal of humanity from all that surrounds it." He briefly mentions the Japanese opposition between *sato* (the inhabited place) and *yama,* the mountain, as "the archetype of an un-inhabited place." Still following Berque, he describes inhabited places and mountains in terms of ritual, in seasonal alternation and spiritual comple-mentarity. And, he deplores the ways in which natural forests in post-war Japan have been replaced with industrial plantations of conifers (Descola [2005] 2013, 45–47). Finally, the Japanese perceive an analogical hierarchy in the role played by ancestors, who are active in the existence of the living, as guardians of norms and values (Descola [2005] 2013, 301).

Jakob von Uexküll (1864–1944), an Estonian German biologist who inspired much of Ingold's work, had an ambitious project of *Umweltlehre* to understand the lifeworlds of organisms ranging from the simplest amoeba to the German nobility and bourgeoisie around him. Like Merleau-Ponty, he began with the perception of organisms as they move through space. For von Uexküll, each organism lives within its own bubble, where it makes sense of its world in its own ways and has to deal with the exigencies of moving through space, obtaining food, avoiding enemies, and having sex. As organisms sense the world around them, they take place in their sur-roundings through perception and effect (action). In what von Uexküll (1980, 39) calls a "function cycle" *(Funktionskreis),* the organism perceives obstacles, food, predators, or sexual partners as receptors of perception, which are then integrated into its inner world *as subject,* after which it takes action. There is a hierarchy of integration levels, beginning with simple cells meeting biochemical needs, to all animals that build their subjective worlds *(Umwelten)* and communicate, and finally to the level of human speech and political passions (von Uexküll 1980, 74–75). As organisms move through space and encounter one another, von Uexküll ([1920] 1926, 84) uses a no-tion of a life tunnel, which corresponds to the length of the animal's life in a way that resembles Ingold's idea of lives as lines. Heralding Ingold, von Uexküll ([1920] 1926, 300–1) calls these relations between lives a "mesh-work," which, presaging Descola, would be best expressed in musical notation as part of the symphony of life itself.

The present chapter is explicitly an intellectual grappling, or *Auseinander-setzung*, with some of these ideas that are relevant to the human-bird relations that I experienced in Japan, as I struggle to understand both the culture of nature and the nature of culture in a specific time and place, all the while trying to bracket off assumptions that nature and culture have radically different ontological statuses. I interpret what happens during birding events in Japan, speculate on what this says to the meaning of organisms moving through space and time, and finally conclude with some reflections on ontology. I think of this as a peripatetic anthropology, in which I learn by walking and attempt to write a guidebook for those who follow after me on the same or similar paths.

While I was in Japan, some of my walking was with thirteenth-generation *yamabushi* master Fumihiro Hoshino, a Shugendo spiritual leader who has the goal of bringing urban Japanese and international guests alike back to nature and back to themselves. On May 28, 2018, on the eve of an event with him at Kumano Sanzan, I joined him and his local supporters in a restaurant. He described his recent trip to Morocco, saying that Islam and Shugendo share the same basic teachings, as the divine is immanent in the world. The difference is that the Middle East and Japan have very different environments. Morocco is lifeless, it is not green, and there are few birds or animals. Therefore, the people relate to the sun. The sun, because there is only one, became the basis of monotheism. By contrast, Japan is full of mountains and is very green. The Japanese relate to many things, which is the basis of their polytheism.[3] Perhaps because I had already discussed my human-bird research with him and because he was familiar with anthropology, he turned to me and offered me the key to understanding Japanese culture. "Aimai," he said, "is the basis of Japanese culture." At his request, since he knew I read Chinese, one of the women wrote down the *kanji* characters for me. Just to ensure that I understood, two people looked up the English equivalent of "aimai" on their smartphones, showing me that it meant ambiguity or vagueness. He gave two examples. The first is that people commonly think of just four distinct seasons, but in fact there are many others, like the moment of our meeting in late May, which was neither spring nor summer. There are also shrines, which always begin with a large

Torii gateway. Trees and forests grace the path, but so do souvenir shops. The Japanese, he said, are comfortable with this ambiguity, the blending of the sacred and the profane. That teaching is a good point of departure for an essay on travelling through the pathways of the world, returning to nature, and the meaning of being Japanese. It also fits nicely into Descola's ([2005] 2013, 300) characterization of analogism as "everything is in everything and vice versa."

The Fieldwork

This chapter is based on ethnographic fieldwork into human-bird relations that I conducted in Osaka and elsewhere in Japan from July 2017 to July 2018 when I was a visiting researcher at the National Museum of Ethnology (Minpaku). My research methods included some interviews but were mostly a particular kind of participant observation that we might call "ethnoethology," spending time in situ with humans as they interacted with other living creatures and discussing what they were experiencing (Brunois 2005). This chapter is derived from my participation in birdwatching expeditions organized by the Osaka branch of the WBSJ. During the course of a year, I went on forty-seven of these, in addition to more photography-oriented trips offered by the professional birding outfitter Y-bird that took me to Taiwan and the Yaeyama Islands of Okinawa that lay just east of Taiwan. I also took a private trip to Hokkaido. I sought out other forms of human-bird interaction by visiting conservation centres and a bird rescue facility, hanging out with duck hunters, watching people fish with cormorants, and even eating crow cuisine in an exclusive French-style restaurant in Nagano. I went to an owl café, where clients interact with and take photographs of themselves with owls, but I found the practice so cruel that I could not bring myself to return. I joined ornithologists for bird banding, including a multi-day expedition to the uninhabited Kanmuri Island in the Japan Sea. I also visited temples and shrines devoted to birds, most notably those dedicated to the worship of the Yatagarasu, a giant three-legged crow who saved the life of the first emperor Jimmu by guiding him out of the forest. I joined in with their major rituals. I attended ornithology lectures and participated in non-birding events of the WBSJ. I also spent time alone observing and photographing birds. This mix of methods was intentionally multi-sensorial, as most of them allowed me to see and hear birds. I was able to touch them while working with bird-banders. In game restaurants,

I tasted crow, bulbul, and quail. I even learned to recognize the scent of some birds, once recording with delight in my field notes that I had correctly identified by smell a cormorant, distinguishing it from a heron, as it flew above me from behind. But my entry into the worlds of birds was made possible by working with the WBSJ.

The Birdwatching Ecology around Osaka

Founded on March 11, 1934, the WBSJ has some thirty-four thousand members and eighty-seven local branches throughout Japan. Its purpose is to protect wild birds and their habitat, to educate people about birds through birdwatching, and to conduct ornithological research. It manages conservation sites and Important Bird Areas. Its first president was the poet, cultural worker, and Buddhist monk Godō Nakanishi (1895–1984), who brought together a group of ornithologists, folklorists, and cultural workers around the common goal of bird appreciation and conservation. At a time when people often kept caged birds in their homes to enjoy their songs or hunted for birds to savour their meat, he encouraged them to seek wild birds in their own milieux. He created the term *tanchōkai,* literally "seeking birds club," which the WBSJ still uses today for its regular birdwatching events. The first tanchōkai was a climb up Mount Fuji. The first incarnation of the WBSJ journal *Yachō (Wild Birds),* published from 1934 until 1944, was a collection of Nakanishi's essays, poems, and photography, blending folklore and ornithology. After he was accused by the more scientific members of the WBSJ of unorthodox practices, such as luring birds into his living room to observe them, and of attempting to establish a religious sect, the journal took a markedly more scientific turn.[4] In its current form, the WBSJ is boldly scientific, albeit more oriented toward public education, conservation, and advocacy than is the Yamashina Institute for Ornithology, which was founded in Tokyo in 1942.

As part of the greater Kansai region of Japan, Osaka has a very diverse ecology and thus a great diversity of birds. Historically a major port and business centre, Osaka Bay is home to sea- and shorebirds, and leads south to the Kii Peninsula. The urban area includes green oases of rather large parks, and in fact Osaka Castle Park downtown, which is only two square kilometres, is one of the best birding sites in western Japan. The city is dominated by the Yodo River, which begins in the north at Lake Biwa in Shiga Prefecture (where it is called the Seta River) and flows through Kyoto (as the Uji River) on its way to Osaka Bay. The rivers and their tributaries nourish the alluvial plains, which are used as fertile paddy fields. To the north are mountains, full of forest birds, but the border zones between foothills and farms, known as *satoyama* in Japanese, host an even wider diversity of birds. The annual spring migration follows a route from Osaka Bay along the Yodo River to Lake Biwa and beyond as birds move between Southeast Asia and Siberia. Participation in tanchōkai is a good way to explore these environments, and to visit historical and cultural sites.

The physical exercise of tanchōkai, although slow and of low intensity, provides an appropriate milieu in which not only to think through, but also to fully experience with the feet and the body, the insights of Merleau-Ponty's phenomenology. His sensual approach reminds us that we humans are embodied and that everything we experience and know comes from the engagement of that body in the world. For him, the body is not an *object* in the world, but a means of communicating with the world. The world, moreover, is not a determined sum of objects, but rather the latent horizon of our experience, always present, even before thought (Merleau-Ponty [1945] 2012, 95). Just as tanchōkai members know from observing the changing position of the sun, checking their watches, and listening to the prompts from the birding guides, experience in the world is temporal. This is full of meaning. As Merleau-Ponty ([1945] 2012, 86–87) writes, "The fusion of soul and body in the act, the sublimation of biological existence in personal existence and of the natural world in the cultural world, is simultaneously rendered possible and precarious by the temporal structure of our experience."

An Urban Tanchōkai

Every three months, WBSJ members receive a schedule of local birding events, which is also available on the branch website. Weekday excursions are offered about three times a month, and there are special events such as joint excursions with plant enthusiasts or child-friendly family outings, but the main events are the regular tanchōkai. These are held on Saturday and Sunday, with two or three options on each day. The general tendency is that one trip will visit the mountains and satoyama areas, whereas the other will be in an urban park or coastal area. The written instructions provide details about where to meet, if hiking shoes are necessary, and whether this particular event will be cancelled in the event of rain. The names of the leaders are also listed, and a cell phone number is provided for anyone who has questions about the outing. There is a cost of ¥100 for members, ¥200 for non-members. Regular participants commonly develop a preference for certain excursions and attend faithfully each month. Some people are attracted to the mountains, with their colourful songbirds. Some become experts in certain birds, such as gulls and other seabirds. And some just want a pleasant outing in the park. The popular stereotype of the birder is of a retired person who has lots of time to scan the trees with a pair of binoculars in hopes of spotting a rarity; and indeed, such people are among the most loyal attendees. But participants also include students with an interest in natural history, busy professionals and businesspeople, and even entrepreneurs. Representatives of companies that sell binoculars, outdoor equipment, or birding tours are very active. Although they never explicitly attempt to sell their products during the outing, they make their brands known simply by using them and will discreetly give their business card to anyone who asks for it. From a sociological perspective, these events are not just opportunities to relate to birds, as Colin Jerolmack (2013, 105) observes in connection with pigeon fanciers. They also enable social relations with other humans.

One of my favourite tanchōkai was the mid-monthly excursion to Tsurumi Ryokuchi Park. I was immediately attracted by the name, which could be literally translated as "a green land for observing cranes." The name recalls one of Japan's largest and most charismatic birds. The park also housed the 1990 International Floral Expo, which, as shown below, lends itself to an archaeology of the physicality of international relations. Boasting an area of 121.7 hectares, Tsurumi Ryokuchi was initially one of four large sites set aside in 1941 to provide refuge from Allied firebombing, a fact that I learned only when I consulted Wikipedia.[5] As it turns out, many of the expansive parks in Japanese cities are remnants of wartime zoning necessity. Taking off from Guam, the US Air Force firebombed Japan's major cities, destroying 26 percent of Osaka (Grayling 2006, xvii). The air raids of 1945 killed 9,246 people in Osaka and 6,789 in neighbouring Kobe (Clodfelter 2008, 559), injuring tens of thousands more and leaving uncounted numbers homeless. Nobody mentioned this to me, so I had to learn to interpret what people omitted, such as the older man who sighed as we walked through this park together and said, "This is not a natural site. It has its history." People did mention that the area had been a landfill before the park was established in 1972. They chuckled as they referred to a small hill as "garbage mountain" because it had been constructed by burying a large pile of waste. Even before they arrive for the tanchōkai in the morning, people already have memories, prior experiences, and at least some notions about both their fellow participants and the land they will explore together.

Everyone starts gathering at the appointed spot about half an hour before the scheduled departure time. Participants are relatively easy to identify, as birders carry binoculars, scopes, and tripods. In terms of dress, men and women alike tend to sport wide-brimmed hats and multi-pocket vests. Some, but not all, carry cameras, usually with a long telephoto lens. The volunteer leaders wear armbands that identify them as WBSJ birders, and regulars will even display their plastic membership cards by attaching them to their daypacks. The leaders collect the fee and ask everyone to fill out a sign-in sheet with name, membership status, and phone number. Each person is given a bird checklist, usually with information about the various species that typically frequent this place during this time of year, and sometimes a route map. The most important thing here is the list of bird names, written in the Japanese syllabic script *katakana,* so that people can make a note of the species they see.[6] Regulars chat among themselves but also welcome newcomers with friendly conversation. They ask unfamiliar people questions such as, "How long have you been birding?" or "Have you come here before?" or even "What do you hope to see today?" As the appointed time arrives, the main leader catches the attention of everyone, introduces themself, and adds a brief welcome. Everyone bows politely. The leader introduces the site and says a few words about migration, nesting, breeding, and other seasonal information regarding the birds. He reminds people of any potentially hazardous features, especially if they involve sharing paths with cyclists or crossing a golf course. If he has read some interesting ornithological research, he may share it. This opening ritual creates the group of people who will spend the next three to six hours together, minds focused on birds.

At the start, people tend to form small clusters. One leader heads the procession and another brings up the rear. Leaders are responsible for informing participants about birds, recording their numbers for the WBSJ database, and ensuring that nobody gets lost. On the Tsurumi Ryokuchi outing, the first challenge is to cross a rather busy thoroughfare with a stoplight and a grassy strip in the middle. As they wait for the light or become stranded in the middle, people begin to notice starlings, pigeons, and other city birds. As they walk along the tree-lined entry to the park, the guide may point out some forest birds such as Japanese Tits. Already, some of the women will exclaim, "kawaii!" (cute). These common birds are an entry, not only to the park, but also to the world of birding. In February at this spot, a leader called my attention to an Oriental Greenfinch and then confessed that he got into birding because he found the sparrows so cute. Once the group passes the fountain and approaches the big pond, the guides begin to introduce more birds. Everyone congregates at the pond as the main leader discusses waterbirds. The leaders set up their scopes on tripods so that those who did not bring their own equipment or who simply desire a closer view can admire the cormorants, herons, and gulls. Crows are ubiquitous, and people strain to identify them from sight, and even by call, trying to determine whether each one is a Carrion Crow or a Jungle Crow.

The day really seems to begin once everyone turns right and passes through a gate to enter the main area of the park, as this is where the smaller birds can be found. They are more difficult to detect and identify than the waterbirds. The group usually strolls along a wooded asphalt path on the east side of the park, sharing it with joggers and dog walkers. The challenge of the woods is seeing the small birds. Unlike the eye-catching ducks, which are commonly quite tame in city parks, they are often well camouflaged and furtive. They do not seem to wait for the birders, crossing their paths in unpredictable ways and appearing and disappearing in a heartbeat. Some people stay on the asphalt path, whereas others step into the trees on dirt paths, which give a view down to a residential neighbourhood. As one moves, the world opens up, along with the beings who share this space. It is no coincidence that Merleau-Ponty chose the birds of his garden to explore this kind of movement through space. Every bird species has its own distinctive way of moving and flying. For example, a crane will fly with its neck outstretched, whereas herons kink their necks as they fly. But it is by the movement, by a particular undulation, that one begins to perceive it, a process by which things are defined first by "behaviour" and not by any static "properties" (Merleau-Ponty [1945] 2012, 288). There is always a movement or perhaps a chirp or call, but at any rate "the difference that makes a difference" is the information that sparks perception (Bateson 1979, 228). During our birding walks, something pre-linguistic happened first, as a participant moved through space and suddenly caught a glimpse of something on the path, a shadowy figure crossing in the air, or a flutter of movement in the leaves. At that point, she would exclaim, "Ah!" or "Eh!" before motioning with her hands for the others to stop and pointing toward what she had seen. Only if she heard the bird's call or saw enough of it to permit confident identification would its name arise, so that she could say, "atori"

(Brambling) or "jōbitaki" (Daurian Redstart), for example. These two winter birds would evoke cries of delight. For common birds, people give a sigh of disappointment and utter a disparaging remark, such as, "It's only a Brown-eared Bulbul." Some people even told me that they hated crows because they ate garbage and leftovers from convenience stores.

This all says something about the nature of perception and communication. Only a few seconds elapse between that first perception of difference as a bird emerges from its background and the formation of a word, but the motions and sounds made during those first seconds are remarkably similar regardless of whether or not the birder is Japanese. It is only secondarily that the word emerges, already translating the initial perception into a symbol, which has a specific place in a cultural system, but this is the crucial moment of recognition. As Merleau-Ponty ([1945] 2012, 183) states, "The designation of objects never happens after recognition, it is recognition itself." The order in which things happen is thus movement, perception, recognition (through naming), and then communication. The group will stop to determine how many birds there are, of which species, and what they are doing. After naming the birds, people start attributing values and meanings to them, which, to the degree in which those are shared, become culture. As ornithology takes over these encounters, the leader verifies the identity of the bird, records its presence on her form, and adds it to the total calculation for the number of birds seen. If it is a rarity or particularly beautiful, people jostle to get a good view or take a photo. If it remains reasonably still for long enough, the leader will set up a scope and encourage people to take a closer look. Usually, the bird will leave the scene before the people do, but if they linger, the leader will eventually say, "Come on! We have to move on!"

Other humans who are interested in birds have their own intentions and ways of attention. The next stop, by the northeast gate of the park, is one of the most intriguing for both birders and anthropologist. We pause at a small pond, set up the scopes, and start searching, all the while keeping a careful distance from a clump of camouflage-dressed humans equipped with folding chairs and even larger cameras – the wildlife photographers. This pond is commonly frequented by the Common Kingfisher, a bird of brilliant blue and orange. Within a few minutes, a kingfisher lands on a branch emerging from the water. Birders excitedly snap photos or look at it through the scopes. A guide asks them to identify its sex, allowing them to guess before revealing that it is a female, as indicated by the orange on the underpart of its beak. "It's her lipstick," he says with a chuckle. Suddenly, the bird dives into the water, and there is a whirr of shutters as the photographers try to get a shot of it in the air or at the nano-second when the beak hits the surface of the pond, creating concentric ripples and sending droplets into the air. There is more excitement if the bird emerges with a small fish in its beak. If it disappears, one or two of the guides may even engage in conversation with some of the photographers, as they know each other from repeated encounters. As we walk away, a guide asks me if I noticed that the branch had intentionally been set in place and that bait had been left on a floating plastic ring in the water. She tells me that setting bait violates the ethics of the WBSJ, which I see as policing the boundary between bird and human, but that photographers do it all the time to control lighting conditions, ensure an uncluttered background, and get the perfect shot. Throughout the year's tanchōkai activities, we repeatedly ran into such groups of photographers, who bring bait or even use recorded sounds to lure birds into the open, another ethical violation in the eyes of the birders. There is a whole community of photographers. One of them told me that they use Instagram to share information about bird whereabouts and photography tips. Unlike the birders, whose goal is to amass the longest list of species, some photographers specialize in only one kind of bird.

Not all of the humans whom we encountered understood what we were doing. Often, as we stopped at the side of the path, cameras and scopes aimed toward a woodpecker in the trees, passersby would become curious. Sometimes, I heard snippets of puzzled conversation. "What are they looking at?" asked one person. Straining to see, her companion retorted, "Nothing at all!" If asked, the birders patiently explained what they were doing. The social distinction between birders and non-birders may be even starker than that between birders and photographers. Birders refer to non-birders simply as *futsū no hito* (ordinary people). They told me that, even outside of the birding context, they can identify non-birders due to the vocabulary they use. Some of it is subtle. For example, non-birders mispronounce the Japanese name for the Black Kite, calling it *tonbi* rather than *tobi*. They also refer to all the ubiquitous herons and egrets in Japan collectively as *sagi*, failing to see the differences between the Grey Heron, Great Egret, Intermediate Egret, and Small Egret. This shows that the tanchōkai focuses human attention on birds in novel ways, but the resulting changes in perception subsequently become ways of making distinctions between humans.

We continue onward, briefly ascending garbage mountain to scan the horizon for raptors before taking a break by the toilets across from the Dutch gardens, with their giant windmill and a vast field ready for the tulip blooms of spring. Since we have been moving slowly, yet burning calories, it is snack time. Someone notes the irony that the foreigner is the only one who has brought a Japanese *daifuku* sweet made of glutinous rice and red bean paste, whereas everyone else is enjoying chocolate bars. All the while, people are scanning the trees near the path for signs of birds and are rarely disappointed. Wagtails forage for food in the grass, and a Pale Thrush materializes from the trees.

Echoing von Uexküll, the guides may explain the existence of *esaba,* the feeding grounds that attract birds. "Esa" means "bait," but these are not human baiting practices like those we saw carried out by the photographers. The word simply refers to the presence of food, such as fruits, that attract the birds across the landscape. Moving on, we linger in the Japanese garden, photographing the Japanese White-eyes, Japanese Tits, Varied Tits, and Long-tailed Tits that flit back and forth between the early-flowering trees. I notice that some young people in historical costume are taking photos of each other, with Japanese architecture in the background. These young women and men, easily identified by the suitcases they pull behind them, ignore the birds that brought us to the garden. The same flowering trees take on different meanings for all of us: food for the birds, natural bait for the tiny creature that birders hope to see, and a culturally appropriate backdrop for cosplay actors.

As we enter the Canadian garden, it is my turn to deliver a cultural performance. I find myself in a familiar milieu, amid maple trees and white pines. Mallards and other ducks swim in the pond at the base of a waterfall. Someone asks me if I feel at home; another refers to the cascade as a miniature Niagara Falls. Inevitably, at this site, someone will reminisce to me about a trip he or she took to Canada. Once, an experienced birder spent a long time looking at a duck with a mottled green head and a black bill. "A very strange-looking Mallard," he muttered before concluding that it was a hybrid between a Mallard and an Eastern Spot-billed Duck.

Yet another human-bird relationship emerged as we reached a large pond fringed by prairie-like grass. This area was full of Grey Herons. Once, I noted the strange behaviour of a heron, which was perched on a bench immediately beside a solitary man. Two other herons and a crow stood near his feet. As my group continued past, I lingered, just to see him slip a silvery fish out of his bag and toss it to the heron. The man was discreet because feeding wild birds is illegal in Japan, but I had seen other people do this. I even became well acquainted with a man in another park, who told me that he had been feeding the crows for forty years, had given them names, and knew their kinship relations. This time, however, I could not stop to learn more, since I had to catch up with my group. I rejoined it just in time to hear the guide explain that some of the herons' bills had turned pink, which he called "lipstick," because they were breeding. Part of the interest in spring birding, when tanchōkai see an uptick in new members, is that we can watch nesting birds, and eventually chicks and fledglings, from a safe and ethical distance so as not to provoke flight.

This is where we always stopped for lunch, a time for more leisurely conversations and sharing of photos that allowed us to create together an understanding of Japan. Inevitably, somebody pointed out the apparent irony that only the foreigner had brought chopsticks and a bento box, whereas everyone else ate sandwiches. Some people were curious about the foreigner in their midst. One man began his conversation in English but switched to Japanese mid-way. "I am happy when foreigners come to Japan to study Japanese culture," he said. "Welcome to Japan." Leaders and regular birders always asked me for an update on my research. Sometimes, they were astonished by the human-bird relations I described, such as eating a Carrion Crow in a restaurant or spending time with hunters and yama-bushi, because these aspects of Japan are beyond their experience. I could also ask them questions. Having noticed that hunters, cormorant fishers, zoos, abattoirs, and even conservation biologists set up commemorative sites and hold an annual sacrifice *(kuyō)* to the souls of birds, I asked if the WBSJ does such things. The answer, which other birders later confirmed, was that commemorating wild birds was unnecessary. This contextualized kuyō for me, letting me see it, not as a ritual conducted because all birds have souls, but as a way of appreciating those particular bird lives that become entangled in human society.[7] Either way, Japanese people display an attentiveness to non-human lives that transcends what I have seen in Western societies or even in Taiwan (where I have done field research for two decades).

Conversations during tanchōkai sometimes speculated on avian minds. When people asked me questions about my reading and writing, I mentioned Eduardo Kohn's *How Forests Think* (2013). Even the title provoked comments such as "but forests don't think!" When I explained his theory of communication, one woman seemed to reflect carefully before giving her opinion that "all animals think, even plants think, but we cannot communicate with different kinds." I asked one elder leader (a retired businessman) whether birds thought. He laughed heartily and said, "Only about food!" Yet, at lunch one day in March, I watched as a woman spoke gently to a lone brambling that was obviously ill, worried that it would not catch up with the other bramblings that had already migrated. In my field notes, I labelled the incident as evidence of an animist ontology because she acted *as if* the bird could understand Japanese.

As we walked through the park, the ornithological lessons were often about bird minds. On February 17, just after lunch, we headed to a former national pavilion from the Floral Expo. A large glass wall loomed up amid the trees. One leader pointed out spots where birds had collided with the glass and even searched the ground for feathers. Holding up a clump of them, he noted that the bird had been a White-bellied Green Pigeon and explained how it had met its end. As he and his colleagues had observed, crows used the wall as a hunting aid. They dove at the pigeons, which scattered, flew into the glass in their efforts to escape, and fell unconscious to the ground, providing a meal for the crows. This example of corvid tool use shows the utility of von Uexküll's theory. Crow and pigeon alike live in their own Umwelten. The pigeon perceives the diving crow as an enemy, which prompts its action of flying away as quickly as possible. The crow sees the pigeon as food, but it also has a theory in mind as to what will happen next. The pigeon does not see the glass, whereas the crow has already learned to use it as a tool. For the birding leader, all of this is a perceptual clue, which draws him to the site to demonstrate his knowledge of bird behaviour and to create a memorable excursion. After passing through a more densely packed series of pavilions, even one for the United Nations and one for the OECD, we stop and watch for shrikes, who perch on poles or branches as they watch for prey. I told one of the leaders that, in Taiwan, I saw people exploit this predictable behaviour to trap shrikes and that I had eaten one. He told me that after the war many Japanese people had to eat starlings and other common wild birds.

Until April 21, after which most ducks had departed for their breeding grounds in Siberia, the climax of the Tsurumi Ryokuchi Park expedition was the pond near the dilapidated Chinese pavilion, where we watched thousands of ducks of eight species. As the leader spotted an *oshidori* (Mandarin Duck), he punned on its name by calling it an *oishidori* (delicious bird). From a distance, the guides pointed out the difference between the Mandarin Duck, Eurasian Widgeon, Mallard, Indian Spot-billed Duck, Northern Pintail, Eurasian Teal, Common Pochard, and Tufted Duck, as well as the occasional hybrid.[8] On February 17, as most participants rushed to the shore where families were plying the ducks, pigeons, and crows with bread crumbs, a few of us followed the leaders to inspect a dead Mallard drake on the grass. One leader was very cautious, holding out her hand to indicate that we should not approach. Another took out his cell phone and called to report the location of the bird. He said that they needed to do this as a precaution against avian influenza.[9] The leaders, however, inspected the carcass carefully, noting that its missing tail had certainly been eaten and thus hypothesized that it had been chased and caught from behind by a raptor. A month later, when they spotted a lone female Mallard, a guide recalled the dead drake seen in February and said that this bird was probably his partner. We all headed toward the shore of the pond, where we could photograph the birds as "ordinary people" fed them. A park employee drove by in a truck, loud-speakers admonishing (to no effect) that feeding the birds was illegal.

Finally, the leaders gathered us together. Sitting on the ground in a circle, we pulled out our bird checklists and pens, eagerly waiting for confirmation of what we had seen. The main leader slowly called out the name of each species and told us how many individual birds we had observed. There were two idiosyncrasies here. First, the ubiquitous Rock Pigeon was not counted. There was usually a separate category where we could note that we had seen it, but the number was not recorded. A leader explained to me that this introduced species was not a wild bird, which meant that it did not count. Second, hybrid ducks were excluded. Even once, when I had photographed a hybrid between a Mallard and an Eastern Spot-billed Duck, which was the only Mallard-type duck we had seen, it was completely excluded from the official records. When I asked why, the leader firmly replied, "Because hybrids are *not* wild birds." So much for Japanese ambiguity.

Each tanchōkai ends much as it begins, with a collective bow, this time accompanied with expressions of thanks from the participants. Every-one heads off in various directions, some going back to the pond to feed the ducks, others walking through the park to the subway station. As I walked alone through the park, I noticed that, in the absence of leaders, participants, cameras, scopes, and binoculars, the birds seemed to recede into the background. Bikers, skateboarders, children playing, and old people chatting on the benches now came to the foreground. For just a few hours, the WBSJ had focused our attention on the lives and names of birds with an emotional intensity that "ordinary people" do not even imagine. It also brought humans into a relationship with one another through conversation and a common experience. From this flux of experience, I conclude with two observations.

Mindful of Birds

A year of participation in tanchōkai made me aware of birds in ways that were new to me. At the end of April, after most ducks had left Osaka, we visited the park. As I described in my field notes:

> As we ate, birds approached us. A Grey Heron came up from the pond and wandered among us, as if looking for food. I said to the guide, "It is used to being fed." He said yes, that is true. There were also bulbuls, starlings, two Japanese tits in the branches just in front of us, sparrows above them, and then a flock of pigeons that strolled over to see if we had bread for them. There was one lonely looking male mallard. As we sat there, a young starling was walking on the ground and seemed to be anxiously looking for something or someone. It cried out several times. Another one on the branch above cried in reply and it flew up to join it. They cooed together as if joyful to be together. There were crows flying above, calling to one another. I realized that, just as Eduardo Kohn had found in the Amazon, we are in a world that thinks.

Tanchōkai taught me to be mindful of the lifeworlds of birds. Reaching across the "soap bubble" that von Uexküll saw as separating all organisms from one another, I learned to perceive avian worlds of hunger and satiation, birth and kinship, death and sorrow. Once, I became so focused on watching a flock of bulbuls that, as they flew away, I felt the sensation of my own soul departing with them, the beating of wings next to my ears, the accelerating ascending motion, and the wind against my face. Was I like the magician imagined by Merleau-Ponty ([1945] 2012, 283), transforming into a bird on his rooftop, all the while maintaining an internal rapport between that which is extinguished and that which is born? I thought about shamans in the Amazon, as I called back my soul, paying attention to my own earthbound body, the breath in my own lungs, the weight of my own arms. Only later did I come to understand this moment, following Merleau-Ponty's ([1945] 2012, 368) notion of intersubjectivity between bodies, which he illustrates with the anecdote of a fifteen-month infant who moved his mouth as he himself nibbled the child's fingers. Merleau-Ponty's point is that perception is less about looking at objects in space than it is about imagining them through the experience of our own bodies. This ability to imagine and to relate transcends the boundaries between species.

Only after we try to translate sensations and perceptions into words do we attach meaning to those experiences and make possible the shared understandings that we know as culture. Maybe in a different culture, or in a different nature, I would have described my sensation of becoming bulbul and been labelled as a shaman-in-becoming. However, in Western naturalist ontology, we tend to emphasize the difference between human and non-human minds. Merleau-Ponty ([1945] 2012, 341) becomes the native informant in his speculations that the difference between humans and animals is that *only* humans have the ability to objectivize the world, to become conscious of themselves, and to understand not just the immediate milieu but an infinite number of possible milieux. I am not convinced of this radical rupture between human and animal worlds. I do not know whether the bulbuls also reflected upon the humans whom they encountered, whether they shared their ideas with other bulbuls, or whether they could become familiar with humans in ways that were meaningful to them.

What I can know is that human and avian birds intersect when it comes to movement. Humans rely on subways, trains, and airplanes to reach distant places, whereas even the tiniest birds can fly long distances solely on the strength of their own wings and lungs. In their movement, human and avian lives become entangled in various ways, enabled by the form of the earth and how they live on it. In Japan, this is most obvious because waterbirds thrive amidst the water that gathers in rice paddies. Only recently, as bird conservationists promote new practices, have farmers begun to flood the paddies during the winter even though no crop is growing. In doing so, they provide a wintering home for migratory birds. As I discovered during my year of tanchōkai, birds can learn to coexist with humans – swallows build their nests in the eaves of traditional Japanese houses, crows build in the electricity infrastructure that powers trains and subways, and a pair of kestrels returns every year to breed in the same air vent in a public building in the suburbs of Osaka where they draw the attention of birders and photographers. In Japan, birding events include a sense of wonder about how all of these bird movements are tied to the four seasons throughout the year. They give us a privileged perch from which to perceive diverse lines of entanglement, which occur as humans and birds move in their own ways as they search for food and livelihoods, sex and reproduction, family and friendship. Tanchōkai is a way of training us to be mindful of bird lives, whether we are taking the subway or climbing Mount Fuji.

These human and avian worlds are not completely separate and incommensurable, as naturalistic notions of "culture" versus "nature" might suggest. Humans and birds rely on one another. This is why Thom van Dooren (2019, 57) calls us to embrace a situated pluralism, in which we seek connection with other kinds of lives, become open to them, and learn to share space well. This does not mean that there are no boundaries to respect. In a year of birding, I saw Japanese people go to great lengths to keep pigeons out of train stations, sparrows out of grocery stores, crows out of garbage cans, and cranes out of broccoli gardens. Part of that work involves the boundary management of forbidding other humans to feed these very birds. There is conflict, as well as a desire to live together harmoniously across species boundaries.

Ever since the founding intellectual work of Godō Nakanishi, the WBSJ has hoped that teaching the Japanese people about birds will convince them to support conservation efforts. I think that the tanchōkai do help their practitioners cultivate a kind of mindfulness, which opens up to a new way of living with birds. This potentially increases support for attempts to conserve birds and their habitat. I am not saying that all participants go out and join environmentalist groups. In fact, I know that many just return to their regular lives and busy jobs. But I think that tanchōkai does provide people with what Ingold (2000, 22) calls an "education of attention," which may be missing from the lifeworlds of non-birders.

There remains the ontological question raised by Descola. Even as the tanchōkai leaders are busy counting species and individual birds, I doubt that the participants whom I met would objectify birds or deny the possibility of their consciousness as categorically as does Merleau-Ponty. In fact, they often speculate on the emotions of birds and make analogies with human traits such as marriage and use of lipstick. But, is that because tanchōkai members are Japanese rather than Westerners? Or is it because they are birders rather than philosophers? Descola equates naturalism, the ontology that humans and non-humans share similar physicalities but differ radically in terms of mind, with Western modernity. This ontology is manifested in the bird lists and use of Linnaean taxonomies, as well as in the good-natured teasing that I endured when I asked people about the thoughts of birds or discussed my readings of Kohn. I also saw evidence of animism, which is often associated with Shintoism, when, like the woman with the sick brambling, people expected birds to understand spoken Japanese or speculated on their intentions. Descola ([2005] 2013, 233) argues that the principles governing the four ontologies are universal, so that by extension they "coexist potentially in all human beings," even as one ontology becomes dominant in any given historical situation. Perhaps it is more appropriate to think of relations between forms of lives in terms of onto-genesis, variations of ontologies arising as people perceive the world during direct interactions with non-human others. Perhaps the ability of tanchōkai participants to toggle between expressions of naturalism and animism is another example of a Japanese tolerance of ambiguity – aimai.

Master Hoshino brought the theme of ambiguity back to me after a day of spiritual practice. He had taken us to see the waterfall from which the Yatagarasu emerged to rescue Emperor Jimmu. As the participants all shared excitedly afterward, everyone had actually seen the Yatagarasu materialize in front of us, casting a shadow as the giant, three-legged crow flew over us into the forest. I saw it just as clearly as everyone else, even if as a Westerner I am supposed to be an avatar of the Enlightenment. There was certainly ambiguity in that moment. Did we really *see* the Yatagarasu, or did we just imagine it? How could all of us possibly have shared the same illusion? As we were preparing to depart, Master Hoshino referred to me in a private conversation as a "scientist." I replied, "There are lots of debates within the discipline if anthropology is a science or a literary genre." "You perceive it that way," he said, "because you [Westerners] are Christian. You think everything is either this or that. Japanese people, on the other hand, accept ambiguity." If perceiving commonalities across established conceptual boundaries is what makes a thought analogist, Master Hoshino brought such thoughts to my mind, as did the birders every time they made analogies between human and bird lives. But it is the thought that is analogist, not the individual who is thinking. Culture is what emerges when such thoughts are shared.

Conclusion

Whether we are regarding birds or other humans, phenomenological approaches have an important contribution for anthropology. Perception arises in living organisms as they perceive the world around them. As subjects, and this is where von Uexküll's Umweltlehre is useful, they focus their attention on the objects of perception and take action. There is surely an education of attention, through which individuals learn from experience, as well as from others, which differences make a difference. Anthropologists tend to focus most on what happens next in human societies: as language takes over, humans enter in conversation with one another, eventually weaving together legends to pass from one generation to another, writing books, performing science and ritual, and creating complex institutions within which they enter into higher-level functional cycles of perception and action. From the same pre-logical world emerge the human ways of organizing the reality that Descola calls ontologies, and then societies produce scientific discourses, art, poetry, and religion according to their own, always interlinking, historical trajectories. Merleau-Ponty's ([1945] 2012, 382) language betokens that of Master Hoshino when he says that all transcendental knowledge springs from no less than the "ambiguous" life.

In connection with birds, the main lessons from phenomenology are that the encounters between living things, in what both von Uexküll and Ingold call the meshwork of life, are the basis of subsequent world making. As avian, human, and other lives meet, some humans in some circumstances perceive a shared subjectivity or soul between themselves and those others. Ingold, Descola, and many others in anthropology tend to identify those ways of organizing perception as animist, associated mostly with non-Western or Indigenous peoples. In anthropology, only Eduardo Kohn stands out by entertaining the idea that this judgment may be an ontological fact. His argument that forests think is an acknowledgment that, in the physical world, "there exist other kinds of thinking selves beyond the human" (Kohn 2013, 94). Even as scientific ornithology, including its most naturalist elements, permeates the WBSJ, tanchōkai still promote mindfulness of birds in ways that its founder, Buddhist monk Godō Nakanishi, would recognize. In those events, I witnessed a specific blend of animism, naturalism, and analogism that anthropologists can legitimately label as expressions of Japanese culture.

At the beginning of this chapter, I quoted Merleau-Ponty's comments that philosophy is about relearning to see the world and that seeing is entering in a universe of beings that show themselves. This is what intersubjectivity is all about; humans and others perceive each other as their various life tunnels intersect. Moving through the world entangles our lives with those of others. On rare occasions, they may even communicate and create a more intimate relationship. In the right context, bird and human lives can be commensurable, as when birds and humans eat together in the park. My hope is that we can do better anthropology and better world making by becoming more mindful and more respectful of the avian and other lives we encounter along the way.

NOTES

1 Haraway (1989, 252) notes that Asquith interviewed over forty Japanese primatologists and found that only Kawai used the term kyōkan. Other Japanese primatologists attributed its use to eccentricity, and Kawai himself said he was unique on this point. Nonetheless, as this essay aims to show, notions such as kyōkan are a form of attention to non-human lives and an awareness of possible cultural difference that emerges from dialogue between some Japanese and Western scholars. This is not a claim that kyōkan is widely accepted by Japanese primatologists.

2 These notions seem pervasive. Even Merleau-Ponty, whose book inspired many of the reflections in this chapter, felt a need to radically other Japan. In a discussion about the corporal expression of emotion, he contrasted "the Japanese person" who smiles when angry with the "Westerner" who may turn red and stamp his foot or turn white and speak in a strained voice (Merleau-Ponty 2012, 195). When I read this, my first reaction was that Merleau-Ponty had spent very little time in Japan or with Japanese people and had even failed to see enough Japanese films. Otherwise, he would have seen that Japanese people express anger in ways that differ very little from those of other humans. Merleau-Ponty's point, drawing upon this unsubstantiated claim about the Japanese and Bronislaw Malinowski's portrayal of paternity in the Trobriand Islands, is that only humans, *in explicit contrast to animals,* create meanings and institutions that transcend anatomical dispositions, even in regard to processes of emotion and reproduction that seem at first glance to be purely biological. Merleau-Ponty's assumption of a rupture between animals and humans, even as he recognizes that human culture emerges from a natural base, is an example of the ontology that Descola ([2005] 2013) calls naturalist.

3 Watsuji (1989) made the same argument, contrasting the fertile and dangerous monsoon climate of Japan to the arid desert of the Middle East, which he saw on his way to study in Germany.

4 This is my summary after reading all the issues of *Yachō* in the University of Kyoto library. I was particularly amused by the photos in which Nakanishi sat at his desk, feeding birds perched on his shoulder, or photographed a cormorant in his salon. When I shared the photos with WBSJ members, they were equally as astounded, as such practices would not be condoned by birders today.

5 Targeting cities that were built largely of wood, incendiary bombs created firestorms, a mass destruction that Mark Selden (2010) terms a "forgotten holocaust."

6 Written Japanese is a combination of three systems. Nouns and stems of verbs, adverbs, and adjectives are usually written in kanji (characters of Chinese origin). The syllabic *hiragana* script is used to write words that cannot be written in kanji, such as verb suffixes and grammatical particles, or to provide a more informal style. An alternative syllabic of katakana is used much like italics in English to provide emphasis but also to transcribe foreign words

(which are commonly used), to represent onomatopoeia (or bird calls), and to write scientific and technical terms, such as (most importantly here) the names of plants and animals. Katakana indicates difference, which is why it is sometimes used in manga to illustrate the Japanese spoken by foreign characters.

7 There is a general idea in Japan that all living things have souls. An anonymous peer reviewer of this chapter generously offered a story about his Japanese grandmother and her pet Java Sparrow, suggesting that I include it as an example of the Japanese belief in animal souls. When his grandmother was old and suffering from lung cancer, her bird passed away. She suddenly felt better than usual and explained that the bird had died on her behalf. Beliefs about wild birds probably differ from those concerning companion birds, but all are seen as having souls and some degree of supernatural potency.

8 On the Yodo River excursion, we also saw the American Widgeon and hybrids between the American Widgeon and Eurasian Widgeon.

9 This kind of behaviour among birders is why Frédéric Keck (2015) studies birders in Greater China as "sentinels for the environment."

WORKS CITED

Ambros, Barbara. 2012. *Bones of Contention: Animals and Religion in Contemporary Japan.* Honolulu: University of Hawai'i Press.

Asquith, Pamela J. 2019. "Multispecies Ethnography from the Perspective of Japanese Primate Social Interaction Studies." *Cahiers d'anthropologie sociale* 18, 1: 37–51.

Bateson, Gregory. 1979. *Mind and Nature: A Necessary Unity.* New York: E.P. Dutton.

Befu, Harumi. 2001. *Hegemony of Homogeneity: An Anthropological Analysis of Nihonjinron.* Melbourne: Trans Pacific Press.

Berque, Augustin. 1986. *Le sauvage et l'artifice: Les Japonais devant la nature.* Paris: Gallimard.

Brunois, Florence. 2005. "Pour une approche interactive des savoirs locaux: l'ethno-éthologie." *Le Journal de la Société des Océanistes* 120–21: 31–40.

Clodfelter, Micheal. 2008. *Warfare and Armed Conflicts: A Statistical Encyclopedia of Casualty and Other Figures, 1494–2007.* 3rd ed. Jefferson, NC: McFarland.

Descola, Philippe. (2005) 2013. *Beyond Nature and Culture.* Translated by Janet Lloyd. Chicago: University of Chicago Press.

Grayling, A.C. 2006. *Among the Dead Cities: Was the Allied Bombing of Civilians in WWII a Necessity or a Crime?* London: Bloomsbury.

Haraway, Donna. 1989. *Primate Visions: Gender, Race, and Nature in the World of Modern Science.* London: Routledge.

Imanishi, Kinji. 2002. *A Japanese View of Nature: The World of Living Things.* Translated by Pamela J. Asquith. London: Routledge Curzon.

Ingold, Tim. 2000. *The Perception of the Environment: Essays of Livelihood, Dwelling and Skill.* London: Routledge.

—. 2011. *Being Alive: Essays on Movement, Knowledge and Description.* London: Routledge.

Jerolmack, Colin. 2013. *The Global Pigeon.* Chicago: University of Chicago Press.

Keck, Frédéric. 2015. "Sentinels for the Environment: Birdwatchers in Taiwan and Hong Kong." *China Perspectives* 102, 2: 43–52.

Knight, John. 2006. *Waiting for Wolves in Japan: An Anthropological Study of People-Wildlife Relations.* Honolulu: University of Hawai'i Press.

Kohn, Eduardo. 2013. *How Forests Think: Toward an Anthropology beyond the Human.* Berkeley: University of California Press.

Laplante, Julie, and Marcus Sacrini. 2016. "Présentation: Poétique vivante." *Anthropologie et Sociétés* 40, 3: 9–35.

Martinez, Dolores P. 2005. "On the 'Nature' of Japanese Culture, or, Is There a Japanese Sense of Nature?" In *A Companion to the Anthropology of Japan,* ed. Jennifer Robertson, 185–200. Malden, MA: Blackwell.

Merleau-Ponty, Maurice. (1945) 2012. *Phenomenology of Perception.* Translated by Donald A. Landes. New York: Routledge.

Selden, Mark. 2010. "A Forgotten Holocaust: U.S. Bombing Strategy, the Destruction of Japanese Cities, and the American Way of War from the Pacific War to Iraq." In *Bombing Civilians: A Twentieth-Century History,* ed. Yuki Tanaka and Marilyn Young, 77–96. New York: New Press.

Van Dooren, Thom. 2019. *The Wake of Crows: Living and Dying in Shared Worlds.* New York: Columbia University Press.

Von Uexküll, Jakob. (1920) 1926. *Theoretical Biology.* Translated by D.L. Mackinnon. New York: Harcourt Brace.

—. 1980. *Kompositionslehre der Natur: Biologie als undogmatische Naturwissenschaft, Ausgewählte Schriften.* Frankfurt a.M.: Propyläen.

Watsuji, Tetsurō. 1989. *Climate and Culture: A Philosophical Study.* New York: Greenwood Press.

Part Two

Birds Are Good to Think With
(Birds in Symbolic Systems)

6

Three Birds, the Emotions, and Cycles of Time in the Central Himalayas

John Leavitt

But why birds? What did the little blighters do that was so compelling? ... Clearly the answer was that birds have a life of their own which, although over large areas irrational and perplexing, isn't quite so irrational and perplexing as the life that human beings have been contriving for themselves of late. Work hard on birds, and you may here and there make some sense of them. This scarcely holds of *homo sapiens*.

– Michael Innes, *Hare Sitting Up*

Birds ... form a community independent from ours, but which, as a result of that very independence, strikes us as an "other" society, and homologous to the one we live in: birds love freedom; they build themselves dwellings where they live as families and nurture their young; they often maintain social relations with other members of their species; and they communicate with them by acoustic means that suggest articulate language.

As a result, all the objective conditions are brought together for us to conceive of the world of birds as a metaphorical human society.

– Claude Lévi-Strauss, *Wild Thought*

THE FOLLOWING REFLECTIONS draw primarily on two sources. First, my own experiences of birdwatching, which I came to rather late, in my late twenties and thirties. Second, time spent in the Indian Himalayas since the early 1980s, involving experiences that, by contrast with those with which I was familiar, taught the relevancy of distinctive patterns of organization of time and activity and the reliance on the real presences of the socionatural world – in this case a world of mountain slopes, river valleys, stone villages, terraced fields, and intervening forests – as markers in such an organization.

Someone with no formal background in biology or natural history already knows that there are different kinds of clearly demarcated natural entities. While, according to biologists, hybrids do occur, they are rare; ravens, owls, and Scarlet Tanagers (I grew up in western Pennsylvania, and the tanagers were unmistakable and unforgettable) look different, act differently, and make different sounds from each other. One meets no dusky red owl-tanagers that come out only during sunset and sunrise, hoot-whistle, and live on a mixture of mice and berries.[1]

One of the first things birdwatching teaches is that this kind of observable demarcation goes much deeper and is much finer than a modern Western layperson generally expects. What one had dealt with as partly overlapping categories of pretty birds, boring birds, tasty birds, noisy birds each resolves not into sub-categories but into kinds, each of which is as clearly, if not as strikingly, demarcated as are ravens, owls, and Scarlet Tanagers. Demarcated kinds exist on different levels, going "down" to that of the very nice distinctions that bedevil birders: Is that a Hairy Woodpecker or a Downy Woodpecker? Even if I can't tell right away, I have read, and am learning to recognize, that it has to be one or the other – and while hybrids do apparently exist,[2] my chances of coming across something between the two are virtually zero.

For someone with a background in a pretty relativistic form of cultural anthropology, this is a salutary lesson. Nature is not a blank slate on which languages and cultures can impose whatever demarcations they "want to" based solely on historically contingent lexical distinctions or what have been called "cultural projects" (Sahlins 1977). This lesson was recognized and run with, particularly from the 1970s through the 1990s, by anthropologists who became convinced that all folk classifications were fundamentally the same because people everywhere and at all times were basing them on the observed discontinuities that the world was presenting to them (e.g., Berlin, Breedlove, and Raven 1973; Berlin 1992). If this is true, it means that our modern scientific classifications of natural beings into genera and species will, with some marginal exceptions, correspond to all the observation-based classifications that human societies have produced. An opposed but equally universalistic position (Atran 1985, 1993) argues that human cognitive propensities are at least as important as, and probably more important than, generic and specific distinctions. An example here is that of the category "tree," which probably exists in all or most languages and cultures but is not recognized in scientific taxonomies.[3]

These views bolstered, and were bolstered by, the rise and intellectual hegemony of a universalistic cognitive science during the same period, promising, specifically, a union of cognitive theory with the "modern evolutionary synthesis" in biology (Ludwig 2018, 416–17). One problem with these views, as with most of the cognitive science of the period, was that while their proponents insisted – against an extreme relativism that they themselves had largely invented to serve as a straw man (for a parallel, Leavitt 2011, Chapter 9) – that neither nature nor the human mind was a blank slate to be written on by languages and cultures, they conversely treated languages and collective conceptions as blank slates to be written on by innate and pre-ordained cognitive patterning and the observation of real natural differences, which would always write the same thing.

But there are no blank slates. Although owls and Scarlet Tanagers and their most striking characteristics are not likely to be confused by anyone ever anywhere, they do not mean the same things everywhere. The owl's great staring eyes are one of its most generally salient points. In the West, this has usually been taken as a sign of wisdom; in South Asia, it is taken as a sign of idiocy, and calling someone "owl brain" *(ullū dimāg)* in a north Indian language is not a compliment.[4]

Any natural being, any natural form or category, has a potentially unlimited number of observable qualities. Some of these are highly salient, which literally means they jump out at you. Such traits are so striking as to be unavoidably, or almost unavoidably, noticed. Others will be more subtle. Since languages and cultures are not blank slates, which qualities a language or a society focuses on or ignores involve factors in addition to observational or cognitive salience.

Lévi-Strauss and Birds

An approach that in my view gives fair consideration both to real salience and to distinctive symbolic patterning is that of Claude Lévi-Strauss, particularly as elaborated in his book *La Pensée sauvage* (translated as *Wild Thought*, 2021), first published in 1962, at the height of the interest in ethnoscience. If there are many ways to classify an entity based on focusing on one or a few of its many properties, then each choice may be expected to be linked into wider and more abstract systems of properties of which these entities may serve as emblems. People, in other words, use concrete entities in combination and opposition to present and discuss not primarily the entities themselves, but the qualities they possess and represent; they serve to emblematize abstract relations. This is what Lévi-Strauss meant by a "science of the concrete." Just which quality is noted depends in part on the system of relations in which the being plays a role. Here, as elsewhere in his work, many of his best examples are birds.[5] In *Wild Thought* (Lévi-Strauss 2021, 63), he discusses a system of divination by birdsong practised by the Iban of Borneo:

> It is clear that the same details might have been given different meanings, and that other traits characteristic of the same birds might have been preferred to these. The system of divination selects only a few distinctive traits, gives them an arbitrary meaning, and restricts itself to seven birds the choice of which is puzzling because of their apparent insignificance. But arbitrary though it be at the level of terms, the system becomes coherent when envisaged in its totality ... There can be no doubt that a considerable number of systems of the same type might have offered an equal degree of coherence, and that no one of them was predestined to be chosen by all societies and all civilizations. Terms never have an intrinsic meaning; their meaning is "positional," a function of history and cultural context, on the one hand, and, on the other, of the structure of the system in which they are called on to figure.

So far, Lévi-Strauss sounds highly relativistic in his privileging of symbol system over nature "in itself." But his avian examples show the recognition that nature is not a blank slate and that some salient properties of creatures, if not always the same ones, are more likely than others to be noted and used. He contrasts the Navajo name of the lark, related to its long spurs, with the English "Horned Lark," which calls attention to its head feathers. He then proceeds with a discussion of why different peoples find woodpeckers and their relatives "good to think" – his phrase, of course, introduced the same year in *Totemism* (Lévi-Strauss 1963). Australian peoples focus on tree-creepers because they live in hollow trees; peoples of the American Prairies say that one never finds a woodpecker's remains, which means that it is protected from birds of prey; the Pawnee, like the Romans, link the woodpecker with storms, the Osage with the sun and stars; and the Iban give the woodpecker a symbolic role because of its "triumphal" song. And we could, of course, add the English word "woodpecker," the Central Himalayan *kaṭhkoṛi*, or the Navajo "one that pounds wood" (Lévi-Strauss 2021, 63), all of which refer to the bird's feeding habits. "To be sure," Lévi-Strauss writes, "we are not dealing with exactly the same birds, but the example helps us to understand how different peoples might make use of the same animal in their symbolism while basing themselves on unrelated features: habitat, associations with weather, cry, and so on." Then he moves to corvids: the agricultural peoples of the southwestern United States see the crow as a pillager of gardens, whereas for the hunting and fishing societies of the Northwest Coast the raven is thought of primarily as a carrion eater. "The semantic charge of *Corvus* is different in the two cases," he writes, "vegetal in one instance, animal in the other; and rivalry with man when they are similar, or antagonism when their behaviors are mutually inverted" (64–65).

In these cases, as in his other analyses of natural kinds used as emblems, it is observable characteristics of a species that are used to evoke and express more systemic and abstract relationships. Even if a woodpecker does potentially offer an infinite number of properties to choose from, this infinity is a different one from the possible properties of a raven. Symbols are constrained in this way to limited infinities. The woodpecker or raven's own observable properties play a role in its classification, along with history, cultural context, and the structure of the system in which it is called upon to appear. And very often, out of the potentially unlimited properties of which any bit of nature is possessed, some are intrinsically more striking than others for human beings.

Some aspects of the world, then, are particularly salient or striking – not necessarily always or everywhere, but often enough to be noteworthy. Rather than a choice between duelling determinisms, between a single extensional world that people simply perceive more or less well versus a multitude of projected or imagined intensional worlds quite independent of an actually perceived universe, we might see such salient characteristics as anchoring points where an intensional world connects into extensionality – that is, into something beyond it. Such a view would mean thinking in terms of the *relative* saliency, the relative "jumping out" to human notice and human use, of bits of the world. This kind of an approach is implied in most of Lévi-Strauss's actual analyses, as well as in his continuing insistence that anthropologists attend to people's observations of nature, so that natural history becomes a part of anthropology. This is not to say that symbol systems cannot override any such salience – only that they impose categories not on a flat tabula rasa, but on an already bumpy table, not on an erased blackboard, but an already multicoloured one.[6]

In fact, challenges to universalizing explanatory strategies regarding natural kinds are not rare, and examples abound of categorizations and especially of important connotations of natural kinds that are profoundly different from modern and scientific ones. Already in 1972, at the height of the universalizing movement, Michelle Rosaldo (1972) was pointing to the way the Ilongot people of Luzon distinguish – or do not distinguish – arboreal orchids based not on their observable characteristics but on the kind of healing spell in which the particular plant will be used, so that exemplars of the same species can be given different names and vice versa. And this fundamental insight, that naming and categorizing natural kinds depends in part on who is doing it and what for, continues to be rediscovered in case after case (Ludwig 2018).

Us and Them

The problems discussed so far represent only a subset of a much wider one, that of the very issue of comparison. What philosophers (e.g., Davidson 1974) call the "principle of charity" – that in dealing with a belief or practice that seems irrational, one should give it the "benefit of the doubt" and assume that it is rational in our terms – is actually about as uncharitable as one can get. It assumes – against the most fundamental rules of science – that our own current knowledge is correct and can never be challenged. It would be far more charitable to assume radical difference and seek to understand in its own terms what initially appears to be, at least in some degree, a different way of cutting things up and putting them together.

Modern and modern-style comparative scholars often attempt what are called cross-cultural studies of a phenomenon that is labelled with a modern Western word and conveys a modern Western concept – genus and species, religion, emotion, class, politics, gender, to give the classical Maussian themes, sacrifice, classification, the body, giftgiving – and see how this concept varies across societies.[7] But this is to take the modern Western idea of, say, religion, as a universal comparand, a kind of centre, and look at the apparently corresponding but not-completely-overlapping concepts of other societies and languages as marginal, as deviations to the extent that they do not overlap with it. Again, a more charitable, as well as more modest, method (Lambek 1991) is to consider a field of variations on a topic that is fixed only provisionally – say, relations with invisible beings or the treatment of living things – and place, as clearly as possible, our own vision as one among many. The only privilege of this particular vision is that we already know it well, and it can thus serve not as the model, not as a centre, but as an evident starting point.

What are the implications of accepting the idea that, at least to some degree, not everyone sees things the same way that "we" do? "We" can be defined in various ways, but here I'll take it as representing secularized Western opinion and generally accepted science. There are four logical possibilities: First, we are right and all those who see things differently are wrong. There is no need to challenge our own views. Second, if we look hard enough at how others see things, we find that they see things the way we do ("principle of charity"). Since everyone in the world and throughout history has always and everywhere seen things in the same way, there is no need to challenge our own views, which are universal. Third, our view is only one of a multiplicity of views and has no particular validity. We should tear down our own biased views. By implication, there is no way to know anything. And fourth, our view is only one of a multiplicity of views, but for whatever reasons, we think it is at least provisionally legitimate. We can seek to understand other views without abandoning our own, or else by "bracketing" our own, abandoning it experimentally to seek a better understanding of other views, with the ultimate hope of improving our own.

The first three positions continue to give our own view special status in relation to those of other people. For the first, if other people do not abandon their views and adopt ours, they are either ignorant or stupid. For the second, if they do not agree that they really think just as we currently do, they are misguided. For the third, if our own way is too seriously challenged, that can only mean that there is no reality, only an ontological flux. The fourth position recognizes the reality of a plurality of ways of seeing things; it says that we share with others a general conviction of the validity of our own way of seeing things and that we can challenge and modify how we see things in a number of ways, including learning about how others do so, without giving up on knowledge – which, however, is always one knowledge in a greater field of possible knowledges. Since we are not gods, I think this is the best we can do.

Birds as Highly Salient Percepts

As stated more generally above, my own modest experience in birdwatching very quickly taught me a lesson in salience: I learned that species exist. Among the various North American spring warblers, for instance, small differences in pattern and behaviour and call can indicate fixed lines of division among endogamous types, lines that are there to be observed if you have the patience. It is in large part this mildly vertiginous sense of discovery of dividing-lines in nature that one derives pretty painlessly from birding that makes me feel that birds as a domain are probably particularly good to think, particularly salient. On the one hand, they represent a relatively easily identifiable grand category, with beaks and feathers and wings and eggs. Though there are always marginal cases, I imagine that most human societies have a category that we would think we recognize as birds and that most prospective birdwatchers in most societies, even given the reality of cultural differences, don't need to start by acquiring a copy of *How to Tell the Birds from the Flowers* (Woods 1907). At the same time, this is a clearly differentiated domain internally, one with many elements that are distinguished by criteria that are relatively easy to observe.

Let me list some of the qualities that mark off birds as a domain. In some ways, this will be a list of clichés, but that's the point.[8]

First, birds fly, or at least a lot of them fly. They are evidently available symbols of access to inaccessible realms, from the shaman's feathers to "Somewhere over the Rainbow." In many *cosmoi,* they serve as mediators between the worlds: the shaman uses bird symbolism to rise up; the Holy Spirit descending is emblematized as a dove.[9]

Second, many bird species are distinguished by noteworthy markings. Feathers are one of nature's great sources of concentrated colour.

Third, birds are good to eat, at least enough birds are, and they play central roles in many ethnogastronomic systems. Who can eat which bird in what circumstances becomes a marker of social distinction, whether we think of a father-to-be bound by couvade, gender restrictions on eating chicken (O'Laughlin 1974), a clan that must or must not eat its totem marker, or the Cambridge college to which the monarch has granted the exclusive right to roast and serve swan once a year. As an extension of this, birds are good to hunt, and, again, who has the right to hunt which birds where takes on symbolic significance.

Fourth, birds are born from eggs, a symbol of beginnings and openings. In many traditions, the universe was born from an egg: in the Central Himalayas, the story is that this was an egg of the *garuṛ,* the semi-legendary eagle or vulture (Oakley and Gairola 1935, 171–72; Jośī 1971, 43–50). In Sanskrit, the word *dvija,* "twice-born," is used for initiated male members of the upper castes, for teeth, and for birds (Monier-Williams 1899, 506).

Fifth, birds often behave in ways that remind human beings of themselves (see the epigraphs for this chapter), apparently expressing joy and sorrow, and, in more complex behaviours, displaying the faithfulness of the turtle-dove or the treachery of the cowbird.[10] Given their observable little families and the relative distinctiveness of bird species, it's not surprising that they should be favoured players in allegories. Such dramas are well known in oral tradition: think of the English folk song "Who Killed Cock Robin?" (Roud Folk Song Index 494), which goes through the murder and the funeral of Cock Robin, assigning different roles to different birds: the owl will dig his grave, the wren will bear the pall, and the dove, his love, will mourn him. In the Kumaoni song of the "Birds' Wedding Procession" *(caṛó ki baryàt,* recorded from Śrī Narī Rām in 1982), a thrush – *musi caṛ,* the "mousey bird," I think it's the Streaked Laughingthrush, *Trochalopteron lineatum* – marries the dove's daughter. The cuckoo presides as priest *(kapu caṛa bāmaṇ chī),* the parakeet is in charge of the wedding songs, and the crow sees to the invitations and leads the wedding procession. The nice differentiation of species in the avian domain also lends itself to philosophical allegory, as in 'Attar's (1984) twelfth-century Persian poem *The Conference of the Birds (Mantiq ut-Tair),* called *Le langage des oiseaux* in Garcin de Tassy's French translation ('Attar 1857). The same is true of Chaucer's *Parlement of Foules* (Chaucer 1937). In both of these, the birds meet to seek enlightenment or to find love, and each species embodies a virtue or vice.

Throughout South Asian history, starting in the *Ṛg Veda* (Hymn to Savitṛ, 2.38; Hymn to the Night, 10.127) and continuing into today's oral performances in the Central Himalayas (see below), the fall of night is heralded by the trope of the scattered birds returning to their nests. This image is put in parallel with that of many beings, particularly human ones, coming back from their diurnal occupations and settling down in their places of rest.[11]

In addition, birds call and sing. That will be the main issue from here on.

Birdsong as Non-Referential Expressive Language

Birds' sounds are often as clearly differentiated as their looks or their behaviour. The calls and songs of many birds involve complex and repetitive patterns that are likely to remind human beings of human language. Indeed, the Vedist Frits Staal proposes that primeval human language, like birdsong, was patterned phonologically and syntactically in repetitive phrases that did not convey referential meaning – a kind of pattern-play in a medium of oral sound. Vedic and other mantras correspond to birdsong in that their sound-pattern is all-important and their referential meaning absent, secondary, or rudimentary and repetitive: "tit willow tit willow tit willow"; *om maṇi padme hum.* Mantras, then, would represent a survival of this earliest linguistic state (Staal 1985).

Without adopting Staal's evolutionary model (although something like it has been argued recently by cognitive scientists: see Miyagawa et al. 2014), we can recognize the salience of birdsong in its language-like patterning and, unlike human language, its apparent lack of much range of specific reference. This is not, of course, always the case. Many traditions tell of birds having a language just like human language; but in the cases that I know, it is always an unusual person, with unusual gifts – the hero who has tasted the dragon's blood or the flesh of the Salmon of Wisdom – who can understand their speech.

What birdsong does for all mortals, as many traditions hear it, is to index, express, and convey specific affective tones, to make emotion audible in something that sounds like, but isn't quite, language. In anthropology, the exemplary analysis of how people hear birdsongs as "emotion-sentences" is to be found in Steven Feld's (1982) work on birdsong and sadness among the Kaluli of New Guinea. But the link between birdsong and emotion is a commonplace in the Western tradition as well, as witness, for English, the whole *Penguin Book of Bird Poetry* (Munsterberg 1980). One example comes at the beginning of the narration of *Perceval*, by Chrétien de Troyes (Chrétien 1959, 3).

> *Ce fu au tans qu'arbre foillissent,*
> *Que glai et bois et pre verdissent,*
> *Et cil oisel en lor latin*
> *Cantent doucement au matin.*
>> 'Twas in the time when trees sprout leaves,
>> When grass and wood and field go green,
>> And the birds in their Latin
>> Sing sweetly in the morning. (my effort at translation)

Birds have their own Latin, but it's a Latin made to epitomize the sweetness of spring, not to give specific referential information.[12] Similarly, in Sanskrit literature the word *vāc,* "speech" or "voice" or "language," is used not only of humans but also of other creatures, especially birds (Staal 1985, 557).

The idea of a language marked by rhythmic or musical patterning and conveying affective tones should be familiar: it's the Romantic and post-Romantic definition of poetry. In South Asia, there is an old tradition of a link between birdsong and poetic language. The most common metre in classical Sanskrit is the *śloka* of two sixteen-syllable lines of two eight-syllable hemistichs each, with distinctive chronometric patterning distinguishing the first and second hemistichs of each line. The great epic the *Rāmāyaṇa,* which is entirely composed in *śloka*s, gives the origin story for this poetic form (*Rāmāyaṇa* 1.2.9–17). The composer of the epic, the sage Vālmīki, happily wandering in the forest, came upon a loving pair of *krauñca* birds.[13] Suddenly a hidden hunter shot the male, and the female, seeing him lying dead, cried out. Vālmīki, deeply moved by seeing the dead bird (verse 11) and apparently identifying with him – both the bird and the initiated sage are here called dvija, "twice-born" – and then by hearing the female's piteous cry (*karuṇāṃ giram,* literally a pity-provoking voice; verse 12), pronounced a curse against the hunter (verse 13). Spoken from the heart, the curse fell into a beautiful cadence of grief and rage. A moment later, Vālmīki realized that his curse had a form that would serve for rhythmic poetry:

> *pādabaddho 'kṣarasamas tantrīlayasamanvitaḥ*
> *śokārtasya pravṛtto me śloko bhavatu nānyathā.*
>> Bound in feet of equal syllables, fit for the beat of stringed instruments,

> What I produced in this access of grief *[śoka]*, let it be
> [called] *śloka*, and nothing else. (*Rāmāyaṇa* 1.2.17; my
> translation, with reference to Gude 1979, 7; Goldman
> 1984, 127–28; Huberman 1994, 21)

The immediate catalyst for the sage's outpouring, and so, within the legend, for the foundation of most of Sanskrit verse, was a bird's cry, heard and affecting as the essence of an emotion. This incident becomes, in later poetics, the parable for all poetic utterance: out of the stress of natural feeling *(bhāva),* an artistic form has to be found or fashioned, a form that will generalize and capture the essence *(rasa)* of that feeling (Ramanujan 1991, 40). The cry of the bereaved female krauñca already expresses that essence; it is a *topos* in Sanskrit literature, the very epitome, the very sound, of grief. Poetic language is language that reproduces this essence in human language, that allows others to taste it.[14]

Himalayan Birds, Their Songs, and the Emotions

The South Asian example given above comes from the most classical of classical traditions. Here, however, we will consider three birds as conceptualized on the borders of contemporary South Asia, in the region of Kumaon, part of the north Indian state of Uttarakhand in an area that geographers label the Central Himalayas. Kumaon is a former kingdom that possesses its own Indo-Aryan language, its own brand of Hinduism complete with local gods and rituals, its own rich and distinctive epic and story traditions, and its own mountain ecology, including flora and fauna that are very different from those of the hotter, flatter, and more heavily populated parts of the subcontinent, notably the great Gangetic plains immediately to the south.

Here, the calls of three birds – cuckoo, crow, and dove – are heard particularly clearly as conveying emotional tones.[15]

Cuckoo, Kaphu Caṛ

In European literary and folk tradition, the cuckoo is the harbinger of spring ("Sumer is icumen in, / Lhude sing cuccu"). These lines even give the title of the chapter on cuckoos in Edward Armstrong's *The Folklore of Birds* (1959, Chapter 12). The cuckoo's arrival in the spring and departure at the end of summer are expressed in English oral "cuckoo calendars" (Munsterberg 1980, 89–90, 322).[16] But this association with the spring often has negative tones (Munsterberg 1980, 26). Chaucer refers to "the cuckoo ever unkind" (Chaucer 1937, l.357). For modern English-speaking Europeans and North Americans, the cuckoo is a bird with a weird call that gives it its name, a name that is used as an adjective to mean "crazy," and a bad reputation for putting its eggs into other birds' nests (see the 1957 science fiction novel *The Midwich Cuckoos* by John Wyndham). In fact, birds of the genus Cuculus are obligatory brood parasites, which means that they have no choice but to lay eggs in other birds' nests. This is the case for both the Common Cuckoo, *Cuculus canorus,* found in Europe, and the South Asian species.

Yet in South Asia, the cuckoo is generally a bird of good omen. In Sanskrit literature, it is associated with springtime and love. K.N. Dave (1985, 128, 129) refers to "the sweet amorous voice of the bird in the Spring" and adds that "no description of *vasanta* [springtime] in Sanskrit literature, but refers to the Sweet Song of the 'thrice welcome darling of the spring'... the *vasanta dūta* [spring-herald] of India." In Act 6, Scene 2, of Kālidāsa's *Śakuntalā* (Kale 1969, 208), the hero, a king, is mourning the loss of his beloved. It is springtime, and all the world should be filled with natural symbols of love and desire. But in correspondence with his plight, the budding flowers fail to form pollen, and

> *kaṇṭheṣu skhalitaṃ gate 'pi śiśire puṃskokilānāṃ rutam.*
> In the throats of the male cuckoos the song falters, even
> though the frosts are past.

This positive view of cuckoos is clearly dominant in the Himalayas. There is even a Kumaoni story of a wicked crow who switches its own offspring with those of the cuckoo. "It is curious," writes E. Sherman Oakley, "to find the cuckoo, a bird of evil reputation in Europe, regarded in India as a virtuous creature and even as an injured innocent" (Oakley and Gairola 1935, 274).

The sub-Himalayan ecology of Kumaon only reinforces the cuckoo's associations with the spring. The cuckoo arrives at the beginning of spring, returning after the long, dark, cold Himalayan winter, and for Kumaonis it epitomizes the many birds whose voices are heard again after long silence. In Kumaon, the one most closely linked with the new spring is the Indian Cuckoo, *Cuculus micropterus,* which arrives early in the season. Its melodious four-note call is heard and repeated by human beings as *kàphav pàko* (the *kàphal* berries are ripe!). This call gives the bird its Kumaoni name of kaphu caṛ, the kaphu bird.[17] Probably the most famous Kumaoni song,

"Beṛu pāko," specifies that the kàphal, colloquially kàphav (bayberry, *Myrica esculenta,* though Osmaston 1927, 517, gives the alternative name *Myrica nagi*), ripen in the month of Cait, the beginning of spring:

> *beṛu pāko bāro māso, naraiṇa,*
> *kàphav pāko caita, meri chaila.*
>> The wild figs ripen all the twelve months, Lord,
>> The bayberries only in Cait, my darling.[18]

As Wikipedia (n.d.) puts it, and I quote Wikipedia because I couldn't say it better myself,

> The theme of the refrain is symbolic. The fig fruit which ripens round the year is not valued much but the deliciously sweet bayberry only appears briefly during the short season in March and April. Thus it is something to look forward to in the midst of an ordinary existence. In a state typified by mountainous terrain the warmth of spring and summer brings a promising bounty of flowers and berries and gladdens the heart ... "Kaphal" not only tastes good but also it happens to ripen around the month when natural beauty touches its extreme. This entire natural beauty instigates childhood memories and fun days within [the singer's] heart.[19]

Hearing the cuckoo's call as kàphav pàko appears to be a secondary interpretation of a name that is originally onomatopoetic. And the name, found in many Indo-European languages, has not undergone the normal sound changes that indicate a common inherited word. This means that it has been renewed through the ages through imitation, even as the language as a whole changed around it (Greppin 1997a, 68).

Crow, Kau or Kauā

Several consultants, when talking about the cuckoo's call as a good omen, contrasted it with that of the crow, a bad omen and a sound "that people don't like to hear." A similar opinion has long been held in the West – Chaucer writes of "the crow with voice of care" (Chaucer 1937, l. 363), and it has been the view in South Asia since ancient times (Dave 1985, 4–5). Kumaonis hear the crow's call as *kau kau* and name the bird kau or kauā. Similar onomatopoeias are used for its name in both Sanskrit *(kāka)* and modern Indo-Aryan languages (Hindi is kauā, Nepali is *kāg*).

The jungle crow, *Corvus machyrhynchus* (Fleming, Fleming, and Bangdel 1979, 174), is a year-long resident in the lower Himalayas, and for most of the year seeing it or hearing its harsh, penetrating voice, though unavoidable, is not a good thing. It has bad habits: it haunts burning grounds and carries off bits of the cremated dead. It steals things and takes them extraordinary distances, and its voice, too, carries extraordinary distances. In some stories, the crow transports people between this world and the next (e.g., Oakley and Gairola 1935, 235).

A proverb says, "If you tie a bell to a mouse, it [the sound] will disappear into a hole; if you tie a bell to a crow, the whole country will know it" (see Upreti 1894, 18).[20] The interpretation given by Pandit Gangā Datt assimilates the crow to the stranger or visitor from afar: "If you do a kindness to a stranger he will praise you for it far and wide; if you help a fellow countryman he will be ashamed to speak about it and will keep silent" (Upreti 1894, 18).

Like that of the cuckoo, the name of the crow in Indo-European languages seems to have been continually refashioned based on its cry (Greppin 1997a, 68).

Dove, Ghughut

The call of the cuckoo is joyful, the crow's cry is harsh and powerful; rural Kumaonis hear the voice of the dove as sad and mournful. This, of course, recalls the Mourning Dove, a species not found in the Himalayas. But the lesson on ornithosymbolic complexity continues here. In the West, the dove is commonly associated with love, as in billing and cooing, and with fidelity: Chaucer refers to it as "the wedded turtle, with her hearte true" (Chaucer 1937, l. 355). For Jews and Christians, the turtledove figures most famously in the "Song of Songs" (2:11–12) as a hallmark of spring, matching the associations of the cuckoo in South Asia: "For lo, the winter is past, the rain is over and gone; the flowers appear on the earth, the time of the singing of birds is come, and the voice of the turtle is heard in our land."

Although classical Sanskrit literature also associates doves with faithful love, it treats some types of dove as inauspicious and dangerous (Dave 1985, 257–64).

A couple of Kumaoni stories recorded at the beginning of the last century explain why the calls of doves and pigeons are so sad (Oakley and Gairola 1935, 271–73). One tells how a sick man died crying out that his family should feed his little brother, who was visiting at the time: the man's last words, *bhai bhūkho,* "Little brother hungry," is the call of the wild pigeon he turned into after his death (see Oakley and Gairola 1935, 272–73; Pāṇḍey 1962, 402–6). Another tells of a mother who mistakenly accused her daughter of stealing some of the wild berries (the text doesn't say which ones) that they had picked together. The mother struck her daughter, who died. Later, she realized that none of the berries were missing and that the heap had only shrunk a little in the heat of the sun. She died of remorse and turned into a "wild dove" that calls *pur putli purai purai*, "They're all there, darling, all there, all there" (Oakley and Gairola 1935, 271–72).

The dove that concerns us here is the ghughut, whose name is derived from its call, the melancholy *ghurr ghurr*. Dave (1985, 259) attributes a call *ghū ghū* to the Red Turtle Dove *(Streptopelia tranquebarica)*, but the Kumaoni ghughut would seem to be the Rufous or Oriental Turtle Dove *(Streptopelia orientalis)*. The ornithologist Sálim Ali (1979, 174) writes that the bird "is common about most Himalayan hill-stations ... Its hoarse, mournful goor ... gūr-grūgroo is one of the more familiar bird voices there. The final groo is especially mournful and uttered as with pulling in of breath."

The dove's associations with separation and sorrow are epitomized in a song composed in the 1970s by Gopāl Bābū Gosvāmī, which, like some of his other songs, became known throughout the region. This song, "Ghughuti na bāsa" (Little Dove, Don't Sing), was high on the local radio hit parade for some years and has been picked up by the oral tradition. When I asked rural Kumaonis to sing a typical Kumaoni folk song, I was more than likely to get "Ghughuti na bāsa" – when it wasn't "Beṛu pāko." The a cappella popular renditions that I heard are sung slowly and lugubriously, fitting the mood of the song, compared with the highly orchestrated and rather snappy version that Gopāl Bābū himself sings in the recording:

> *teri ghuru ghuru suṇi, teri ghuru ghuru suṇi, maĩ lāgo udāsa*
> *svāmī merā paradesa bārphilo lādākha*
> *ghughuti nā bāsā, ghughuti nā bāsā āme kī ḍāīmā.*
>
>> When I hear your ghurr ghurr, when I hear your ghurr
>> ghurr, I'm struck by sadness;
>> My lord is in a faraway land, in snowy Ladakh.
>> Little dove don't sing, little dove don't sing in the mango tree.

> *ritu aige bhali bhali, ritu aige bhali bhali, garami caitaikī*
> *yāda makaĩ bhaute aige āpaṇo pati kī*
> *ghughuti nā bāsā, ghughuti nā bāsā āme kī ḍāīmā.*

The lovely, lovely season's come, the lovely, lovely season's
come, of warm Cait.
The memory of my lord has come to me intensely.
Little dove don't sing, little dove don't sing in the mango tree.

teri jasi maile hūno, teri jasi maile hūno, uṛibera jānō
svāmī ko mukaṛi kaĩ jī bhari dekhanō
ghughuti nā bāsā, ghughuti nā bāsā āme kī ḍāīmā.
If I were like you, if I were like you, flying away I'd go,
My soul would be filled up to see my lord's face.
Little dove don't sing, little dove don't sing in the mango tree.

uṛi jā tū o ghughuti, uṛi jā tū o ghughuti, nhai jā tū laddākha
hāla myāra batai diye svāmī kā pāsa
ghughuti nā bāsā, ghughuti nā bāsā āme kī ḍāīmā.
Fly away, little dove, fly away, little dove, go to Ladakh.
Tell of my condition there where my lord is.
Little dove don't sing, little dove don't sing in the mango tree.[21]

Here the forlorn young wife asks the dove first not to sing in (its nest) in
the tree, then to sing its song when it goes far, far away, so that her husband
can hear how sad she is.

In a comparable tale of a travelling dove, the bird goes to the Underworld,
where its sad song melts the heart of Lord Yama, the king of the dead (Oakley
and Gairola 1935, 279–80).

The dove's associations with separation and regret stand in clearest contrast
with the associations of the parakeet (*su* in Kumaoni, here primarily the
Plum-headed Parakeet, *Psittacula cyanocephala*), the local love-bird par
excellence. In Kumaoni women's ritual art, wall-paintings done for marriages
depict a pair of parakeets, symbols of wedded bliss (Hart 1995).

A Regional Cosmology

Cuckoo, crow, and dove have onomatopoetic names derived from their
calls; for each of them, the call is heard as expressing, and as provoking or
intensifying, a clear emotional state. In this part of the world, emotional
states themselves are interpreted in terms of a shared set of assumptions
about movement in the world.

Kumaonis have ways of talking, thinking, and acting with reference to processes in the world that I think have enough coherence to be called at least a fragmentary cosmology. These idioms, if I may call them that, seem to derive, in part at least, from more ancient and widespread South Asian patterns. Central in many domains of life is an opposition between degrees of movement and interaction: too much movement and interaction is bad, not enough is bad, a balance is good. Greater movement and interaction is often expressed in idioms of heating, less movement and interaction in idioms of cooling. This contrast marks traditional Kumaoni ethnophysics, sociology, calendrics, medicine, gastronomy, and psychology; I don't know where its limits lie. The ideal in all of these domains is a proper balance of hot and cold qualities, and such a balance means a proper productive flow, experienced as health and happiness for the person, peace and prosperity for the family and the village, order and growth for "this mortal sphere." Just where the appropriate balance lies, however, depends on who you are, in terms at least of caste and gender. Warriors (ṭhākur) are relatively hot in nature; it is appropriate for them to engage in a high degree of interaction with others, whether in fighting, in hunting, in ploughing the earth, or in sexual activity. Ideal-typically, they eat meat and drink alcohol, both heaty substances. Brahmans (bàmaṇ), on the contrary, should stay cool and be very careful about interactions. Ideally, they should not eat meat, and the most strict avoid all kinds of heaty foods, including onions and garlic; they do not drink alcohol, although they may well use cooling products such as cannabis as an aid to meditative withdrawal from social interaction. Those who can afford it do not plough the earth, a violent interaction, but hire others to do it for them (Sanwal 1976, 45). Women are appropriately hotter than men, which means that they are more involved, more loving, and also more prone to anger.[22]

Happy life in "this mortal sphere" is conceptualized in proverb, song, and story as ongoing balanced activity shifting between relatively high movement and interaction during the day and in the summer and relatively low movement and interaction during the night and in the winter, these corresponding to periods of relative light and darkness. This whole process of ongoing life, called saṃsāra, the "flowing together," in Sanskrit (sansār in modern north Indian languages), is also referred to in Kumaoni as yo mṛityu maṇḍal, "this circle of death" or "this mortal sphere," or as jugak pheṛ, "the turning of the age."

Sometimes the world stops turning. I was able to record a myth in which the god Saim, the creator of this mortal sphere, the mother's brother of all beings – Uncle Saim – is offended; he goes to the Underworld, taking the chariots of the sun and the moon with him. The circle of the world stops turning, and the bard Kamal Rām Āryā presents the situation in a series of epitomizing scenes:

> *ki mrityu maṇḍal mẽ, isvar mero bābā, / ki rāt kilai rāt hai ge; /*
> *ki din kilai rātai hai ge; / ki aiso andhkār hai go chī / ki goṭhe ki*
> *gāi goṭhai mẽ rai ge chī; / ki bāṭi baṭauv ko ḍyār jo chī bāṭai rai*
> *gai chī, isvar mero bābā. / ki godi ko bālak jo chī godai rai go chī*
> *... / ki aiso andhkār hai go chī / ki ghās ki ghasyār jo chī ghāsai*
> *rai he chī.*

> In this mortal sphere, Lord my father, / night became night, /
> day too became night. / There was such darkness / that the
> cow of the cowshed stayed in the cowshed, / that the traveller
> on the road stayed camped on the road, / that the child of the
> lap stayed in the lap ... / There was such darkness / that the
> grass-cutting girl stayed [out] in the grass.

Saim's favorite nephew Goriyā goes down to the Underworld to fetch him, sits on his lap, and gives him a hug. This starts to warm up Uncle Saim. He emerges from his meditative withdrawal, becomes happy, and releases the chariots of the sun and the moon:

> *ki goṭh ki gāi jo chī, isvar, godi ko bālak jo chī, khel lāgaṇ phai*
> *go chī. / ki bāṭi ko baṭauv ko ḍero cal go chī ... / ki jhal jhal kā*
> *ujyāv ho chyau.*

> The cow of the cowshed, Lord, the child of the lap started
> to play. / The traveller on the road moved his camp ... /
> jhal-jhal! there was dawn.

The same idioms of movement and rest are cited in possession rituals called *jāgar*, "vigils" or "wakings."[23] These take place at night and have the goal of calming an angry, overly moving regional deity by inducing him or her to possess a human medium and, once in the human body, to dance and so become calm, happy, and well disposed. The jāgar begins with an evocation of the twilight, *sandhyā,* in a long recitative that includes a series of images of the transformations of the activity of different beings "at evening time":[24]

> *jhulani sandhyā mẽ kyā kām hai rĩ, isvar mero bābā? sandhyā*
> *kā bahat mẽ, isvar mero bābā, gāi bachan kā bādan lāgĩ, ghol*
> *ki cai jo cha ghol mẽ lhai gai cha, isvar mero bābā, sandhyā kā*
> *bahat mẽ.*
> *bāṭi baṭauv ko dyār jo cha, isvar mero bābā, bāṭai bādi go,*
> *isvar mero bābā. sandhyā kā bahat mẽ godi ko bālak jo cha*
> *god mẽ sukālo hai go, isvar mero bābā, sandhyā kā bahat mẽ*
> *tumāro nām lhinũ, isvar mero bābā.*
> *ki gāi bachan kā bādan lāgĩ, isvar mero bābā, ghol ki cari ghol*
> *lhai ge, isvar mero bābā, sandhyā kā bahat mẽ tumāro nām*
> *lhinũ, isvar mero bābā, sandhyā kā bahat mẽ.*

> In the swinging twilight what works are going on, Lord
> my father? At twilight time, Lord my father, the cows and
> calves have been tied up, the little bird of the nest has gone
> into the nest, Lord my father, at twilight time.
> The traveller on the road, Lord my father, has pitched his
> camp on the road, Lord my father. At twilight time the
> child of the lap has become happy in the lap, Lord my
> father, at twilight time we take your name, Lord my father.
> The cows and calves have been tied up, Lord my father,
> the little bird of the nest has gone into the nest, Lord my
> father. At twilight time we take your name, Lord my father.

This series of riffs follows the same pattern as those from the myth of Saim. This time, instead of the whole world stopping disastrously, we have a picture of evening swinging over the lands of the village and of all creatures settling in for the night. Notice, on this happier and more modest scale, the little birds, who here again serve as a metaphor for human society, settling into the nest, while domestic animals, an extension or metonym of human society, go into the basement of the human house to pass the night. Here, interaction and withdrawal are relative and healthy; the jāgar itself will take place during a period of relative withdrawal, implying a turning away from the movements of this world so that the possessed medium and the attending family and friends are ready to receive the deity, who him- or herself arrives full of movement, "like the wind" *(hàv jas)*.

The same idioms are also used to characterize emotions. Negative emotions represent excess or insufficiency; happiness is balance. Anger is generally thought of as hot. A local policeman, not a hot warrior by caste or nature, told me that he needed to drink a lot of alcohol, a heating substance, to become angry enough to yell at suspects and beat them up, a normal and necessary part of his duties. But in a cold being, anger, though hard to provoke, may take the form of a disastrous excess of coldness, of withdrawal, as in the case of Saim's descent to the Underworld. Sorrow and sadness, conversely, are generally thought of as cold. They are stereotypically associated with separation, whether in the case of a young man leaving his family to take the vows of a yogi or a young bride whose husband is far away. Here again, however, a hot being may react hotly to grief; in one legend, a mother whose son is leaving her to become a yogi beats her knees on the ground and weeps hundreds of gallons of tears (Leavitt 1996). Similar oppositions between excessive movement and insufficient movement or flow also characterize different kinds of divine and demonic beings; they help to explain medical practice and possession ritual, among many other things.

The voice of each of the three birds considered here is located at a highly marked point along the excess-balance-insufficiency range: the cuckoo is at a point of balance expressed in happiness, the dove at a point of insufficiency lived as sadness and separation, and the crow at a point of excess heard as anger.

Three Birds in the Pattern of the Year

These three birds have clearly marked roles in the pattern of the rural year, which, not unexpectedly, is marked by variations in hot and cold (Leavitt 2000). The changing year also involves changes in expected feelings, and in some transitional moments such changes are marked by these birds and their calls.

The year in Kumaoni conception is fairly clearly divided into seasons. The transitional, and so well-balanced, seasons of spring and autumn are thought of positively. The other seasons have stereotypical associations with discomfort and suffering – they are respectively too hot and too cold. In the legend of Gaṅganāth, a prince who abandons his home to become a wandering ascetic, his prospective guru tries to dissuade him by describing the seasonal hardships of life on the road:

> "Being a yogi is a great hardship," he said. "You have to suffer the frosts of [the months of] Māgh and Pus. You have to suffer the dust of Jeṭh and Baisākh. You have to suffer the mud of Sauṇ and Bhadav."[25]

The rainy season gets particularly, and deservedly, bad press for its sudden and horrible explosion of bloodsucking bugs. The poet Gaurdā even composed a satirical "Praise of the Rainy Season" *(Cāturmāsya mahimā)* detailing each of the insects one is likely to become intimate with (Pāṇḍe 1965, 140–44). But the birds that concern us here are linked to spring (cuckoos) and to midwinter (doves and crows).

We have already seen that the joyful character of the cuckoo's call is closely associated with early spring, with its new light and warmth and freedom of movement and the ripening of the kàphav berries, the first wild fruits of the new year. In the month of Cait, which runs from mid-March to mid-April, young people of Kumaoni villages go wandering in the woods during the lengthening afternoons, grazing the family's cows and buffalos, munching on the ever more abundant kàphav berries, swinging on forest swings, and making romantic assignations far from the usual constraints of village and household life. Behind this new sense of ease lies the fact that the wheat harvest is beginning in this month, so staple food, as well as wild food, is suddenly more abundant after the lean winter.

The first day of the solar month of Cait is the festival of Phūl Dhoi (Flowers on the Threshold).[26] On the morning of this day, children go from house to house scattering flowers on the threshold of each, singing a song wishing prosperity to the householder and receiving a coin or a sweet:

> *phūl dheli, cammā celi,*
> *daiṇo dyār, bhār bakār,*
> *tvi dheli saũ namaskār.*
>> Flowers on the threshold, daughters dancing,
>> Mustard flowers in the doorway, a full granary,
>> A hundred greetings on your threshold.

Given these associations, it is not surprising that the cuckoo's voice is felt to be lucky in itself. In the course of the possession ritual, the phrase "the voice of the cuckoo," *kaphuvā ki bāg,* is a frequent formula uttered by the inspired oracle in the voice of the possessing god: "May the voice of the cuckoo be fruitful" or "be successful," *kaphuvā ki bāga saphal hai jo.* The word for "voice" used here, bāg, is the derivative of Sanskrit vāc.

The sharpness of pleasure in the springtime is accentuated in this country, which lies at an altitude of three to seven thousand feet. Here, winter is long, dark, cold, snowy, hungry, and boring. Birds are scarce and hungry. By what Hindus take to be the winter solstice, which falls on the first day of the month of Māgh in mid-January, people are settled in for a long haul. This day, Makar Sankrānt, "the juncture-day of Capricorn," is celebrated all over the Hindu world with fairs, particularly the great Kumbh Melā, which takes place every twelve years in the sacred cities of Allahabad and Hardwar. This is the shortest and darkest day of the year, but it is also when the sun turns northward and days will start to get longer. For this reason, it's called Uttarāyana, the turning-north.

In Kumaon, the day, Uttaraini in colloquial Kumaoni, is celebrated with bathing and purifying the body and the house. One eats rich, heating, and sustaining foods. Mothers spend the afternoon making little cakes of wheat dough sweetened with sugarcane sap. Made in the form of a loop with a twisted end, these ghughut or "doves" – of all things – are fried in oil and become hard. Once they're cooked, children string them around their necks as necklaces. The next day is Ghughutiyā, the festival of these fried dove-cookies. At daybreak, the children take their ghughut and other fried snacks onto the slate roofs of the houses and call the crows, who usually flock around to be fed.[27] S.D. Pant (1935, 234–35) wrote that "the feast affords a very welcome relief to the half-famished and cold-bitten birds, which are almost starved on account of the severity of the winter. Men, women, and children eat rich and heat-giving food, because hunger is abroad, and digestion most vigorous owing to the cold ... The children on this day are in the highest spirits."

This is the single moment of the year when seeing and hearing an abundance of crows is a good thing – the more of them, and the louder they caw, the better. The children cry "khā le kauvā" (Come eat, crows!) and "khā le, khā le ghughutī" (Come eat, come eat little doves!), and they chant rhymes:

le, kauv, baṛ. makaī di jā sunuk ghvaṛ.
Take, crow, a cake. Bring me a golden horse.

le, kauv, khīr. itai huri phir.
   Take, crow, rice pudding. Hurry here already.
le, kauv, lagaṛ. makaĩ di jā bhai baiṇi dagaṛ.
   Take, crow, frybread. Bring me little brothers and sisters too.

Boys ask for a wife:

   le, kauv, kyauli. makaĩ di jā bhali bhali bhyauli.
      Take, crow, a little banana. Bring me a good, good bride.

Girls ask for a husband:

   le, kauv, kyauv. makaĩ di jā bhal bhal bhyauv.
      Take, crow, a banana. Bring me a good, good groom.

For children, especially, this is an exciting occasion – up on the roof or out in the courtyard in the cold, stuffing oneself and dozens of screaming crows with these hard cookies with their distinctive molasses flavour tasted only on this day of the year. One consultant assured me that Ghughutiyā is the most memorable festival of the year for rural Kumaoni children.

Why such good treatment of bad birds? Why feed fake doves to real crows at midwinter? My interpretation, as you might imagine, draws on the perceived nature of these birds, on the qualities for which they are emblematic in Kumaon, and on the place of these qualities in the pattern of the year. Feeding doves to the crows transforms birds of cool sorrow, of separation, of insufficient movement, into nourishment for birds of heaty anger, of excess, of dangerous connection, and this at the moment of greatest cold, darkness, and stillness of the year, when the sun is farthest away, when a good shot of movement is needed to get the year rolling again. And at this time, the crows, of all beings, are asked to fulfill our wishes, to bring us bright magical things, such as golden horses, or the things that should come to us in a balanced world: brothers, sisters, brides, and grooms.

Comparisons

Other traditions seem to use comparable avian terms as elements in cosmo-logical patterns involving movement through the shifting year. Examples of cold-weather crow feeding may be found elsewhere in the Himalayan region, both in northern Pakistan and in Nepal, although the dove connection seems unique to Kumaon.[28] Looking farther afield, we find comparable links between birds and the shifting year, links that may suggest the existence of implicit cosmological patterning of the type I have been discussing. In early Irish poetry, to cite another fairly well-developed ethno-ornithological system, found at the other end of Indo-European–speaking territory, cranes lament in the frigid spring. In summer, "dust-coloured cuckoos call aloud," and the blackbird sends his note flying across lakes and plains; then is a good time to travel. Winter in Ireland is presented not as a time of silence, as in Kumaon, but of great noise and violence. In Kumaon, violent, noisy crows are called upon to reverse the stillness; in Ireland, ravens, noted here again for their noise, as well as for their violent behaviour, reproduce, echo, and seem to reinforce that of winter. They are winter incarnate:

> *Dubaib rathib rogemrid*
> *robarta tond túargabar*
>   *íar tóib betha blái.*
> *Brónaig eóin cach íathmaige*
> *acht fiaich fola forderge*
>   *fri fúaim gemrid gairg,*
> *Garb dub dorcha dethaite.*
>   In the dark seasons of deep winter
>   heavy seas are lifted up
>   against the sides of the world.
>   Sorrowful every bird of the meadowlands,
>   except the red and bloody raven,
>   at the roar of rude winter,
>   rough, black, dark, smoky.
>   (translation slightly modified from Meyer 1914, 2–5)

What bird, one may ask, figures in midwinter ritual in Ireland? On the day after Christmas, groups of boys used to catch and kill a wren and bear its body in state from house to house, singing, in one version,

> The wren, the wren, the king of all birds
> On St. Stephen's Day was caught in the furze;

Though his body is little, his family is great,
So rise up, landlady, and give us a treat. (Danaher 1972, 244)[29]

Why is the wren the king of all birds, and is there a link between this status and its role in midwinter ceremonies involving the distribution of rich food? There is an old story about this. It's attributed to Aesop (Plutarch, *Moralia* 806e) and continues to circulate as a folktale in many parts of Europe. It figures in the Grimm fairy tales (no. 171) and is particularly well attested in Ireland.[30] When the birds were choosing their king, they decided the crown should go to the highest flyer. It was the eagle, not surprisingly, who flew the highest. But the tricky little wren had hidden on its back. At the zenith of the eagle's flight, the wren leapt up, trilling in his triumph, and so became king of the birds.[31] This also means that the wren, of all the birds, came closest to the sun. A little shot of heat, then, as the sun turns north.

This last is a very modest proposal for interpreting a bit of the elaborate ritual complexes that have grown up around the wren at midwinter. There are far more ambitious interpretations, which have the virtue of covering many other elements of the complex. The problem with them is, precisely, their immodesty: their authors feel called upon to treat the wren complex as a survival of postulated earlier stages of civilization in which kings were killed to make the crops grow (Frazer 1915), or as the expression of universal human drives (Róheim 1930), or as a combination of both (Muller 1993; Lawrence 1997). All of them, in other words, derive the specifics of the ritual from much broader and less easily defensible purely hypothetical models, ones not based on specific regional cosmologies. What I am proposing, on the contrary, sticks close to the material itself and requires no such vast presumptive schemes; it is also, of course, only an initial proposal. But it suggests that we may have hold of the end of one strand in a skein of cosmological association that underlies a great deal of European, even Eurasian, belief and practice, both seasonal and ornithological, and that may result in a different weave elsewhere, as in the pieces of patterning I think I discern in Kumaon.

Conclusion

Feeding doves to crows at midwinter and calling on the voice of the cuckoo as the very sound of blessing are examples of the use of creatures in the world as conduits for conceptual and affective associations, drawing on implicit ethnotheories, or rather more or less elaborated implicit ethnotheoretical fragments.

The birds presented here are symbols or emblems, but they are also birds. Their choice is neither forced on Kumaonis by nature nor entirely free from nature: it is a social choice among natural properties. These particular birds are not considered good to eat; but in their clear differentiation and their fit with an assumed cosmological pattern of properties, they are good to think. Yet this pattern is not a purely conceptual one: it not only explains, but also evokes emotions. Certain emotions are appropriate and expected in certain situations and at certain times of the year, and some, at least, are condensed, are sent out as, or are heard as pure affective tones in birdsongs. Such tones need be neither direct expressions of some universal feeling body nor completely reducible to the systems of meaning in which they take their place (Leavitt 1996), any more than natural categories are purely reflections of objective differences or purely linguacultural impositions. The world speaks, but we don't all hear exactly the same thing; we respond to the world, but not always in the same way. As affectively charged natural-symbolic terms, birds are good to think, but they are also good for making us feel.

ACKNOWLEDGMENTS

Thanks to Harriet Whitehead, the late Paul Friedrich, Lynn Hart, Greg Forth, and Scott Simon for comments on earlier versions of this chapter. Research in Kumaon was funded by the Social Sciences and Humanities Research Council of Canada, and analysis was facilitated by the Groupe de Recherche Interuniversitaire sur le Tibet et l'Himalaya, supported by the Fonds de Recherche du Québec – Société et Culture.

NOTES

1 One anthropological tradition sees such imagined mixtures as monsters, sometimes sacred monsters. See E.R. Leach (1964); Mary Douglas (1966); and Dan Sperber (1996).
2 See, for instance, http://birdhybrids.blogspot.com/2014/06/downy-woodpecker-x-hairy -woodpecker.html.
3 For an overview and discussion of these and related debates, see Glauco Sanga and Gherardo Ortalli (2003).
4 See the reaction when one of Donald Trump's American supporters, speaking to an Indian audience, referred to him as "wise like an owl, or as you say, *ullū*." "Trump Is 'Wise Like an *Ullu*': Celebrity Video Has Twitter in Splits," NDTV World, August 25, 2020, https://www. ndtv.com/world-news/wise-like-an-ullu-donald-trumps-celebrity-supporter-tomi-lahren -stirs-laughter-on-twitter-2285039.
5 Throughout his career, many of Lévi-Strauss's central arguments were built around birds: hunting eagles from a hole in the ground (Lévi-Strauss 2021); the unhappy birdnester, stuck halfway up a cliff, who launches the *Mythologiques* (Lévi-Strauss 1969), which finish

(Lévi-Strauss 1981) with the insane Loon Woman destroying the world; the goatsucker, or "wind-gobbler" as it is called in French, who provides a reference point for *The Jealous Potter* (Lévi-Strauss 1988). These are in contiguity relations with the person; in terms of similarity, Lévi-Strauss looked like a bird, specifically a heron. A lean figure with a beak on him, he paced slowly and deliberately back and forth as he lectured, absorbed, looking a little downward, like a heron after fish.

6 Such an approach is not deterministic in any simple way, and there's plenty of evidence that even the most salient aspect of a bit of nature can be overridden by the requirements of a given symbolic system. An example I like is from phonetics. A history of laboratory experiments found that speakers of many languages associate high front vowels such as [i] with small, bright, fast referents, low back vowels, [o, a], with large, dark, slow referents (Sapir 1929; for an apparent instantiation in the naming of animals, see Berlin 2003). But, as Benjamin Lee Whorf (2012, 341–43) points out, an obvious exception to this model will be found in English: the word "deep," with its high front vowel, carries the connotations not of its sound symbolism, but of its meaning in English, and so to English-speakers the word "sounds" dark, heavy, low: deep. This may be taken as proof of the power of system over intrinsic salience. But note, conversely, that salience does not disappear. It continues to lurk, pouncing on any invented English "words" ending in [-i:p]: "queep," "zeep," and "meep" all suggest light, small, fast referents. See Roman Jakobson (1960, 372–73); and Leanne Hinton, Johanna Nichols, and John J. Ohala (1994).

7 For an extended critique of such "cross-cultural" methods in social psychology, see Claude Faucheux (1976).

8 I'll relegate most examples here to endnotes. I give them at all only as an indication of some of the sources of my own thinking and feeling about this domain.

9 One of the many names for birds in Sanskrit is *antarikṣaga,* the one who "goes in the space in-between" – that is, in the space between heaven and earth. That birds are inhabitants of the air and so closer to God motivates their identification with twins for the Nuer (Evans-Pritchard 1956, 128–33). And see Gaston Bachelard's discussion of birds in literature in *Air and Dreams* ([1943] 1988, Chapter 2) and Christopher Moreman's (2014) of birds as psychopomps.

10 A troubadour lyric by Bernart de Ventadorn (Pillet and Carstens 1933, number 70.43) begins

> *Can vei la lauzeta mover / de joi sas alas contra.l rai,*
> *que s'oblid e.s laissat chazer / per la doussor c'al cor li vai.*
>> When I see the lark moving her wings with joy against the light,
>> Who forgets herself and lets herself fall for the sweetness that goes to her heart.

11 The word for "nest" in many Indo-European languages, including English, Sanskrit, and Kumaoni, is derived from the root *sed-* "sit, settle," with the prefix *ni-* "down" or "alone" (Greppin 1997b).

12 In the poem "When Lilacs Last in the Dooryard Bloomed," his lament for Abraham Lincoln, Walt Whitman (1977, 351–59) weaves the song of a hidden Hermit Thrush together with emblems of springtime and sunset:

> Sing on, sing on you gray-brown bird,
> Sing from the swamps, the recesses, pour your chant from the bushes,
> Limitless out of the dusk, out of the cedars and pines ...
> You only I hear ...
> From deep secluded recesses,
> From the fragrant cedars and the ghostly pines so still,
> Came the carol of the bird.
> And the charm of the carol rapt me,

As I held as if by their hands my comrades in the night,
And the voice of my spirit tallied the song of the bird.

The transition from the individual referential speech of human beings to the common non-referential language of birds takes place in one of Yeats's last poems, "Cuchulain Comforted" (Yeats 1950, 395–96). The hero is dead and has descended among the shades, where all heroic individuality ends. As he is told, here "all we do / All must together do." His comforting is to lose his own separateness, which he had fiercely defended all his life:

They sang, but had nor human tunes nor words,
Though all was done in common as before;
They had changed their throats and had the throats of birds.

13 The dictionaries define the krauñca as the curlew, *Numenius arquata*, and Robert Goldman (1984) accepts this in his translation of Book 1 of the *Rāmāyaṇa*, but some authorities identify the bird with the Sarus Crane, *Grus antigone* (Dave 1985, 311–16; Huberman 1994), which is found throughout South Asia (Fleming, Fleming, and Bangdel 1979, 32). I lean toward the latter view, since the *Rāmāyaṇa* calls the bird *tāmraśīrṣa*, "red-headed" (in a verse left out of the critical edition, cited in Dave 1985, 314), and of these two birds only the crane has a red head. The Sarus Crane also has a habit that makes it a likely symbol of conjugal love: "The call is a fine trumpet uttered mornings and evenings, and if the pair happen to feed apart during the night they keep in touch by constantly calling to each other" (Dave 1985, 316).

14 In a nice example of creative misremembering, I have "known" for years that Vālmīki's curse was spoken in the very rhythm of the bird's cry, so that Sanskrit poetry would be a transposition into human language of the pattern of birdsong. I don't know where this idea came from; there isn't any evidence for it, as far as I can tell. But it is noteworthy that krauñca birds have been specially associated with speech and with the goddess Vāc (Speech) since Vedic times. There is a Vedic hymn-melody called *vāṅnidhanakrauñca*, "a krauñca melody 'ending in speech'" (Staal 1985, 557). And krauñca birds are the appropriate sacrifice to Vāc (Huberman 1994, 24). On the krauñca question, see Jeffrey Masson (1969).

15 I am taking it as given that what we call emotions are not unique to each individual, but to some degree are marked for our (and other) species and to some degree are culturally and socially defined, both in terms of what they mean and how they feel (Leavitt 1996). Here again, the key arguments were laid out by Michelle Rosaldo (1983, 1984) in essays published only after her death. The social and collective nature of emotions marks much recent "affect theory" (e.g., Flatley 2008; Gregg and Seigworth 2010).

16 The cuckoo calendars are the inspiration behind Simon and Garfunkel's 1966 song "April, Come She Will."

17 In Nepali, the bird is called the *kāphal car* (Turner 1931, 87). Its call is rendered *kaiphal pakkyo* (Fleming, Fleming, and Bangdel 1979, 112). It should not be confused with another of the Cuculidae, the Asian Koyal or Koel, *Eudynamys scolopaceus*, whose sweet single note, a staple in South Asian romantic poetry, announces the rainy season in Kumaon.

18 Composed in the early 1950s, with music by Mohan Upretī and lyrics by Brijendra Lāl Sāh, "Beṛu pāko" was quickly adopted as a virtual regional anthem for Kumaon. For a version sung by Gopāl Bābū Gosvāmī, see "Bedu Pako," Himalayan Creative Workshop, https://www.youtube.com/watch?v=oTBdLisrElk.

19 The Kumaoni song values bayberries over figs (*Ficus palmata*, the Fegra fig or wild fig or Punjab fig) because the former are available only in the spring, whereas the latter are supposed to ripen all year. By contrast, figs are specifically marks of springtime in the "Song of Songs" (2:13): "The fig tree putteth forth her green figs." The reference here seems to be to *Ficus carica*, the common fig. Both species bear initial fruit in the spring on the previous

year's shoots, then another main crop in August, which stays on through the winter. This gives two opposed interpretations. In Kumaon, this is interpreted as figs always being available. The Biblical reference seems to be to the new figs of the spring.

20 *musā ghāni lagai, dulā paiṭh. kavā ghāni lagai, des phir.*

21 The song may be heard at "Aam ki dai ma ghughati na basaa by Gopal Babu Goswami," Dev bhumi Uttrakhand, https://www.youtube.com/watch?v=xsQETnQIfek. For a printed version, see Gopāl Bābū Gosvāmī (1982, 42). YouTube also offers a large selection of covers and dramatizations.

22 The idea that different castes and activities are marked as more or less interactive corresponds to what McKim Marriott (1989) calls the dimension of "mixing."

23 These texts are from jāgars performed by the bard Kamal Rām Ārya in 1981 and 1982. I am grateful to him for permission and encouragement to reproduce them.

24 This trope is very old; it is found in, and may be borrowed from, verses 4–5 of the Vedic Hymn to the Night (*R̥g Veda* 10.127):

> *sā́ no adyá yásyā vayáṃ ní te yámann ávikṣmahi /*
> *vr̥kṣé ná vasatíṃ váyaḥ //*
> *ní grā́māso avikṣata ní padvánto ní pakṣiṇa /*
> *ní śyenā́saś cid arthínaḥ //.*
>
> As today thou [hast come], at whose coming we have come home
> As birds (*vā́yaḥ,* see Mayrhofer 1996, 507) to their dwelling on the tree.
> Home have gone the villagers, home those with feet, home birds
> (*pakṣíṇaḥ* "winged ones").
> Home even the eager hawks.

This figure is discussed at greater length in John Leavitt (2022).

25 The Kumaoni text as I recorded it goes *"ki jogi huṇ mē̃ / ki baṛ kaṣṭ hū̃," kuni. / "ki māgh pus ki ta tusār sādhan paraī. / ki jeṭh baisākh ki ta dhūp sādhan paraī. / ki sauṇ bhadav ki ta him sādhan paraī."*

26 On this festival, and on the joys of spring in Kumaon, see S.D. Pant (1935, 231–32); Trilocan Pāṇḍey (1962, 130–31); and John Leavitt (2000, 51–52). Pāṇḍey gives more Phūl Dhoi rhymes on page 359. YouTube offers a number of musicalized performances under various romanizations, particularly "phool deyi."

27 I participated in Ghughutiyā in 1982 and 2009; an idea of the stability of its observance may be gained from comparing this description and that in Leavitt (2000, 64–65) with that of Edwin T. Atkinson (1884, 872), which is based on the Makar Sankrānt of 1878:

> The *Makar* or *Mágh sankránt* ... is also known as the *Ghugutiya, Phúl,* and *Uttaráyini* or *Uttraini sankránt.* The name *"Ghugutiya"* is given from the small images of flour baked in sesamum oil or ghi and made to resemble birds which are strung as necklaces and placed around the necks of children on this day. On the morrow or the second day of Mágh the children call the crow and other birds and feed them with the necklaces and eat a portion themselves.

Some more or less bollywoodized versions of these practices may be found on YouTube.

28 In Nepal, the days just before the Autumn Divālī cycle (October–November) are called *tihār,* "festival," and the first of these is Kāg Tihār, the Crow Festival, when "no one may eat ... before the crows have been fed" (Turner 1931, 286). Among the Magar of central Nepal, rice is left on the roof for the crows, who are considered beneficent messengers (Lecomte-Tilouine 1993, 122–23). Among the Kalash of the Hindu Kush in northern Pakistan, the only group in the region to have maintained a form of archaic Indo-Aryan religion and not converted

to Islam, midwinter (celebrated in December) involves several days of ritual, including *kagāyak,* "Crow [day]." On this day, the crows are called and fed: *klak jo klak jo, ric kagā,* "Make noise, make noise, shit-crow!" (pers. comm., Kavi Khosh Nawaz, Rumbur, Pakistan, 1976). The crows are asked for things, too:

> O crow, sharp-horned bulls bring!
> O crow, four-horned sheep bring!
> O crow, quadruplet (-bearing) goats bring!
> (Morgenstierne 1973, 36; see Loude and Lièvre 1984, 310–18)

M.N. Srinivas (1952) reports a comparable practice among the Coorgs of south India, but associated with the life cycle rather than the annual cycle. On the eighth, ninth, and tenth days after a funeral, food is left for the crows on a post in the yard before the mourning-house. The spouse of the deceased claps his or her hands and shouts "'kā, kā' (in imitation of the cawing of crows)" (Srinivas 1952, 114–15). I presume this practice is related to the crow's role as messenger to the realm of the dead.

29 Videos of Wren processions may be found on YouTube under the search term "Wren Boys." See also Lisa O'Neill (2019).

30 "The Election of Bird-king" is Tale Type (ATU) 221 (Uther 2011). Antti Aarne and Stith Thompson (1961, 74) note thirty-nine versions in the archive of the Irish Folklore Commission. "Wren as king of birds. Wins contest for kingship" is Motif B242.1.2 in the *Motif-Index of Folk-Literature* (Thompson 1955–58, vol. 1). On the wren as king of the birds, see Edward Armstrong (1959, 135–36); on the midwinter Wren Hunt, "among the most elaborate bird rituals surviving in Europe" (141), see Armstrong (1959, Chapter 9).

31 In Latin, the wren is *regulus* (little king), which gives calques in the French *roitelet* and the German *Zaunkönig,* the "hedge-king." See the treatments of wren ritual and myth in western Europe by Sylvie Muller (1993) and Elizabeth Lawrence (1997), the first of which includes massive documentation. The fact that wrens make their nests in holes has given the Eurasian Wren, the only European species, the designation *Troglodytes troglodytes.*

WORKS CITED

Aarne, Antti, and Stith Thompson. 1961. *The Types of the Folktale: A Classification and Bibliography.* Folklore Fellows Communications 184. 2nd revision. Helsinki: Finnish Academy.

Ali, Sálim. 1979. *Indian Hill Birds.* Delhi: Oxford University Press.

Armstrong, Edward Allworthy. 1959. *The Folklore of Birds.* Boston: Houghton Mifflin.

Atkinson, Edwin T. 1884. *The Himálayan Districts of the North Western Provinces of India.* Vol. 2. Allahabad: Government Press.

Atran, Scott. 1985. "The Nature of Folk-Botanical Life Forms." *American Anthropologist* 87, 2: 298–315.

–. 1993. *Cognitive Foundations of Natural History.* Cambridge: Cambridge University Press.

'Attar, Farîd-Ud-Dîn. 1857. *Mantic uttair ou Le langage des oiseaux.* Translated by Joseph Garcin de Tassy. Paris: Imprimerie Impériale.

–. 1984. *The Conference of the Birds.* Translated by Afkham Darbandi and Dick Davis. London: Penguin.

Bachelard, Gaston. (1943) 1988. *Air and Dreams: An Essay on the Imagination of Movement.* Translated by Edith R. Farrell and C. Frederick Farrell. Dallas: Dallas Institute of Humanities and Culture.

Berlin, Brent. 1992. *Ethnobiological Classification.* Princeton: Princeton University Press.

–. 2003. "Tapir and Squirrel: Further Nomenclatural Meanderings toward a Universal Sound-Symbolic Bestiary." In *Nature Knowledge: Ethnoscience, Cognition, and Utility,* ed. Glauco Sanga and Gherardo Ortalli, 119–27. New York: Berghahn.

Berlin, Brent, Dennis E. Breedlove, and Peter H. Raven. 1973. "General Principles of Classification and Nomenclature in Folk Biology." *American Anthropologist* 75, 1: 214–42.

Chaucer, Geoffrey. 1937. "The Parlement of Foules." In *The Complete Works of Geoffrey Chaucer.* Edited by Walter W. Skeat, 101–10. London: Oxford University Press.

Chrétien de Troyes. 1959. *Le roman de Perceval ou le Conte du Graal.* Edited by William Roach. Geneva: Droz. [Textes Littéraires Français, 71.]

Danaher, Kevin. 1972. *The Year in Ireland.* Dublin: Mercier.

Dave, K.N. 1985. *Birds in Sanskrit Literature.* Delhi: Motilal Banarsidass.

Davidson, Donald. 1974. "On the Very Idea of a Conceptual Scheme." *Proceedings and Addresses of the American Philosophical Association* 47: 5–20.

Douglas, Mary. 1966. *Purity and Danger: An Analysis of Concepts of Pollution and Taboo.* London: Routledge and Kegan Paul.

Evans-Pritchard, E.E. 1956. *Nuer Religion.* London: Oxford University Press.

Faucheux, Claude. 1976. "Cross-Cultural Research in Experimental Social Psychology." *European Journal of Social Psychology* 6, 3: 269–322.

Feld, Steven. 1982. *Sound and Sentiment: Birds, Weeping, Poetics, and Song in Kaluli Expression.* Philadelphia: University of Pennsylvania Press.

Flatley, Jonathan. 2008. *Affective Mapping: Melancholia and the Politics of Modernism.* Cambridge, MA: Harvard University Press.

Fleming, Robert L., Sr., Robert L. Fleming, Jr., and Lain Singh Bangdel. 1979. *Birds of Nepal.* 2nd ed. Kathmandu: Avalok.

Frazer, J.G. 1915. *The Golden Bough: A Study in Magic and Religion.* 3rd ed. London: Macmillan.

Goldman, Robert P., ed. and trans. 1984. *The Rāmāyaṇa of Vālmīki.* Vol. 1. Princeton: Princeton University Press.

Gosvāmī, Gopāl Bābū. 1982. *Uttarāñcal rahasya.* Vol. 1. Nainital: B.K. Press.

Gregg, Melissa, and Gregory J. Seigworth, eds. 2010. *The Affect Theory Reader.* Durham, NC: Duke University Press.

Greppin, John A.C. 1997a. "Birds." In *Encyclopedia of Indo-European Culture,* ed. James P. Mallory and Douglas Q. Adams, 66–68. London: Fitzroy Dearborn.

–. 1997b. "Nest." In *Encyclopedia of Indo-European Culture,* ed. James P. Mallory and Douglas Q. Adams, 393. London: Fitzroy Dearborn.

Gude, Raymond J. 1979. "'Metamythopoesis' in the Vālmīki *Rāmāyaṇa.*" *Chicago Anthropology Exchange* 13, 2: 4–23.

Harris, Roy, and Talbot J. Taylor. 1989. *Landmarks in Linguistic Thought.* London: Routledge.

Hart, Lynn M. 1995. "Three Walls: Regional Aesthetics and the International Art World." In *The Traffic in Culture,* ed. George E. Marcus and Fred R. Myers, 127–50. Berkeley: University of California Press.

Hinton, Leanne, Johanna Nichols, and John J. Ohala, eds. 1994. *Sound Symbolism.* Cambridge: Cambridge University Press.

Huberman, Eric A. 1994. "Who Is Vālmīki? The Ādi-Kavi and the Origins of Lyric Poetry." *Journal of Vaiṣṇava Studies* 2, 4: 17–30.

Jakobson, Roman. 1960. "Linguistics and Poetics." In *Style in Language,* ed. Thomas A. Sebeok, 350–77. Cambridge, MA: MIT Press.

Jośī, Kṛṣṇānand. 1971. *Kumāū̃ kā lok-sāhitya. Paricayātmak saṅgrah.* Bareilly: Prakash Book Depot.

Kale, M.R., ed. 1969. *The Abhijñānaśākuntalam of Kālidāsa*. 10th edition. Delhi: Motilal Banarsidass.

Lambek, Michael. 1991. "Treading beyond Objectivism: Introduction to *From Method to Modesty: Essays on Thinking and Making Ethnography Now.*" *Culture* 11, 1–2: 3–14.

Lawrence, Elizabeth Attwood. 1997. *Hunting the Wren: Transformation of Bird to Symbol*. Knoxville: University of Tennessee Press.

Leach, E.R. 1964. "Anthropological Aspects of Language: Animal Categories and Verbal Abuse." In *New Directions in the Study of Language*, ed. E.H. Lenneberg, 23–64. Cambridge, MA: MIT Press.

Leavitt, John. 1996. "Meaning and Feeling in the Anthropology of Emotions." *American Ethnologist* 23, 3: 514–39.

–. 2000. "The Year in the Kumaon Himalayas." *Cosmos: Journal of the Traditional Cosmology Society* 16: 43–88.

–. 2011. *Linguistic Relativities: Language Diversity and Modern Thought*. Cambridge: Cambridge University Press.

–. 2022. "A Trope of Time: Twilight Swings across the Central Himalayas." In *Tropological Thought and Action: Essays on the Poetics of Imagination,* ed. Marko Živković, Jamin Pelkey, and James W. Fernandez, 44–66. Oxford: Berghahn.

Lecomte-Tilouine, Marie. 1993. *Les dieux du pouvoir. Les Magar et l'hindouisme au Népal central.* Paris: CNRS.

Lévi-Strauss, Claude. 1963. *Totemism*. Translated by Rodney Needham. Boston: Beacon Press.

–. 1969. *The Raw and the Cooked: Mythologiques*. Vol. 1. Translated by John Weightman and Doreen Weightman. Chicago: University of Chicago Press.

–. 1981. *The Naked Man: Mythologiques*. Vol. 4. Translated by John Weightman and Doreen Weightman. Chicago: University of Chicago Press.

–. 1988. *The Jealous Potter*. Translated by Bénédicte Chorier. Chicago: University of Chicago Press.

–. 2021. *Wild Thought: A New Translation of* La Pensée sauvage. Translated by Jeffrey Mehlman and John Leavitt. Chicago: University of Chicago Press.

Loude, Jean-Yves, and Viviane Lièvre. 1984. *Solstice païen. Fêtes d'hiver chez les Kalash du Nord-Pakistan*. Paris: Presses de la Renaissance.

Ludwig, David. 2018. "Revamping the Metaphysics of Ethnobiological Classification." *Current Anthropology* 59, 4: 415–38.

Macdonnell, Arthur A. 1917. *A Vedic Reader for Students*. London: Oxford University Press.

Marriott, McKim. 1989. "Constructing an Indian Ethnosociology." *Contributions to Indian Sociology* 23, 1: 1–40.

Masson, Jeffrey Moussaieff. 1969. "Who Killed Cock Krauñca? Abhinavagupta's Reflections on the Origin of Aesthetic Experience." *Journal of the Oriental Institute* (*Baroda*) 18: 207–24.

Mayrhofer, Manfred. 1996. *Etymologisches Wörterbuch des Altindoarischen*. Vol. 2. Heidelberg: Carl Winter.

Meyer, Kuno. 1914. "The Guesting of Athirne." *Ériu* 7: 1–9.

Miyagawa, Shigeru, Shiro Ojima, Robert C. Berwick, and Kazuo Okanoya. 2014. "The Integration Hypothesis of Human Language Evolution and the Nature of Contemporary Languages." *Frontiers in Psychology,* June 9. https://doi.org/10.3389/fpsyg.2014.00564.

Monier-Williams, Monier. 1899. *A Sanskrit-English Dictionary*. 2nd ed. Oxford: Oxford University Press.

Moreman, Christopher M. 2014. "On the Relationship between Birds and Spirits of the Dead." *Society and Animals* 22, 5: 1–22.

Morgenstierne, Georg. 1973. *Indo-Iranian Frontier Languages*. Vol. 4, *The Kalasha Language*. 2nd ed. Instituttet for Sammenlignende Kulturforskning, series B, issue 58. Oslo: Universitetsforlaget.

Muller, Sylvie. 1993. "Le roitelet: vie et mort dans le rituel et les contes irlandais. Essai sur l'évolution des représentations des rapports nature-culture et homme-femme." PhD thesis, Université de Nice Sophia Antipolis.

Munsterberg, Peggy, ed. 1980. *The Penguin Book of Bird Poetry*. Harmondsworth: Penguin.

Oakley, E. Sherman, and T.D. Gairola. 1935. *Himalayan Folklore*. Allahabad: Government Press.

O'Laughlin, Bridget. 1974. "Mediation of Contradiction: Why Mbum Women Do Not Eat Chicken." In *Women in Culture and Society*, ed. Michelle Z. Rosaldo and Louise Lamphere, 301–18. Stanford: Stanford University Press.

O'Neill, Lisa. 2019. *The Wren, the Wren*. Digital EP, Rough Trade Recordings, London, RLR008DS2.

Osmaston, A.E. 1927. *A Forest Flora for Kumaon*. Allahabad: Government Press.

Pāṇḍe, Cāru Candra. 1965. *Kumāŭnī kavi "Gaurdā" kā kāvya darśan*. Almora: Deśbhakt Press.

Pāṇḍey, Trilocan. 1962. *Kumāŭ kā lok sāhitya*. Almora: Sri Almora Book Depot.

Pant, S.D. 1935. *The Social Economy of the Himalayans*. London: Allen and Unwin.

Pillet, Alfred, and Henry Carstens. 1933. *Bibliographie der Troubadours*. Halle: Niemeyer.

Ramanujan, A.K. 1991. "Three Hundred *Rāmāyaṇa*s: Five Examples and Three Thoughts on Translation." In *Many Rāmāyaṇas: The Diversity of a Narrative Tradition in South Asia*, ed. Paula Richman, 22–49. Berkeley: University of California Press.

Róheim, Géza. 1930. *Animism, Magic and the Divine King*. London: Kegan Paul.

Rosaldo, Michelle Zimbalist. 1972. "Metaphors and Folk Classification." *Southwestern Journal of Anthropology* 28, 1: 83–99.

–. 1983. "The Shame of Headhunters and the Autonomy of Self." *Ethos* 11, 3: 131–51.

–. 1984. "Toward an Anthropology of Self and Feeling." In *Culture Theory: Essays on Mind, Self, and Emotion*, ed. Richard A. Shweder and Robert A. LeVine, 137–58. Cambridge: Cambridge University Press.

Sahlins, Marshall. 1977. *Culture and Practical Reason*. Chicago: University of Chicago Press.

Sanga, Glauco, and Gherardo Ortalli, eds. 2003. *Nature Knowledge: Ethnoscience, Cognition, and Utility*. New York: Berghahn.

Sanwal, R.D. 1976. *Social Stratification in Rural Kumaon*. Delhi: Oxford University Press.

Sapir, Edward. 1929. "A Study in Phonetic Symbolism." *Journal of Experimental Psychology* 12, 3: 225–39.

Sperber, Dan. 1996. "Why Are Perfect Animals, Hybrids, and Monsters Food for Symbolic Thought?" *Method and Theory in the Study of Religion* 8, 2: 143–69.

Srinivas, M.N. 1952. *Religion and Society among the Coorgs of South India*. London: Oxford University Press.

Staal, Frits. 1985. "Mantras and Bird Songs." *Journal of the American Oriental Society* 105, 3: 549–58.

Thompson, Stith. 1955-58. *Motif-Index of Folk Literature*. 6 vols. Bloomington: Indiana University Press.

Turner, R.L. 1931. *A Dictionary of the Nepali Language*. London: Kegan Paul.

Upreti, Gaṅgá Datt. 1894. *Proverbs and Folklore of Kumaun and Garhwal*. Lodiana: Lodiana Mission Press.

Uther, Hans-Georg. 2011. *The Types of International Folktales: A Classification and Bibliography, Based on the System of Antti Aarne and Stith Thompson*. 3 vols. Folklore Fellows Communications 284–86. Helsinki: Finnish Academy.

Whitman, Walt. 1977. *The Complete Poems*. Edited by Francis Murphy. London: Penguin.

Whorf, Benjamin Lee. 2012. "Language, Mind, and Reality." In Benjamin Lee Whorf, *Language, Thought, and Reality*, 2nd ed., 315–44. Cambridge, MA: MIT Press.

Wikipedia. n.d. "Bedu Pako Baro Masa." Wikipedia. https://en.wikipedia.org/wiki/Bedu_Pako_Baro_Masa.

Woods, Robert Williams. 1907. *How to Tell the Birds from the Flowers: A Manual of Flornithology for Beginners*. San Francisco: Paul Elder.

Yeats, W.B. 1950. *The Collected Poems of W.B. Yeats*. Second edition. London: Macmillan.

7

Time, Space, and Typhoons in Ibaloy Birdlore (Philippines Cordillera)

Frédéric Laugrand, Antoine Laugrand,
Jazil Tamang, and Gliseria Magapin

"When the brolga sings out, the catfish start to move," said one of my Aboriginal teachers, Daly Pulkara ... "You didn't know that?" he asked me. "That's really culture, that one."

– Deborah Bird Rose, *Oiseaux de pluie*

IN SOUTHEAST ASIA, scholars have extensively studied the relationships between birds and humans, and Pierre Le Roux and Bernard Sellato's 2006 compendium *Les messagers divins: Aspects esthétiques et symboliques des oiseaux en Asie du Sud-Est* (Divine messengers: Bird symbolism and aesthetics in Southeast Asia) remains a key reference. Some studies were conducted earlier in Papua New Guinea (see Bulmer 1967; Feld 1982), Borneo (Metcalf 1976), and Indonesia (Forth 1996, 2004, 2006a, 2006b, 2007, 2008, 2009a, 2009b, 2010). Taxonomy, naming systems, and divination were important topics in these works. More recently, new studies have discussed birds in Indigenous cosmologies in Taiwan (Cauquelin 2006; Simon 2015) and in the Philippines (Gonzalez 2011). Birds are also well-known emblems (Simon 2015) and metaphors (Chapter 8 in this volume).

Today, many people believe that birds have their own senses or wisdom (see Birkhead 2008, 2012; Tidemann and Gosler 2010). However, birds are always perceived by specific people and from the lens of human culture. They exist on their own terms, but when humans interact with them, they occupy a place within a cosmology. With the ontological turn, birds are now referred to as "non-human persons" or "more-than-human entities" (see Rudge 2019). The Ibaloy, who inhabit a huge mountainous territory in the province of Benguet, in the Philippine cordillera on the island of Luzon, and who are the subject of this chapter, believe that birds, just like humans, have a *karashowa* (a soul), but they do not believe that birds share the same subjectivity. They do not communicate with birds, but they do observe them, respect them, and listen to their sounds very carefully. In the past, wild birds were frequently eaten, but this is no longer the case, as the Ibaloy do not practise hunting. Sometimes, when they hear certain bird calls, such as the *bokaw* (hawk), they still follow taboos and perform rituals, especially when they are connected to the death of a person.

Drawing on eleven years of joint research with the Ibaloy of Upper Loacan on various topics, notably elders' narratives, this chapter focuses on their birdlore at a time of climatic and environmental changes. The Ibaloy have a substantial body of knowledge about their local birds, so the notion of entanglement is highly relevant here.[1] Their knowledge is such that they can reproduce the sounds of many birds and recognize and distinguish them easily. In the past, birds were hunted with slingshots *(palsi-it)* or trapped *(solo)* to be eaten.[2] Another technique, the *akikan,* consisted of making a *pedded* – a cage structure with a hole in the side – beside which hunters would wait with their whips, ready to strike the birds. The hunters would kindle a fire in the cage, and the birds, drawn to the light, would try to enter the hole (Lolo Màrcial and Lolo Nardo, cited in Laugrand et al. 2019c).[3] Moss (1920, 229) observed that technique in action.[4] However, these practices have vanished. Some caged birds are still kept inside the house, such as the *martines* (Crested Myna; also known as *martinez* in Tagalog), a Sturnidae that can be raised as a pet and trained to speak any language.[5] Elders share numerous stories about martines imitating human voices. Some even point out that this bird can become a messenger if needed: "That is their talent as a bird. It can be trained to speak different languages. It can be trained to speak Tagalog or English. These birds also know how to make remedies if it is needed so that they will not die" (Laugrand et al. 2019c, 60). Thus, the Ibaloy knowledge of birds is extensive.

During their hunting expeditions, in their gardens, or when they walk in the mountains,[6] the Ibaloy observe birds. They learn their songs and watch them moving around. Lolo Nardo, an elder from Tolibeng, related an anecdote showing how much they would learn from birds: "They [the Elders] told us that if the bird *beshing* [White-bellied munia] eats the fruit of the *anggowad*, the bird will get drunk. That is why people knew that it could make people drunk" (Laugrand et al. 2019a, 120). The Ibaloy still pass on these traditions, and they see birds as essential and sentient beings to be respected. According to Lola Margarita, an elder from Tolibeng, certain birds are helpful because they remove pests: "The *pamoltongan* [a kind of Pied triller] can help us; that is why I don't like them to be hunted or to be trapped, because they can help us in removing the worms of plants, especially the vegetables" (Laugrand et al. 2019c, 52). Lolo Nardo stated that this also applied to the *talal* (a bird classified by the Ibaloy as another kind of Pied Triller). The talal can drive away other birds from the rice fields. It is friendly because it can help in removing worms (Laugrand et al. 2019c, 52).

According to Lolo Melanio (an elder from Anteg-in), there is no origin myth for birds: "Birds were created by God and are living on earth just like humans, they were created for them to be used" (Laugrand et al. 2019c, 62).

The Ibaloy use some birds in their rituals, especially chickens and ducks. Lolo Edward, a *mambonong* (a ritual officiant or shaman), mentioned that the duck was used for healing purposes, especially if a person had been affected by the *somjang* or the *topja* (kinds of sickness resulting from witchcraft) (Laugrand et al. 2019c, 46).

Bird symbolism reaches its highest level in the *tayaw* dance, in which the men imitate a gliding eagle while their female pair stays behind and follows. The *tolsho*, the big eagle, has disappeared from their area, but many people recall its ability to fly off with a small pig clutched in its talons. The eagle still appears as an inspiring animal that humans imitate when they dance in the rituals. The tayaw is performed in various contexts and is considered a powerful means to connect with the deceased and with the *kabunian*, the divinities. In this respect, the Ibaloy share similar practices with many other ethnic groups in Southeast Asia, where birds and funeral rituals are interconnected (Le Roux 2006, 64). At funerals, a *balon to* (a lunch box) is prepared for the deceased, and eggs are added to its chicken and rice. But as Le Roux (2006, 60) and Marie-Madeleine Davy (1993) suggest, the extent to which birds are symbols of the human soul is unclear. They are undoubtedly connected to the deceased, as they are in contact with another world. Among the Ibaloy, they are not emblems, as they are in many nearby countries such as Taiwan (Simon 2015), Papua New Guinea, or Indonesia. They are connected to where they live, but their role is in anticipation and prediction. This is also the case in neighbouring groups such as the Blaan of Mindanao and the Alangan Mangyan of Mindoro, with whom they sometimes share names for birds (see Laugrand, Laugrand, and Tremblay 2018a, 2018b). Overall, it appears that birds are most marked in terms of temporality.

During several projects to help pass on traditional knowledge from elders to youths, we had the opportunity to work with the Upper Loacan community (Itogon, Benguet). We conducted fieldwork each year starting in 2012, and we organized three workshops on the intergenerational transfer of knowledge in 2017, 2018, and 2019 with over twenty elders and around ten youths. Jazil Tamang and Gliseria Magapin, two young Nabaloy-speakers, helped a great deal in this research, especially by organizing the workshops and interpreting, transcribing, and translating the transcribed verbatims, as well as co-authoring the present discussion. Antoine Laugrand conducted additional fieldwork from February to July 2020 for his PhD and to learn the Nabaloy language.

Setting up knowledge-transfer workshops for elders and youth was based on work conducted with the Inuit between 2000 and 2011 by Frédéric Laugrand and Dutch anthropologist Jarich G. Oosten. Their purpose was to record the richness of regional traditions and take all local variations into account. Although the workshop format looks simple, it is not easy to set up. Once all participants agree on its objectives and the agenda, various topics are listed. Then, roundtable discussions can start, and each elder is invited to share his or her experiences on the selected topics. Special procedures ensure that all participants are allowed the time they need to explain their point of view and share their experience. For each session, various roundtables are proposed. All participants can share their views or ask questions. The sessions are video recorded to facilitate transcription and to preserve the participants' words. During the sessions, the young people are invited to ask questions, with the hope of triggering the elders' memories or developing additional points of interest.

As with the Inuit, an important feature that contributed to the Ibaloy workshops was that most participants were related to each other. This familiarity facilitated a relaxed atmosphere. It allowed them to discuss issues in-depth and to share their personal experiences in detail. Elders involved themselves wholeheartedly in the sessions. They enjoyed the opportunity to develop an agenda that reflected their interests in discussing and preserving Ibaloy traditions. They appreciated being challenged by their companions and allowed to hear each other's stories. Knowledgeable but modest, they chose to speak only of events that they themselves had experienced. They spoke with great sincerity. Their knowledge was vast and rooted in practice. It could not be qualified as "traditional knowledge" as it had been updated throughout their lives.

During the workshops, elders showed substantial knowledge of bird sounds. According to Lolo Marcial, for example, they recognized the *ngoweg* (Philippine quail) through its call, "Hooh! Hooh! Hooh!" This bird was also referred to as the *akop* (a kind of owl), for its similar "Koop! Koop! Koop!" sound. According to Lolo Melanio, "the sound of the *ot-ot* (zebra dove) is 'Ot ot ot ot ot ot ot ot ot,'" and that of the *jadjaran* (Grey Wagtail) is "Sitik! Sitik!" (Laugrand et al. 2019c, 49, 55). Nicole Revel (1992) in Palawan and Gregory Forth in Indonesia also observed that birds are often named after the sounds they produce. Many Ibaloy names for birds are thus "phonological iconisms." Unlike the Batek of Malaysia studied by Alice Rudge (2019, 5), the Ibaloy do not believe that the birds are uttering their own names. They acknowledge that the names come from humans. Bird chants indicate messages intended for the living.

Ibaloy medicine includes some analogical reasoning. The case of the *pato,* the duck, is an interesting example, as it illustrates how much analogy shapes some Ibaloy ways of reasoning about birds. Lolo Nardo explained,

> When the duck eats, it immediately defecates, so they used to say that it is not good for a mother who just gave birth to eat it because it will affect the offspring. The child can be like the duck who will immediately defecate after eating, or it will follow that the baby will keep on eating and defecating. (Laugrand et al. 2019c, 46)

When humans eat birds, they acquire their characteristics. Lolo Melanio noted that there are two types of talal birds. If the *taynan* (a kind of Pied Triller) type is fed to a baby, the child will grow up and be talkative, but if a baby eats the *omel* (another kind of Pied Triller), it will be mute (Laugrand et al. 2019c, 51).

Lola Apolonia, an elder from Sabkil, also made an analogical connection:

> I have an experience with the bird *jadjaran*. We had a garden before and when we started weeding and clearing the land, there was a bird who was tame and gentle. I wanted to catch the bird but when I got closer, it would fly away. The bird stayed there in our garden until we finished digging and preparing the land for planting. It even stayed there until we finished

planting the vegetables; it seemed as if it was watching us. When our vegetables grew, I noticed that our vegetables were very good, and the garden was fruitful. This bird was only gone when the typhoon came, and it died. I observed that when that bird died, our crops also died. Before it died, we would always see it every morning and afternoon in our garden. I saw that our crops were very good at that time when it was still alive. This bird was gentle. I wanted to catch it but when you got closer, it would move to the other side, as if it did not want to be caught. (Laugrand et al. 2019c, 55)

According to Lola Apolonia, this wagtail represented the vitality of her garden, which was fruitful until the bird died after a typhoon. Analogical thinking is widespread in Asia and combined with animism. Birds are seen as beings who possess their own agency.

In what follows, we will examine the role of birds in three domains: as predictors of the weather, typhoons, and death; as agents connected to the deceased; and as guides passing along messages.

Birds, Weather, and Typhoons

The Ibaloy of Upper Loacan acknowledge birds for their capacities to indicate the rhythm of the day and the seasons. Birds are vocal at certain times, as Lola Margarita noted in reference to the ot-ot (Zebra Dove):

There is a time. At ten o'clock in the morning, it will produce its sound. At four o'clock in the afternoon, it will again produce its sound. I heard it when I was in Nueva Vizcaya and that is what I observed about this bird. It says, "Ot ot ot ot ot ot!" (Laugrand et al. 2019c, 49)

The appearance of birds and their position in the sky are meant to predict the weather. One must be aware and carefully watch and listen for this.

Some Ibaloy statements evoke the traditions of Indigenous Australians, as described by Deborah Bird Rose (2009, 194), who writes about rainbirds: "They tell what is going to happen. People are quite explicit in saying that other creatures know things that we don't know because they inhabit regions that we do not inhabit." She also mentions the swift: when the wet season begins, it flies low, but when the wet season is over, it flies high. Both Australian Aborigines and Indigenous peoples of the Philippines refer to this knowledge as real culture. But perhaps there is more to it. Birds do not inhabit a visible territory; they come from elsewhere or from another temporality.

In the cordillera, Lola Augustina Etop observed, "We have the *kiling*, red in colour. If this kind of bird makes a sound, it means that it is the end of rainy season. We also have the *talal* birds. When these birds come out, it means that it is the start of the summer" (Laugrand et al. 2019b, 87).

Another key element is the movement of birds. Lolo Edward explained how elders used birds to count the months, the seasons, and the typhoons. An excellent example here is the jadjaran bird, which moves up and down when it travels from place to place:

> The Ibaloy word *jadjaran* means moving up and down ... but its other name is *sisiw* (a kind of wagtail). It comes out in June. In the past, the elders used the birds to know the cycle of the whole year because they kept on counting the birds. The people usually observed the birds that successively came out within a year, especially the birds that go together with the typhoons. (Laugrand et al. 2019c, 54)

Table 7.1 summarizes two examples of birds and their associated predictions.

Table 7.1 Two birds and their predictions		
Name of bird	*Movement*	*Prediction*
Jadjaran	Up and down	First typhoon of the season
Kiling	When it first appears	Summer season

Birds are described as seasonal animals. Lolo Edward commented on their capacity to predict the weather, particularly typhoons, through their successive appearances:

> A long time ago (when the elders would see a *jadjaran*) they would say, "Asus! There will be a *powek* (a typhoon), on the fifteenth or the twentieth of this month." That was the Elders' prediction. If the bird *alishog* came out, they would say, "There are the *alishog*." In September, they would say that there will be a typhoon ... The last typhoon of the year is predicted by the bird *kiling*. After the typhoon disappears, it means that there will be no other typhoon in the same place (Laugrand et al. 2019a, 74).

The appearance of certain birds informs the Ibaloy of the month in which a typhoon will arrive.

If a kiling is spotted, the next typhoon will be the last of the season. Birds indicate the end of the rainy season and the beginning of the next one, the rice-planting season. As Lolo Edward recalled,

> In November, the bird *kiling* would sound and the people would say, "Asus! There will be one more typhoon that will come." We can eat this bird. After this bird comes out, the bird called *tigwi* [the White-bellied Sea Eagle], which goes together with the *bokaw*, will be observed by the elders. It will keep on producing sounds above the sky during the planting of rice. "Tigwi! Tigwi!" When these birds fly around above the sky, it is the planting season of the *kintoman* rice. (Laugrand et al. 2019c, 54)

Lolo Nardo explained that certain birds followed each other, just as the months did:

> Those birds are what we call the seasonal birds. They appear at the beginning of September. The bird *jadjaran* appears in July. The next bird will be the *elshas* [a kind of Pied triller], it is like the *talal* [but smaller]. The bird *kiling* will appear in November when it is the strong typhoon, super typhoon. There is also what we call *ag-agojot;* we call it the *powek ni esib.* It [means that it] will always rain every day, and it is a sign indicating that it is the last typhoon of the season. Those birds will disappear in June and appear again in July or August because they are seasonal birds. (Laugrand et al. 2019a, 74)

Here, temporality is marked, notably in connection with the jadjaran bird. Time changes, as does the weather. According to the elders, typhoons are no longer restricted to a certain season:

> In today's situation, the weather has changed because the typhoon strikes our place at any time. It was very different in the past because if they (the bird) said that there will be a typhoon coming, it will become true. But today, it is different because if you watch the television, the typhoons just keep on coming in any month, which is not normal in our place. In the past, the typhoons would only start in August; then the elders would always check the weather ... In the past, people would always

observe the birds, unlike today; it is very different, and it was slowly being forgotten. In September, the bird *alishog* will come out. That is one of the birds that the people counted long ago, but it is not done in today's generation because the typhoons come anytime, in any month. (Laugrand et al. 2019c, 54)

Table 7.2 lists various birds that are linked to typhoons.[7] In some instances, a single bird species can be connected to more than one.

Table 7.2 Connections between birds and typhoons		
Typhoon	*Time*	*Latin name of the bird*
powek ni jadjaran	June-July	*Motacilla cinerea*
powek ni elshas	July-August	*Lalage nigra*
powek ni alishog	September	Unidentified
powek ni talal	September-October	*Lalage nigra*
powek ni tigwi	September-October	*Haliaeetus leucogaster*
powek ni omel	September-October	*Lalage nigra*
powek ni kiling	November	Unidentified
powek ni esib	December	*Anthus novaeseelandiae*

As Lolo Marcial and Lolo Edward pointed out, now that typhoons are given human names rather than those of birds, they have grown more destructive: "Now, we use the names of people in naming the typhoon, so the typhoons are strong, as if they are very angry" (Laugrand et al. 2020b, 120). This statement suggests that typhoons originate from an agency that is able to react emotionally or that they themselves possess an agency to which birds are attached. Connecting typhoons to humans instead of to birds results in a cosmological disorder, as if it withdraws the proper position of birds as announcers and agents of typhoons and relegates the categories of "humans" and "birds" to a place where they do not belong. Lolo Edward added that

the typhoons now are named using people's name. The people are the ones who name the typhoon now. Before, we only have a few typhoons like *powek ni esib, powek ni jadjaran, powek ni alishog* and *powek ni talal*.

Every time the birds would come out, the people knew that a typhoon would come and call them, *"Powek ni jadjaran."* If they see the bird *bokaw,* they will call it *powek ni tigwi.* In November, a strong typhoon which we call *powek ni kiling* would come and the people were afraid of it. Right now, we have so many religions created by different people, and we also have many soil erosions in the mountains, especially here in our place. That is what I observed and witnessed since I was young and until now that I am seventy-seven years old. (Laugrand et al. 2020b, 120)

Lola Tarcela agreed as well:

There were many casualties because the name of the typhoon is a name of a person. For me, it is not good to name the typhoon using the name of a person because it causes death. It is good if they will return the name of the birds as the name of typhoons because maybe, the typhoons will not be as destructive as what we experienced these recent years and there will be no casualties even though there will be landslides. (Laugrand et al. 2020b, 121)

The elders connected weather changes, the worsening typhoons, and soil erosion to the fact that typhoons now bore human names. According to Lola Alice, these new developments were linked to a cultural loss: "People are becoming worse, and they do not care about what they do. People do not believe in our beliefs, so we are experiencing disasters. It is like the Lord got angry with us, so he gave us disasters because we do not believe in our own culture and tradition" (Laugrand et al. 2020b, 121).

Birds and the Deceased

A few questions can be raised here: Do birds come from another world in time or space, allowing them to forecast the weather? Are they travelling and connected to the invisible world from which they bring signs and warnings? Like many other groups in Southeast Asia, the Ibaloy associate birds with the deceased and the spirits of ancestors.

Lolo Melanio told a story that stressed the capacity of two bird species – the jadjaran and the kiling – to predict the weather, comparing the strength of the typhoons to the way they danced the tayaw:

These two birds came to a place where there was a *keddot,* a ritual. The people said, "You let *jadjaran* dance the *tayaw.*" When the *jadjaran* danced, he enjoyed it very much and he kept on moving up and down so the people decided to let him dance longer. After the *jadjaran* danced, they let *kiling* be the next. "*Kiling* will dance next." When *kiling* danced, he was very fast, and all the things were thrown everywhere because he kicked them while dancing. The people immediately stopped him from dancing. The meaning of that story is about the typhoon. If we say typhoon *kiling,* it means that it is the twenty-four-hour-strong typhoon that is coming. The typhoon *jadjaran* is not that strong but it lasts longer than the *kiling.* That was the meaning of the dances of the *jadjaran* and the *kiling.* The *jadjaran* enjoyed his dance; that is why it took him to dance longer while *kiling* stopped dancing immediately because he was stopped by the people. We can eat both of these birds. (Laugrand et al. 2019c, 55)

The pace and vigour of the dance thus correlate with those of the typhoon. The birds' dancing skills are connected to the destructive power of the storm. The story also suggests the power of words.

Interestingly, the tayaw is one of the moments in which the living and the dead mix, as the dancers are said to be carrying the deceased on their shoulders and dancing for them. It is performed during several rituals involving the dead, such as in the *kail,* the exhumation of human remains, or *batbat,* a feast for the dead (see Laugrand et al. 2020a). Surrounded by a crowd of family members, neighbours, and friends, a couple follows three musicians bearing small gongs, who move in single file. All five dance in a circle, accompanied by rhythmic beats from two drummers who sit close by. After two turns, the spectators shout the *owag:* "Ooooway! Ooooway! Wooh! Wooh!" Afterward, the dancers stop to drink the rice wine offered by the mambonong. Each dancer represents a *kedaring,* a deceased relative. Men drape a blanket loosely over their shoulders, and women roll one around themselves. The men imitate a flying and gliding eagle. With arms outstretched, they open their hands and spread their fingers to draw in and gather blessings and luck from the kedaring, as well as the kabunian, the Ibaloy gods. Drinking the rice wine allows the dancers to imbibe the gift of luck given by the kedaring. The dance aims to bless the living family for which the ritual is performed and to give them luck and a long life.

The tayaw can also be done during festivities such as weddings, anniversaries, and birthdays. In any case, if the drums are played, words must be uttered, asking the kedaring to come and join the humans in the feast. The kedaring, who are believed to hear the music, would make people sick if they were not invited to dance.

According to Jazil Tamang, an Ibaloy-speaker of Tocmo, if the bird *doriyan* calls "Toooooreeet" at night, it warns that a ghost is nearby. If it sounds "Kiw! Kiw! Kiw!" (if male) or "At! At! At! At!" (if female) early in the morning, it has something to tell you. Lolo Edward added that the *bowet* related to the deceased through its colour: "We have a belief that if the *bowet* enters our house with a *dabang* [bicolour] colour, it is the same as the blanket of a deceased person, which is the *banshala* [flag]. This is what I heard from the Elders. The colour of the *bowet* is compared to the blankets of the deceased" (Laugrand et al. 2019a, 117).[8]

The ngoweg might also be related to the deceased, as suggested in a story told by Lolo Melanio:

> If you will see the eggs of this bird on the land, you are lucky because it predicts goodness. You collect the eggs and perform the ritual *sangbo* (to accept the blessing) because it means good life and good health. There was a story before about someone from Daclan who married a resident living in Bakong. He died in that place and people decided to inform the family in Daclan, so they walked. There were groups of people who walked. The first group performed the *sangbo* ritual when they saw a *tilay* (monitor lizard) on their way. They passed by the barrio of Apalan, Loacan, and they roasted the *tilay*. The second group of people performed the ritual *sangbo* when they saw the eggs of the *ngoweg* bird in the barrio (village) of Doting, Loacan. They gathered the eggs, and after performing the ritual, they became rich. That is the story about the eggs of the bird *ngoweg*. This bird has small eggs. Some people perform the *sangbo* regarding the eggs and they became rich. These people came from Daclan, and they were lucky. The eggs of this bird are like the eggs of the bird *pugo* (barred buttonquail). (Laugrand et al. 2019c, 45–46)

The eggs embody the luck that one can receive from the deceased. Those who performed the sangbo ritual were meant to accept the blessing and become rich.

Similarly, the bird *kodibanga* is related to death. If a group of kodibanga is spotted and enters a house, it means luck will be bestowed upon the owners of the house. The latter should perform the ritual sangbo to thank the dead, who are responsible for this gift. Lolo Edward noted,

> If you perform the ritual *sangbo* because of this bird, the elders will say a *madmad* [ritual way of addressing the dead] like, "It is good. You will get rich because you will sell something to others," if your business is selling products. This bird stays in the trees. If it sounds, it goes like this: "Yeet! Yeet!" This bird has different colours like there is coloured *dabang*. If they fly in a group and enter your house, you may perform the ritual *sangbo*. (Laugrand et al. 2019c, 53)

Seeing certain birds in certain places or finding their eggs can bring luck, if the humans perform the right ritual to accept the gift from the deceased. Thus, the dead communicate with the living through birds, as Lolo Edward pointed out in connection with the *manok,* the rooster: "It is not only during morning and lunchtime that a rooster will crow. It can also crow in the afternoon, but it means that it is calling the soul of a living person [which can wander around]" (Laugrand et al. 2019c, 48).

Yet, most birds can figure as omens, both good and bad; they warn humans about a potential danger. Lolo Edward remembered being warned and guided by a bird. He referred to this as *palti-ing,* a bird's prophecy:

> If you have belief, it will happen. One belief about birds is that if you are going to one place and a bird crosses your path, you must go back because it is a sign that something bad will happen to you. You need to say a *madmad* if you see a bird flying across your path or flying in the direction of the place where you came from. But if the bird is following your path and someone says it is okay, it will be good. I experienced this when we went to Isabela. We were on our way when a bird called *martines* met us. The bird was flying to the place where we came from. We did not have any idea that it was a sign for us to go back. Instead of going back, we continued our trip, going to Didipio, Isabela. When we arrived at that place, my younger brother, Buligon, got sick, so we went back home immediately.
>
> There was a time that I went to Bitnong. In the past, there were no houses along the way because it was a forest. I didn't know the way to

Bitnong because there were lots of junctions and crossings. Suddenly, I saw a bird called *talal* singing, and it was following my way together with other birds. I uttered a *madmad:* "Please guide my way to where is the way." After that, the bird suddenly followed the road. The bird flew up in the direction of the road, so I followed it. On my way, I saw another bird called *tudki* in the *sapsap,* the runo reed grass, saying, "Kew! Kew! Kew!" I thought of going in the direction where I heard the sound. When I stepped on top of a rock, I saw the house where I needed to go. That is why I learned that birds could give us signs, but you must know how to follow these signs. (Laugrand et al. 2019b, 37–38)

If a bird crosses one's path or flies in the opposite direction, it is a bad omen, but if it goes in the same direction it is believed to be guiding you. Hence, birds tell humans if they are going in the right direction and warn them of the danger of continuing in the wrong way. Moss (1920, 351) also reported this belief. According to Lolo Edward, these interactions with birds were compatible with Christianity. In this context, birds were mediators to communicate with God:

It is the same with the birds that give signs and are *ipajos,* omen in the sense that they let you feel or see what will happen. You are going to ask from God above the guidance. You will say, "My Lord in heaven, take care of us. Show us the way from the east, west, north and south direction. This is my first time in this place so please show us the way through your creations like the birds or any animals." Those were the stories about birds and snakes, and why they are used as signs and symbols to predict things or incidents. (Laugrand et al. 2019b, 38)

Lolo Nardo also added a story about the red *pitpit:* "If it crosses our way, it is telling us that something bad will happen. We need to go back from where we came from if a bird crosses our way twice because we are going to meet an accident if we continue" (Laugrand et al. 2019b, 66). Lola Rosita indicated that if a bird flew across one's path, it was called *bakwad:* "You must not continue your journey. Return and take a bath. Then, you may continue your journey the next day" (Laugrand et al. 2019b, 109).

Lola Margarita stated the importance of following a bird's signs and the dangers of ignoring them:

These topics about *bakwad* are true because my younger sibling experienced this. The sibling of my sister's husband died, and they buried her yesterday. In the morning, my sister and her husband went out to repair the television. They went out but they just walked for a few metres before their child saw a big bird cross their path. Their child said, "Hey, Mommy! There is the big bird. I saw it and it has an unusual colour." They took it for granted and continued their way; they did not return home. When they were near the riprap of the river, the car they used fell down the river. We were glad that they were okay because they only had a few injuries. My sister's husband got dizzy for some time because he was a family member of the deceased. And the day they travelled was the *debben,* the day just after the burial. It was a few days before he felt better because he was the one who got injured. The television that they were about to bring to the repair shop was damaged. That is why it is not good to travel during the day of *debben* even though the place is far from yours, if it is your relative or family member who was buried. We must not go out during the day of *debben.* (Laugrand et al. 2019a, 80)

In this story, it was as if the bird were reminding the family to respect social rules. Lolo Marcial Monang added another example of a death prediction, this time in connection with the bokaw, the hawk:

It is the bird that produces a sound like this: "Towik! Towik!" It also gives a prediction. It can predict that someone is going to die, or someone has died in that place. If the *bokaw* is flying around above, you will know that someone died at the same place where the bird is flying around. It can predict that there will be an accident, or someone will die in the area where the bird is flying around or near our place. (Laugrand et al. 2019b, 136)

The belief that birds can foresee and announce events is common to many Southeast Asian groups. The Blaan and Alangan Mangyan know of a bird, called *lmugan* and *kuykuruan,* which indicates through the rhythm of its chant whether continuing on a journey is safe or if one must wait for a while before going.

The musical sound, be it from a gong or the vocalization of a bird, seems to be a powerful means to communicate with the deceased. The tone and pace of the bird's call, and even the time at which it is heard, thus inform humans of occurrences.

Birds as Predictive Agents and Guides

The movements of birds can provide a lot of information to the Ibaloy. Their position in the air, the direction of their flight, and the time when they appear guide the living or warn them of danger. These signs should not be ignored, as they can predict serious accidents and even death. Table 7.3 shows some examples mentioned by the elders.

Table 7.3 Predictive signs of birds			
Bird	*Sound*	*Movement/direction*	*Prediction*
Jadjaran	Unrecorded	Moving up and down	First typhoon of the season
Kiling	Unrecorded	Appearing	Summer season
Pitpit	Unrecorded	Crossing your path	Danger; cancel or postpone the journey
Martinez	Unrecorded	Going in the opposite direction	Danger; retrace your steps and take a bath
Talal, tudki, pamoltongan	Unrecorded	Flying in the same direction	The bird is guiding you
Doriyan	Kiw! Kiw!	Flying in the same direction	The bird is guiding you
Doriyan	Tooooореeet	Appearing at night	There is a ghost
Bokaw	Towik! Towik! Kowiw! Kowiw!	Flying above; appearing in groups in daytime; following humans	A relative will die in three days
Tigwi	Tigwi! Tigwi!	Flying above	The place where someone will die
Dabaan	Kowik! Kowik!	Flying above	Good or bad premonition
Akop	Koop! Koop!	Getting near the house or heard in the daytime	Someone will die after three days
Ot-ot	Ot o tot ot ot!	Entering the house	Brings luck if the sangbo is performed
Kosding	Kosding! Kosding!	Flying in a group	Brings luck if the sangbo is performed

Lolo Edward gave an account in which the bokaw (hawk) warned of deadly danger:

> If *bokaw* are flying above [in] the sky and are numerous in the daytime; then it means that there will be an incident at night. I experienced it myself because it happened when I was in Kalinga, particularly in Law-angan. My cousin looked up above the sky and he asked why there were *bokaw* flying in the sky. At night, some unknown men came and shot the houses on top of the mountains. Even the companions of my cousin were hit because the unknown men used big guns pointing at the houses. I forgot the date when it happened, but I remember that the birds were making a sound above the sky. My nephew named Juanito noticed the birds at that time, and he was asking me what the premonition about the birds was. Then, at night, there were New People's Army came and shot at the houses on top of the mountain, so the people living in that area died. The bird *bokaw* can show us a premonition. In the past, when the *bokaw* were flying above the sky producing sound "Kowiw! Kowiw!" the people would sit down for a while under the trees and smoke because there might be an incident or accident that would happen along the way. They would say, "If there is any sign, show us so that we will know if we will come back." (Laugrand et al. 2019c, 47)

Lolo Nardo added that there are two kinds of bokaw: the tigwi and the *dabaan* (a kind of hawk), both of which have red on their back. When the dabaan is seen, it is a sign that someone is near death. Usually after three days, "we will hear that someone has died" (Laugrand et al. 2019c, 47). According to Lolo Melanio, the tone of the bird's call conveys different messages:

> It can give a negative premonition or prediction, but it can also be used positively. If the *bokaw* keeps on shrieking in a high pitch but a loud manner, it means that a female person is nearly dying. If the bird keeps on screeching at a low pitch and in a deep tone but a loud manner, it means that a man is nearly dying. There was another sign given to us by this *bokaw* bird ... If you go to the river and you notice that the bird *bokaw* keeps on shrieking above the sky, you will know that there is many edible fish that you can catch in the water. That is a story about *bokaw* that I heard from the elders. (Laugrand et al. 2019c, 47)

Lola Margarita emphasized that the bokaw followed humans to tell them about a dying relative:

> Even if we are in a distant place, the bird *bokaw* can tell us something. They can follow us anywhere we are, especially if we have a relative who is nearly dying. After I heard the shriek of the *bokaw* within three days, I heard that someone died: "Your relative died." The people will notify us even if we are far from each other. That is a story about this *bokaw* when it shrieks. After three days, you will hear that someone has died. (Laugrand et al. 2019c, 47)

The akop, the owl, can also predict death, though it is generally said to bring luck. Lolo Edward stated,

> The *akop* bird tells us that one of our relatives is nearly dying. We can notice it especially if it keeps on saying, "Koop! Koop! Koop!" If it gets close to your house, it means that it is telling us something or it is a sign of someone who is nearly dying. After three days, we can hear that someone died or one of our relatives died. If you go out to another place to sell something, you may say, "We will collect using our hands the good luck and the wealth." After that, you will observe that you will have additional income. If you are selling something, you will be lucky because you will sell more than what you usually sell. (Laugrand et al. 2019c, 49)

Lolo Edward explained that signs also appear when a night bird is heard during the day:

> If you hear the sound of *akop* during the daytime, you will know and expect that there is someone who is nearly dying. That is what the *akop* can tell us. In Labilab, when some people were cutting a tree for the coffin of Ateban, there was an *akop* that produced sound. After a few days, we heard that someone had died. (Laugrand et al. 2019c, 50)

Lola Alice gave the following account:

> The story of *baktad* is true and it is not good because there was an incident that happened during the wedding of the child of Lido at Nueva Vizcaya. When we were on our way going to the church, a blackbird flew across

our way. The people insisted that we would go to the church, so we went there. What I observed was that the couple got married at that time, but their marriage did not last long as they separated. They even had two children. The bird I mentioned was black with a bigger size than usual. (Laugrand et al. 2019a, 80)

Conversely, diurnal birds that were seen or heard at night were also portentous. According to Lolo Melanio, if the *doriyan* bird "sounds in the evening while you are walking, it means that it is a ghost. That is one of their signs." Its call is "'Tooooreeet.' It is like there is an echo of the sound. 'Teeeerrrrtttt.' Then you will know that there is a ghost as long as that is the sound at night." Lolo Edward added that "the bird is poisonous because it goes together with the ghost. This bird is loved by the ghost" (Laugrand et al. 2019c, 61).

If birds were sent by the deceased, they could bring luck, but only if the recipients performed the sangbo, a ritual to accept the gift. Lola Margarita remarked that "if the *ot-ot* enters your house, you can perform the *sangbo* ritual because they are wild ones. They don't usually come closer to people. When it enters the house, you can perform the ritual *sangbo* because it can give luck" (Laugrand et al. 2019c, 49).

Lolo Edward also made the connection between birds, luck, and the sangbo:

Many kosding birds fly and perch on the trees, especially pine trees. Others call this bird the *bosbosjag.* These birds fly in groups. I saw them in the part of Na-jen, Philex, and I witnessed that people there performed a ritual because of these birds. The elders would say their prediction during the ritual: "It will follow these birds that they fly as a group." They would predict something positive about it and some people who worked in the mines became rich. Bador and Dignay [two elders] performed the ritual *sangbo* because of these birds. If these *kosding* birds enter your house, the elders would say, "Oh, you perform the ritual *sangbo.*" "Kosding! Kosding!" is the sound of this bird; that is why it is called *kosding.* (Laugrand et al. 2019c, 52)

The akop (owl) could also bring luck, but failing to respond with the appropriate ritual had consequences, as Lolo Edward explained:

Yes (the *akop* bird tells us bad and good omens). It is the same that if an *akop* enters your house, then it will defecate, and you must perform the ritual *sangbo*. In the past, the people performed rituals wherein they perform the *sangbo* ritual. Like the story of the elder sister of Benito, the *akop* entered her house and defecated on the cooked rice placed on the floor. The family did not perform any simple ritual like *peltik* or *madmad*. They immediately threw it outside. If they had performed the *peltik,* their family might be rich right now. They had luck but they did not strictly follow the right process; they did not fix it properly. They had received some amount of money but not for a long period because their luck in gardening immediately disappeared. The elders say that the family did not perform the *ngilin* properly. If you are working and you have luck in the garden, you must perform a ritual so that you will be given luck by your own ancestors' spirits. You must do the ritual and follow the procedures. (Laugrand et al. 2019c, 49–50)

Lolo Edward connected birds with luck and wealth, which the spirits of the ancestors convey when they are pleased, but only if the living share their wealth and perform the right rituals.

Certain birds also act as guides, and one should ask them the way and follow them if lost. According to Lolo Edward,

There are other predictions given by birds. I experienced it when I went to Isabela. I was confused about which path I should follow, so I said, "Oh God, can you show me a sign for me to follow the right path?" After that, the bird *doriyan* came and landed on a tree near me. The bird was moving its wings and producing its sound. Then, I followed the path where the bird was facing.

There is another incident again in Nueva Vizcaya when I went there. I didn't know which way I should follow. Then, suddenly, the bird *talal* came flying, so I said, "Show me the right way so that I will follow." The bird followed a road, so I followed the direction of the bird. When I came up, the bird *doriyan* appeared, moving by flying its wings. I came closer and I saw downstream that there was a house, so I said, "Ah, it is here where I will go." (Laugrand et al. 2019a, 74)

Lolo Edward mentioned the pitpit, known as the leader of the birds:

We also call it *pitpit*. For us Ibaloy, we have different terms for one bird. If this bird crosses your way, it means that you are affected by the *bakwad or baktad*. This bird has a signal because if this bird enters your house, the elders will say that it is trying to tell you something. People would say, "Maybe this bird is telling us that something bad will happen." In the mountains, they said that this bird is the leader of other birds. If this bird sees us coming, it will say, "Pit! Pit! Pit!" Then all the other birds will fly away; that is why they call this bird the captain or the leader. If this bird produces its sound repeatedly, all the other birds will fly away. They always follow the bird *pitpit*. (Laugrand et al. 2019c, 58)

This bird cannot be eaten. It is a sign that one must turn around and go back to where they came from. If it enters your house, the elders say that something bad will happen, so they advise you to consult a *mansi-bok* (a person who has the gift to read and interpret signs).

Lolo Edward added more detail about the pitpit, which is also known as the *tadistis:*

If this bird *tadistis* died inside the house, the family must perform the *ngilin,* but that was a long time ago. Maybe, if that happens today, the young men or the adult will just say that it is normal. Before, the people performed the *ngilin*. If the bird crosses your path while walking or while on your journey, you must go back or you have to stay for a while and say a *madmad* before leaving because something bad will happen. But it is better to go back and continue your journey tomorrow. That is what they used to say about a bad sign with regards to the *pitpit* bird. (Laugrand et al. 2019c, 58)

All these statements suggest the connection of birds with the deceased and the afterlife. Among the Ibaloy, it is assumed that the dead play an important role for the living, exchanging luck and blessing for offerings, as well as respect and good care of their remains. In this, birds act as their messengers, bringing luck from them or warning people about danger. Not listening to the birds – to the kedaring – results in a range of negative consequences, including disasters.

Conclusion

Ibaloy knowledge about birds has eroded with time. Lolo Nardo stated, "There are songs, but they are forgotten. Maybe if it had been taught in school, it could be sung right now." He underlined the good feelings that birdsongs inspired:

> These birds, especially the ones living in the forest, are very good for us. They are good especially when they sing, and when you hear them while walking alone and sad, you will feel better, and your mood will be lifted. Our government right now is trying to protect our nature and the animals living in the forest, so they always remind us that we must not kill and catch those animals like the birds and any other living creatures. Birds have a very good melody when they sing that can lift our sad feeling. (Laugrand et al. 2019c, 63)

Birds can evoke strong emotions in humans and can diminish sadness. In this, Ibaloy beliefs regarding birds evoke those of the Kumaonis of the Himalayas, especially regarding the cuckoo, the crow, and the dove, as discussed by John Leavitt in Chapter 6 of this book.

Lola Julie added that birds were very helpful and pressed for their conservation:

> These birds can help us, people, especially in clearing the *bigis* (a kind of pest) that destroy our plants and crops. Other birds can also remove the lice of other animals such as the cow and carabao. The birds are very friendly because they help us. In the past, people always say that we must not burn the mountains so that the birds and other animals will not die. We must not hunt birds using our slingshot so that they will not all disappear or be gone. (Laugrand et al. 2019c, 63)

Thus, birds are prayed to for aid. In addition to announcing future events, they attack the insect pests that feed on crops, but the Ibaloy do not venerate them, unlike in Japan, as described by Atsushi Nobayashi in Chapter 9 of this book.

Birds are marked by their orientation in space (directions, position) and the times when they appear. If they are heard at the wrong time, someone will die soon. If they are seen in the wrong place, a gift of luck usually follows. Regardless of whether they foretell a good outcome or a bad one, the living must follow their advice and perform the right rituals. When birds lose their place, as when human names are given to typhoons, these disasters become more devastating. In Ibaloy cosmology, every being occupies its own place and is embedded in relationships with other beings. This entanglement persists as long as each occupies the right place: birds as messengers and bringers of seasons, the weather, and typhoons, and humans as believers who follow taboos and perform rituals of exchange conducted for the deceased, who give blessings, luck, and wellness. When they lose their place, or when people stop believing and practising rituals, disasters ensue.

In *Habiter en oiseau,* Vinciane Despret (2019) brilliantly connects birds to space, suggesting that, unlike humans, they do not live in territories with clear boundaries. Instead, they are more likely to share a space with others and to occupy it with their songs. The Ibaloy connect birds to temporality. Time and space are closely linked, yet the Ibaloy perceive many birds as seasonal animals, coming in and out, coming from afar and moving from an invisible space to a place inhabited by humans. To be informed about the invisible world, one must carefully observe birds, their movements, their directions, and their appearance in time, and must listen to their sounds.

Birds are the great masters of rhythm, and this also applies to birds among the Blaan and the Alangan Mangyan (see Laugrand, Laugrand, and Tremblay 2018b). Following Marcel Mauss's (1906) majestic essay on seasonal variations among the Inuit, we argue that birds carry the social rhythms of the Ibaloy, notably the high and low moments characterized by vitality and death; they convey the coming of the seasons. They signal the right time to plant rice or when to prepare for the destruction of crops. A succession of phenomena follows from bird behaviour and sound. Bird knowledge is undoubtedly woven into Ibaloy culture. In many places in Southeast Asia, this capacity of birds is marked. They are the masters of time. Gregory Forth (2007, 506) discusses how the story of the pigeon and the friarbird articulates with eastern Indonesian mythology concerning the origin of temporal processes. Steven Feld and Alexandrine Boudreault-Fournier (2019, 197) compare birds to clocks, providing the pace of the daily space-time in Papua New Guinea. Everywhere, birds are perceived as able to indicate hours and seasons. Feld (1982) also connects birds to spiritual entities, to beings who should be listened to on an everyday basis. The Ibaloy do observe and listen to birds when they walk in the forest, but they have no interest in classifying them as Western societies do. They no longer hunt them for food but do not turn them into symbols either, except for the eagle that they imitate in their dances. Though there is no standardized system, such as that of the Kantu in Indonesia, where several forest birds have foreknowledge of human events (see Dove 1993), Ibaloy birds provide important messages.

Among the Ibaloy, beliefs about birds are not considered superstitions; they are truth. Birds are signs and beings that have the capacity to anticipate coming events; they cannot be fooled and must be respected. Listening to them provides favourable conditions for a good life, for individuals, and for the community. In a living exchange with the deceased, they remain interconnected, thanks to an entangled chain of relationships. In Ibaloy cosmology, every agent must occupy its proper place, aware that everything is linked in time and space.

ACKNOWLEDGMENTS

We thank the Upper Loacan elders as well as Lolo Melanio Billit and Lolo Edward Bante. We also thank the Fonds National de la Recherche Scientifique (FNRS, grant number F. 6002.17), the Talos-ARC (UCL), as well as the Fonds pour la recherche scientifique en sciences humaines (FRESH-FNRS) and the Fonds de recherche du Québec – Société et culture (FRQSC) for awarding a doctoral scholarship, which paid for part of Antoine Laugrand's fieldwork. Additional support was provided by a SHRCC project directed by Scott Simon. Warm thanks to Scott Simon and to our colleagues at the LAAP, UCLouvain (Belgium).

NOTES

1 Robert Kennedy et al. (2000) provide many illustrations of birds from the Philippines. We used this book extensively with the elders. For additional information on birds in this country, see Nicole Revel (1992), who did fieldwork in Palawan. Except for her exemplary scholarship, few works have examined Philippine birds from an anthropological perspective. See also our own work on bird knowledge among the Alangan Mangyan of Mindoro and the Blaan of Mindanao (Laugrand, Laugrand, and Tremblay 2018a, 2018b). See also J.C.T. Gonzalez (2011).
2 Charles Moss (1920, 229) observed that already in the early 1920s, the Ibaloy no longer used bows and arrows.
3 In the Ibaloy language, *lolo* and *lola* are gender terms used to address male and female elders respectively.
4 Moss (1920, 229) also describes various traps: "*apad,* a large trap on the ground for catching wild chickens; *solo,* a small trap of the same kind; *katig,* a trap for small birds attached to post; *bagodo,* a similar trap attached to the branches of a tree."
5 The *sabag,* a wild chicken, can also be raised as a pet, but this rarely occurs.
6 When they are not working in their terraces or in the city, the Ibaloy enjoy walking in the mountains *(shontog)* to gather wild mushrooms, berries, and other fruits.
7 In his work, Moss (1920, 279) does not refer to wild birds predicting typhoons but to the chicken, when it catches lice under the house.
8 Bokod – a myth recorded by Alfonso Claerhoudt (1930) – explains why the crow has black feathers and became jealous of all the other birds since they were beautifully feathered.

WORKS CITED

Birkhead, Tim. 2008. *The Wisdom of Birds: An Illustrated History of Ornithology.* London: Bloomsbury.

–. 2012. *Bird Sense: What Is It Like to Be a Bird?* New York: Walker.

Bulmer, Ralph. 1967. "Why Is the Cassowary Not a Bird? A Problem of Zoological Taxonomy among the Karam of the New Guinea Highlands." *Man* 2, 1: 5–25.

Cauquelin, Josiane. 2006. "Paroles d'oiseaux à Puyuma (Taiwan)." In *Les Messagers divins: Aspects esthétiques et symboliques des oiseaux en Asie du Sud-Est,* ed. Pierre Le Roux and Bernard Sellato, 191–209. Paris: Éditions connaissances et savoirs.

Claerhoudt, Alfonso. 1930. "Why the Crow Has Black Feathers: An Ibaloi Tale." *Primitive Man* 3, 3–4: 75–77.

Davy, Marie-Madeleine. 1993. *L'oiseau et sa symbolique.* Paris: Albin Michel.

Despret, Vinciane. 2019. *Habiter en oiseau.* Paris: Actes Sud.

Dove, Michael R. 1993. "Uncertainty, Humility, and Adaptation to the Tropical Forest: The Agricultural Augury of 'the Kantu.'" *Ethnology* 32, 2: 145–67.

Feld, Steven. 1982. *Sound and Sentiment: Birds, Weeping, Poetics and Song in Kaluli Expression.* Philadelphia: University of Pennsylvania Press.

Feld, Steven, and Alexandrine Boudreault-Fournier. 2019. "Relations sonores: Entretien avec Steven Feld." *Anthropologie et Sociétés* 43, 1: 195–210.

Forth, Gregory. 1996. "Nage Birds: Issues in Ethnoornithological Classification." *Anthropos* 91: 89–109.

–. 2004. *Nage Birds: Classification and Symbolism among the Eastern Indonesian Peoples.* London: Routledge.

–. 2006a. "Sounds, Spirits, Symbols and Signs: Birds in Nage Cosmology." In *Les Messagers divins: Aspects esthétiques et symboliques des oiseaux en Asie du Sud-Est,* ed. Pierre Le Roux and Bernard Sellato, 579–614. Paris: Éditions connaissances et savoirs.

–. 2006b. "Words for 'Bird' in Eastern Indonesia." *Journal of Ethnobiology* 26: 177–207.

–. 2007. "Pigeon and Friarbird Revisited: A Further Analysis of an Eastern Indonesian Mythicoornithological Contrast." *Anthropos* 102: 495–513.

–. 2008. "Friarbird on Roti." *Anthropos* 103: 541–45.

–. 2009a. "Symbolic Birds and Ironic Bats: Varieties of Classification in Nage Folk Ornithology." *Ethnology* 48, 2: 139–59.

–. 2009b. "Transformation and Replacement: A Comparison of Some Indonesian Bird Myths." In *Pika-Pika: The Flashing Firefly: Essays to Honour the Life of Pauline Hetland Walker (1938–2005),* ed. Anthony R. Walker and Pauline H. Walker, 385–402. New Delhi: Hindustan.

–. 2010. "What's in a Bird's Name: Relationships among Ethno-Ornithological Terms in Nage and Other Malayo-Polynesian Languages." In *Ethno-Ornithology: Birds, Indigenous Peoples, Culture and Society,* ed. Sonia Tidemann and Andrew Gosler, 223–37. London: Earthscan.

Gonzalez, J.C.T. 2011. "Enumerating the Ethno-Ornithological Importance of Philippine Hornbills." *Raffles Bulletin of Zoology* 24: 149–61.

Kennedy, Robert, Pedro C. Gonzales, Edward Dickinson, Hector C. Miranda Jr., and Timothy H. Fisher. 2000. *A Guide to the Birds of the Philippines.* London: Oxford University Press.

Laugrand, Frédéric, Antoine Laugrand, Gliseria Magapin, and Jazil Tamang. 2019a. *Connecting Life and Death: Rituals, Prohibitions and Spirits. Ibaloy Perspectives (Itogon, Philippines).* Verbatim 2. Louvain-la-Neuve: Presses universitaires de Louvain.

–. 2019b. *Life Stories of the Ibaloy from Upper Loacan, Itogon (Philippines).* Verbatim 1. Louvain-la-Neuve: Presses universitaires de Louvain.

–. 2019c. *Looking for Signs: Animals, Spirits and Death Rituals. Ibaloy Perspectives (Itogon, Philippines).* Verbatim 3. Louvain-la-Neuve: Presses universitaires de Louvain.

–. 2020a. "Exchanges with the Dead: Exhuming Human Remains among the Ibaloy of Upper Loacan (Philippines)." *Bijdragen tot de taal-, land- en volkenkunde / Journal of the Humanities and Social Sciences of Southeast Asia* 176, 4: 475–503.

–. 2020b. *Mapping the Land of Upper Loacan: Trees, Plants and Incidents (Itogon, Philippines).* Verbatim 4. Louvain-la-Neuve: Presses universitaires de Louvain.

Laugrand, Frédéric, Antoine Laugrand, and Guy Tremblay. 2018a. "Chants d'oiseaux, cris de cochons et bruits des petites bestioles: Les sons de la divination chez les Alangan de Mindoro (Philippines)." *Anthropologica* 60, 1: 278–92.

–. 2018b. "Lorsque les oiseaux donnent le rythme: Chants et présages chez les Blaans de Mindanao (Philippines)." *Anthropologie et Sociétés* 42, 2–3: 171–98.

Le Roux, Pierre. 2006. "La femme et l'oiseau. Approche esthétique et symbolique des oiseaux en Asie du Sud-Est." In *Les Messagers divins: Aspects esthétiques et symboliques des oiseaux en Asie du Sud-Est*, ed. Pierre Le Roux and Bernard Sellato, 25–117. Paris: Éditions connaissances et savoirs.

Le Roux, Pierre, and Bernard Sellato, eds. 2006. *Les Messagers divins: Aspects esthétiques et symboliques des oiseaux en Asie du Sud-Est.* Paris: Éditions connaissances et savoirs.

Mauss, Marcel, with H. Beuchat. 1906. "Essai sur les variations saisonnières des sociétés eskimos: Essai de morphologie sociale." *L'Année sociologique* 9: 39–132.

Metcalf, Peter. 1976. "Birds and Deities in Borneo." *Bijdragen tot de Taal-, Land- en Volken-kunde / Journal of the Humanities and Social Sciences of Southeast Asia* 132, 1: 96–123.

Moss, Charles R. 1920. "Nabaloi Law and Ritual." *University of California Publications in American Archaeology and Ethnology* 15, 3: 207–342.

Revel, Nicole. 1992. *Fleurs de paroles: Histoire naturelle de Palawan.* Vol. 3. Paris: Peeters.

Rose, Deborah Bird. 2009. *Oiseaux de pluie.* Marseille: Wildproject.

Rudge, Alice. 2019. "The Sounds of People and Birds: Music, Memory and Longing among the Batek of Peninsular Malaysia." *Hunter Gatherer Research* 4, 1: 3–23.

Simon, Scott. 2015. "Émissaires des ancêtres: Les oiseaux dans la vie et la cosmologie des Sadyaq de Taiwan." *Anthropologie et Sociétés* 39, 1–2: 179–99.

Tidemann, Sonia, and Andrew Gosler, eds. 2010. *Ethno-Ornithology: Birds, Indigenous Peoples, Culture and Society.* London: Earthscan.

8

Birds as Metaphors and More in a Changing Indonesian Community
Gregory Forth

IN THE ASIA-PACIFIC region, as in other parts of the world, people identify birds with spiritual beings. A well-known example from the Western canon is Aristophanes's play *The Birds*. A major premise of the play is an idea announced by the main human character Pisthetaerus, that the birds were the original gods and that, with his assistance, they can regain their position and replace the (very human) gods of Olympus. Pisthetaerus himself eventually becomes the king of the gods. But significantly, in order to do so, and in accordance with his plan, he must himself become a bird.

Throughout the play, the birds reveal an apparent equality. Before Pisthetaerus's plan can be put into effect, the king of the birds, the hoopoe *(Upupa epops),* must gain the approval of all the other birds, which is to say, birds of all kinds. A general equality is also revealed between humans, birds, and the Olympian gods. For one thing, the hoopoe king is a metaphorphosis of a human king. But more than this, the two main human characters – Pisthetaerus and his companion, another Athenian – transform into birds, after which they and all the other birds become gods.

In this overall parity between the three comprehensive categories of beings, anthropologists might glimpse an example of the evidently universal ontological "trichotomy" of humans, animals, and spirits identified by Geoffrey Lloyd (2011) as components of religious or symbolic cosmologies around the world. Moreover, in the processual equivalences implicit in Aristophanes's plot, a more specific comparison might be found in a recent approach to ontology, in which several authors have recently redeployed

E.B. Tylor's famous term to label one ontological tendency as "animism." On the other hand, this animism is conceived in opposition to naturalism (see Descola 2013), a perspective on the world that, somewhat ironically in the present example, is supposed to have got its start in ancient Greece. But whatever the parallels, *The Birds* is a comic play, and as such it need not entail cultural *beliefs* connecting spirits with birds or birds with humans, in the same way as cosmologies incorporating birds as supernatural entities or agents presumably do.

Issues in the Study of Nagé Bird Symbolism

Of course, representing birds as creatures identified with spiritual beings is hardly the only way in which they figure in what can broadly be called symbolic thought. The ethnographic subjects of this chapter, the Nagé of Indonesia – indigenous cultivators, stock raisers, and occasional hunters whose folk zoological knowledge and practice I have explored elsewhere – certainly connect particular birds with particular sorts of spirits. Yet they also employ birds in a large number of conventional metaphors. Found in all languages, conventional metaphors are metaphorical expressions of a more or less invariant form that appear not only in special performances (including literate works, in societies with writing) but equally, and indeed more often, in everyday speech. English-language examples would be describing something as a bird in the hand or someone as a silly goose or a hawk, or a person's appearance as owlish or speech as parroting. In literate cultures, and especially in poetry, new metaphors of the same form can be invented (as in the title of Harper Lee's novel *To Kill a Mockingbird*). But both these and more prosaic conventional metaphors contrast with conceptual metaphors – pervasive themes that find expression often in a number of conventional metaphors and sometimes in a large number and variety. One example is "human is animal" (Kövecses 2010, 152–54), which of course underlies the majority of conventional animal metaphors (though not quite all) and thus, more specifically, bird metaphors.

As I have shown elsewhere (Forth 2019), conventional metaphors differ in important ways from a use of "metaphor" (one might say a metaphorical use of the concept) that became popular in twentieth-century anthropology. Following the lead of Roman Jakobson, structuralist anthropologists began to apply metaphor to relations between entities involved in one of two major forms of magical practice (identified by James Frazer as homeopathic magic;

Jakobson and Halle 1956), and to the identity between human members of a totemic clan and their totem animal (Lévi-Strauss 1963). However, it is not difficult to see how such metaphorical relations involve belief – for example, how contagious magic entails a belief in, or an unquestioned assumption of, some mysterious connection between a wax effigy, say, and the person it represents, and therefore the possibility of affecting the second by acting on the first.

In contrast, and as I've also shown, Nagé entertain no such assumption or belief when they employ metaphors describing a person as a bird (Forth 2019, 49–52). Accordingly, in what follows I employ "metaphor" exclusively to refer to usages where a stated identity between a human and an animal is recognizably figurative, or metaphorical in the sense used in ordinary English. Other representations, where the identity is not figurative, I call beliefs. Thus, the Nagé idea that owls or other birds of prey can embody malevolent spirits is a belief, whereas the Nagé metaphor describing humans as "chickens of god" is explicitly not. (This last usage will again become relevant later on.) "Belief" has been perennially problematic in anthropology at least since Rodney Needham (1972) raised questions about the essentially European concept more than fifty years ago. All I'll say for the moment is that I use the term to refer not only to deeply held convictions but also to any proposition that people generally accept as true (and thus non-figurative) or about which they do not usually entertain serious doubts.

In English, as I expect in most languages, the majority of animal metaphors employ mammals as their vehicles. But birds are likely to come a close second. For example, Robert Palmatier's (1995) dictionary of English animal metaphors lists 42 kinds of birds, and as it deals mainly in American metaphors, a number of further instances can be added from other parts of the anglophone world (Forth 2019, 367n3). The same pattern occurs among the Nagé. In fact, Nagé metaphors include a larger number of bird kinds than Palmatier records for English – 49 in all (Forth 2019) – and the total significantly exceeds the number of domestic and wild mammals they employ in conventional metaphors. At the same time, this apparent predominance of birds partly reflects the relatively small number of recognized mammal species on Flores Island, just fifteen in all. Also, Nagé metaphors employing birds, of which there are 178, are easily outdone by the 240 mammal metaphors. (The total of all Nagé animal metaphors is 566.)

My recent study of animal metaphors produced several conclusions that touch on issues relevant to the study of metaphor in general. Not just Nagé

Figure 8.1 Common Hill Mynah (top) and Black-naped
Oriole. The Nagé name for the oriole is oriole python. |
Artwork by Donna McKinnon

bird metaphors but also a large majority of their animal metaphors have
human beings as their referents, as I suspect do most animal metaphors in
other languages. Others then occur in the naming of other animals (such
as the eagle porcupine or the oriole python, see Figure 8.1), plants (such as
the dove coconut), times of the day and year, meteorological phenomena,
and as we shall see, certain spiritual beings. Nagé have their own term for
"metaphor" (that is, conventional metaphors), *pata péle* (covering [separat-
ing, screening, protecting] speech), and they recognize all propositions that
fall under this heading as figurative, or consciously symbolic. By the same
token, they are able, for example, to distinguish a metaphorical pig *(wawi
péle)* from a real pig *(wawi tebhe)* when using "pig" to refer to a human
being (specifically in this instance, when requesting a bride). Related to this,
Nagé do not understand a person who is described as a particular kind of
bird or as behaving like the bird, as actually being a bird or as sharing some
essential property of the bird (as, for example, might people in some totemic
societies whose totem is a bird). Nor do such metaphors require that birds,
or for that matter any animal, must be essentially similar or identical to

humans for the metaphor to work. In the same vein, Nagé recognize metaphors as epistemologically different from statements of belief that can link a particular bird with a spiritual being or a human witch.

At the same time, certain birds as it were do double duty by serving both as vehicles of conventional metaphors and as the objects of spiritual belief – specifically as natural creatures actually linked in some hidden or mysterious way to supernatural beings. Indeed, this is the case with most of the birds whose metaphorical use I examine below. To be clear, most Nagé metaphors employ animals that lack any specific spiritual significance, and where they are significant in this way, the metaphorical sense rarely has anything to do with their supernatural aspect. Otherwise stated, Nagé animal metaphors typically do not reflect spiritual beliefs concerning the same animals. All this, of course, is consistent with their understanding of conventional metaphors (pata péle) as figurative expressions and as thus distinct from spiritual beliefs. These points are most clearly illustrated by snakes. Nagé consider snakes more than other sorts of animals as manifestations of forest spirits (beings they call *nitu*) and as guises the spirits might temporarily assume. Yet not one of their twenty-two snake metaphors is motivated by this spiritual connection. By the same token, whereas among snakes, pythons are the most likely to manifest forest spirits, they provide the vehicle of just one of over twenty metaphors (a metaphor referring to a greedy person, by reference to the python's ability to swallow prey whole), the remainder then employing either "snake" *(nipa)* or other particular kinds of snakes.

In implicating beliefs about spiritual beings, the bird metaphors I discuss below are thus somewhat exceptional. Nagé bird metaphors incorporate a far larger number of bird kinds (forty-nine in all) than do snake metaphors (in which just five named kinds appear, in addition to nipa, the general word for "snake"). Nevertheless, one could argue that, more than other animals, birds challenge the contrast of "metaphor" and "belief," or between figurative metaphor and non-figurative forms of symbolic representation. And even though the challenge by no means nullifies these distinctions, they still require qualification especially in regard to potential ways in which people might interpret their own metaphors.

In Forth (2019, 325), I classified animal metaphors reflecting spiritual beliefs as members of a broader category of metaphors motivated by cultural factors, which included both utilitarian and symbolic values of the animals concerned. There were 110 of these, or just 19 percent of the total of 566 for all animal metaphors, so in the remaining 81 percent the motivation recognized by Nagé commentators comprised empirical – that is, morphological or behavioural attributes – of the zoological vehicle. As a subset of metaphors reflecting symbolic values, I further identified a category labelled "cosmological, mythical, magical significance," which largely included animals involved in Nagé spiritual belief. There were 15 metaphors of this sort, and 7 or nearly half concerned birds rather than mammals, other non-mammalian vertebrates, or invertebrates. Birds are also prominent in a distinct type of spiritual metaphor (which I therefore counted separately), where spiritual beings are named after animals. There are just 4 of these in the entire Nagé corpus, and birds appear in 3 of them. For example, *manu ke'o,* which translates literally as "speckled fowl (or chicken)," denotes a supernaturally powerful creature assuming the form of a large snake with a cock's head that Nagé understand as a particular manifestation of forest spirits. The only non-bird metaphor among the 4 is earth buffalo *(bhada tana),* which ambiguously refers to either the soul or the corpse of a recently buried person. The metaphor is interesting because it also reflects a Nagé spiritual belief – specifically that, two nights after a burial, witches (including the one responsible for the death) will transform the deceased, either the body or the soul, into a buffalo and then slaughter and devour it in a nocturnal feast (Forth 1998, 251–52).

The prominence of birds in metaphors that appear motivated by spiritual beliefs might suggest that, in contrast to all other sorts of animals, birds for Nagé are especially spiritual creatures. In a cross-cultural perspective, we know that in many places, including in the Western Christian tradition, birds are identified with the human soul or with spirits or spirit. Think, for example, of the Holy Spirit descending as a dove. These associations may derive from birds' power of flight and possibly also from the quality of their many and varied cries. However, in the totality of Nagé spiritual cosmology, it is not so much birds specifically as non-mammals in general that are associated with things spiritual. In fact, Nagé regard birds as visible or vocal manifestations of spiritual beings no more than they do snakes. And rather than birds, it is reptiles and invertebrates that they mostly represent as manifestations of spirits and especially of human souls.

Spiritual Birds in Nagé Metaphors

In only one Nagé metaphor is a bird selected as the vehicle because of its identification with human souls. This is the *cio woza,* the Black-faced

Figure 8.2 Black-faced Cuckoo-shrike. |
Artwork by Donna McKinnon

Cuckoo-shrike (*Coracina novaehollandiae*, Figure 8.2), a greyish bird with a black mask and a strongly undulating flight, whose distinctive call (replicated in *cio*) reveals the soul of a dead relative who has come to summon a living person to death. Heard mostly in planting songs, the metaphor is "(when the) cuckoo-shrike calls, only tears will fall." But even here, there is a disparity between this metaphorical use and the more general symbolism of the bird. As an augury, the call of the cuckoo-shrike and the direction in which the bird flies can convey a variety of meanings, and by no means all of these are bad or presage death. For what follows, I should also mention that though the English word "shrike" denotes carnivorous birds of the family Laniidae, the cuckoo-shrike (named by anglophones because of its supposed resemblance to both cuckoos and shrikes) is mainly insectivorous and not carnivorous. Besides the cuckoo-shrike, the only other birds Nagé associate with human souls are a small unidentified passerine called *deza kela* and possibly the Bare-throated Whistler *(Pachycephala nudigula)*, or *kete dhéngi*, which they speak of as transformations of aborted fetuses and dead newborns (Forth 2004, 87–89). And of these, only the whistler occurs in a conventional metaphor, where it describes a mistreated child (Forth 2019, 239–40).

According to the interpretations given by Nagé themselves, none of the remainder of metaphors featuring "spiritual birds" are selected because of a bird's significance in spiritual belief. Rather, their motivation lies solely in empirical features of the birds (such as the nature of their cries or mode of flight). As noted, the birds in question are mostly birds of prey. Together with scavenging birds (including two species of crows), Nagé identify all birds of prey – both nocturnal and diurnal, thus owls as well as eagles, hawks, and falcons – as members of a symbolic class linked with witches *(polo)* and other malevolent spirits, mostly identified as *bapu, nitu bapu, ga'e bapu,* or *polo bapu* (polo bapu combines the two categories of malevolent supernaturals; see Forth 2004, 63–79). Nagé designate birds of this class simply as polo, "witch(es)," but when speaking Indonesian, the national language, they refer to them as "witch birds" *(burung suanggi).* Since witches are, in one respect, no more than individual human beings whom others identify as witches, it should be mentioned that the connection between them and malevolent spirits follows from a Nagé belief in their identical homicidal and anthropophagous (or cannibalistic) proclivities. Indeed, witches can be parsimoniously defined as malevolent spirits in human form, and Nagé believe that people become witches mainly through dealings with malevolent spirits (Forth 1993, 1998). For Nagé, witches are, above all, maleficent beings who kill fellow humans and devour their flesh. Thus, their association with carrion birds and more especially, raptors, many of which kill and consume other birds, is easy to understand.

Two witch birds (the Flores Crow, *Corvus florensis,* and an unidentified night bird called *koa ka*) do not feature in Nagé metaphors. One that does is the owl. As by far the most central member of this symbolic class, owls provide an especially clear example of birds whose spiritual significance plays no part at all in their metaphorical use. Owls appear in just two metaphors. One is "eagle owl" *(po kua),* a term that denotes a large owl whose plumage resembles that of an eagle. The bird is probably a Barn Owl, *Tyto* spp., and should not be confused with the various species of eagle owl that inhabit Palearctic regions. As applied to a person, however, "eagle owl" describes someone with a blanket or garment pulled over the head to keep warm, something typically done at night. Nowadays, the head covering is often the hood of a hooded jacket, or hoodie, or a balaclava (Forth 2019, 224–25). The comparison is often made jokingly, or in mild derision.

The second owl metaphor, "hawk-owl pretends to be close" *(je podi we'e),* describes a person who "feigns friendship with someone in order to take advantage" of them (Forth 2019, 225). The metaphor is motivated by the reputation of this particular owl, apparently the Brown Hawk-owl *(Ninox scutulata)*, for alighting on a branch where chickens are roosting, sidling up to them while making a piping sound like a young chick, and then seizing one. Whether academic ornithologists have ever observed this behaviour in hawk-owls I have never been able to establish. What is more certain, however, is that the metaphor has no connection with the spiritual associations of owls. In fact, perhaps because the bird is named distinctively from *po* (the term for all other owls), Nagé sometimes express doubt as to whether the hawk-owl is a witch bird.

The Eagle and the Goshawk

Whereas in owl metaphors the distinction between metaphorical referents and the significance of the same birds in spiritual belief is quite clear, with another three metaphors incorporating witch birds, all diurnal birds of prey, things are not so straightforward. This is partly because the three metaphors occur in Nagé songs of mourning performed at funerals and thus pertain to matters of death.

In two of the three, Nagé understand the birds, the eagle *(kua)* and the goshawk *(sizo),* as metaphorically representing mourners, and the recognized motivation lies in their specific cries, designated respectively as *no'i* and *io.* For the most part, witch birds as a class are also detected by their vocalizations. However, these calls are heard only at night and are collectively named *po,* also the onomatopoeic name for most local species of owls. According to Nagé, not just owls but all other witch birds are equally capable of producing the nocturnal po sounds, even though they possess individual cries of their own (including no'i and io). Admittedly, these distinctions may seem somewhat fine. Yet they are important, for contrasting vocalizations are one of several factors distinguishing representations of the same ornithological species as objects of spiritual belief, on the one hand, and as vehicles of conventional metaphor, on the other.

Sounds Nagé attribute to particular birds are one of a variety of empirical features that motivate the adoption of birds for metaphorical ends. But as will soon become clear, Nagé names for the birds themselves can provide another kind of motivation. Specifically, I refer to the way that names of certain birds function prosodically – producing either rhyme, assonance (a correspondence of vowels), or alliteration (a correspondence of consonants) – in combination with other terms included in complete metaphorical expressions. Prosody is especially evident in conventional metaphors forming parts of songs, and as mentioned, the three metaphors incorporating diurnal birds of prey occur in Nagé mourning songs.

One passage in these songs conjoins the eagle and the goshawk. As noted, Nagé interpret these two birds as referring to mourners, who primarily comprise the weeping relatives of someone who has recently died. The two component phrases are as follows:

Eagle calls seaward from the top of a lontar palm, pitying the father (man) who died before his time (*Kua* [eagle] *no'i* [calls] *lau lobo koli* [lontar palm], *mesu ame ulu mata po'i* [(die) before time]).
Goshawk cries upstream from the top of a coconut palm, pitying the mother (woman) whose death was premature (*Sizo* [goshawk] *io* [cries] zéta lobo nio [coconut palm], *mesu ine ulu mata 'ibo* [premature (death)]).

In the first phrase, kua can refer to several species of eagle that occur in Nagé country, none of which they distinguish with a more specific name. Translated as "goshawk," sizo refers to at least two birds, probably both of the genus *Accipiter,* one of which is larger and higher-flying than the other. The larger kind is usually known simply as sizo, though it can be distinguished as *sizo kaju* (tree sizo). Like the eagles, it is also a witch bird. By contrast, Nagé sometimes doubt whether the smaller hawk, called *sizo awu* (earth sizo) is a witch bird as well, especially as it flies close to the ground – thus contrasting with other raptors – and because, according to some Nagé, it eats only insects. (Also suggesting that the bird's name refers primarily to the larger, carnivorous variety is the fact that, as a verb, "sizo" means "to sweep down and seize," the characteristic action of raptors when taking prey.)

As regards metaphorical referents, the phrase involving the eagle refers specifically to the death of a man, whereas that incorporating the goshawk refers to the death of a woman. Even so, both phrases are sung together regardless of the gender of the deceased, as they are intended to recall all the relatives whom the mourners have lost. For analytic convenience, I have translated the bird names in the singular. But since they refer to a large group of mourners, they could just as well be rendered in the plural as "eagles" and "goshawks." (Like many Austronesian languages, Nagé does not regularly distinguish singular and plural.)

As indicated earlier, the words no'i and io in the two phrases function as verbs and refer to the cries of the eagle and goshawk. More specifically, they denote particular cries of raptorial birds, mewing or other high-pitched sounds reminiscent of the weeping and keening of mourners. Io is a variant of *ie,* which also denotes the whinnying of a horse and further appears in *io wea* or *ie wea,* the onomatopoeic name of the Common Hill Mynah (*Gracula religiosa,* Forth 2004, 74; see Figure 8.1). As funerary metaphors, therefore, eagles and goshawks are invoked owing to the quality of specific cries and their resemblance to sounds made by humans. As words, however, both no'i and io have a palpable prosodic value, as they rhyme or are assonant with both the names of the birds (as in sizo, goshawk, and io, cries) and the names of the two palm trees (as in sizo and *nio,* coconut palm). By the same token, it is clear why Nagé employ io rather than ie to refer to the cry of the goshawk. Assonance or rhyme is further evident in words denoting the cries of the birds and the palms – as in no'i (the eagle's cry) and *koli* (lontar palm) and io (the goshawk's cry) and nio (coconut palm) – as well as between other elements in the two expressions, including *po'i* ([to die] before one's time) and no'i and koli, and sizo, io, nio, and *'ibo* (premature [death]). Also noteworthy in relation to prosodic qualities is the way in which the vowels of the component terms in each expression are reversed in the other, so that in three instances the combination /o/ and /i/ (as in no'i) becomes /i/ and /o/ (as in nio).

Interestingly, only the name of the eagle (kua) does not have prosodic value. This may not seem very significant, as not all components of such expressions, especially ones as lengthy as these two, can be expected to produce prosodic effects. All the same, the exception of the eagle's name suggests that the selection of this bird is motivated by physical or behavioural features of the eagle itself or by symbolic values of this bird unrelated to its name. What is more, it could suggest that the eagle has priority over the goshawk in this context, a precedent that accords with the fact that the phrase incorporating the eagle is typically sung first.

By the same token, the value of the goshawk in the complementary expression lies mainly if not entirely in the phonological character of its name, sizo. Thus, one might speculate that, were the goshawk named otherwise, the phrase would have featured a different bird. Noteworthy here is the Nagé use of ie – a variant of io, denoting the goshawk's cry – to refer to sounds made by another raptorial bird, the kite *(jata)*, which as we shall see figures in another mortuary metaphor. Rather more indicative of the partly arbitrary character of the goshawk as the specific vehicle of the present metaphor is the possibility of substituting sizo with *mole sio,* a dialectal name for the previously mentioned cuckoo shrike, which is usually named cio woza in central Nagé. Sio in mole sio, corresponding to cio in cio woza, is part of the bird's name, unlike io, which designates the goshawk's cry or act of calling. Yet Nagé recognize sio as onomatopoeic (Forth 2004, 18), so on this ground it is suited to substitute for io (itself a possible onomatope). Sio of course maintains the prosody with nio and 'ibo, whereas, unlike sizo, mole (in one name for the cuckoo-shrike) does not.

A more important point is that, as a substitute for the goshawk, the cuckoo-shrike represents living human mourners, whereas, as mentioned above, it refers to a deceased soul in another metaphor. Also, in the more general context of Nagé supernatural belief, its cries and movements convey omens, including but not restricted to death omens. Unlike the goshawk and eagle, the cuckoo-shrike is not a witch bird, and in view of its augural significance as well, it may be considered a better metaphorical vehicle for mourners than is the goshawk. On the other hand, the cuckoo-shrike is not a bird of prey, so in this empirical respect it does not complement the eagle nearly as well as does the goshawk. Nevertheless, the possibility of substituting the cuckoo-shrike for the goshawk in this context underlines how the recognized meaning of the paired metaphors in these phrases does not depend on Nagé spiritual belief concerning the two birds of prey.

Another manifest feature of the expressions incorporating the eagle and the goshawk is the fact that, together, they exemplify the parallelism that is widely encountered in eastern Indonesian ritual speech, oratorical performances, and other formal genres (see, for example, Fox 1988). In the present instance, we thus find the pairs eagle//goshawk, cries//calls (no'i//io), seaward//landward, lontar palm//coconut palm, father//mother, and (die) before time//(die) prematurely. If, as suggested, the appearance of the goshawk is somewhat arbitrary in relation to the eagle – indeed, there seem to be no other instances in parallel speech where the two birds occur together – then the same applies to two other pairs of terms. Specifically, nothing in the behaviour or ecology of Flores birds suggests why eagles should be associated with the seaward (or downstream) direction or goshawks with landward (or upstream) locations. (Grammatically, it is worth noting that *zéta,* "landward, up, above," contrasting with *lau,* "seaward," serves a double purpose in the second expression, as it refers to both the goshawk's notionally landward, or inland, location and its position "at the top," *lobo,* of the lontar palm.) In fact, neither eagles nor goshawks are coastal birds, both occurring in parts of central Nagé where I recorded the metaphors, which do not extend to the sea. Also, whereas kua, as a reference to several eagle species, should include the White-breasted Sea Eagle *(Haliaeetus leucogaster),* a coastal raptor similar to the North American Bald Eagle, there is nothing to show that, in the metaphor, kua refers specifically to this bird. The association of one raptor with the lontar palm and the other with the coconut palm is equally arbitrary. On the other hand, lontar palms do indeed grow on or near the coast, not so much in contrast to coconut trees but more in contrast to the other major palm from which Flores Islanders tap juice (or toddy), the Arenga palm.

Since Nagé animal metaphors are entirely or for the most part motivated by morphological or behavioural features of the creatures concerned, the two funerary metaphors, drawing largely on qualities of names of the birds (or one of the two birds) in relation to other terms, as well as names of their cries, are thus somewhat exceptional. But the more important point is that, according to the interpretations of Nagé themselves, the appearance of raptorial birds in neither expression has anything to do with spiritual beliefs concerning the same birds – or specifically their status as witch birds. Expressed with reference to purely empirical features, in both metaphors the two birds represent humans mourning deceased relatives by virtue of particular vocalizations. By contrast, in Nagé belief the same species appear as witch birds and thus death-dealing spirits owing to their sharp beaks and claws, predatory nature, and carnivorous diet (Forth 2004, 63–79).

The Kite as Soul

Many of the points that apply to the eagle and goshawk metaphors apply equally to another mortuary metaphor employing another bird of prey – the kite, a kind of large hawk. Also heard in songs of mourning, the expression is "high-flying kite sits atop the nest." As Nagé explain, in this metaphor the kite represents the soul of someone recently buried, and the "nest" is the grave, above which the deceased's soul hovers or circles, like a bird of prey. It must be stressed, however, that in Nagé spiritual belief neither kites nor any other bird of prey are identified with human souls. In this respect, then, the kite in this metaphor contrasts with the cuckoo-shrike, as well as with a variety of insects and arachnids and even snakes and house-lizards, which Nagé situationally identify with souls. Like eagles and goshawks, on the other hand, kites figure in Nagé spiritual cosmology as instances of witch birds and thus as manifestations of malevolent spirits.

The complete metaphorical expression incorporating the kite is as follows:

> High-flying kite sits atop the nest
> *Ana jata jawa zéta wawo sa*
> The wind rocks the liver (heart) making it unsettled and sad
> *angi wa wéjo ate zéze zeo*
> Have pity on my younger brother of former days
> *Mesu e wai azi nga'o nebu ke*
> His roof ridge is already of grass, his walls are already of earth
> *Ghubu ne wai ku, naja ne wai tana*
> His sleeping mat is already of earth, his headrest is already
> of stone.
> *Te'e ne wai tana, lani ne wai watu.*

Placed before the bird's name *(jata jawa), ana* (child, member of a collectivity, specimen) has no particular significance. In fact, the word (which contextually can also mean "animal, creature") is often placed before the names of birds and other animals to singularize the zoological referent. In the second line, *ate* (liver) is what Nagé, like many other Malayo-Polynesian speakers, consider the organic site of emotions or feelings, character traits, and the like – thus corresponding to English "heart" (as in soft-hearted). Interestingly enough, in central Nagé "ate" closely resembles *'ate* (grave), distinguished only by an initial glottal stop (cf. dialectal *rate*), but this may be merely coincidental. In the third line, "younger brother" can be replaced by other kin terms, as appropriate. Referring to sleeping mats and headrests, the last line was described as an alternative to the fourth – and indeed, both refer to a grave – but I'm not sure it is not sometimes incorporated as an additional line. (Actually the reference to "grass" in the fourth line is curious because Nagé graves, laid in a village plaza that should be clear of vegetation and covered with stones, are typically not overgrown with grass.)

As a folk ornithological category, jata jawa requires comment. Jata alone normally denotes the Brahminy Kite *(Haliastur indus)*, a large mostly rusty-red hawk that is quite central to the class of witch birds. Accordingly, Nagé situationally interpret a Brahminy Kite that hovers and circles but does not ascend as a temporary embodiment of a malevolent spirit out in search of human victims to slaughter in the form of spirit water buffalo (Forth 1998, 151, 2019, 45–48). When necessary, the Brahminy Kite can be distinguished as the White-headed Kite *(jata ulu bha),* after its white head and breast. In contrast, jata jawa denotes another, less common kind of kite with variegated or speckled plumage, in which respect the meaning of jawa as "foreign, exotic" or "strange, unusual" appears relevant. Nagé describe raptors of this kind as high-fliers, and thus I translate jata jawa in the mortuary metaphor as "high-flying kite"; at the same time, it is unclear how far the birds differ from the Brahminy Kite in this regard.

Despite the distinction of the two kites, there is no evidence that Nagé systematically exclude jata jawa from the witch birds – believed to manifest malevolent spirits by their cries or visible forms. Nor does it mean that for some Nagé (particularly the good number that seem unaware of the distinction between the two sorts of kites), jata jawa does not evoke the Brahminy Kite. However, the fact that the metaphor specifies the jata jawa is arguably consistent with the fact that Nagé interpret the bird in this case as a reference to a deceased soul rather than a malevolent spirit – an entity more closely associated with the Brahminy Kite (jata).

According to Nagé commentators, kites represent the human soul in this metaphor because of the way these birds will hover over a spot for a time before flying away in a particular direction. Worth mentioning, then, is the bird's name, jata, which also means "to turn, wind; spinning wheel." In the same way, Nagé say, the soul of a dead person remains for a while near the body and the grave before departing for the land of the dead. "Sitting on the nest" is further metaphorical inasmuch as the interpretation specifies a kite hovering or circling in the air. Actually, the Nagé expression contains no explicit reference to sitting, describing the bird simply as being "on" or "on top of" *(zéta wawo)* the nest *(sa).* Nonetheless, "sits" is implied insofar as the preposition suggests some contact or connection between the nest and the bird, just as Nagé conceive of the soul remaining connected with the body for several days after death. The references to a roof ridge and a wall (of grass and earth) of course refer to the grave and more specifically to a grave conceived as a house. The sleeping mat and headrest in the alternative or additional line have the same referent but represent the grave as a more individual or personal space within a dwelling. The terms further imply a symbolic equation of death with sleep or rest.

At the same time, prosody plays a part in all these expressions, although to a lesser extent than in the metaphors employing the eagle and the goshawk.

Noteworthy are the partial rhyme of jata (kite) and zéta (up, upward) and of jawa (the qualifier of jata) and wawo (on top of, above; upper [part], surface); and the assonance of ana, jata, jawa, and sa (nest), of *wéjo* (rock, shake) and *zeo, ghubu* (roof ridge) and *ku* (grass), and *naja* (walls) and tana (earth); and the alliteration in *zéze zeo* (unsettled and sad).

Sea Fowls and Domestic Pigeons

Two final examples involve birds that are not raptors, but like the kite, appear in mourning songs as metaphorical references to the soul of the deceased. Since the two expressions are often conjoined parallelistically in this context, they are also comparable to the expressions regarding the eagle and the goshawk. The first is

> Sea fowl cries pitying itself (or: mourning its body)
> *Ana manu mesi polu kasi weki.*

"Sea fowl" *(manu mesi)* can be understood either as a metaphorical name for a spiritual entity (the soul) or as a bird that, like the kite (jata jawa), refers to the soul only in this mortuary metaphor. Although in other languages of central Flores, "sea fowl" (or sea chicken, *manu* is "chicken, domestic fowl") names various large waders or smaller shorebirds, in central Nagé it refers to a bird of no particular kind. According to one local interpretation, in this expression it refers instead to any sea or coastal bird that might occasionally wander far inland but that, owing to its nature, must eventually return to the sea. "Sea fowl" therefore provides an apt metaphor for a human being, whose time on earth is limited and whose soul must ultimately return to its place of origin, which Nagé identify with a creator divinity (Déwa or more completely Ga'e Déwa; see Forth 2019, 176–77). Almost certainly relevant, then, is the identification in yet another mortuary metaphor, of humans as "chickens of god," *ana manu déwa* (172). That is, they are fowls belonging to the divinity, whose lives – just like those of their own poultry – are in the hands of their owner, who determines when they will die. Here, it should be noted that Nagé do not conceive of humans or their souls as ever taking the form of chickens, in contrast to the belief that, in the spirit world, people take the form of sacrificial water buffalo belonging to spirits called bapu or nitu bapu (Forth 1998, 2019, 42–48). The difference thus underscores once again the importance of distinguishing metaphor – that is, conventional metaphor – from spiritual belief.

The word ana in both ana manu déwa (god's chickens) and ana manu mesi (sea fowl) has the same significance as in the metaphor incorporating the kite. In this expression, assonance is revealed in *mesi* (sea) and *weki* (body), and mesi forms an imperfect rhyme with *kasi*. (The unaccented /e/ is always the schwa in the first syllable of bisyllabic words.) Also, it is probably significant that mesi is very similar to *mesu* (pity, sympathy; what a pity, it's a pity), a word virtually synonymous with kasi. Indeed, it complements kasi in the standard phrase *mesu kasi* (sympathy, cf. Indonesian *kasih sayang,* "love and affection").

Incorporating the name of a pigeon *(kolo dasi),* the complementary phrase is semantically identical to the phrase involving the sea fowl, although in my experience, it is less fully interpreted by Nagé commentators. It runs as follows:

> Pigeon down by the ocean waves at Mbai
> *Ana kolo dasi lau bata Bai.*

Bai (or Mbai in the pronunciation and transcription used in the national language) is a location on the north coast of Flores. So far as I could determine, it has no special connection with pigeons. Kolo dasi specifically denotes the introduced domestic pigeon or Rock Dove, *Columba livia.* (Ana preceding the name has the same significance as it does in ana manu mesi.) As kolo alone refers to small wild doves of the genera *Streptopelia* and *Geopelia,* Nagé suggested that the qualifier dasi, the meaning of which is uncertain, is inserted in this expression mostly to correspond with Bai, a notion perhaps referring to a limited assonance. But as mentioned elsewhere (Forth 2019, 177), dasi more closely resembles *tasi,* denoting the sea, one of a number of places where, Nagé say, souls go after death. Once arrived there, they do not take the form of pigeons. On the other hand, a story concerning a famous Nagé shaman relates that, after his death (some time in the middle of the twentieth century), two domestic pigeons whose derivation was a mystery briefly appeared and alighted on the roof of his house before flying off in the direction of the Ebu Lobo volcano. The volcano is also associated with deceased souls. However, the narrators, including the man's son, did not explicitly make this connection (Forth 2004, 91–92).

Reviewing the two expressions together, as part of the name of the pigeon dasi appears equally illuminated by other prosodic considerations – namely, the way it rhymes with kasi and forms an imperfect rhyme with mesi, part of the name of the sea fowl (manu mesi). Yet it is not only prosody that qualifies the two birds as vehicles for two metaphorical expressions referring to the human soul. Both domestic pigeons (kolo) and domestic fowl (manu) are birds that people keep, raise, and also slaughter just as the divinity does with human beings, the chickens of god. Contextually, kolo can refer to birds in general, whereas, in languages related to Nagé, manu occurs in compounds denoting particular kinds of wild birds and thus with something approaching the general sense of "bird" (Forth 2006). Thus, it may be more than a coincidence that the two names are incorporated in two parallel phrases of essentially the same meaning. Even so, the status of chickens and some pigeons as domestic birds is evidently more germane to their combination in the two complementary metaphors.

Conclusion

As demonstrated, mortuary metaphors incorporating the sea fowl and domestic pigeon are, semantically, virtually identical to the metaphor employing the kite and very similar to those featuring the eagle and goshawk. Yet it is useful to reiterate this similarity, for it shows that metaphors relating to human death and the funeral, including the metaphor employing the cuckoo-shrike, do not rely solely on ornithological vehicles comprising death-dealing birds (or witch birds), birds that moreover prey largely on other birds. To that extent, the similarity affirms that the predatory nature of the birds of prey is not essential to their deployment in any Nagé conventional metaphor. By contrast, the character of eagles, kites, and goshawks, as birds that kill animals (including other birds) and consume their flesh, is indeed essential to their representation as embodiments of malevolent spirits, including human witches. Thus, to attain a proper understanding of either, it is imperative not to confuse and to keep analytically separate the part these birds play in metaphor, on the one hand, and in other forms of symbolic representation and especially spiritual belief, on the other.

At the same time, it would seem almost disingenuous to argue that the significance of predatory birds in spiritual belief is completely disconnected from the use of the same birds in metaphors that relate to death. This may apply particularly to the eagle and the goshawk, which according to the conventional interpretation of mortuary metaphors, refer to relatives who mourn the newly deceased, although it concerns the kite as well. In other words, it cannot be ruled out that the identification of these three birds with death-dealing spirits, and thus in Nagé cosmology as the common agents of human deaths, is somehow relevant to their metaphorical interpretation of the same birds either as victims of these spirits, in the case of the kite, which represents the deceased's soul, or as the deceased's survivors, in the case of the eagle and goshawk.

Viewed another way, one might discern two possible interpretations of what the three birds of prey stand for and how Nagé deploy them in songs of mourning. The first pertains to conventional metaphor, where Nagé understand the birds, in accordance with a standard interpretation, as creatures that, by way of either their calls or their patterns of flight, evoke either mourners or the soul of the person mourned. In a second and less conventional way, by contrast, the three birds might be apprehended as symbols – that is, symbols as distinct from recognizably figurative expressions. In this respect, the predatory birds on the contrary call to mind witches and other spiritual agents of death, an identification that, far from being a figurative representation, is for Nagé a matter of spiritual belief.

To be clear, Nagé do not entertain the latter interpretation when commenting on the metaphors (or, at least, not in discussions with me). For them, in other words, the spiritual status of the birds does not motivate the metaphors; nor is it in any way essential to their motivation or, therefore, their comprehension. Nevertheless, this last interpretation is potentially present, not just in mortuary performances but also in the wider context of death, including human susceptibility to death by malevolent spiritual forces. Accordingly, the identification of the eagle and goshawk as ornithological embodiments of these forces can persist as a connotation of the metaphors that accompanies their denotative reference to human mourners.

Insofar as the two interpretations (mourning kin and death-dealing spirits) are present together, their combination creates an irony – thus another distinctive mode of symbolic thought (Fernandez 1991). By the same token, in the Nagé denial that the metaphors invoke deadly spirits, we might further glimpse an instance of the "blocked exegesis" that Victor Turner (1967, 38) identifies in his analysis of ritual symbols, whereby meanings of symbols that contradict social harmony and reflect a community in a negative light are suppressed in the articulation of meanings, both among community members and for the benefit of ethnographers. In this case too, the ironic plot as it were hatched by the raptorial birds is not just a product of external analysis, but is discernible in Nagé social relationships. According to Nagé, witches may be the ultimate cause of all deaths or were so in the past (Forth 1993, 108). What is more, Nagé witchcraft accusations (which nowadays at least, tend to be private rather than public) make it clear that witches who are accused of causing the death of a person tend to be found among the victim's co-resident clan-mates – including in the case of a man or an unmarried woman, the person's most closely related agnates (Forth 1993, 116–18). It is precisely these relatives who, at the funeral, comprise the principal mourners. Thus, it is in effect the mourners who are commonly conceived as including the homicidal witch, while witches are identified with the predatory witch birds that, in the case of goshawks and eagles, also metaphorically weep and keen over the deceased.

Yet important differences remain. Not only do Nagé deny the second, spiritual interpretation – the one that makes for the irony – but as the analysis shows, in the first interpretation, where the birds are understood purely metaphorically, they simply resemble human mourners, specifically by way of cries that resemble human weeping. By contrast, in Nagé spiritual belief, the very same birds, in some mysterious way, *are* the human witches who caused the death. This distinction nicely exemplifies another general point borne out by the study of Nagé metaphor (Forth 2019, 15–16, 315–16), that animal metaphors typically draw on just one or two physical or behavioural features (in birds, a specific tail shape, manner of flight, and so on). Or to put it another way, their vehicles comprise only a part of an animal, just as their referents often concern only a part of a human being (a particular facial appearance, a harsh voice, a manner of walking), whereas in spiritual belief it is typically an animal in its entirety that is identified with the "whole" of a spiritual being. It then follows that witches and mourners become identical only when both interpretations are brought together in an ironic – one might also say cynical – synthesis. But this synthesis exists not only as an insight of an external analyst, but, for Nagé, also as a potential double understanding – and not only of their own symbolic forms, but, as shown, equally of the ways in which they conceive of their own society as working.

As the foregoing should suggest, Nagé bird metaphors provide especially intriguing and illuminating illustrations of several important issues pertaining to conventional metaphors in general and their relationship to other kinds of symbolic representation. Moreover, they evidently do so more than metaphors employing other sorts of animals. As noted, snakes, for example, serve as vehicles for twenty-two Nagé metaphors (Forth 2019, 244–54), and snakes are also closely identified with spirits. Yet none of the snake metaphors provides the possibility of two kinds of interpretation – non-spiritual and spiritual – as do the bird metaphors treated above.

Why birds might be special in this way, or why bird metaphors should appear especially rich in regard to possibilities of metaphorical interpretation, I am not entirely certain. Aristophanes might provide some clues, especially in regard to the continuity (partly instanced by the possibility of transformation) revealed in his famous play between birds, humans, and spirits (gods). Alternatively, an answer might be found in the original sense of the Greek *metapherein* (metaphor), meaning "transfer" and more specifically denoting a carrying over from one domain to another. Of all sorts of animals, it might then be considered that birds, with their distinctive power of flight and thus the ease with which they pass between distant places, are the most closely associated with this sort of conceptual passage.

In any event, the birds of Nagé country have taken me some distance toward understanding how their human neighbours construct and interpret metaphors, and have provided essential insights into ways that metaphors in general, as recognizably figurative or consciously symbolic expressions, differ from non-figurative symbols or beliefs. In addition, Nagé conceptual uses of birds reveal how conventional metaphors, by employing zoological vehicles that are simultaneously the objects of spiritual beliefs, might sometimes be interpreted "unconventionally," as incorporating symbolic relations that the metaphors, as metaphors, seemingly disallow. In this respect, such metaphors might be conceived as like birds, which are less constrained than other animals and after remaining perched or on the ground for a time will, on being closely approached, quickly fly away.

Postscript

As an addendum, it seems appropriate to point out that birds serve the Nagé not only as metaphors and objects of spiritual belief but, as might be expected, in various practical ways as well. As objects of the hunt, they provide food and, in the case of both domestic cocks and some wild birds, feathers for ceremonial decoration. Also, bird vocalizations, and less often movements, serve as chronological signs, marking parts of the day and night and changes in the seasons. In fact, fifteen Nagé metaphors turn on the value of an animal as a chronological sign, and in all of these the vehicle is a bird. For example, two species of migratory cuckoos, whose calls announce the approach of the wet season and the time when people should prepare their gardens for planting, serve as metaphors for people who provide crucial assistance to others but who (like the cuckoos, which do not consume the resulting crops) themselves receive no benefit from their actions (Forth 2019, 167 68).

To be sure, unlike the cuckoos, some birds are valued negatively, as they feed on rice grains or newly planted seed, maize, or other cereals (as in the case of crows, cockatoos, parrots, doves, and various small passerines). Similarly, raptors prey on chickens. For decades now, Nagé, and especially people living in more densely settled areas, have noted with dismay the reduction of many bird species and the local disappearance of some. This they attribute, quite accurately, to several linked factors of economic change and "development," including deforestation, expanding human populations, and the availability of new technology for killing birds, most notably air rifles. Some birds, including cockatoos, mynahs, and thrushes, have also locally disappeared as a result of trapping for the export trade (Forth 2016, 181–84).

Ironically, it may be thought, Nagé mourn the relative or absolute loss not only of these birds but also of several birds of prey, including Brahminy Kites and other large raptors, the main enemies of chickens, as well as crows and cockatoos, birds they describe as formerly occurring in large flocks that would lay waste to fields of ripening maize. That Nagé do not celebrate the disappearance of these birds would indicate that they value birds in ways other than the practical. And the reason, I suggest, can be found in the various respects, including but not limited to their occurrence in metaphor and spiritual beliefs, in which birds recall for Nagé an indigenous culture that has passed or is now passing. Since many birds are known partly by their calls – which nowadays are heard no longer or only rarely – an aspect of this change is a new silence or a range of ornithological sounds that is largely replaced by new sounds (many of a motorized variety). As human vocalizations are partially derivative of bird vocalizations (replicated, for example, in onomatopoeic bird names or words denoting their cries), bird metaphors may be expected to decline in tandem with the reduction or disappearance of the birds themselves. In other words, one might anticipate a parallel cultural decline in the meaningful use of birds not just as metaphors but also as objects of spiritual belief. And indeed, older Nagé regularly complain that younger people are less familiar than people once were with local birds and their local names, as well as with the indigenous culture in which birds occupied a not inconsiderable place.

On the other hand, evidence shows that new metaphors, some incorporating birds, are emerging all the time. Examples are birds whose crests or tails provide metaphorical names for modern hairstyles now worn by some younger Nagé (see Forth 2019, 189, 192). Hence, there is reason to believe that, as long as there are birds and other wild creatures, their significance as vehicles of metaphorical or other symbolic expression will survive. All the same, if some birds are no longer commonly seen or heard, it may also be expected that older metaphors and other symbolic representations involving them will gradually lose their force and that the metaphors may eventually become as dead as some bird species have become or are becoming. If so, this too is reason to mourn – if not to the same extent as the demise of the ornithological species themselves or the loss of deceased fellow humans.

WORKS CITED

Descola, Philippe. 2013. *Beyond Nature and Culture.* Translated by Janet Lloyd. Chicago: University of Chicago Press.

Fernandez, James W., ed. 1991. *Beyond Metaphor: The Theory of Tropes in Anthropology.* Stanford: Stanford University Press.

Forth, Gregory. 1993. "Social and Symbolic Aspects of the Witch among the Nage of Eastern Indonesia." In *Understanding Witchcraft and Sorcery in Southeast Asia,* ed. C.W. Watson and R.F. Ellen, 99–122. Honolulu: University of Hawai'i Press.

—. 1998. *Beneath the Volcano: Religion, Cosmology and Spirit Classification among the Nage of Eastern Indonesia.* Leiden: Royal Institute (KITLV) Press.

—. 2004. *Nage Birds: Classification and Symbolism among an Eastern Indonesian People.* London: Routledge.

—. 2006. "Words for 'Bird' in Eastern Indonesia." *Journal of Ethnobiology* 26, 2: 177–207.

—. 2016. *Why the Porcupine Is Not a Bird: Explorations in the Folk Zoology of an Eastern Indonesian People.* Toronto: University of Toronto Press.

—. 2019. *A Dog Pissing at the Edge of a Path: Animal Metaphors in an Eastern Indonesian Society.* Montreal and Kingston: McGill-Queen's University Press.

Fox, James J., ed. 1988. *To Speak in Pairs: Essays on the Ritual Languages of Eastern Indonesia.* Cambridge: Cambridge University Press.

Jakobson, Roman, and Morris Halle. 1956. *Fundamentals of Language.* The Hague: Mouton.

Kövecses, Zoltán. 2010. *Metaphor: A Practical Introduction.* 2nd ed. Oxford: Oxford University Press.

Lévi-Strauss, Claude. 1963. *Totemism.* Boston: Beacon Press.

Lloyd, Geoffrey E.R. 2011. "Humanity between Gods and Beasts? Ontologies in Question." *Journal of the Royal Anthropological Institute,* n.s., 17, 4: 829–45.

Needham, Rodney. 1972. *Belief, Language, and Experience.* Oxford: Blackwell.

Palmatier, Robert. 1995. *Speaking of Animals: A Dictionary of Animal Metaphors.* Westport, CT: Greenwood Press.

Turner, Victor. 1967. *The Forest of Symbols: Aspects of Ndembu Ritual.* Ithaca: Cornell University Press.

Part Three

Birds Are Good to Craft With
(Birds in Material Culture)

9

From Good to Eat to Good to Make

Ethnographic Archaeology of Bird Representations in Ancient Japan

Atsushi Nobayashi

MUCH RESEARCH ON relations between humans and animals has assumed that the consequences of these interactions for human societies are primarily economic or symbolic (Mithen 1999), or that researchers easily understand the meaning of each (Andersson et al. 2014). As Bronisław Malinowski and Claude Lévi-Strauss suggest, animals have generally been analyzed as either "good to eat" or "good to think" (see also Bowman n.d.).

When people discuss issues relating to humans and animals, they express differing viewpoints on the relationship. Some adopt a "human versus animal" approach, seeing the relationship between humans and animals as confrontational (DeMello 2012, 4; Kompatscher, Spannring, and Schachinger 2017, 23–24), but other researchers are critical of assuming an oppositional structure (McFarland and Hedinger 2009; Boddice 2011; Birke and Hockenhull 2012; Roscher 2016). The concept of "non-human personhood," such as not singling out human beings, and multi-species research provide a new anthropological arena for the debate on human-animal relations (Descola 2005; DeGrazia 2006; Hill 2013; Locke 2017; Morton 2017).

On the other hand, an ecological approach is still useful because animals, including humans, are members of ecosystems that change both naturally and artificially. Alterations in the environment can cause changes in behaviour among both animals and humans. The resulting changes in their relationship are discernible in anthropology, though long-term observation is required to determine whether they are fixed or temporary. Fortunately, archaeology can investigate human-animal dynamics at varying timescales (see Hussain 2018) and may contribute to the formation of "anthrozoo-technical relations" (Doré and Michalon 2017) that chart the intersections and interdependencies between tangible and non-tangible human-animal relations.

When we think about the relationship between birds and humans, we must consider that birds differ in striking ways from other creatures. They can fly, travelling through the sky and sometimes covering extraordinarily long distances. Apart from some species of bats and a few insects, such as the famous monarch butterfly, no other animals are capable of long-distance flight. This fact can be correlated with the wide geographical distribution of birds. The relationship between birds and humans, therefore, can be more extensive than our relationships with other animals.

We must also pay attention to the localized historical ties between birds and people. As defined by the binomial system of species description established by Carl Linnaeus in the mid-eighteenth century, 11,032 extant bird species and 162 extinct species are currently known on Earth.[1] Although the classification is based on broad geographical divisions, such as North America and Africa, 9,940 bird species (about 90 percent) do not span regions. Although this does not preclude the possibility that every area has a story to tell about birds and people, we cannot forget that some values and viewpoints transcend regional boundaries. The so-called civilized way of dealing with nature has made the link between humans and nature unidirectional; in other words, *Homo sapiens* aims to conquer nature.

In the Pleistocene era, humans had long-lasting biological connections with other species before they could adapt culturally; in the latter part of the Pleistocene, humans developed cultural relationships with other species as they spread across the world; and in the Holocene, they attempted to subdue nature. Now in the Anthropocene era, we can travel the globe and our activities affect the environment. Our current relationships with birds may be more dependent on anthropogenic, or human-created, conditions than on ecological ones.

What is critical in considering the association between birds and humans is its diversity, which is determined by the conditions of time and space. Specifically, since change involves the passage of time, a particularly effective approach is to analyze phenomena that are likely to capture changes in our relationships. With his concept of *fūdo*, Tetsurō Watsuji ([1935] 1979) concluded that the interdependence of climate, geography, society, and technical change contributed to the evolution of cultures. He suggested the importance of time in considering human existence or the connection between humans and nature. The entangled lives of birds and humans are part of that process.

This chapter focuses on changes in the human use of birds during the Jomon and Yayoi periods of Japan as an attempt to examine these issues in more detail. The main differences between the two periods are twofold. The former involved a hunter-gatherer lifestyle, whereas the latter was agrarian, relying on the cultivation of rice paddies. Also during the Yayoi period, an influx of migrants from continental Asia brought new cultures to the Japanese archipelago.

The two periods differ in terms of the number of bird remains found in archaeological sites and the objects representing them. As previous studies reveal, birds were a food item during the hunter-gatherer Jomon period, though they were rarely depicted in art or on pottery. In the Yayoi period, they were still used for food, but their appearance as figurines increased overwhelmingly. This indicates that during the transition between the two periods, birds may have become not only "good to eat" but also "good to think about."

Working from previous studies, this chapter outlines the differences between the Jomon and Yayoi periods in the use of birds as food and the motifs of bird sculptures (Figures 9.1 and 9.2). It then introduces two examples of ethnographic and folk beliefs that may provide background for the Japanese view of animals as "good to think": the hunter-gatherer Ainu

Figure 9.1 Wooden bird carvings of the Yayoi period, excavated at the Ikegamisone site in Osaka. The largest one *(topmost figure)* is thirty-four centimetres long (see https://www.youtube.com/watch?app=desktop&v=poO4yQvSb-4).

Figure 9.2 A replica Yayoi building at Ikegamisone, Osaka. Two carved wooden birds adorn the roof.

view of birds as the incarnation of deities and the continental farmers' view of birds as messengers from deities. This is a story of the entanglement of land, humans, birds, and other lives that co-evolved to become Japanese civilization.

Chronology of the Jomon and Yayoi Periods

The Jomon period began about sixteen thousand years ago and continued for about thirteen thousand years until the beginning of the Yayoi period when rice paddy farming was adopted. The Jomon period lasted from the late Pleistocene (melting ice age) to the Holocene. It is characterized by pottery that is decorated with rope patterns, the spread of pit houses, and the appearance of shell mounds that differ from those of the previous Paleolithic period. The Jomon period can be divided into six subperiods based on the form of pottery: the pioneer period (14000 BC–9000 BC), the beginning period (9000–5000 BC), the early period (5000–3400 BC), the middle period (3400–2500 BC), the late period (2500–1200 BC), and the end period (1200–800 or 500 BC).

In the early Jomon period, the climate was warmer than that of the Last Glacial Maximum, though it was still cold. Sea level was a few tens of metres lower than at present. Later, the climate warmed and sea level neared its present position. By the mid-Jomon period, however, it was two to three metres higher than it is today due to global warming, and in the plains, the coastline extended inland, known as the Jomon Marine Transgression. Despite these climatic changes, basic subsistence patterns, such as hunting and gathering and living in pit houses, did not change significantly in the Japanese archipelago. Even so, regional diversity existed, particularly in northern Kyushu and Hokkaido, where exchange with continental Asia could potentially have occurred.

Full-scale rice paddy farming began during the second half of the tenth century BC. With the beginning of the Yayoi period, most elements of Jomon culture, including alimentation, settlements, tombs, pottery, and stone tools, were discarded. Means of subsistence and alimentation changed from hunter-gathering to rice farming, and pit settlements were replaced by moat-encircled communities with defensive capability. Graves were supplanted by stone tombs and wooden coffin tombs, earthenware was replaced by open field firing, and the earlier style of stone tools gave way to a new continental type of polished stone tools.

It is generally understood that these new cultural elements came from the Korean peninsula. During this period, cultures from the continent, both material and spiritual, were introduced to the Japanese archipelago. Perhaps one of them featured some kind of belief involving birds. What is important here is that the bird became "good to make." As we shall see, a typical example is the wooden bird-shaped carvings found at several Yayoi sites.

The Jomon period did produce clay figurines of birds, the first bird artifacts found in Japan, but they are few in number, and there is little evidence that birds were used symbolically at the time. By contrast, characteristic bird-shaped wooden carvings from the Yayoi period have been unearthed in many parts of Japan. The first five were discovered in 1970 at the Ikegamisone excavation site in Osaka. Japanese archaeologist Hiroshi Kanaseki (1975) speculated that they might be used for the bird poles known in Korea, northeastern China, and Siberia. In the 1980s and 1990s, as more wooden bird carvings were discovered in various parts of the country, they attracted the interest of archaeologists.

Animal Artifacts of the Jomon Period

Pottery and clay figurines are typical artifacts of the Jomon period, but most figurines are humanoid, and few extant examples depict birds or animals.

The most frequently excavated animal-shaped clay products portray wild boar, deer, bears, monkeys, and dogs (Fujinuma 1997, 119). However, they are not realistic, and researchers differ regarding their subject matter. For example, some researchers concluded that a particular artifact represented a turtle, whereas others thought it was a small animal such as a *gengorō* (Diving Beetle, *Cybister japonicus*) or a tadpole.

Among these objects, boar-shaped clay products from the latter half of the middle to the late period were excavated all over Japan and accounted for more than half of all animal-shaped clay products of the period. No later examples have been found. There are only a few instances of deer-shaped earthenware, which were excavated from archaeological sites with wild boar clay products. Many researchers believe that the boar artifacts are associated with hunting rituals, such as praying for a safe hunt, since boars are among the most hunted animals in human societies, but can also be dangerous to the hunters.

Interestingly, bird-shaped clay products often comprise only the head, unlike those depicting other animals, which commonly include the whole body. They could have been attached to pottery, where they functioned as handles, and for this reason are sometimes called birdhead handles. They are presumed to represent birds of prey or waterfowl, but snakehead handles were also common, and it is not always easy to distinguish between them. An illustrative example is an early mid-Jomon bowl excavated at the Mawaki site in Ishikawa Prefecture. Known as "Tori-san" pottery, it is small, about the size of a rice bowl. The surface of the earthenware is engraved with a sharp bamboo spatula. An animal head, forming a convenient handle, protrudes above its lip, and traces of red pigment remain on the eyes. It may represent a bird or a pit viper, which are rare in pottery of this period. It has been suggested that the bowl may not have been used to boil food or water but for some other special purpose.[2]

One of the best-known bird-shaped clay items from the Jomon period is a piece of earthenware depicting a saw-whet owl. Dating from late in the period and found at the Kusagasawa site in Iwate Prefecture, it is 7.6 centimetres tall and it sports the characteristic ear tufts of the owl family (Fujinuma 1997, 126). It is worth noting that, in this particular artifact, the entire body of the bird is represented, which is unusual. Given the limited number of finds, it is unlikely that many of these were produced. However, attributing the choice of the owl solely to the personal preference of the sculptor would be misleading. As discussed below, the owl is a spiritual animal for the Ainu people of Hokkaido. As hunting birds, owls sometimes compete with humans for food, though hunters can also observe them to help them find prey. Thus, although researchers have found some bird-shaped artifacts from the Jomon period, the number is small. The reason for their scarcity is difficult to uncover. Perhaps the Jomon did not create symbolic forms of animals, apart from the wild boar. Animism, which imbues animals and natural objects with a spiritual essence, may have involved avoiding the reproduction of animal forms. This world view evolved since the beginning of the Yayoi period, and one of these changes is seen in the appearance of wooden bird-shaped carvings.

Carved Wooden Bird Figures in the Yayoi Period

Wooden objects tend to be ephemeral in older archaeological sites, with the result that there are few reports of wooden figures from the Jomon period. In contrast, archaeological digs in Yayoi sites have unearthed characteristic carved wooden statues, including those in the shape of birds.

Some of these bird carvings are rounded, some are flat, but what they all have in common is that they are carved from a single piece of wood. Many are not particularly realistic, and it is not clear which species they represent. Their classification is based on whether they are viewed from the side or from above, the depiction of behaviour (in flight or at rest), or form (perforated and attached to a pole, or without perforations) (Ametani and Sato 2000, 11).

Researchers suggest that these carvings are associated with religious beliefs (Kanaseki 1975). In an analytical study, Kana Hirayama (2009) reviewed previous research on bird-shaped wooden carvings, particularly from the Yayoi period. She collected data on these objects and examined them by morphological category, period, and region. Thanks to her work, we know that there is a great diversity of bird-shaped wooden products and that determining their function or the particular bird represented is difficult.

The Function of Bird Carvings

After reviewing earlier research on Yayoi bird-shaped woodcarvings, Hirayama proposed five theories regarding their use: attached to bird poles, which have sometimes been called *Sote;* to mark boundaries; not for Sote;

in funerary rituals; and for multiple purposes. Hirayama (2009, 23–25) herself supported the final option of the five.

The Sote, or Bird Pole

Kanaseki (1975) put forth a hypothesis about a wooden bird-shaped object from the Yayoi period that was excavated at the Ikegamisone site in Osaka. He suggested that such carvings were used in bird poles, wooden poles that featured a carved bird perched at the top, which occurred in Korea, northeastern China, and Siberia. He also pointed out that bird poles were associated with shamanism, that they originated in China, and that they played a role in the early stages of agrarian society in ancient East Asia.

The beliefs associated with these bird carvings have also been discussed in connection with the sote beliefs in the Korean peninsula (Kokubu 1983). On the peninsula, "sote" may refer to the bird pole itself or to the site where a wooden doll *(changsun)* is attached to the sote (Hagiwara 1996, 28). Historically, the word sote, with the same pronunciation, appears in the ancient Chinese document *Wei-zhi dong-yi-zhuan,* the book of Wei (554–59) (Hagiwara 1996, 29). The sote site was the area where ancestral spirits and grain gods were worshipped during the spring sowing and autumn harvest (Hagiwara 1996, 29).

The practice of building bird poles is still widely disseminated, occurring in the Korean peninsula, Northeast Asia, and Southeast Asia. They are erected at the entrances to villages and temples, in tomb huts, in paddy fields, and especially in the inhabited areas of marginal ethnic minorities. Their use in the shaman tent of the Evenki people in Siberia and at the gates of the Akha people in northern Thailand is well known (Uno 1938).

On the other hand, the bird pole might have spread from China to the Korean peninsula with grain rituals. Paddy rice cultivation was already widespread on the peninsula by this time, so it is safe to assume that the pole was built on the site where agricultural rituals were practised. It was also used in agricultural rites during the Yayoi period, as revealed by examples found in paddies (Yamada 1996).

The relationship between birds and agricultural rituals is connected with the tradition of the ear-dropping god, a myth about the origin of grain that spread throughout East and Southeast Asia. A tradition in many parts of Japan is that cranes (migratory birds) bring ears of rice. However, no wooden carvings from Yayoi sites can be confidently identified as depictions of cranes.

Boundary Marking

As with the previous hypothesis, boundary marking recognizes a ritual function for the carved wooden bird, a continuation of Kanaseki's idea that they create sanctuaries. Archaeologists such as Masayoshi Mizuno (1982) and Makoto Watanabe (1995) argue that the carvings were tools for establishing boundaries, emphasizing the fact that they were found in ditches surrounding settlements and that sote had a boundary-marking function. The main difference between this hypothesis and the previous one is whether the carvings are related to agricultural rituals.

The Non-sote Theory

This theory suggests that bird-shaped woodcarvings are not related to bird posts. Hirayama's (2009, 24) analysis shows that seventeen of the ninety-one carvings she examined (18.6 percent) had holes or grooves in them, which suggests that they could have been attached to a pole or a rod. Note, however, that this is only speculation.

Funeral Rites

The fourth theory is based on the attributes of the sites where the carvings were excavated and on a suggestion from Yasuhiro Yamada (1996). The artifacts have been found in cemeteries, which naturally suggests that they have a funerary function.

The Multipurpose Theory

This idea posits that the carvings may have been used for a variety of purposes. It encompasses the uses discussed above and suggests that the objects had different functions at different times and in different regions, and that many of them were involved in rituals (Hirayama 2009, 24–25).

Ultimately, the five hypotheses contend that the bird-shaped wooden carvings of the Yayoi period were either mounted on poles or attached to a structure (such as a gate) and used for ritual purposes (such as praying for a good rice harvest or as an indicator of a sacred area). Exactly which birds are represented has been the subject of some debate among archaeologists; however, identifying the species or type solely on the basis of morphology would be difficult. The only consensus is that the objects have a ritual significance that did not exist in the Jomon period, when hunting and gathering were the basis of subsistence.

Distribution and Morphology of Bird-Shaped Wooden Carvings

Hirayama's (2009) study examined the classification of forms, periods, and regions. Working from her earlier research, she analyzed the data for bird-shaped wooden carvings found at Yayoi sites and clarified their characteristics such as their form, size, and materials. Figure 9.3 shows the locations of the sites and the number of carvings that she assessed. The box-plot diagram in Figure 9.4 shows the total length of each piece. The average length is 26.2 centimetres, with the smallest being 6.1 centimetres and the largest being 89.4 centimetres. Hirayama's (2009) classification criteria for total length were

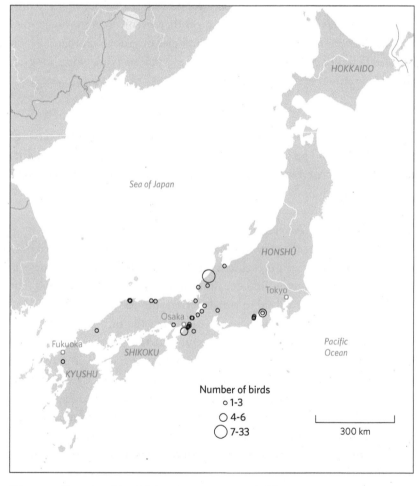

Figure 9.3 Sites where Yayoi bird carvings were excavated. | Cartography by Eric Leinberger

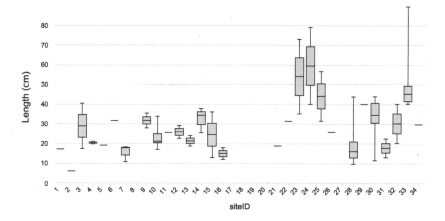

Figure 9.4 Sizes of bird carvings found at Yayoi sites. Horizontal lines indicate that only one sample has been measured, no horizontal line indicates that no sample could be measured.

"small," between 5 and 25 centimetres; "medium," between 25 and 45 centimetres; and "large," longer than 45 centimetres. However, in terms of the overall distribution represented in Figure 9.4, it is possible to divide the data into two groups (less than 40 centimetres and more than 40 centimetres).

Sites 1 to 17 are in western Japan, west of the Kinki region. Relatively large carvings were found at the Ohinui and Kamoda sites (site 24) on the eastern shore of Lake Biwa in Shiga Prefecture and at the Tana-Murayama site (site 25) in Fukui Prefecture, with one object each. The former is 79.0 by 40.0 centimetres, the latter 31.5 by 56.5 centimetres, and both are classified as types whose morphology, viewed from the side, resembles that of a bird. Carvings found in sites 30 to 32, in the Tokai region of Aichi and Shizuoka, are generally between 20.0 and 40.0 centimetres long. Six carvings were excavated at site 33, with an overall size that was larger than in the other Tokai region sites. One cannot argue that there are marked regional differences when it comes to length, but this may reflect the fact that the sites are relatively few in number. The differences between the Sea of Japan side (facing the Korean peninsula) and the Pacific side are unremarkable.

Although the classification of the carvings has changed over time, it is common among many researchers. I modified the classification method adopted by Hirayama (2009). Examining each carving from the side and from directly above, I classified it into one of three types: type 1 resembled a bird when viewed from the side, type 2 looked like a bird when viewed

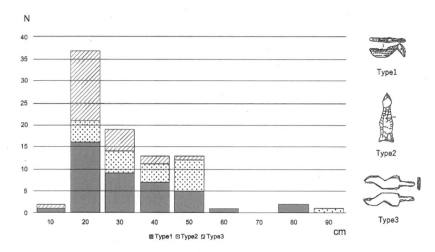

Figure 9.5 Size and morphological types of Yayoi bird carvings.

Figure 9.6 Imagined use of Yayoi bird-shaped carving.

from immediately above, and type 3 was a combination of types 1 and 2 with other components. Type 3 carvings became less abundant as size increased (Figure 9.5). The use of type 1 and type 2 bird-shaped wooden carvings is relatively easy to guess, and it is thought that they were probably mounted on poles (Figure 9.6).

It is not known which birds these carvings represent, although there are regional variations in size and shape. The archaeological material shows that bird figures, rare during the Jomon period, were made with care in various regions during the Yayoi period. This suggests that the relationship between humans and birds may have changed as the Jomon transitioned into the Yayoi.

Ecological Role of Birds in the Jomon and Yayoi Periods

From the point of view of "good to make," we can understand that human attitudes toward birds changed when the Yayoi period began, as people began carving birds in greater numbers. I also consider another perspective, that of "good to eat"; in other words, the ecological roles of birds. During the hunter-gatherer Jomon period, humans recognized natural resources as ecological resources and either used them or systematized their knowledge of them.

Compiling a list of bird bones found at various Jomon and Yayoi sites, Tomoko Niimi (2008) finds that many pheasant and duck bones were recovered from the Jomon sites, except for those in Hokkaido, where pheasants do not live. Niimi (2008, 227) estimates that pheasants and ducks together accounted for 50 percent of all bird bones found in the Jomon sites. Other than these, waterbirds inhabiting lakes, seas, and rivers – such as geese, cormorants, albatrosses, petrels, and little grebe – were excavated, as were crows, eagles, and hawks. Niimi (2008, 227–28) attributes the preponderance of pheasants and ducks to the fact that they are among the heaviest birds and have a lot of meat, making them a valuable food source. It is believed that crows were also targeted for the same reason. Eagles and hawks are thought to have been used for purposes other than food, as their feathers were added to arrows (Niimi 2008, 231). Only a few sparrow and pigeon bones were found, perhaps because their tiny size makes them difficult to detect in a dig, though it is possible that these birds were not commonly hunted. On the basis of these results, Niimi (2008, 232) speculates that Jomon bird hunting may have systematically concentrated on waterfowl.

Niimi (2008, 235–37) notes that Yayoi sites yielded fewer bird bones than Jomon sites and that the types of bones varied as well. Pheasant bones decreased, whereas those of geese and ducks increased, as did those of cranes. This may be because the paddy fields were situated in wetlands, where human activities overlapped those of waterbirds. Because ducks often dabble for seeds sown in the shallow water of paddies, Yayoi duck hunting was probably a way of putting supper on the table while protecting the rice crop at the same time.

Ainu, Hunter-Gatherers, and Birds in Japan

On the basis of excavated bird remains, we can conclude that the pattern of eating birds changed from the Jomon to the Yayoi period, meaning that forms of natural resources also changed. The major shift was away from a subsistence pattern based on hunting and gathering toward establishing an economy based on paddy rice cultivation. It cannot be said, of course, that all areas of the country made this shift during the Yayoi period. However, humans increasingly settled in the basins of large rivers and lowland wetlands, which were most suitable for growing rice. Along with this, the types of birds that people saw in their daily lives and used for food also changed during the Yayoi period.

Although climatic geography and historical processes must be considered, an examination of the Indigenous Ainu people of Hokkaido – where paddy rice cultivation was not introduced for many years – can provide some insight into the cultural dynamics of a natural-resource-using group that relied on hunting and gathering. John Batchelor (1855–1944) wrote a detailed ethnography of the Ainu way of thinking about and using birds (Batchelor 1901). A British missionary who lived among the Ainu from 1877 to 1941, Batchelor contributed to the documentation of their culture by writing Ainu-English dictionaries. He believed that the Ainu were very interested in birds, and he recorded their bird lore.

According to Batchelor (1901), the Ainu classified birds according to criteria such as whether their calls could be imitated and where they lived. For example, as he put it, some birds belonged in heaven above, some dwelled only on the earth below, and some had their proper home in Hades under the earth. There were five special birds whose cry should not be imitated by anyone: the cuckoo, the woodpecker, the nighthawk, the goatsucker, and the owl. These birds had the power to bewitch people, so imitating their cry would bring misfortune. To mimic the cry of any unknown bird was also prohibited. Strange birds were often sent by the devil, carrying the seeds of disease. The eagle-owl was seen as a deity. To imitate its cry would therefore be blasphemous.

Geographer Dal Williams (2017) has also written on the ethnobiology of the Ainu, basing his book on previous research and his own fieldwork. He describes fifty-six species of birds found in Hokkaido and gives their Ainu names and meanings (Williams 2017, 197–98). Of course, there is regional diversity in Ainu culture, and Williams's account is incomplete. Nonetheless, it does give us an idea of the kind of bird the Ainu named the *kamuy*, which refers to a high spiritual being with divine status. They bestowed the name Kamui on thirteen birds: Blakiston's Fish Owl, Scops Owl, Ural Owl, Jungle Nightjar, Steller's Sea Eagle, kingfisher, Greater Pied Kingfisher, Black Woodpecker, wren, Japanese Crane, Laysan Albatross, Eurasian Tree Sparrow, and Eurasian Jay.

The most prominent of these is the Blakiston's Fish Owl, which in Ainu culture ranks alongside the bear as a high deity among land creatures. It is thought to protect villages, as suggested by its Ainu names – *kotan koro kamuy* (village god) and *kamuy chikap* (god bird). Batchelor (1901) also left a detailed record of Ainu beliefs regarding this eagle-owl. The Ainu gave it five names: *humhum okkai kamui* (the divine male who calls hum kamuy), *kamui ekashi* (the ancestor of the gods), *kamui chikappo* (divine little bird), *ya un kontukai* (the servant of the world), and *ya un kotchane guru* (the mediator of the world).

The fourth name – ya un kontukai, or the servant of the world – is significant, as the bird was believed to help a hunter, directing his movements and leading him to his quarry, while also alerting him to impending danger by calling "humhum." If it hooted loudly, danger was approaching, whereas quiet and regular calls signified peace and good luck. The day before departing for a hunt in the mountains, hunters erected wooden ceremonial staffs *(inau)*. If an owl came and sat on them overnight, making a loud noise, this was a sign of danger, and the hunt would be cancelled. When the hunter pursued his quarry, he worshipped the bird, praying with the inau, asking the bird to assist and watch over him, and drinking wine in its honour.

Batchelor also left an interesting account of the wildness and divinity of birds. A captured eagle-owl chick would be raised in a cage like a bear. Eventually, it was sacrificed and its spirit was sent as a special messenger to

God. The Ainu are known for conferring divine spirituality on birds, various animals, and plants. According to Kan Wada (1959), however, they may have avoided creating religious images of them. The Ainu perceived idols of human and animal forms as "horrible things" because they had souls and became monsters (Wada 1959, 93). They did fashion animal carvings, but apart from the wooden figures made as souvenirs during the Ainu tourism boom of the 1970s, these were sparse. The creation of items that were not intended for the tourist trade may be related to the shamanism of Siberian peoples, particularly to the images of totems as the cause of illness and death, and their shamanistic use in curing disease (Wada 1959, 76–77).

Discussion

The difference in bird artifacts between the Jomon and Yayoi periods can throw an important light on the question of cultural lineage in Japan. We might say that during the Jomon period, birds were seen as good to eat and good to think, and that the Yayoi period added a new cultural element to this relationship, of birds as good to make.

Most would agree that the practice of carving wooden birds was introduced to Japan from continental Asia during the Yayoi period. To understand their purpose, it is important to consider their social context in mainland China and its periphery. Determining whether a similar custom occurred on the continent during the same period is especially germane.

An important clue is the depiction of birds on bronzes. One example is a relic found in a warrior tomb in Gaozhuang, Huaiyin City, Jiangsu Province, near the base of China's Shandong Peninsula, which is engraved with an image of a bird attached to a pole (Hagiwara 1992). The artifact dates from the fifth century BC, which coincides closely with the Yayoi period. During the Spring and Autumn Warring States period in Chuxing, shamanistic elements and animal worship were common, and the Miao people of today were believed to have some connection to them. We do not know whether birds featured in the Miao faith system or whether the practice of representing them on objects moved from the centre to the periphery or vice versa. Comparative ethnographic research is necessary to discover how the peoples of each region acquired these customs.

In some Miao areas, a wooden pole with a carved bird at the top was erected in the middle of the square and people danced around it (Hagiwara

1996, 70–74). The bird may have represented the silver pheasant *(Lophura nycthemera)* or the phoenix. Of particular significance was the direction in which it faced, toward the sunrise, so that it could call out to the sun. Birds were thought to have the power to welcome the sun and ensure a good rice harvest.

On the other hand, ethnographic examples of bird iconography, for which a direct relationship to the fertility of harvesting is not easily discernible, also occurred among ethnic minorities in peripheral areas of China. The best-known are the carved wooden birds placed on gates at village entrances. The Hani and Akha ethnic groups from China and Thailand, respectively, followed this custom. The gate marks an obvious boundary between the outside and the inside, but the function of the carved bird is unclear (Inamura 1992).

From the ethnography and folklore in the periphery of Japan, we can understand that birds played differing roles in human life, and it is not easy to find an absolute reason as to why their images appeared in artifacts, even when people saw them as good to make. The hunter-gatherer Ainu developed animism because of their awareness of the diversity of natural resources. They saw birds, including migratory birds, not only as divine messengers but also as deities, and they believed that if they made an idol of a bird, the real bird, or God, would leave them. Nevertheless, as mentioned, some Ainu did make figures of birds and other animals, perhaps because the influence of shamanism promoted the practice. In contrast, agrarian groups seem to have viewed the creation of bird images in a positive light. Because birds played such a clear role in bringing wealth, the practice was constructive and was maintained. It is also possible to conceptualize the worship of a single object in the context of the development of agriculture. The difference between the hunter-gatherer Jomon period and the agrarian Yayoi period may have altered perceptions of animals. A trace of this can be seen in the differences in the shapes of bird artifacts.

Conclusion

Bird-shaped wooden carvings first appeared in Japan during the Yayoi period, when rice paddy cultivation was introduced to the archipelago. Perhaps this change was due to the migration of rice farmers from the continent. In any event, though the woodcarvings excavated from various Yayoi sites can be divided into two groups, large and small, this is no guarantee of significant regional or typological differences. This suggests that the carvings introduced to Japan were not diverse and that regional variations may have occurred after their arrival.

The process by which regional differences emerged needs further investigation. Considering how local groups developed their attitudes toward birds and animals may be a starting point. The Jomon economy relied on hunting and gathering, which may have had an animistic character grounded in a diverse perception of nature. The Ainu, a hunter-gatherer group in Hokkaido, had a rich awareness of nature and an associated animism. They avoided making animal idols out of respect and awe for nature. On the other hand, due to the influence of shamanism from the northern ethnic population, some Ainu may have created animal idols to visualize the causes of bad luck.

In continental Asia, bird statues for religious purposes existed concurrently with the Yayoi period. Ethnographically, the creation of the statues has been based on the relationship between the rice harvest and birds, as seen in the Miao custom.

Comparing the ethnographic examples of modern agrarian peoples to hunting-and-gathering-based groups may provide hints for thinking about the relationship between humans and birds in the Jomon and Yayoi periods. We can assume a change in natural resource use as the view of birds changed: from being good to eat and good to think, they also became good to make. The material artifacts reflect how people related to birds in an environment that they had modified due to technological innovation.

This pattern is not limited to Japan; in fact, it may be typical of many human groups that transitioned from hunting and gathering to farming, and who changed from a mobile to a sedentary lifestyle. Another possibility is that the species of birds seen every day differed depending on where human populations lived. For example, the birds that frequent the water-rich areas that are suitable for growing rice, as in Japan, will differ from those that live in regions favoured by slash-and-burn farmers, who need much less water but who require an extensive territory as they move from place to place. With the fast pace of environmental change in the Anthropocene, the birds we see every day may also change. The question of what we should think about them today can, in part, be answered by exploring our past relationships with them.

NOTES

1 See "IOC World Bird List," https://www.worldbirdnames.org/new/.
2 For an image of the bowl, see the second photograph at Mawaki, http://www.mawakiiseki.
jp/survival%20-%20p.html.

WORKS CITED

Ametani, Hajime 飴谷一, and Kimiyasu Sato 佐藤公保. 2000. "Tokaichihou no torigatamokuseihin" 東海地方の鳥形木製品―本川遺跡出土例の検討 [The wooden bird-shaped figures
in the Tokai area]. *Aichiken Maizobunkazai Center Kenkyukiyo* 愛知県埋蔵文化財センター
研究紀要 1: 9–18.
Andersson Cederholm, Erika, Amelie Björck, Kristina Jennbert, and Ann-Sofie Lönngren.
2014. "Editor's Introduction." In *Exploring the Animal Turn. Human-Animal Relations in
Science Society and Culture,* edited by E. Andersson Cederholm, A. Björck, K. Jennbert,
and A.-S. Lönngren, 5–11. Lund: Pufendorf Institute of Advanced Studies.
Batchelor, John. 1901. *The Ainu and Their Folk-lore.* London: Religious Tract Society.
Birke, Linda, and Jo Hockenhull, eds. 2012. *Crossing Boundaries: Investigating Human-Animal
Relationships.* Leiden: Brill.
Boddice, Rob. 2011. *Anthropocentrism: Humans, Animals, Environments.* Leiden: Brill.
Bowman, Chellie. n.d. "Towards an Anthropology of Birds: A Critical Review." Academia.
https://www.academia.edu/9637206/Towards_An_Anthropology_of_Birds_A_Critical_
Review.
DeGrazia, David. 2006. "On the Question of Personhood beyond Homo Sapiens." In *In
Defense of Animals: The Second Wave,* ed. Peter Singer, 40–53. Malden, MA: Blackwell.
DeMello, Margo. 2012. *Animals and Society. An Introduction to Human-Animal Studies.* New
York: Columbia University Press.
Descola, Philippe. 2005. *Par-delà nature et culture.* Paris: Gallimard.
Doré, Antoine, and Jérôme Michalon. 2017. "What Makes Human-Animal Relations
'Organizational'? The Description of Anthrozootechnical Agencements." *Organization*
24, 6: 761–80.
Fujinuma, Kunihiko 藤波邦彦. 1997. *Jomon no Dogu* 縄文の土偶 [Figures of Jomon]. Tokyo:
Kodansha 東京：講談社.
Hagiwara, Hidezaburo 萩原秀三郎. 1992. "Nichi・chou・chuuu no torizaoshuuzoku kara
mita Yayoijidai no shamanizumu" 日・朝・中の鳥竿習俗からみた弥生時代のシャーマニズム
[Shamanism during the Yayoi period as seen from a comparison of the custom of Chokan
in Japan, Korea, and China]. *Hikakuminnzokukenkyu* 比較民俗研究 [Asian folklore studies]
5: 101–11.
–. 1996. *Ine to Tori to Taiyo no Michi* 稲と鳥居と太陽の道 [The road of rice, birds and the sun].
Tokyo: Taishukan 大修館.
Hill, Erica. 2013. "Archaeology and Animal Persons: Toward a Prehistory of Human-Animal
Relations." *Environment and Society* 4, 1: 117–36.
Hirayama, Kana 平山加奈. 2009. "Yayoi jidai no noukougirei" 弥生時代の農耕儀礼―鳥形木
製品の役割を中心に. *Koji* 古事 [Ancient Matters] (Annual Bulletin of the Department of
Archaeology, Tenri University) 10: 15–33.
Hussain, Shumon T. 2018. "MAMMOTHSTEPPE-LIFE. Mammoths, Owls and Other
Creatures: Sketching the Trail towards a Comparative Investigation of Human-Animal
Situations in the European Upper Paleolithic." In *The Situationality of Human-Animal*

Relations: Perspectives from Anthropology and Philosophy, ed. Thiemo Breyer and Thomas Widlok, 83–111. Bielefeld: Transcript.

Inamura, Tsutomu 稲村務. 1992. "Hani zoku no sonmon: shisanpanna Hanizoku no kaisou to riniji no doutai" ハニ族の村門—西双版納ハニ族の階層とリニジの動態 [Village gate of the Hani people: Xishuangbanna Hani hierarchy and Lineage dynamics]. *Hikakuminnzokukenkyu* 5: 175–86.

Kanaseki, Hiroshi 金関恕. 1975. "Yayoi jin no seishinseikatsu" 弥生人の精神生活 [Spiritual life of the Yayoi people]. In *Kodaishi Hakkutsu 4: Inasaku no Hajimari* 古代史発掘4稲作の始まり [Excavation of ancient history 4: The beginning of rice cultivation], eds. Makoto Sahara 佐原眞 and Hiroshi Kanaseki 金関恕, 80–86. Tokyo: Kodansha.

Kokubu, Naoici 古代日韓関係の一面を窺う. 1983. "Yayoi shakai to soto kei shinko Kodai Nikkannkankei no Ichimen wo ukagau" 弥生社会と蘇塗系信仰 [Yayoi society and the soto-beliefs: A glimpse into ancient Japan-Korea relations]. *Gekkann Kankoku Bunka* 月刊韓国文化 [Korean culture monthly] 6: 21–26.

Kompatscher, Gabriela, Reingard Spannring, and Karin Schachinger. 2017. *Human-Animal Studies: Eine Einführung für Studierende und Lehrende.* Münster: Waxmann.

Locke, Piers. 2017. "Elephants as Persons, Affective Apprenticeship, and Fieldwork with Non-human Informants in Nepal." *HAU: Journal of Ethnographic Theory* 7, 1: 353–76.

McFarland, Sarah and Ryan Hedinger, eds. 2009. *Animals and Agency: An Interdisciplinary Exploration.* Leiden: Brill.

Mithen, Steven. 1999. "The Hunter-Gatherer Prehistory of Human-Animal Interactions." *Anthrozoös* 12, 4: 195–204.

Mizuno, Masayoshi 水野正好. 1982. "Yayoi jidai no matsuri." 弥生時代のまつり *Rekishikouron* 歴史公論 82: 60–62. Tokyo: Yuzankaku 雄山閣.

Morton, Timothy. 2017. *Humankind: Solidarity with Non-Human People.* Brooklyn: Verso Books.

Niimi, Tomoko 新美倫子. 2008. "Tori to Nihonjin" 鳥と日本人 [Birds and Japanese people]. In *Hito to Doubutsu no Kankei* 人と動物の関係 [Human-animal relations], ed. Toyohiro Nishimoto 西本豊弘, 226–52. Tokyo: Yoshikawakobunkan 吉川広文堂.

Roscher, Mieke. 2016. "Zwischen Wirkungsmacht und Handlungsmacht: Sozialgeschichtliche Perspektiven auf Tierliche Agency." In *Das Handeln der Tiere: Tierliche Agency im Fokus der Human-Animal Studies,* ed. Sven Wirth, Anett Laue, Markus Kurth, Katharina Dornenzweig, Leonie Bossert, and Karsten Balgar, 43–65. Bielefeld: Transcript Verlag.

Uno, Harva. 1938. *Die religiösen Vorstellungen der altaischen Völker.* Helsinki: Suomalainen Tiedeakatemia. (Translated by Tanaka Katsuhiko, as *Shamanis: Arutai kei shominzoku no sekaizo.* Tokyo: Sanseido, 1971.)

Wada, Kan 和田完. 1959. "Karafuto Ainu no Guzo" 樺太アイヌの偶像 [Figures of Karafuto Ainu]. *Studies from the Research Institute for Northern and Arctic Culture* 14: 43–78.

Watanabe, Makoto 渡辺誠. 1995. "Kankoku no soto to yayoi jidai no torigata mokuseihin" 韓国の蘇塗と弥生時代の鳥形木製品 [Soto of Korea and wooden bird-shaped figures in the Yayoi period]. In *Kofunbunka to sono Dentou* 古墳文化とその伝統 [Kofun culture and its traditions], eds.Hiroshi Kanaseki 金関恕 and Masaaki Okita 置田雅昭, 661–82. Tokyo: Benseisha 勉誠社.

Watsuji, Tetsurō 和辻哲郎. (1935) 1979. *Fūdo: Ningentekikousatsu* 風土——人間的考察 [Climate and culture: A philosophical study]. Tokyo: Iwanami Shoten 岩波書店.

Williams, Dai. 2017. *Ainu Ethnobiology.* Boston: Society of Ethnobiology.

Yamada, Yasuhiro 山田康弘. 1996. "Torigatamokuseihin no saikentou" 鳥型木製品の再検討 [Re-examination of bird-shaped wood products]. *Shinano* 信濃48, 4: 1–27.

10

Birds as Figurative Patterns and Artifacts as Efficient Agents

Agency and Ritual Behaviour among the Mentawaians of Bat Rereiket (Siberut, Indonesia)

Lionel Simon and Syarul Sakaliou

As CHELLIE BOWMAN's (n.d.) synthesis work demonstrates, the consideration of avian fauna in anthropological literature reflects the evolution of theoretical axes through which animals in general have been problematized for nearly a century. Birds, as anthropological objects, are thus witness to the epistemological questions that have shaken up the anthropological field. What has come to be called the "ontological turn" (Latour 1991; Viveiros de Castro 1998, 2009; Ingold 2000; Descola 2013) is in this respect entirely symptomatic of the novel ways of conceptualizing relations between humans and their environments. Highlighting the agency of "non-humans" has fostered the idea that interactions are not guided by an opposition between subject and object. The notion of companion species (Haraway 2003), the fungal trajectories organized by the "mushroom at the end of the world" (Tsing 2015), or the semiotic dimension of a shared engagement within the world (Kohn 2013) are notable examples of the increasing complexity of studies pertaining to systems of relations among beings. They strive to illuminate the interdependence and ordinary entanglements that connect individuals and collectives – including in the social and political realms of their lives – to beings that surround them.

It seems to us that the present volume attests to this renewing of the anthropological perspective and, more generally, of ways of problematizing human and non-human relationships (Laugrand and Simon 2020). In doing so, it extends Pierre Le Roux and Bernard Sellato's (2006) explicit illustration of the importance of avian fauna in Southeast Asia. The authors point to the significance of birds and their symbolic importance in ceremonial and ritual practices but also in myths and artistic creations. These contributions showcase how diverse and multiform these interests in birds can be.

In our contribution to this endeavour, we propose to illustrate the plurality of expectations that the Mentawaians of Siberut Island, Indonesia, express regarding avian fauna. This involves documenting and proposing a first analysis of the ways in which birds intervene in the interactions that humans weave with their environment. In proposing three entry points – divination in a ceremonial context, cynegetic (hunting) practices, and iconography – this essay strives to link birds to three related modes of apprehension: as individuals, as identified species, and as "life forms" (winged bipedal animals).

Siberut and the Mentawaians

This chapter is grounded in data gathered in 2018 and 2019 during three research trips with the Mentawaian populations living in Bat Rereiket, in the south of the island of Siberut (150 kilometres off the island of Sumatra). Scattered in the dense tropical forest that covers an island of roughly four thousand square kilometres, the Mentawaians are organized in exogamous patrilineal clans (termed *uma*) among egalitarian group entities comprising no centralized figure of power or political authority (Wallace 1951; Schefold 2001; Hammons 2010, 2–15). They are subjected to increasing pressures from government land-use planning schemes (Schefold 1998; Reeves 1999; Figueras 2010, 19-20; Yulia, Zulfa, and Naldi 2018), alternative tourism projects (Persoon 2003a; Bakker 2007), and various pervasive influences, particularly of a mercantile (Persoon 2001, 2003a) and religious nature (Persoon 2004; Delfi 2013; Hammons 2016). Today, they number only two thousand or so in Siberut's dense forest *(ka leleu)*. They are disseminated along river branches from which the clans generally derive their names. The clans assemble a variable number of nuclear families *(lalep)* around a collective house (the uma) where the great ceremonies *(puliaijat)* are held. But day-to-day activities take place within the nuclear family according to a gendered division of labour, although few of them are the privilege of a single sex.

The Mentawaians derive most of their diet from horticulture.[1] They grow a wide variety of fruit trees and tubers,[2] but it is the *sagu,* small baguettes made of the processed pulp of the sago tree trunk *(Metroxylon sagu),* that constitutes the staple food at the centre of all meals. These are usually supplemented by river fishing,[3] small-game hunting (for birds or rodents), gathering, or harvesting for larvae *(tamara)*. The Mentawaians also practise animal husbandry. Livestock – mainly chickens (*Gallus gallus domesticus,* or *goukgouk* in Mentawai) and pigs (*Sus domesticus,* or *saina*) – are reared for important events and consumed in ceremonial occasions.[4] Sporadically, deer *(Rusa timorensis),* wild pigs *(Sus barbatus),* and the island's four endemic primate species are the favoured prey of hunting activities.[5] Hunting is now subject to government limitations imposed in the name of biodiversity preservation. It is therefore mainly practised to underscore important ritual acts.

Omens and Divination: Birds as Species

In anthropological literature, birds frequently figure as partners in ritual action or as important actors in predictive activities (Laugrand and Simon 2018). In Taiwan, Scott Simon (2018) notably showed how profoundly Truku mantic activity draws from the "lived worlds" of birds to formulate omens. Using their knowledge of ordinary bird behaviour, people can distinguish salient comportments to evaluate imminent dangers or to portend misfortune. Like Gregory Forth (2007) and Michael Dove (1993) – who work with the Nage and Kantu of Indonesia, respectively, Frédéric Laugrand, Antoine Laugrand, and Guy Tremblay (2019) highlight an identical phenomenon in the Philippines, in the ethnographic contexts of the Blaans of Mindanao, the Ibaloy of the cordillera, and the Alangan Mangyan.

Centred on avian rhythms, these omens do not require specific devices to emerge. On the contrary, such cases exemplify a widespread tendency, that of detecting auguries through variations in the milieu – in this case, through animal behaviours. The Mentawaians also adopt this posture of attentiveness to modulations in the environment. They too sometimes believe that outlying events foretell future outcomes, granting predictive roles to specific species. In particular, the songs of the *kuliak* (the Ashy Tailorbird, *Orthotomus ruficeps*) and of the *kemut* (the Greater Coucal, *Centropus sinensis*) provoke certain ways of acting (Forestier et al. 2008, 62–63). The former is a land bird endemic to the island of Siberut, common in all biotopes, from primary and secondary forests to mangroves, and from coastal wooded areas to horticultural zones (Kemp 2000; Meyers 2016, 72, 136).[6] The latter is not endemic but breeds on the island. It lives in humid forests and swamps, as well as in areas that are subject to human activity, occasionally inhabiting mangrove or lowland forests. The songs of these two birds foster caution. The song of the kuliak prohibits leaving the house, warning of dangers lurking outside; that of the kemut suspends all activity (Forestier et al. 2008, 62–63). The Mentawaians thus prove attentive to these birds' vocalization, whose predictive powers depend on "the contingency of their own lived world," to use a formula from Scott Simon (2018, 152, translated by Laura Shine).

It remains challenging to isolate the mechanisms driving individuals to distinguish these species from the realm of living things or to establish the causal links that lend a prophesizing quality to the songs of these birds. Often, men and women refer to "the way elders acted" to justify and legitimize this type of knowledge. The attention paid to the songs nevertheless denotes an attentiveness that confers an annunciatory function to a sound. The songs here figure in a semiotic relationship wherein an occurrence – a behaviour or a sound – refers to a signified. Whether the relationship between sound and omen is indexical or symbolic brings us back to the causal regime binding these two elements. Whether the noise is understood as the codified expression of a message (the meaning of which stems from the conjunction between an occurrence and the moment when it takes place) or as an indication of an event in progress (as a tangible manifestation of the omen) is difficult to establish and would require a specific in-depth inquiry. In any case, it is worth noting that this type of inference is widespread in both the geographical area covered by this volume (Southeast Asia or the Austronesian area) and largely beyond.[7] This denotes a specific way of involving oneself in the world, a propensity to apprehend incidents as reflections (or heralds) of current or future phenomena. It also denotes a sensory knowing of the environment and an inclination to interpret some of its variations as resulting from entanglements between disparate phenomena (a sound and a future incident).

Beyond this attentive posture, one that recognizes and interprets signs based on avian behaviour, the Mentawaians also frequently resort to specific devices to predict outcomes. These devices form an integral part of all ceremonies *(uliat)*. They differ from "spontaneous" omens in attaching divination to an active stance, rather than a more passive foreseeing. It relates more directly to "making it happen" than to "seeing it coming." This mantic could be understood as a "constraining" action on the course of things. It relies on chickens (goukgouk) and pigs (saina), to which the Mentawaians express their wishes. They grab the hens or crouch down beside the pigs to

Figure 10.1 Aman Naru, a shaman from Butui, holds the mesentery of a chicken and reads the auguries, a form of divination that is performed at all ceremonies. If the auguries are good, the bird will contribute to the realization of human projects.

explain what is expected of them. The animal is circulated to everyone present to point out the beneficiaries of the requests. The Mentawaians then break the hens' necks (or slit the throats of pigs). This killing is understood to convert the victims into beings capable of fulfilling the stated aspirations. Following the sacrifice, the hearts of pigs or the ventral mesenterium of chickens *(lauru)* are extracted (Figure 10.1). The signs thus rendered visible are meant to reflect the intentions of the sacrificed animals, manifesting their desire (or lack thereof) to accomplish the tasks assigned to them. In a serious tone, the assembly member reading the organs pronounces "maeruk!" (it's good!) or "tamaeruk!" (it's not good!) to establish the omen.[8] A bad outcome launches a new sacrificial process, since the realization of human desires depends entirely on assistance from the animals.

In this context, animals are no longer "listened to"; they are truly petitioned as beings that are capable of influencing the course of individual lives. The hens figure at the centre of intersubjective relationships, as partners and privileged interlocutors. As Salomo, an elder from Butui, stated during an interview on November 26, 2018,

> I cannot tell you why it's like that [why the future doesn't appear in animals' viscera if we don't ask them before they are killed]. But what I do know is that when you don't tell the hens, you don't see anything. There is nothing to see. But when you talk to them, you can see the lines. It's like that.

For the Mentawaians, a peaceful passage in the world is thus unthinkable without resorting to animals. Indeed, their practices suggest the attribution of singular characteristics to hens and pigs. Foreseeing a happy or unhappy future is possible precisely because the animals' sacrifice generates their ability to carry out human desires. They are differentiated beings, ones that allow humans to compensate for their inability to fully control their existence. They reflect a complex inscription in a world that remains inhospitable without a recourse to beings possessing qualities that humans do not. Without the support of these animals, rituals are bound to remain unsuccessful. As sacrificial beings, hens are intermediary figures between humans and the forces shaping their lives.

The Animist Scheme in a Cynegetic Context: A Discernment That Upholds Relations

As we have just seen, the roles the Mentawaians attribute to birds in mantic activities single them out as subjectivities (they are interlocutors) and as species (they are differentiated beings).

Other avian species highlight the animist scheme (Descola 2013; Århem and Sprenger 2016) that upholds relations with animals in general.[9] If the Mentawaians prove rather exhaustive in their attribution of intentional qualities to non-humans, this attribution is modulated by a notable discernment linking hunter and prey. Indeed, not all animals are liable to being treated as subjects, and only some of them elicit attentive precautions. This is most apparent in cynegetic practices, which distinguish two types of hunting and two types of prey.

The first type of hunting serves to supplement a diet based on horticulture. It complements sago palm baguettes (sagu), as does river fishing. The latter constitutes the most systematic procurement method, yielding small fish, frogs, and shrimp. Hunting destined to enrich meals – or to fill young men's spare time – takes place close to the house and does not require any preparation. It is often practised with air guns. The victims – rodents or birds – elicit no great precaution. A few feathers or tails are taken from the slaughtered specimens and hung on the roof mats that cover houses, almost perfunctorily and without much attention. We have seen people inadvertently forgetting to do so, without fearing great consequences. These quiet gestures thus appear to be of moderate importance to the Mentawaians. However, they are not without effect on the quality of the relationships that humans maintain with animals. As part of a broader management of the environment and its inhabitants, they are meant to demonstrate a parsimonious use of resources. They reveal the hunters' good disposition toward and respect for their prey. This benevolent attitude is thought to induce the favours of Tai ka leleu – the "master of the forest," the personified being synthesizing its diversity – in turn generating successful hunts. Though this type of hunting does not engender complex relationships, the management of resources is broadly included in a type of moral order. This is also evident during the consumption of animals. All parts of animals are systematically eaten, and meat is distributed in a strictly equitable way,[10] testifying to this desire for frugality and balance. These attentions contribute to the harmonious inclusion of humans in their environment.

To explain the care with which they hang feathers on their roofs, our interlocutors also frequently mentioned the desire to make the house "happy." Understood as an entity synthesizing everything it contains, the uma, enlivened by its new adornments, is then said to foster a positive momentum for all its occupants, human and non-human. Although subtle, these attentions differ by the enmeshment of multiple purposes. These refer to a complex system of relationships that generate particular living conditions, a system characterized by the imbrication of levels of conditioning, each level being indispensable for the fulfillment of a serene life. We will return to this idea later. Let us note for the moment that the individual, the house as a living whole, and the surrounding environment constitute nested stories that such gestures actualize. The birds here reveal a hierarchical arrangement of levels of inclusiveness and constraint.

Figure 10.2 A Mentawaian hunting camp. This makeshift shelter, a wooden structure roofed with banana leaves, protects against rain during the night.

But as suggested, the simplicity of these quasi-"mechanical" gestures contrasts with the hunting excursions that the Mentawaians conduct "in the forest" (ka leleu), which involve spending several days at a hunting camp (*sapo,* Figure 10.2). They require more sophisticated devices to manage three pillars of the successful predatory act (L. Simon 2020a). The first two mandate ritual sequences carried out in the forest, at the start of the hunt. Addressing Tai ka leleu and forest trees in succession, these rituals aim to secure the support of all those who can facilitate the hunt.[11] Tai ka leleu is asked to free the animals, to make them available. Presented as the master of the ecosystem, this being synthesizes the forest space and all its occupants. The presence of prey in the hunters' path is thus understood to stem from its will. Similarly, the Mentawaians ask that trees (or the ground) send them prey to fulfill human aspirations. Their contribution is explicitly demanded: "Look, these are the hunters you must send the animals to; look at these weapons, send them the monkeys."

Again, these ritual acts denote the entrenchment of multiple levels of constraint and the intervention of various interlocutors. They illustrate the prevalence of an asymmetric animist scheme posited by Kaj Århem (2016a, 2016b) when he distinguishes between a "symmetrical animism" – based on egalitarian precepts and best exemplified by Amazonian societies (Descola 1996; Viveiros de Castro 1998) – and an "asymmetrical animism," predominant in Southeast Asia. The latter specifically includes hierarchical hunting relationships in which the game appears as the "livestock" of a master spirit. This leads to a trade-based relationship differing from the intersubjective relationships that Amazonian societies maintain with their prey. Among the Mentawaians, the centrality (or the omnipresence) of Tai ka leleu reveals this asymmetrical relationship, much like the hunting rituals aiming, in part, to offer food and material to the master of the forest to encourage him to free his animals. The relationship is thus understood as an exchange. Yet hunting rituals are not devoid of intersubjective relationships between humans and animals, even in the absence of shamanic actions to "de-subjectify" the quarry and eliminate the risks of counter-predation.[12]

Indeed, the presence of animals in human pathways does not guarantee a successful hunt. For the Mentawaians, the animal must consent to be caught and must offer itself to their poison arrows. This aspect we wish to examine more closely. Although hunters do pursue several types of game (such as small birds, pangolins, and rodents), some are more preferable than others: the island's four species of primate, deer, wild pigs, bats *(leitua)*, and two bird species – the *kailaba* hornbill and the *kotkot*. When killed and eaten, they are treated in a specific manner. Their skulls are positioned in a significant location on the central beam *(lelengan kelabaga)* of the uma (Figure 10.3). Thus, placed in the centre of the house, they are meant to attract their living fellows by attesting to the good care bestowed upon them by humans. Adequate treatment of the skulls is understood to guide the behaviour of future prey, encouraging it to surrender to humans.

To ensure the collaboration of the dead animals, the Mentawaians provide special care to their skulls. They speak to them, intersperse leafy bouquets harvested on successful hunting trips, and adorn the most imposing skulls with artifacts covered in painted motifs. They describe the latter as "toys" for the animals (*umat simagre*, "toys for their souls"), and the bouquets are presented as fresh leaves gathered in the forest they once roamed: "Look at the beautiful leaves I brought you." They are meant to keep the skulls happy and make them comfortable.[13] The effectiveness of these acts, the causality that unites the success of future hunts and the care provided to the skulls, rests on the idea that animals, dead or alive, keep on communicating with each other. Ensuring the comfort and pleasure of the victims must thus influence the messages circulating between house and forest. This fosters enthusiastic talk about the treatment of game animals, making future prey more inclined to accept a seemingly dire fate and integrate human dwellings.

Figure 10.3 In a house at Butui, the skulls of a deer, a wild pig, and primates killed during the hunt sit on a beam. Parts of the pig skull have been painted with red and black lines, a carved bird on a pole is attached to the deer skull, and bunches of leaves hang throughout. These decorations testify to the hunters' respect for their prey.

This highlights an understanding of animals as thinking individualities: as beings endowed with intentionality, each one of them must be contented. What's more, these appeasements are assumed to affect independent and specific groups. Touching the skull of a wild pig has no bearing on macaques, gibbons, or deer, and inversely. Each animal is seen as a member of a collective that is separate from others. The care provided to skulls hence simultaneously actualizes the links binding each individual to its species – grounding the practices' effectiveness – and the ontological divide between species.[14] Hunters see themselves as operating in a compartmentalized world. It is animals' existence as parts of discrete groups, as well as the continuity between members of these groups, that they act upon to foster successful future pursuits.

The Mentawaians thus mobilize connections between live and dead animals to serve their own purposes. The manifest impact of their care and consideration on future hunts is rendered plausible by this very connection. In this context, animals are embedded in a general animist scheme: they are intentional beings, privileged interlocutors, subjectivities inscribed in a closed collective delineated along speciated lines. Through their different modalities, hunting practices and their accompanying precautions highlight the modulations of this animist scheme, as preferred species are subject to different behaviours. This scheme does not imply that all beings, dead or alive, give rise to complex intersubjective relations, even when, as for the Mentawaians, intentionality and affects are attributed to non-humans in a highly systematic way.[15] Birds testify to this discernment, which rests on distinction between species and criteria such as size.[16]

Birds are taken as part of a species, not yet as a particular "form of life." This departs from a feature we wish to examine more closely, one that emphasizes the avian form as a distinctive attribute.

Birds as a Figurative Theme: Replicating the Forest Space and Assuming Acts of Predation

The House as Arrangement: Reproducing the Forest Ecosystem
The third focal point we here propose surveys figurative strategies, in which birds *(sia'gou)* hold an important place. The richness of Mentawaian iconography and their aesthetic attentions have long fascinated travellers (Crisp 1799) and researchers (Schefold 2002, 2017; Persoon 2003b; Wagner 2003; Delfi 2015; Figueras 2020) alike. The ornamentation of bodies and the graphic complexity of their artifacts – be they technical or decorative objects – are indeed quite remarkable and worthy of interest. In these pages, we draw the outlines of an initial analysis to showcase the complexity of relations imbricated in Mentawaian *decorum*.

Figure 10.4a, b, and c Birds as architectural adornments, Alimoi. These figurative pictures are typical of the decorations found in Mentawaian homes throughout the Rereiket region.

We examine one of the most explicit manifestations of this aesthetic care – the creation of architectural adornments. These comprise garlands and vegetal festoons, often made of sago palm leaves. Houses also contain animal representations. These can be simple evocations or complex designs using various techniques – most often sculpture, painting, or bas-relief. They hang from gables and decorate walls, roofs, and shelves (Figure 10.4a, b, c). Birds are the most varied forms and, along with monkeys *(joja)*, the most often depicted. Lizards and turtles are also represented, though less visibly. All these motifs are notably realistic. Beyond forms and proportions, this preoccupation is most evident in the movement and postures of depicted monkeys. Wooden birds are, for their part, usually situated higher up, suspended from ceilings or placed on horizontal beams.

Some objects, such as the *sia'gat batak* (wooden teeth), demonstrate the aesthetic preoccupations behind the production of ornamental artifacts (Figure 10.5). They were shown to us as replicas of Mentawaian teeth that had been sharpened to points. According to the most spontaneous Mentawaian commentators, their purpose is to make the house more hospitable. Vegetal festoons serve a similar purpose. But limiting ornaments to simple aesthetic or artistic functions seems too restrictive.[17] As Wilfried Wagner (2003, 199, emphasis added) underlines regarding corporal modifications, the "beauty" associated with form among the Mentawaians always surpasses the sensible and is thus never limited to purely aesthetic qualities: "beauty

Figure 10.5 Sia'gat batak, Butui. Terminating in a bird's head, these wooden carvings represent the sharpened teeth of the Mentawaians.

is a form of self-perception and a life-concept. *When beauty has been achieved, it is connoted with other qualities.* It forms the visible, sensory side of something transcendental."

Similarly, Mentawaian vocabulary suggests that the agency (Gell 1998) of artifacts does not rest solely on their adherence to canons of beauty, important though this may be (Schefold 2017). Whereas the word *makire* (good, fine) reflects the fine craftsmanship of objects and their formal intrinsic qualities – their similitude to prototypes – notions of *maeru* (good) and, more significantly, of *mateu,* refer to the "efficacy" of artifacts. As Schefold (2017, 149) explains,

> There is one more seminal term the Mentawaians use to judge the esthetic value of an object: *mateu.* In contrast to *makire, mateu* is not an absolute statement, as it is directed toward the relationship of a given object with a perceived context. This term is perhaps best translated by equating it with the word "fitting." A huge carved bird in a small house is not *mateu,* even if by itself it is so well made that it would deserve to be called *makire.* It simply does not fit. A clumsily carved bow in the hands of an experienced hunter is not *mateu* either, as it does not harmonize with its owner … Consistent with this idea is the fact that the words for "good" and "beautiful" are the same in Mentawai – *maeru.* When the term is used, only the context can make it clear whether it describes an object's technical qualities or its esthetic aspects.

Fine craftsmanship is thus always subservient to "function" (functionality, usage, utility), and creations cannot be abstracted from their destined uses or the context in which they will be exposed.[18] It is of course the very nature of this function that we seek to illuminate. Many comments we collected regarding these ornaments can help do this.

The Mentawaians propose a causal link between decorative artifacts and household well-being. They most commonly seek to "make the house happy," wherein the building serves as a metonym for its parts and what it contains. This preoccupation was mentioned to us during an important *gurut uma* (an inauguration ceremony for umas) while a new house was being built in Butui. The owner, Aman Naru, explained, "Everything works better [when ornaments are plentiful and uma rituals are performed correctly], it's like the sun, it shines. Everything is well: utensils work well, people are happy, the house too."

Following this idea, ornaments are apprehended through their inscription in an environment; they contribute to its harmony as a system. Meaningfully, the Mentawaians call these figurines – like the collection of decorative items a house contains – umat simagre, which is usually translated as "toys for souls." As such, they are meant to contribute to the well-being of the house (and to that of all its parts) and are required for the fulfillment of the diverse beings gathered within it. They contribute to the success of its inhabitants; in short, they provide positive momentum. Bird figurines, like monkey paintings and bas-reliefs, are parts of a sum (the house) of which they modify the features (they provide a positive momentum). They acquire value from the context in which they are presented, since the quality of their craftsmanship and their aesthetic dimensions are in the service of a larger composition. It is through their inscription in a larger arrangement – the house – that they must first and foremost be understood.

The house thus evokes a specific type of figuration that refers to an analogic scheme,[19] as explained by Descola (2006, 179, emphasis added, translated by Laura Shine):

> In short, the figurative aim of analogism is, first and foremost, to *render present networks of correspondence between discontinuous elements,* which largely supposes multiplying components of the image to better de-individualize its subject. In this way, and independently of the analogic figuration's level of detail, it *does not so much strive to imitate an objectively presented "natural" prototype as to reinstate a thread of affinities within which the prototype takes on meaning and acquires a certain type of agency* ... What analogism seeks to make apparent in images is even more abstract than what other modes of identification strive to figure: not a relationship between subject and subject, as in animism, or a relationship of shared inherence to a class, as in totemism, or a relationship between subject and object, as in naturalism, but a *metarelationship, meaning an encompassing relationship which structures disparate relationships.*

Taken as elements of a greater whole, ornaments thus showcase the model that their arrangement strives to reproduce. Descola's work invites us to connect modes of figuration and ontological schemes, in that the image gives rise to features associated with the beings it represents. It is worth noting that rather than representing or figuring specimens by exposing some of their ontological features, Mentawaian artifacts are tasked with replicating, within the domestic space, the general structure of a forest ecosystem represented in a state of harmony.[20]

Two elements uphold this idea. First, Mentawaians readily state that decorative objects are like a piece of forest: "It's like a piece of forest, so the house is happy," explained Teorepako, a sikerei (shaman) from Atabai. Second, it is significant that all depicted animals live in the forest and that they are often designated through generic monikers, such as sia'gou (bird), joja (monkey), and bate (lizard or monitor). As "types of beings" or "life forms" rather than identified species, the animals contribute to the replication of the forest as a system, assembling to figure its general composition.

A Substitution Effect: Managing the Morality of Predation

The preceding discussion suggests the notion of "ritual image," which is defined as a complex system of actions and relations (Severi 2007, 2009, 12–41; Charlier 2012) not solely aimed at signification, and whose agency is not limited to fostering aesthetic fascination. Nonetheless, figurative strategies are not analogous to ritual imagery. They do not endeavour to allow a tangible (and ritually orchestrated) reunion between ontologically differentiated beings, but rather to artificially produce a microcosm in the image of the forest. Admittedly, the apparatus (the house) as a whole works toward neatly differentiating between species, but it does not aim to transcend ordinary ontological segmentations. As we would now like to demonstrate, it seeks to substitute a replica to the forest prototype it represents.

Having shed light on the overall effect engendered by the "animalform" ornaments, we can problematize the realism that is integral to their craftsmanship. Indeed, though the overall composition is of great importance, the paintings, sculptures, and bas-reliefs draw part of their agency from their formal qualities. These explicitly uphold evocations through their evident mimetic dimension. Their shapes, sizes, placements, and postures attest to a genuine attempt at replication. There is no meaningful work on scales: the figurines are not miniaturized, their size roughly analogous to that of the actual birds and monkeys. This allows us to hypothesize that their creation also aims for a substitution effect, that the ornaments strive to supplement the prototypes they represent. As mentioned previously, the Mentawaians readily claim that figurines and paintings are like "a piece of forest" in dwellings. Moreover, in a specific context, this substitution effect is rendered explicit.

Figure 10.6 Manai built for the inauguration ceremony of a new house, Butui. A carved wooden bird perches on the crossbar, and figurines representing monkeys also appear. One is on the middle of the crossbar and another at the top of the right-hand post. They are made of palm fibre.

During gurut uma – inauguration ceremonies for umas – Mentawaians construct a gateway *(manai)* in front of their new homes (Figure 10.6). On these structures, they place bird figurines and dolls made of *paula* palm fibres that represent monkeys *(joja paula)*. These objects are described as a sort of "contract" binding the owner to his house, as he pledges to bring home the same number of animals he has placed on the manai. More generally, the manai displays the care with which the household will ensure the continuous influx of skulls to hang on the lelengan kelabaga beam. The skulls of forest animals are also understood to enliven the house. The manai thus aims to guarantee vitality in the dwelling.[21] As the hunter returns with a monkey or bird, he can remove the corresponding artifact from the manai. In this ceremonial context, the substitution effect thus becomes particularly explicit, like the relational dimension that characterizes the inscriptions of individuals within their uma.

Birds here feature as terms of a family's relationship with its home. What is made apparent are the conditions for a harmonious and fecund fulfillment of beings. The house thus adorned aims to replicate the ideal of the forest ecosystem. As a sizeable ornamental apparatus, it reproduces an interlacement uniting ontologically distinct beings (since, as previously examined, individuals are siloed in species-collectives) into a coherent ensemble,[22] a condition for each being's fulfillment.

We can further associate these ornamental apparatuses with the moral order in which the Mentawaians generally situate all their acts of predation. Hunting and gathering plants is always subject to significant precautions. Much as when they hunt down animals, the Mentawaians adopt a respectful posture when cutting down trees to build their homes. Referring constantly to the parts and the whole, they speak to the selected tree, explaining the aims of the felling. This allows them to maintain a harmonious relationship with the other members of its species-collective and with the forest as a whole. "We cannot cut a tree for no reason," they explain, or "the forest is upset if we are not respectful." The Mentawaians readily justify such attentions as appeals to Tai ka leleu (who personifies the forest as a whole). Procuring adequate care to the house – always understood as an assemblage of the trees felled for its construction – thwarts the destructive nature of the predatory activity, offering as a counterpoint a replication of the original forest ecosystem within the home.

This probably explains why artifacts are described as umat simagre, as toys for the souls of all household beings. Figurative practices would hence serve as counterpoints to the tree felling that is necessary to build the uma. The relational well-being economy that the ornaments actualize would thus find part of its raison d'être in its compensatory effect. It could also be argued that the dynamic postures of the figurines translate the vitality they are meant to provoke in the household. Moreover, in light of this "compensatory" effect and the relational dimension that upholds the ornamentation, the craftsmanship itself plays an important role and takes on a performative function. Engaging in this craft attests to humans' good dispositions toward trees, the forest, and related beings. The very act of making becomes one of the terms of a relationship that must be tended to. Beyond their iconicity, part of the efficiency of the figurines and paintings stems from their "indiciality," from their translation of humans' good dispositions. They show the efforts made to ensure the well-being of the house and its inhabitants; they render explicit a desire to respectfully remain invested in the forest ecosystem.

This first analysis – which needs further refining – sheds light on the imbrication of numerous levels of agency that place figurines at the core of a complex relational weave. The attention paid by families to the well-being of their home reveals how parts and the whole commingle in a "generalizing synecdoche." The happiness of the uma influences the adequate functioning of the objects it contains and the beings that inhabit it. As part of the assemblage they contribute to, the bird-shaped ornaments showcase the play of scales in which the forest is reproduced (in its "structure" or its overall composition) within the house. The adorned dwelling is a demonstrative apparatus that shows visitors – human or otherwise – the owner's artistic competencies but also, in doing so, his moral qualities. Through their figurines, the Mentawaians actualize and confirm their full inscription in an environment wherein well-being depends on the preservation of the ecosystem and on the quality of humans' inscription within it.

Conclusion: Imbrication and Encompassment Effects, or the Replication of Harmony

As demonstrated throughout this chapter, birds figure at the centre of multiple trajectories and relations for the Mentawaians. In each context, they play an important role and shed light on certain transversal logics underpinning the Mentawaians' interactions with their environment.

In the hunt, they uphold an animist understanding of the environment. Quotidian hunting necessitates no particular precaution, but forest hunting (*uraurau ka leleu*) is underpinned by complex rituals that illustrate the attribution of intentional qualities to prey. Certain birds have the potential to abet human projects. Chickens are solicited to ensure a promising future, whereas the songs of Ashy Tailorbirds and Greater Coucals are interpreted as auguries. As decorative objects, birds appear more as "life forms," though homeowners sometimes identify the species depicted (Schefold 2017). Inserted in the household, they replicate the forest ecosystem,[23] are implanted in the moral dimension of predation, and unite humans to their dwelling and to the environment. In this context, they are part and parcel of a constant game that metonymically transfers from part to whole. Central actors in an ecology-economy of well-being, they contribute to the successful inscription of individuals in the dwelling and, more largely, in the general space. In a word, their preponderance as an iconographic theme reflects their supposed role in the forest ecosystem: they enliven, brighten, and allow beings to shine.

Notwithstanding the heterogeneous modes of apprehensions related to birds, we can unravel a transversal logic, a hierarchical imbrication or encompassment of varying levels of constraint and the importance of a metonymical scheme that ceaselessly articulates parts and the whole. The uma appears as a replica of the forest, not only because it reproduces the forest ecosystem, but also because the material from which it is built remains connected to its original context and maintains its intentional properties. Because of this persistence, it cannot be mistreated without provoking the wrath of Tai ka leleu and of the assemblage it subsumes. In this way, the Mentawaians' considerations for their uma are meant to generate a chain reaction of wholes and parts: good care affects the house, all the elements and objects it contains, its inhabitants and its visitors, but also the encompassing forest as well as all of its parts.

This logic of imbrication is probably rendered most explicit through cynegetic activity because the associated rituals attend to each level of constraint. One must tend to relations with skulls so that members of their species-collective allow themselves to be killed; the entire forest, through its trees and soil, is petitioned to send animals to the hunters; finally, exchanges with Tai ka leleu are needed to free his livestock for humans. Birds are, as we showed, at the core of all these trajectories that allow us to consider their singularities (singular and specific) and their complex inscriptions in a world understood as a relational enmeshment.

NOTES

1 For a synthesis of Mentawaian arboriculture and horticulture, see Hubert Forestier et al. (2008, 82–101). See also Hadi et al. (2009). For a more general synthesis of the acquisition and production of means of subsistence, see Gerard Persoon (2001, 69–72); and Darmanto Darmanto (2020).

2 Trees include jackfruit (*Artocarpus heterophyllus,* or *pegu* in Mentawai), durian *(Durio zibethinus, doriat),* banana (*Musa* spp., *mago*), and coconut *(Cocos nucifera, toitet).* Tubers include yam (*Dioscorea* spp., *laiket*) and taro (*Colocasea esculenta, gettek*).

3 River fishing comprises three main activities: *paligagra* (diurnal dip netting practised by women), *pangacla* (diurnal fishing practised by men), and *pangiou* (nocturnal fishing).

4 See, for instance, Edwin Loeb (1929a, 1929b); and Reimar Schefold (1982, 2001).

5 The primates are the Siberut macaque (*Macaca pagensis,* or *bo'koi* in Mentawai), the pig-tailed langur (*Simias concolor, simakobu*), Kloss's gibbon (*Hylobates klossi, bilou*), and the Siberut langur (*Presbytis potenziani siberut, joja* or *simagalei*).

6 See also Tri Haryoko et al. (2020).

7 For example, Lionel Simon (2020b) demonstrates how this "listening" – a non-anticipatory posture that apprehends events as signs to interpret – grounds the understanding of phenomena among the Wayuu of Colombia. In this ethnographic context, it upholds the types of relations binding humans with animals (L. Simon 2017).

8 This task is not necessarily fulfilled by a shaman *(sikerei)*.

9 "Animism" here refers to the notion as it has been revisited, in particular, by Philippe Descola (2013), who defines it as an identification scheme that grants non-humans an intentionality analogous to that of humans. "Physicalities" here take on the role of ontological differentiators (Descola 2013, 129–43). Kaj Århem and Guido Sprenger (2016) examine manifestations of this animist scheme in Southeast Asia, from which Århem "draw[s] a general conclusion ... that the predominant form of animism in Southeast Asia (the prototype) differs in significant respects from the current standard concept and therefore suggests an alternative to the standard notion – a broader concept of animism, understood as a continuum of phenomenal forms, ranging from an egalitarian or horizontal form (the standard notion) to a hierarchical or vertical type – what we refer to as hierarchical animism" (Århem 2016b, 4).

10 Ethnologists living among the Mentawaians have long been enthralled by their obsession with sharing (Bakker 2007; Figueras 2010, 202).

11 For a description of these ritual sequences, see especially Lionel Simon (2020a).

12 On counter-predation in Amazonian animist areas, see especially Carlos Fausto (2007).

13 There is more at stake than the freshness of the leaves and the enthusiasm they are meant to generate among the skulls. The Mentawaians carefully choose the plant species on the basis of their purported qualities, which are also said to influence the success of future hunts. This subject lies outside the scope of the present discussion, however.

14 These two ideas refer to an animist scheme, as defined by Descola (2013, 129–43): an identification scheme that distributes beings by ascribing to them an interiority similar to that of humans (they are thinking beings) and by making bodies the ontological differentiators between species. Their interiority is analogous, but their physical attributes are distinct.

15 As we will see, the attribution of such qualities is not limited to fauna and flora. It also extends to artifacts and, through encompassing personifications, to environments.

16 Small prey, including among the same species, usually elicit fewer precautions. This is what Salomo, a sikerei (shaman) from Butui, explained to us following a quick ritual performed after he had killed a small wild pig. When we questioned him about the limited motions, he explained that since the pig was small, the habitual rituals could be whittled down to a simpler version.

17 We here refer to the separation between "aesthetic" and "artistic," as summarized by Denis Laborde (2000, translated by Laura Shine): "According to a distinction endorsed by art historians, I differentiate the artistic from the aesthetic on the basis of intentionality. The aesthetic implies an emotional mobilization, whether or not it is intentional. The artistic refers to any intentionally aesthetic creation (independently of the attributed 'value')."

18 As Bernard Charlier (2015, 125, translated by Laura Shine) puts it, "Neither text nor image has first and foremost an artistic finality. This is not to say that the ritual image has no aesthetic value, but rather that its production is not primarily aimed at generating the inference of aesthetic valuation. Moreover, its primary function is not to signify, to produce symbols submitted to interpretation. Again, this is not to say text and drawing have no signification, but rather that the production of signification is not the raison d'être of the ritual."

19 Descola (2013, 201) defines analogism as "a mode of identification that divides up the whole collection of existing beings into a multiplicity of essences, forms, and substances separated by small distinctions and sometimes arranged on a graduated scale so that it becomes possible to recompose the system of initial contrasts into a dense network of analogies that link together the intrinsic properties of the entities that are distinguished in it."

20 It is also worth noting, though we cannot analyze it in detail here, that in itself, the dwelling's spatial organization replicates the distinct conceptual and organizational axes of the world. The neat separation of the skulls of domestic and wild animals reproduces the distinction between garden and forest (L. Simon 2021), much like the distribution of objects along a right-left axis actualizes a distribution of features associated with this axis. The house as a whole thus replicates the global arrangement of the world in "classes" of objects.

21 The owner also needs to demonstrate his "cynegetic vitality" by embarking on a hunt before the end of the gurut uma. As Aman Naru explained to us, this forest outing "makes the house happy." This is because, he said, "it knows I will always bring animals home. The house is happy when we bring back lots of animals."

22 On this issue and the resolution of issues related to this enclosure, see Lionel Simon (2020a).

23 We find, to borrow Bernard Charlier's (2012, 20) phrasing, "simplified ideal traits of a world in miniature."

WORKS CITED

Århem, Kaj. 2016a. "Animism and the Hunter's Dilemma: Hunting, Sacrifice and Asymmetric Exchange among the Katu of Vietnam." In *Animism in Southeast Asia*, ed. Kaj Århem and Guido Sprenger, 91–113. New York: Routledge.

–. 2016b. "Southeast Asian Animism in Context." In *Animism in Southeast Asia*, ed. Kaj Århem and Guido Sprenger, 3–30. New York: Routledge.

Århem, Kaj, and Guido Sprenger, eds. 2016. *Animism in Southeast Asia*. New York: Routledge.

Bakker, Laurens. 2007. "Foreign Images in Mentawai: Authenticity and the Exotic." *Bijdragen tot de taal-, land- en volkenkunde* 163, 2–3: 263–88.

Bowman, Chellie. n.d. "Towards an Anthropology of Birds: A Critical Review." Academia. https://www.academia.edu/9637206/Towards_An_Anthropology_of_Birds_A_Critical_Review.

Charlier, Bernard. 2012. "Dessiner pour consacrer. Interprétation d'un rituel de consécration d'animaux en Mongolie de l'ouest – Drawing to Consecrate: Interpretation of a Ritual of Consecration of Animals in West Mongolia." *Les Annales de la Fondation Fyssen* 27: 7–20.

–. 2015. "Ecrire, dessiner et révéler la personne par le texte et l'image en Mongolie de l'ouest." In *La lettre et l'image. Enquête sur les territoires du visible*, ed. Carl Havelange and Lucienne Strivay. El Jadida: Presses universitaires d'El Jadida.

Crisp, John. 1799. "An Account of the Inhabitants of the Poggy, or, Nassau Islands Lying off the Coasts of Sumatra." *Asiatick Researches* 6: 77–91.

Darmanto, Darmanto. 2020. "Good to Produce, Good to Share: Food, Hunger, and Social Values in a Contemporary Mentawaian Community, Indonesia." PhD thesis, Leiden University.

Delfi, Maskota. 2013. "Islam and *Arat Sabulungan* in Mentawai." *Al-Jāmi'ah* 51, 2: 475–99.

–. 2015. "Tattoos in Mentawai: Markers of Identity and Contemporary Art." International Indonesia Forum Working Paper Series 3. https://iif.or.id/wp-content/uploads/2015/10/03-Tattoos-in-Mentawai-Maskota-Delfi.pdf.

Descola, Philippe. 1996. "Constructing Natures: Symbolic Ecology and Social Practice." In *Nature and Society: Anthropological Perspectives*, ed. P. Descola and G. Pálsson, 82–102. London: Routledge.

–. 2006. "La fabrique des images." *Anthropologie et Sociétés* 30, 3: 167–82.

–. 2013. *Beyond Nature and Culture*. Chicago: University of Chicago Press.

Dove, Michael R. 1993. "Uncertainty, Humility, and Adaptation in the Tropical Forest: The Agricultural Augury of 'the Kantu.'" *Ethnology* 32, 2: 145–67.

Fausto, Carlos. 2007. "Feasting on People: Eating Animals and Humans in Amazonia." *Current Anthropology* 48, 4: 497–530.

Figueras, Raymond. 2010. *Au pays des hommes-fleurs. Avec les chamans des îles Mentawai.* Paris: Éditions Transboréal.

—. 2020. *Mentawai. Les sages de la forêt.* Bordeaux: Éditions Elytis.

Forestier, Hubert, Dominique Guillaud, Koen Meyers, and Truman Simanjuntak. 2008. *Mentawai. L'île des hommes fleurs.* Marseille/Sommières: IRD/Romain Pages Éditions.

Forth, Gregory. 2007. "Pigeon and Friarbird Revisited: A Further Analysis of an Eastern Indonesian Mythicoornithological Contrast." *Anthropos* 102: 495–513.

Gell, Alfred. 1998. *Art and Agency. An Anthropological Theory.* Oxford: Clarendon Press.

Hadi, Susilo, Thomas Ziegler, Matthias Waltert, and Keith Hodges. 2009. "Tree Diversity and Forest Structure in Northern Siberut, Mentawai Islands, Indonesia." *Tropical Ecology* 50, 2: 315–27.

Hammons, Christian. 2010. "Reciprocity, Mimesis, and the Cultural Economy of Tradition in Siberut, Mentawai Islands, Indonesia." PhD thesis, University of Southern California.

—. 2016. "Indigenous Religion, Christianity and the State: Mobility and Nomadic Metaphysics in Siberut, Western Indonesia." *Asia Pacific Journal of Anthropology* 17, 5: 399–418.

Haraway, Donna. 2003. *The Companion Species Manifesto – Dogs, People and Significant Otherness.* Chicago: University of Chicago Press.

Haryoko, Tri, et al. 2020. "Recent Ornithological Expeditions to Siberut Island, Mt. Talamau and Rimbo Panti Nature Reserve, Sumatra, Indonesia." *Treubia: A Journal on Zoology of the Indo-Australian Archipelago* 47, 1: 13–38.

Ingold, Tim. 2000. *The Perception of the Environment: Essays in Livelihood, Dwelling and Skill.* London: Routledge.

Kemp, Neville. 2000. "The Birds of Siberut, Mentawai Islands, West Sumatra." *Kukila* 11: 73–96.

Kohn, Eduardo. 2013. *How Forests Think: Toward an Anthropology beyond the Human.* Berkeley: University of California Press.

Laborde, Denis. 2000. "Éditorial." *Socio-anthropologie* 8. http://journals.openedition.org/socio-anthropologie/116.

Latour, Bruno. 1991. *Nous n'avons jamais été modernes. Essai d'anthropologie symétrique.* Paris: La Découverte.

Laugrand, Frédéric, Antoine Laugrand, and Guy Tremblay. 2019. "Lorsque les oiseaux donnent le rythme. Chants et présages chez les Blaans de Mindanao (Philippines)." *Anthropologie et Sociétés* 42, 2–3: 171–97.

Laugrand, Frédéric, and Lionel Simon. 2018. "Présentation: Deviner, prévoir et faire advenir." *Anthropologie et Sociétés* 42, 2–3: 9–35.

—. 2020. "What Do Animals and Plants Know, Predict and Transmit?" *Anthropologica* 62: 15–25.

Le Roux, Pierre, and Bernard Sellato, eds. 2006. *Les messagers divins: aspects esthétiques des oiseaux en Asie du Sud-Est* [Divine messengers: Bird symbolism and aesthetics in Southeast Asia]. Paris: IRASEC.

Loeb, Edwin M. 1929a. "Mentawei Religious Cult." *University of California Publications in American Archaeology and Ethnology* 25, 2: 185–247.

—. 1929b. "Shaman and Seer." *American Anthropologist* 31, 1: 60–84.

Meyers, Susan. 2016. *Wildlife of Southeast Asia.* Princeton: Princeton University Press.

Persoon, Gerard A. 2001. "The Management of Wild and Domesticated Forest Resources on Siberut, West Sumatra." *Antropologi Indonesia* 64: 68–83.

—. 2003a. "Conflicts over Trees and Waves on Siberut Island." *Geografiska Annaler* 85, 4: 253–64.

–. 2003b. "The Fascination with Siberut: Visual Image of an Island People." In *Framing Indonesian Realities: Essays in Symbolic Anthropology in Honour of Reimar Schefold*, ed. Peter J.M. Nas, Gerard A. Persoon, and Rivke Jaffe, 315–31. Leiden: KITLV Press.

–. 2004. "Religion and Ethnic Identity of Mentawaians on Siberut (West Sumatra)." In *Hinduism in Modern Indonesia: A Minority Religion between Local, National, and Global Interests*, ed. Martin Ramstedt, 144–59. New York: Routledge-Curzon.

Reeves, Glenn. 1999. "History and 'Mentawai': Colonialism, Scholarship and Identity in the Rereiket, West Indonesia." *Australian Journal of Anthropology* 10, 1: 34–55.

Schefold, Reimar. 1982. "The Culinary Code in the Puliaijat Ritual of the Mentawaians." *Bijdragen tot de taal-, land- en volkenkunde* 138: 64–97.

–. 1998. "The Domestication of Culture: Nation-building and Ethnic Diversity in Indonesia." *Bijdragen tot de Taal-, Land- en Volkenkunde* 154, 2: 259–80.

–. 2001. "Three Sources of Ritual Blessings in Traditional Indonesian Societies." *Bijdragen tot de Taal-, Land- en Volkenkunde* 157, 2: 359–81.

–. 2002. "Stylistic Canon, Imitation and Faking. Authenticity in Mentawai Art in Western Indonesia." *Anthropology Today* 18, 2: 10–14.

–. 2017. *Toys for the Souls: Life and Art on the Mentawai Islands*. Bornival: Primedia.

Severi, Carlo. 2007. *Le principe de la chimère. Une anthropologie de la mémoire*. Paris: Rue d'Ulm.

–. 2009. "La parole prêtée. Comment parlent les images?" *Cahiers d'anthropologie sociale* 5: 11–41.

Simon, Lionel. 2017. "Ce qu'évoquent les petites bêtes. Hétérogénéité des modes d'appréhension et d'(inter)action chez les Wayùu de Manaure (Colombie)." *Recherches amérindiennes au Québec* 47, 2–3: 149–59.

–. 2020a. "Composer avec les esprits et contraindre l'état ordinaire des choses. Modalités de l'action rituelle chez les Mentawai de Siberut (Indonésie)." *Cargo: revue internationale d'anthropologie culturelle et sociale* 10: 37–56.

–. 2020b. *Écouter les résonances du monde. Rapports aux humains et aux non-humains chez les Wayùu de Colombie*. Paris: Karthala.

–. 2021. "Les contraintes douces. Hospitalité et relations interspécifiques dans la chasse et l'élevage (Mentwai, Indonésie)." *Anthropozoologica* 56, 13: 197–213.

Simon, Scott. 2015. "Émissaires des ancêtres. Les oiseaux dans la vie et la cosmologie des Sadyaq de Taiwan." *Anthropologie et Sociétés* 39, 1–2: 179–99.

–. 2018. "Penser avec des oiseaux. L'ornithomancie et l'autochtonie à Taiwan." *Anthropologie et Sociétés* 42, 2–3: 151–69.

Tsing, Anna. 2015. *The Mushroom at the End of the World: On the Possibility of Life in Capitalist Ruins*. Princeton: Princeton University Press.

Viveiros de Castro, Eduardo. 1998. "Les pronoms cosmologiques et le perspectivisme amérindien." In *Gilles Deleuze, Une vie philosophique*, ed. Éric Alliez, 429–62. Paris: Le Plessis-Robinson.

–. 2009. *Métaphysiques cannibals*. Paris: PUF.

Wagner, Wilfried. 2003. "The Mentawaian Sense of Beauty: Perceived through Western Eyes." *Indonesia and the Malay World* 31, 90: 199–220.

Wallace, A. 1951. "Mentaweian Social Organisation." *American Anthropologist* 53, 3: 370–75.

Yulia, Refni, Zulfa Zulfa, and Hendra Naldi. 2018. "Improving the Government Policy on the *Arat Sabulungan* Tradition in Mentawai Islands." *TAWARIKH: Journal of Historical Studies* 10, 1: 59–74.

11

Environmental Shift and Entangled Landscapes
Use of Birds in Amis Ritual Practices of Taiwan
Yi-tze Lee

THE NANSHI AMIS, an Indigenous people who live in the Eastern Rift Valley of Taiwan, developed their ritual practices under the leadership of shaman groups, using materials from wild animals, most prominently birds.[1] Their rituals follow a yearly cycle and are linked to millet sowing, pest control, weeding, and the harvest. However, the loss of their traditional territories, the urbanization of ritual locales, and new means of acquiring animals used in ritual, especially birds, have created an "environmental shift" in ceremonial practices. For example, pheasant tail feathers, indispensable for age group rituals, are now imported from Vietnam due to the scarcity of local birds. As a result, the ritual landscape in which birds are involved has been heavily transformed.

Introducing the Amis People

Numbering about 250,000, the Amis are the largest Indigenous group in Taiwan. Living mostly in the eastern part of the island, they traditionally practised horticulture and fishing as their subsistence strategy. They observe the seasonal cycle in their daily and ritual lives, both of which depend on animals and plants for various purposes. For example, miscanthus grass (also known as Chinese silver grass) is used as a ritual gate in funerals, and the pith from its stem is eaten during the memorial feast. Also, though fish is a dietary staple, eating fish is taken as a symbolic ending of a ritual celebration. The Amis have a long relationship with birds, the animal that is most commonly used in their rituals: feathers decorate the elaborate head-dresses worn by men, birds send messages to deities, and they are eaten during the November feast. The Amis live with their bird neighbours; waterfowl and migratory birds are important messengers and correspondents in ritual activities. These close relationships with nature are derived from and reflected in Amis legends. In mythical tales, birds speak the Amis language.

The seasonal rituals of the Amis revolve around sowing millet, weeding, cleaning the field, controlling pests, harvesting, storing the crop, and fishing (Table 11.1). Although ceremonial activities characterize their daily lives, these have changed over time due to the scarcity of certain animals, altered subsistence strategies, and urbanization, which limits access to traditional territories. The interconnection between these factors has resulted in the transition of the landscape or "deterritorialization" (Buchanan 2008) of the Nanshi Amis on their own land, which in turn reshapes the ritual landscape. The Amis are constantly on the move due to environmental and working conditions. They often construct *taluan* (traditional shelters) for habitation or tool storage, either for fishing or hunting activities or for field cultivation. Building a taluan can be seen as an ontological means of "reterritorialization," compensating for continuous relocation. Just as birds make shelters when they move to a new territory, so do the Amis. In a ritual sense, they decorate themselves with feathers to acquire the abilities of birds; in daily life, they adapt and relocate due to modernization, just as birds adjust to seasonal change and habitat loss. The Amis embody the stamina of birds via ritual and symbolic activities and relocate due to outside pressures, just as birds do.

The Amis calendar in Table 11.1 illustrates the ritual cycle and the rhythm of relations among humans, plants, and animals throughout the year. Birds and humans alike are parts of a multi-species meshwork that gains meaning to humans in rituals. In this chapter, I apply two major concepts in analyzing the ritual landscape of the Amis and their relationship with birds.

The first is multi-species ethnography (Kirksey and Helmreich 2010), a field of anthropology that attends to the other-than-human creatures whose lives are entangled with our own. Through multi-species ethnographic think-ing, we can approach an understanding of birds from the Amis perspective and extend our understanding of Amis-bird relations. The second concept is environmental shift, which refers to the changes in the relationship be-tween human culture and the environment due to transitions in physical arrangement. For the Amis, these include changes in the administrative

Table 11.1 Yearly ritual cycle of the Nanshi Amis

			Month									
	Dec	Jan	Feb	Mar	Apr	May	Jun	Jul	Aug	Sep	Oct	Nov
Season	Kasi'nawan (Cold season)			Kafalawfawan (Windy)			Kacidalan (Dry and sunny)		Kabaliusan (Typhoon)		Kafalian (Windy)	
Event	Midiwai		Misatuligun		Miva'va	Mivalidath	Miladis	Miadop		Malalikit	Mirecuk	Malahok to Liliw
Activity	Millet sowing		Weeding, growing yams		Dispelling pests, birds, and ghosts	Harvesting and storing millet	Fishing ritual	Hunting for the harvest festival		Harvest festival	Shamanic rejuvinating rituals	Bird feast
Animals/ plants involved	Millet, rice		Yams		Insects, birds	Millet, Arenga palm	River or sea fish	Chicken, shrike, Muntjac deer		Pheasant, pigs	Pigs	Migratory birds

boundaries of villages due to urbanization, decreased access to undeveloped areas on the seashore and in the hills, and the differing availability of environmental/ritual kin, such as animals and plants. Entangled in the symbolic view of environmental shift, species become interlocutors in the understanding of the ontological view of the Indigenous world (Kohn 2013). In employing the concepts of multi-species ethnography and environmental shift, I propose that contemporary Amis keep their relationship to nature through retrospective memories and constructive interaction in symbolic meaning with various species, especially birds.

Amis Migration Routes and Livelihood Transition

According to traditional oral narratives, the ancestors of the Amis sailed across the seas and settled in various regions of Taiwan hundreds of years ago (Huang 2005). Regardless of the migration routes delineated by the oral traditions, the first pioneers explored the island several times before they settled there, eventually swayed by its beauty and abundant natural resources, such as numerous plants and animals that inhabited low hills. The impact of this new environment and the interactions and intermarriages with other people that it enabled were bound to affect Amis culture by incorporating different kinds of animals and plants in their legends. In a mythical tale of the Nanshi Amis, after their settlement, demonic giants called Alikakay were constantly taking over their land. The giants could transform into men and have sexual relations with Amis women. They were immune to conventional weapons – only a *porong,* a knot made of miscanthus grass, could hurt them. To locate them, Amis warriors learned to make the *takal,* an elaborate headdress decorated with the long white tail feathers of the Swinhoe's Pheasant, which enabled them to fly. Finally, they defeated the Alikakay. This tale informs us that the Amis were new settlers on their current territory, that they will fight for the land, and that they learned to use local plants and animals. Amis traditional knowledge, if not all derived from legend, reflects multi-species interaction and survival.

For a long period, the Amis sustained themselves by hunting, fishing, gathering wild vegetables, and cultivating millet. They developed a sophisticated cycle of ritual practices that was in harmony with seasonal rhythms and based on the availability of natural resources. Their traditional lifestyle changed during the Japanese colonial period (1895–1945) when they were forced to cultivate japonica rice in paddy fields. The introduction of japonica rice and other cash crops provided the Amis with an additional harvest cycle, which conflicted with local rituals but – alongside the millet cycle – better supported their dietary needs. Moreover, the Amis were eventually mobilized into the wartime supply system, which demanded plantation efficiency, forced labour to build railways and harbours, and heavy taxation (Tsurumi 1977; Ka 1995). In addition to these changes in subsistence strategy and labour, the Amis also faced conflicts relating to religion and the modern educational system. Their traditional life, based on natural resources, began to dissolve as the environment changed and modern infrastructure prolifer-ated throughout Taiwan. Now, new generations of Amis are increasingly alienated from their ancestral knowledge of nature. Fortunately, some rituals and elders remain, allowing us to explore this changing culture and its adaptations to the environment. The Amis relationship with birds was also altered by modernization. In many ways, the use of birds reflects how the Amis have adapted to the environment throughout history.

Fieldwork Background and Birds in Ritual

The fieldwork on which this chapter is based was conducted by the author in Lidaw, an Amis village in northern Hualien City near the mouth of the Cikasuan River. Lidaw is a major tribal community of Nanshi Amis. Of its 1,500 residents, about half are Amis (or Pangcah, as the Amis living in the north call themselves; see note 1). My fieldwork in Lidaw since 2015 covered two terms of male initiation ceremonies (which occur every eight years) and several yearly rituals based on seasonal cycles. Lidaw's urbanization trajectory differs from that of other major Nanshi Amis communities such as Pokpok and Nataoran near Hualien City, which resulted in its unique ritual land-scape and daily life. In the past, Lidaw provided the Nanshi Amis with salt and access to the ocean, and its extended territory ranged from the current residential district to the area of low hills (Yenliao) and across the Hualien River to the south (Figure 11.1). Lidaw residents pastured their water buffalos at Yenliao while they themselves constantly shuttled between the village, the seashore, and Yenliao as they searched for waterbirds, seafood, and plants. However, after the Second World War, due to the military conflict and restric-tions on access to the coast, the people of Lidaw were confined inland to the area between Lidaw and Yenliao. My studies on the contemporary rituals of the Lidaw Amis reveal the connection between the biota of the foreshore zone and Yenliao with ritual landscapes where the Amis live with animals and

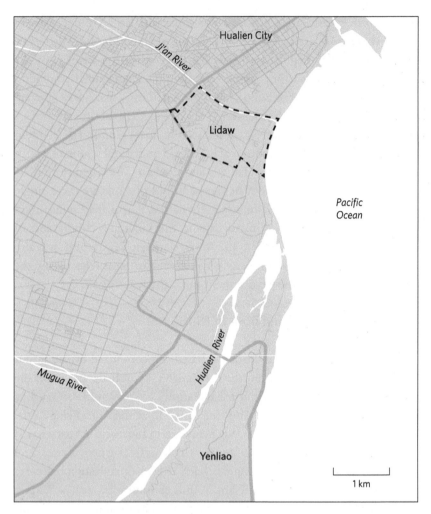

Figure 11.1 Lidaw (enclosed by dotted lines) and its environment to the seashore and mouth of the Hualien River. The area of dunes and low hills at the bottom right is called Yenliao. | Cartography by Eric Leinberger

plants. Ceremonies and subsistence strategies are woven together in the setting of the natural environment and the availability of ritual materials.

Whereas the other Nanshi Amis communities, Pokpok and Nataoran, were affected by urbanization and Han Chinese culture after the Second World War, the cultural life of Lidaw remains relatively untouched by modern changes. Unlike most Indigenous communities in Taiwan, Lidaw did not have a prominent missionary presence or a mass conversion to

Christianity after the war. Furthermore, it retains its seasonal rituals under the leadership of the *sikawasay,* the traditional shaman group. The sikawasay lead rituals for land cultivation, village cleansing, and familial worship. Another traditional organization, the *slal* (called *kapah* in Southern Amis), or male age group, has great importance for the public service of the village. Holding initiation ceremonies at regular intervals and leading ritual activities during public affairs, the slal is the rubric of community affairs, covering activities from military training, exchange labour, ritual practice, and social welfare. The sikawasay and the slal are instrumental in preserving tribal memories and actions, and both have important relationships with birds, as explained below.

Nature provides fundamental "infrastructure" for ritual activities, and the practices of both the sikawasay and the slal require products from the environment, either animals or plants. For the sikawasay, pigs are the vehicle of deities in rituals, and betelnuts and ginger leaves are vessels for the deity's blessings. Nonetheless, birds represent the ability to get beyond the boundary and break the fast after their rejuvenating rituals. For the slal, which consists solely of men, pheasants and chickens are the messengers of the male Protection God, miscanthus grass is made into ritual gates, and fish are important to expel evil after rituals. The idea of multi-species interaction is embodied in the daily and ritual life of the Amis. Among the various animals that are used for rituals, birds – both physical and symbolic ones – are important to the Amis. They represent energy and agility. In addition, they form a key ingredient in the rice harvest feast, which, in the Amis system of reciprocal labour, recognizes the contribution of those who helped with the work. The symbolic meaning of birds is revealed in their ability to cross borders and their life-giving power during shamanic rituals. The multispecies ethnography of the Amis hinges on bird-related activities and extends from the understanding of birds from the Amis perspective to the birds' understanding of the Amis.

From Ritual to Landscape: Environmental Shift in Contemporary Settings

The meaning of landscape is sustained by animals and plants in Amis ritual life. However, environmental conditions have been altered due to changes in infrastructure and ongoing urbanization, which resulted in the reconstruction of Amis relationships with their non-human kin. In Lidaw, the most prominent rituals of the year include Midiwai at the end of December (to announce millet sowing), Misatuligun in March (field cleaning on the farm, weeding, and growing yams), Miva'va' in April (pest control), Mivalidath in May (harvesting millet), and Miladis in June (fishing, which marks the end of the planting cycle). Equally important is Malahok to Liliw (bird catching/eating), which once occurred in May but was rescheduled to November with the transition to rice cultivation. These ceremonies reveal the relationships between humans and non-humans within a particular landscape. However, contemporary ritual activities have formed a new arena for cultural revitalization. Rituals still follow traditional cycles, but their content has been amalgamated with government-sponsored cultural festivals, political mobilization, and new ways of promoting community solidarity. How do the Amis retain their connection to ritual animals and their multi-species lifestyle? My argument is that, through repeated ritual practice, the cultural landscape is constantly reshaped with new meanings and active components. Although the traditional lifestyle of the Amis is irretrievable, changes in their relationship with animals and plants can shed light on how landscapes are constructed through Indigenous memories (as conjured through ritual) and through local biota. Lastly, contemporary transitions in the ritual landscape are the consequence of capitalist infrastructural expansion, which operates within the colonial legacy of human-animal relationships that characterize the Anthropocene. In certain ways, to understand the extension of the contemporary lifestyle of the Amis, we must look at the revitalization activities related to non-human elements in the presentation of ritual landscapes.

In the literature on ritual activities and landscapes, the latter are taken as historical discourses or references for collective action (Turner and Turner 1978; Bell 1992). Ritual activities define the boundaries between ethnicities and therefore represent identities and reconstitute collective memories symbolically. As such, landscapes are products of ritual engagement with the world. Nevertheless, a third aspect of the cultural landscape has not been examined in previous discussions: the ritual landscape as constituted by networks of human-animal or human-plant interactions. Although anthropologists have studied the animals and plants used in rituals, there has been virtually no discussion about the relationship between these life forms and the people using them, or the way that they participate in the construction of cultural landscapes. In his classic discussion of the ecological implications of religious practice, anthropologist Roy Rappaport (1967) points out the important relationship between ecological pressure and ritual warfare, as mediated through networks such as that between the symbolic rumbim tree and domestic pigs, the interrelations of which complete the ritual cycle of sustainability. Plants and animals are not only the objects of rituals but are also the agents that invest meaning in ritual actions.

Contemporary environmental shifts due to urbanization and changes in infrastructure result in the disappearance or alteration of bird migration routes. During the 1930s, Nanshi Amis bird-catchers could take quail and skylarks with their bare hands in the bushes near the coastal region, about a fifteen-to-twenty-minute walk from their village. Nowadays, the mangroves, ponds, and irrigation canals that once provided rich bird habitat are gone. If a bird-catcher wishes to obtain waterfowl for the late November feast, he must journey far to the south, where aquaculture ponds and irrigation canals shelter them, an example of environmental shift based on infrastructure change. "Infrastructure" creates new territorial activities and spurs the movement of materials (Larkin 2013), but it also transforms the human-animal relationship in the Anthropocene (Whyte 2017). In the case of the contemporary Amis, transformations such as road construction in the lower-altitude forests, replacing farmland with factories, and building sea walls near the harbour since the Second World War have excluded them from their ancestral area and prevented their contact with birds.

Living with Birds

The Amis categorize birds as either residents or migrants, but they have local names for the ones that provide them with feathers and food or that carry messages. Many different birds appear in folklore and myth, as the following examples demonstrate (Sayama [1921] 2005, 15–21, Amis names are in parentheses):

- Pheasants *(tolok)* and eagles *(kalebis)* were present at the creation of humans. After the great deluge at the beginning of human history, they acted as scouts in the search for an Amis homeland, behaving with bravery. Symbolizing intrepidness, their feathers decorate the takal, the ritual headdress worn by Amis men.
- The wagtail *(howacuko)* taught the Amis how to reproduce. Since the sole survivors of the deluge were the brother and sister Sera and Nakao, they were unable to have sex due to the shame of incest. The wagtail

taught Sera to disguise her appearance so that her brother could marry her and they could have children without shame.

- The Black Drongo *(kori)* raised the sky in the age of the burning sun. After the great deluge, the sun was so hot that it scorched the earth. The bird volunteered to fly high and raise the sky for the benefit of humans.
- The Black Drongo also provided fire for humans. Like the Bunun people of Taiwan, who credit the *haipis* (Black Bulbul) with bringing fire, the Amis recognize the Black Drongo as a brave friend who took the seed of fire to dispel the darkness for human beings.[2]
- The Long-tailed Shrike *(tilu)* warned the Amis to labour in the field before the deities became angry. A messenger from the gods, the bird warned a lazy couple of Amis to harvest before the crops were over-run with pests. This shrike is consumed during the November bird-catching feast.
- A naughty young husband failed in his duty to send his wife's message to the villagers. As a result, he was turned into a heron *(aletac)* that can eat only at night.
- A lazy child who disrespected the elders was turned into a crow *('anekak)* that had to search for food by itself.
- When the death of his lover saddened a young man, villagers turned him into a dove *(tolatolaw)* so that he could follow her.
- Doves and pheasants represent couples and the protection of the family.

All these folktales highlight the intimacy between birds and the Amis. The type of bird may vary, but their messages are clear, marking a specific meaning of human-bird entanglement: they represent bravery, benevolence, and loyalty (for metaphors involving birds, see Chapter 8 in this volume). On the other hand, humans who are lazy, self-indulgent, and mischievous may be turned into birds. Birds are a special type of animal that can reach both heavenly deities and mundane humans. Furthermore, they easily cross boundaries, a special capacity and agency to which humans aspire. Sometimes, they are tricksters, mimicking the sounds of other animals to mislead humans. When encountering heavenly power, they are not intimidated or seduced; when facing human failure, they do not betray their friends or deliver false messages. Birds are loyal and honourable, and there-fore can be considered a test of human integrity and environmental aware-ness. This is also the message that contemporary Amis face when their environment and rituals are changed due to urbanization, capitalist development, and infrastructure construction.

During my fieldwork at Lidaw, young boys underwent a period of training before progressing to the initiation ceremony that marked their passage into manhood, sleeping outdoors and hunting for food. Sleep deprivation and hunger were fairly common aspects of this week-long experience, and almost every participant reported the feeling of joining the birds dancing and thus lightening the tiresomeness of the ordeal. Any bird they caught, usually a quail, would be a welcome treat, and the novice who caught the most birds would be recognized as the leader of his age grade as a lifetime honour. After passing through the training period, the boys are finally allowed to wear the takal in public to show their agility and energy. This headdress and the lively high-stepping dance that goes with it are instantly recognizable, whether they appear at traditional festivals or in the media. Amis pop singer Suming wrote a song titled "Kapah o A'tolan" (The Male Age Group of A'tolan, 2018) to praise the novices. The accompanying music video has a great image of them taking their trophy feathers and "flying" in the field, just like the pheasants that provide the feathers.[3] These experiences make birds a great representative of the Amis people, especially the men.

Male Age Groups and Birds as Boundary-Crossing Agents

The male age group (slal) is the basic organizational unit of Amis society. Every Amis *niyarow* (village) has its own age group naming systems and interval for the recruitment and training of novices. Candidates who successfully endure the hardship of the initiation period receive their age group names and are recognized as real men (Huang 2005). Every seven years (in what villagers usually refer to as "eight years cycle," which includes the first and last year of the interval), a cohort of young men is initiated, obtaining the status of adulthood. As they undergo this process, they wear white shirts and white towels on their heads, representing the male Swinhoe's Pheasant, a bird with a sapphire-blue body and a long white tail. Although currently rare, this species, which is endemic to Taiwan, was common during precolonial times, when Amis hunters could catch it in the wild fields or on millet farms (Furuno [1934] 2005).[4] Swinhoe's Pheasant has been extirpated in the Lidaw area since the Second World War, however, and the lands where they were once hunted are now dominated by paddy rice farms. The image of the pheasant is now embodied only in the takal worn during harvest rituals (Figure 11.2). In the past, Amis males would take the two longest

Figure 11.2 White pheasant feathers crown the headdresses of Amis dancers who are recently initiated. Photo taken in Lidaw, 2020.

feathers from the bird, some of which can reach twelve inches. The lower layer of decoration is made from the downy plumage of the Taiwan Bamboo-partridge, and other feathers come from the eagle or various raptors. When I first saw the headdress, I asked, "Why do Amis male hunters use blue pheasant feathers rather than raptors to symbolize their bravery?" As he worked on his headdress, Amis elder Butal of Lidaw replied, "Raptors are rare and usually act by themselves. It is not a good virtue that the Amis appreciate. Pheasants seem peace-loving, but they fight for their nest together with other pheasants as a group. The most important thing is that pheasants act in couples, which Amis husbands should always remember." For the Amis, working together is more important than being aggressive and audacious.

Although Ring-necked Pheasants do occur near the Nanshi Amis residential area, their feathers are not considered the most desirable for the male headdress, and pheasants are no longer hunted for their feathers. Since the 1990s, specialized Indigenous dress and decoration shops have met the demand for the festival outfit. Traditionally, a full-fledged headdress for a young man required twelve white long tail feathers from the Swinhoe's Pheasant. Nowadays, supplies from retail outlets are especially needed for the headdresses of young men in their twenties due to stricter hunting regulations and the reduced number of wild pheasants. Nowadays, the feathers come from the Vietnamese Pheasant (which also has long white feathers) and are imported from Vietnam. Every ten-feather set costs US$70. With plumage from doves, bamboo partridges, and goose quills attached to a framework of bamboo and rattan, the headdress can weigh up to five kilograms and cost over US$200. Although the price seems high, it is a necessary expense for young men who wish to be initiated into manhood.

During their training period, the boys must stay in the field for a week without returning home; in the past, they would have stayed for a month. While there, they must locate edible roots and tubers, make reed straws to drink water from the river, gather wild plants for sustenance or medicinal purposes, and, most importantly, catch birds with a traditional bamboo snare or small net, for protein and as trophies on their takal. Achieving success on this last point is critical: they will be recognized as real men only if they catch some kind of bird for the group during the training week and add its feathers to their headdress in the public dancing event. On the last day of training, the boys run a race from the village entrance to the coastal area where elders keep their fishing boats. An elder who bears the same age grade name as the boys runs behind them, carrying a white chicken (in the past, a Swinhoe's Pheasant).[5] Anyone who cannot outrun him and is grabbed by the chicken foot is said to be under the shadow of *pakaros,* which means the footprint of the resting birds. Mama Ripon, the leader of Lidaw village, explained the rules for age group training:

> Young men should run like a flying bird; if anyone runs even slower than the elder, he is not qualified to acquire the new name of the age group and should come back again seven years later in the next cycle. *Karnis* (a special white pheasant) is the guardian and transformation of the male deity *Maladaw;* anyone caught by *Maladaw* needs to sacrifice a chicken and rejoin the training cycle.[6]

As either training trophies or guardians, birds symbolize the ability to cross boundaries. For young Amis males transitioning from childhood to membership in the slal, the pheasant is a symbol of flying, dancing, and crossing physical boundaries. Because its feathers are rare locally, overseas trading is another form of boundary crossing linked to the bird. Carrying pheasant feathers not only transforms animal materials into human virtue, but also represents the common fate of Amis labour forces in the capitalist era. During colonial times, when Amis men were forced to work outside of their communities in harbour and railroad construction, they could only look at birds and dream of returning home.

Birds and Shamans

The second type of relationship between birds and the Amis people occurs in shamanic practice. A major deity in Amis rituals is Ansurai, the "Falcon God." Interestingly, he is not the protector of bird-hunters and does not provide an abundant harvest for the bird feast. Surprisingly, he is the guardian of the boat ritual that is part of male initiation and of the fish catches that follow throughout the man's adulthood. It is said that a few hundred years ago, five boats came to establish the Lidaw community, and one of the legendary boats was an incarnation of Ansurai, the Falcon God. In Mirecuk, the rejuvenating ritual of shamanic magical power in October, the offerings are arranged as planted crops in the field. The Falcon God Ansurai is worshipped to oversee the growth of ginger root stems in the symbolic farm represented by offering settings with betelnuts, sticky rice cakes, and piper betel leaves; the ginger root stem protects shamans against contamination from impure contact during ritual processes. In this case, birds (in the form of Ansurai) symbolize the transition from the mundane to the sacred realms.

Another shamanic ritual connects birds more deeply with the Amis ceremonial cycle and ecological perspective. In October, after a week of the

Figure 11.3 A shaman ritually prepares the teker.

shamanic rejuvenating ritual separated from daily life, Amis shamans go to the farmland surrounding the village (usually after the harvest), perform a cleansing ritual, and undergo a "reintegration" back into everyday life. This process is called the *tala omah,* which literally means "going to the farm" in Amis. It coincides with Arnold van Gennep's ([1960] 2004) idea regarding rites of passage, in which individuals are separated from routine life, transformed with spiritual power, and then returned to normality. As offerings are prepared for worship in the field, ginger leaves are tied to bird traps called *teker,* which are made from bamboo sticks with a string attached to one end. Normally, if the teker are to retain their sacred effect, only males can touch and use them. However, in the shamanic usage of the teker, the initiator and those who perform the ritual are female shamans (Figure 11.3). As the leading female shaman, Sera Ingui, told me,

> This ritual is to thank our deity *Ansurai,* and also to bring the birds back in the field for later harvest. During our ritual, *Ansurai* (the falcon) is always present so all the birds are hiding. Now we need to release them back to the field so that all our crops can freely grow, and the birds can feast after the harvest.[7]

In the "bird releasing" ritual, shamans tie ginger leaves to the teker, which represents captive birds. After worship is done, the shamans (both female and male) remove the leaves from the teker and take them to the riverbank, facing eastward to release the leaves from their hands (Figure 11.4). In this act, the symbolic birds are sent back to the field. This ritual shows that birds are agents to connect males and females; when a woman uses a trap that is normally the exclusive preserve of men, the meaning of bird-catcher is transformed into bird-releaser. Among the various animals caught or related to Amis hunters and catchers, such as mountain mammals or fish, only birds can enable such a transformation.

Birds have transformative power in various ways. In mythical tales, birds and human beings are interchangeable in achieving tasks that deities impose upon them. The Amis do not see birds as harmful pests even though their crops may be consumed by birds; instead, after the crop has been harvested, they follow the ecological cycle to symbolically capture birds in the shamanic ritual, release them afterward, and anticipate their return when they can be caught again. As this symbolic action goes, birds have taken the Amis people from niyarow to *omah* (village to farmland), from *vavayinai* to *vavahi*

Figure 11.4 Shamans throwing ginger leaves to represent releasing birds.

(male to female), and from *taiyo* to *ayam* (ginger to bird; plant to animal). Bird traps (teker), a device used by men, further transform newly initiated boys into men when they wear the feathering crown (takal) after the initiation ritual. The whole process can be understood as the symbolic Amis ecological transition of the production cycle. The power of non-human beings is carried out, particularly via the action of birds, which recognize new identities and new lives.

Birds, Sworn Siblings, and Reciprocal Labour

Sworn siblings (*liliw* in Amis) initially consisted of age group cohorts but later expanded to include kin, classmates, and co-workers who have an obligation and responsibility to help each other, such as when a house is built, the land is cultivated, or the harvest is taken in. Whereas the slal is exclusively male, the liliw is an economic unit founded on reciprocal labour that can cross gender and generations. Nowadays, it usually comes into play during certain milestones, such as for marriage banquets, renovating a house, or holding a retirement gathering. Sworn siblings also gather on a monthly basis for leisure and communication. By contrast, the slal is more recognized for one's identity and cultural belonging. Birds are connected to both groups, though their relationship with the Amis via the liliw differs from that of the slal.

When farm work ends in the winter, the Amis who live in the north of the Eastern Rift Valley hold a festival. Known as *Pakalahok to Liliw* (the bird-catching and eating festival), it is a unique celebration of the Nanshi Amis.[8] During this collective leisure activity, which occurs in late November, farming teams from each village hunt and capture birds in various fields to "wish for a good harvest" in the coming year (Figure 11.5). Year-round bird hunting is illegal in Taiwan, and the hunters must obtain a "temporary ritual hunt permit." In addition, they must immediately release any species protected under the Wildlife Conservation Act.[9] Sparrows, quail, common moorhen, and bamboo-partridge are abundant and can be hunted, but the Swinhoe's Pheasant, Giant Eagle (which may be extirpated locally), and Long-tailed Shrike are protected and should not be caught. The notion of targeting only certain birds both takes into account the environment and reflects the culture of the festival. During the breeding season, the Amis refrain from hunting wild birds, leaving them undisturbed to raise their chicks. Therefore, bird-catching activities are not only a kind of living custom but also a part of the life festival, including ecological awareness, life education, and cultural heritage.

The types of birds that are usually visible and accessible in Amis territory reveal the transitions in lifestyle and subsistence strategy. In the past, birds that were hunted were *masamaamaanay a 'ayam*, which means "the birds that move back and forth (near the farmland)." These included sparrows *(cirociro)*, swallows *(suwik)*, shrikes (tilu), doves/pigeons *(tolatolaw/banul)*, quail *(pulu')*, moorhens *(tikukuway/aka "karate")*, herons *(aletac)*, and wild ducks *(dadok)*. All are especially favoured not only for their fatty meat but also because they are seen as "making a contract" with the Amis: present in November, they are consumed during the feast of that month, when individuals join the liliw (group of reciprocal labour), becoming sworn siblings. While birds are taken as part of the connection, the Amis contract with migrant birds as sworn siblings with the feast. The loyalty of migratory bird visits and their moving in groups, along with their foraging activities, make the Amis particularly fond of them compared to resident birds. They are mostly called *sical* in Amis and are referred to as "credible shrike" (which also encompasses other migratory birds).[10] In the past, they visited the Hualien area around September, just before the Malalikit dancing festival after the millet harvest. However, their numbers are plummeting and urbanization has destroyed much of their habitat in the Hualien area. The same process of habitat loss has obliged the Amis to leave the farm and look

Figure 11.5 Making a bird trap with bamboo and string.

for wage labour in the city. We thus see a symmetry between migrant birds and the Amis, as both have been disenfranchised, becoming a parallel reference for each other.

A Local Museum and the Struggles of Bird Spirits

The Amis contract with migratory birds as sworn siblings, yet they still eat birds during the reciprocal labour feast in November, when they treat the people who helped bring in the harvest. The bird was not only considered a friend in age group hunting activities but was also the messenger of the deity Maladaw (a male protector) and therefore the companion of the shaman. Such practices reveal the transitional livelihood of Indigenous people in urbanized conditions.

In 2022, the Nataoran Local Museum in Ji'an County, which is devoted to Nanshi Amis culture, mounted an exhibition that featured the November bird-catching feast. Its theme was "Following the Trajectory of the Bird Spirit." The show was organized by the Nataoran Amis Cultural Association, a body transformed from a traditional age group to interact with modern bureaucracy. The museum, originally a male gathering house, opened its doors during the 1980s. In any case, the transition of a traditional organization into a modern one seems inevitable.

The exhibition revealed birds as the still image caught by an Amis hunter, performing the act of bird watching activities through binoculars or devouring them at the feast. The show included the takal headdress worn during the harvest festival (Figure 11.6), as well as photos of Amis bird-hunters with their traps in hand. However, all the shots of birds were of a type loved by birders (and wildlife photographers) the world over – crisply focused portrayals of the entire body and the plumage. Not a single one showed a bird in a net or a trap. Elders who visited the display expressed doubts about the photos: "Those birds do not look like the way we catch them; they are too quiet." For some viewers, the exhibition felt like a "tamed version" of Indigenous hunting knowledge. The photographs were shown in a nostalgic tone, with captions such as "Conundrum between traditional heritage and contemporary regulation" or "A feather crown is the display of male power and capacity, also the sign of maturity." In many senses, the exhibition was the very symbol of entanglement between the Amis and the government

Figure 11.6 A takal on display at the Nataoran Local Museum.

Figure 11.7 The bird feast outside the Nataoran Local Museum.

since this is a county government–funded event for the sake of "preserving the Amis tradition." The images of birds reflected the knowledge and conservation-oriented perspective of modern society. However, the curator organized a bird feast outside the museum to show the authenticity of the birds' relationship with the Amis (Figure 11.7).

Nowadays, most Nanshi Amis no longer farm, but the custom of reciprocal labour still applies in other aspects of their lives. Eating birds is just one shared activity. Liliw members are friends who will loan each other money and help in house construction; when boys are initiated into manhood, the liliw is the workforce that provides ritual helpers for gift giving; sons and daughters of liliw members have a marked propensity for becoming couples. Although sworn siblings still gather for the November festival, the museum presentation of the celebration in the photos of "birds views" revealed little about the limitations on the ability of Amis hunters. Amis bird-catchers are subtle hunters who do not carry guns. Rather, they determine which farmland areas are most likely to attract migrant birds and then set bamboo or wire traps or nets to catch them. In the museum show, the captions labelling bird-catching activities reveal the forgotten wisdom and the weakened authority of traditional obligations. In portions of their traditional territories that have been privatized or seized by the government, the Amis no longer hunt for birds. Even though bird catching is no longer a subsistence practice due to environmental shift, people in the liliw still uphold their contracts with other group members, as well as with birds. While remaining within the liliw, the Amis try to catch up with the changing world.

In discussing the dreams of hunting dogs belonging to the Runa people of Ecuador, Eduardo Kohn (2007) writes that the dogs symbolize the domination of Western settler colonialism in Runa country. Amis bird-catching activity also shows a similar struggle against the Han Chinese settler government's animal protection regulations, as well as land-grabbing economic development. The extirpation of bird species in the Nanshi Amis area parallels the loss of Amis land, farming, and the right to hunt. Here, the bird is the witness to the cultural entanglement brought about by an environmental shift. Birds symbolize the limited freedom and imagined self-governance of the Amis people in urbanized life. For the Amis, the Wildlife Conservation Act, which specifies where, when, and how they can hunt, functions like a constricting net. Living in an urban environment, governed by laws that are not their own, and forced to undertake wage labour if they wish to stay out of debt, the Amis are like birds caught in a mesh of modernization. To them, birds as the source of feathers for the takal or as treats to be consumed during a feast are more appealing than the static photos presented by the museum. With bird spirits (adingo no ayam) in the field, those hunting and eating activities can carry Amis cultural memories into the intimate form of social solidarity, whereas the static images of birds were staged in the museum to acquire government funding in the wave of animal conservation. On the one hand, the Amis exhibition and public performance are funded by the government to revitalize their cultural identity; on the other hand, the display and unsustainable way of bird feasts without reciprocal labour remind the Amis that they are like birds entwined in the nets of modernization and urbanization. The museum exhibit thus vividly revealed the struggle of the bird spirits in this entangled ecology.

Conclusion: How Birds Speak to the Amis about the Entangled Ecology

For the Amis, birds are good to think (Tambiah 1969), and birds are also ritually connected and offered to the ancestors (Rappaport 1967). However, with the challenges posed by urbanization and the environmental shift, the Amis have been ensnared in modern regulations and a lack of accessibility to birds, just as the birds themselves are caught in Amis nets. What I refer to as "entangled ecology" recognizes the environmental shifts such as species availability and changing infrastructure. It also reveals the ecological views of the Amis, along with modern policies and landscape changes. Marlene Castellano (2004) refers to Indigenous traditional knowledge as an "arboreal structure." In this metaphor, the canopy is comprised of individual behaviours, branches are traditional customs, leaves and twigs are ethical conduct, and the trunk signifies values and behavioural norms. At the bottom, the roots anchor the entire structure, which represents the multiplicity of species, the spiritual world, and the cycle of sustainable livelihood. The knowledge tree is challenged by the entanglement of Indigenous people, culturally meaningful species, and modern governments. Due to shifting subsistence strategies in the environment, animals used in rituals have been greatly changed. The symbols for the collective work of the male age grade are fish from the sea and birds from the mountain. When the government restricted public access to the sea, Amis males turned to fishing in the river estuary or even in the pond of a tourist park where their traditional territory had been privatized. Birds traditionally caught for the harvest feast are now purchased commercially, and the feathers for the takal are imported from Vietnam. Coming from an ancestral viewpoint but creating retrospective innovations by renewing the tradition resembles what James Clifford (2004) calls "traditional futures." As we can see, these changes are environmental shifts that mark different settings and means of acquiring animals for ceremonial purposes.

However, the challenges presented by multi-species ethnography entail more than reflecting the cultural meaning through species on their entanglement with environmental issues; it also includes how we think about the world differently in terms of emergent conditions regarding human-animal relationships. Working from the example of the Runa people's relationship with their dogs, Eduardo Kohn (2007, 21) presents his idea of "multinatural ontology" to show the collaboration of animal beings and the Runa epistemology of knowing the world. If Kohn represents an ontological turn involving species, Paul Nadasdy (2021) questions its universality. Tracking hunting policies in Canada, he vigorously challenges the "multiple-worlds thesis," which refers to a physical environment that fosters many possible world views. Rejecting the thesis as plagued by theoretical problems, he argues for an alternative approach – "indeterminacy" – which incorporates contingent situations such as conditions of environmental or anti-colonial politics (Nadasdy 2021, 359). Here, what birds reveal in the Amis world echoes Nadasdy's argument, showing how ritual authenticity, museum curation, and working with government-funded cultural revitalization projects all co-create an indeterminate arena for both Amis elders and youth, and for Indigenous ritual and public exhibitions. If only the Amis-bird relationship in the multiple worlds were taken into account, we could represent the Amis as enjoying a more intimate world than other peoples in relation to birds, which is not the case for contemporary Amis. Indeterminacy here refers not only to the understanding of the human-bird relationship as historically rooted, but also as challenged by the larger framework of colonial discourse that provides further struggle and interpretation within various political arenas and mobilizations. The ambivalence of Amis elders regarding the Nataoran Local Museum exhibition, as well as the governance and restrictions that apply to Amis bird-catchers, reframes the interaction between the Amis and birds in the political world. If we apply the indeterminacy approach, the agency of non-humans (birds in this case) is revealed from the net of meaning cast by human beings.

At the beginning of this chapter, I mentioned that in Amis legends, birds can speak the language of humans. If a bird from legendary times were magically transported to the current day, would it speak differently to the Amis? Birds are the most sensitive actors in the environment, whether as symbolic figures in male initiation practices, as mediators of gender and role transition in shamanic rituals, or as witnesses to conflicts over land and hunting legislation. These ritual activities, landscape memories, and daily experiences of Amis cultural boundaries are critical elements in multi-species networks. Birds in Amis ritual life embody culture and make it function as a whole. Ritual is not only the engaged domain of public discourse but also a realm that encompasses all possible differences in ethnic relationships. To deal with the contested issues of entangled ecology, birds in rituals have been in "dialogue" with cultural beliefs and government restrictions upon the Amis. In this chapter, I use three examples of bird-Amis relationships to show the understanding in ritual gradually expanding from the traditional ontological view of symbols to the unavailable land and change of sworn siblings or gender roles and finally to the conflict of cultural revitalization and legal pressure on bird consumption. That birds in legend can speak the Amis language refers to the mutual adaptation and understanding between the two; however, the contemporary situation, as discussed above, shows that birds may not be able to speak as their ancestors did, while the Amis themselves are challenged by their means of communication to birds due to the entanglement with the man-made environment.

From multi-species ethnography to indeterminacy, birds have taught both the Amis and ethnographers about the world and its constituents via rituals, age grade spirits, popular music, hunting activities, and museum collections. The multi-species approach questions the centrality of human meaning, and the Amis-bird relationship further challenges the mapping of traditional ecological knowledge onto such an entangled environment. Entangled ecology features neither a retrospective push toward cultural revitalization nor a detached historical account about contemporary regulations; rather, it shows how birds have survived through the entanglement of natural habitats, cultural representations, and industrial/cultural infrastructures. Although we see the disappearance of ritual animals, we also see efforts of "substantialized" images of ritual symbols as tokens of actual animals or plants. This provides a local mechanism for resilience and sustainability in a setting of public participation and cultural identity struggle. The Amis practice with birds documents and records ritual activities via environmental shift and entangled ecology to show the impact of urbanization, environmental degradation, and changing subsistence strategies.

The Anthropocene reveals the critical issue of human survival, from both the historical and the philosophical perspectives. Indigenous philosopher Kyle Whyte (2017, 210) has turned the challenge of climate change and its environmental impact into the notion of "renewing relatives," considering non-human actors in Indigenous surroundings as meaningful relatives to provide survival needs and networking support. In the case of birds and their relation to Amis practices, I would also consider "infrastructural renewal" as part of an extensive understanding of networking between humans, various species, and space. Birds are persistent actors in the environment. In folklore, they seem to be the messengers for a human companion from the sky. For the Amis, they possess two key characteristics. They are agile leaders that young men aspire to emulate and embody, as epitomized by the takal. They are also the guardians of shamanic power and crop growth. In this, they are both the competitors and the feeding agents for a harvest of spiritual power and for cultivating the harvest. In these cases, the Amis-bird-field connection is the key to the Nanshi Amis, showing the renewal of relationships based on changing surroundings. What birds can tell us about the Amis is embodied in the work of the male age groups, sworn siblings, and shamans; what we can see about the birds in this entangled presence, with its catching and releasing rituals, the Wildlife Conservation Act, and display of images, artifacts, and feathers in a museum, has created an indeterminacy for the Amis to re-enact their lives with birds. The contemporary Amis have more to speak to their feathered interlocutors.

NOTES

1 The Nanshi Amis are one of the five groupings of Amis people in Northeastern Taiwan. The Amis living in the North, including the Nanshi, call themselves *Pangcah*. Because their traditional territory is based on the Nanshi plains in the Northern Hualien region, Japanese scholars have used the ethnonym "Nanshi" for this subgroup of the Amis.

2 There is evidence that certain raptors may actually pick up burning twigs and drop them elsewhere, with the probable intent of starting a fire and flushing out prey. Many Indigenous peoples, in addition to the Amis, see this as the origin of the human use of fire. Some Indigenous peoples in Australia re-enact avian fire spreading in Dreaming fire ceremonies (Bonta et al. 2017, 705).

3 YouTube clip of "Kapah o Atolan," https://www.youtube.com/watch?v=kX6RWEoaR3M.

4 Swinhoe's Pheasant *(Lophura swinhoii)* is also known as the Taiwan Blue Pheasant. The Amis usually refer to it as the common pheasant or the white chicken. Feathers from Ring-necked Pheasants are used in the headdresses of elders. Traditionally, the long white tail feathers of Swinhoe's Pheasant are used only in the headdresses of young men to signify the virtues of purity and intrepidness.

5 There are nine age group names in the Nanshi Amis system: *Alamay, Aladiwas, Alabangas, Alemet, Rarao, Maoway, Maolac, Maorad, and Matabok*. The names of the age groups are passed on in cycles. Therefore, the elders who have the same age grade name as a new crop of novices would be at least sixty-three years old.

6 Interview with Mama Ripon, fieldnotes taken on August 14, 2022.

7 Field note from shamanic activity, October 13, 2015.

8 Differing from place to place, the name is variously Pakalahok to Liliw, Malahok to Liliw, Miliwliw, or Malaliliway.

9 *Wildlife Conservation Act*, 2013, https://law.moj.gov.tw/ENG/LawClass/LawAll.aspx?pcode=M0120001.

10 However, the exact meaning of "sical" needs to be clarified. Does it apply generally to any migrant bird, or does it refer specifically to shrikes? In general, shrikes visit southern Taiwan around October and November. The records for shrikes in Hualien fluctuate because the birds stay for only a few weeks before heading south.

WORKS CITED

Bell, Catherine M. 1992. *Ritual Theory, Ritual Practice*. Oxford: Oxford University Press.

Bonta, Mark, Robert Gosford, Dick Eussen, Nathan Ferguson, Erana Loveless, and Maxwell Witwer. 2017. "Intentional Fire-Spreading by 'Firehawk' Raptors in Northern Australia." *Journal of Ethnobiology* 37, 4: 700–18.

Buchanan, Brett. 2008. *Onto-Ethologies: The Animal Environments of Uexkull, Heidegger, Merleau-Ponty, and Deleuze*. Albany: State University of New York.

Castellano, Marlene Brant. 2004. "Ethics of Aboriginal Research." *Journal of Aboriginal Health* 1, 1: 98–114.

Clifford, James. 2004. "Traditional Futures." In *Questions of Tradition,* ed. Mark Phillips and Gordon Schochet, 152–68. Toronto: University of Toronto Press.

Furuno, Kiyoto 古野清人. (1934) 2005. *Gaoshazu de jiyi shenghuo* 高砂族的祭儀生活 [Ritual life of the Takasagosoku in Formosa]. Translated by Huang Mei-yin 黃美英. Taipei: Academia Sinica 台北：中央研究院民族學研究所.

Huang, Shiun-wey 黃宣衛. 2005. *Yizuguan, diyuxing chabie yu lishi: ameizu yanjjiu lunwenji* 異族觀、地域性差別與歷史：阿美族研究論文集 [Images of others, regional variations and history among the Amis]. Taipei: Institute of Ethnology, Academia Sinica 中央研究院民族學研究所。.

Ka, Chi-Ming. 1995. *Japanese Colonialism in Taiwan: Land Tenure, Development, and Dependency, 1895–1945.* Boulder: Westview Press.

Kirksey, S. Eben, and Stefan Helmreich. 2010. "The Emergence of Multispecies Ethnography." *Cultural Anthropology* 25, 4: 545–76.

Kohn, Eduardo. 2007. "How Dogs Dream: Amazonian Natures and the Politics of Transspecies Engagement." *American Ethnologist* 34, 1: 3–24.

–. 2013. *How Forests Think: Toward an Anthropology beyond the Human.* Berkeley: University of California Press.

Larkin, Brian. 2013. "The Politics and Poetics of Infrastructure." *Annual Review of Anthropology* 42: 327–43.

Nadasdy, Paul. 2021. "How Many Worlds Are There? Ontology, Practice, and Indeterminacy." *American Ethnologist* 48, 4: 357–69.

Rappaport, Roy. 1967. *Pigs for the Ancestors: Ritual in the Ecology of a New Guinea People.* New Haven: Yale University Press.

Sayama, Yukichi 佐山融吉. (1921) 2005. *Fanzu guanxi diaocha baogaoshu diyice: Amei Nanshifan* 蕃族慣習調查報告書第一冊：阿美族南勢番 [Investigation reports on traditional customs of Aboriginal Formosa, book 1: The Nanshi branch of Amis]. Taipei: Academia Sinica.

Tambiah, Stanley J. 1969. "Animals Are Good to Think and Good to Prohibit." *Ethnology* 8, 4: 423–59.

Tsurumi, E. Patricia. 1977. *Japanese Colonial Education in Taiwan, 1895–1945.* Cambridge: Harvard University Press.

Turner, Victor W., and Edith L.B. Turner. 1978. *Image and Pilgrimage in Christian Culture: Anthropological Perspectives.* New York: Columbia University Press.

Van Gennep, Arnold. (1960) 2004. *The Rites of Passage.* Translated by Monika Vizedom and Gabrielle Caffee. London: Routledge.

Whyte, Kyle. 2017. "Our Ancestors' Dystopia Now: Indigenous Conservation and the Anthropocene." In *The Routledge Companion to the Environmental Humanities,* ed. Ursula Heise, Jon Christensen, and Michelle Niemann, 206–15. London: Routledge.

Epilogue
The Emergence of Ethno-Ornithology
Andrew G. Gosler

A STUDENT ONCE asked me, "What are birds for?" Somewhat taken aback, I replied, "What are you for?" Although my answer may have gotten me out of a lengthy debate, the question led me to a deeper reflection. This was not so much on the purpose of life in general, or birds in particular, but on the cultural assumptions I had made about the student who asked the question. Had I projected onto this student my concern that, somehow, the failure to recognize that a living organism could have value independent of human perceptions might lie at the root of all the challenges of the Anthropocene, so that my somewhat defensive response reflected that? Although I shall never know what prompted the question (it didn't follow a lecture in either ornithology or ethno-ornithology), I had viewed it through a certain prism of knowledge that sensitized me to its apparent anthropocentricity.

My prism was undoubtedly influenced by my knowledge of the decline in direct experience and first-hand knowledge of nature among young people, increasingly documented around the world, in both Indigenous and post-industrial societies. I was researching this subject at the time in terms of student knowledge of natural history. The waning of nature-connection had become a broader concern after the publication of Richard Louv's *Last Child in the Woods* (2005). It has been framed in a number of ways, including the "extinction of experience" (Soga and Gaston 2016), but we need to understand more about the way in which such knowledge is held in, and regarded by, communities. By studying the knowledge of biology students, Stephen Tilling and I had discovered that natural history knowledge in Britain took the form of traditional and local ecological knowledge. Rather than reflecting formal education, the possession of natural history knowledge was strongly influenced by vertical transmission through generations and was contextualized locally both culturally and ecologically on a need-to-know basis. What was considered necessary knowledge was strongly influenced by parents and grandparents, and this in turn influenced the relative salience of birds and other organisms (Gosler and Tilling 2021). Although research has focused on the knowledge and interests of young people, the diminishing salience of nature is not exclusive to them. Here lies a problem. If many who live in post-industrial societies no longer see nature as relevant, and yet humanity is as dependent on a functioning biosphere as ever (Chivian and Bernstein 2008; Ninan 2009; Everard 2021), a cognitive dissonance exists between salience and reality, between the ontological and the epistemological. The Anthropocene is defined formally in terms of its geological legacy (Zalasiewicz et al. 2010), but it is perhaps this dissonance that is its defining feature.

All this (I believe) influenced my assumption that, in asking "What are birds for?" the student was not asking a biological question about the ecological services that birds performed through their relationships with plants and other animals. Rather, I assumed that the query was shorthand for "What purpose do birds serve for us humans?," on which framing rests two further questions: "What is the *value* of birds to humans?" and, consequently, "Why should we care about birds?" Furthermore, given some knowledge of the cultural anthropology of Britain, I had also assumed that the student was not asking a metaphysical or theological question about God's justification for creating birds, the answer to which could have included both an ecological and an anthropocentric framing of the question. Such a theological approach would cast as questionable the ethics of requiring any organism to justify its existence to humanity. Nevertheless, since 2005, when the United Nations Environment Programme's Millennium Ecosystem Assessment introduced the Ecosystem Services framework (MEA 2005), conservationists have been encouraged to adopt an overtly anthropocentric perception of nature. This is perhaps the more peculiar because the MEA explicitly recognizes that the diversity of life (species, genetic, and ecosystem diversity) has evolved over billions of years to the present (MEA 2005, section 4.1.2), so that although humanity depends on the "services" provided by ecosystems, the argument that this provision gave purpose to ecosystems would be difficult to sustain. Nevertheless, bound up with the framing of ecosystems as servicing humanity has been the development of valuative approaches to nature, such as TEEB (The Economics of Ecosystems and Biodiversity),[1] which attempt to demonstrate the economic value of nature. In its crudest forms (such as endeavouring to place a monetary value on a species), this can lead to unsustainable bias (Martín-López, Montes, and Benayas 2008), but it may be of use applied at an ecosystem level. It remains controversial, however, both morally and because of its questionable ability to deliver sustainable ecological benefit (Rodríguez-Labajos and Martínez-Alier 2013).

The declining salience of nature now characterizing the Anthropocene does not merely reflect a change in the perceived priorities of post-industrial humans over the past fifty years. It reflects a deeper change in human perception of life that has its roots in the development of pastoralism and agriculture some ten thousand years ago (Ingold 2022c) and the domestication of plants, animals (Ingold 2022b), and humans (Wilson 1988). Tim Ingold (2022c) draws on the work of Nurit Bird-David (1990, 1992), Colin Turnbull (1965), and others to recognize two significant shifts in human perception associated with these developments. The first is a sense of human separation from the rest of life, of "nature" as a term referring to that part of the biosphere that is not human. The very existence of such a word expresses that sense of distinction, and establishes an apparent contrast with "culture" as a discrete domain of human affairs. It is also from this contrast that Charles Darwin (1859) assumed a distinction between what he called "artificial" and "natural" selection, whether evolution occurred "artificially" through human agency or not. Indigenous forest-dwelling people have no such concept of nature since their perception of the world is founded on an *ontology of dwelling* and an understanding of their relationship with the forest to be one of mutual dependency (Ingold 2022c). The second shift in perception, characterized by Ingold (2022b) as "from trust to domination," is a belief in or assumption that life is dependent on humans, a view that might be framed as the paradigm of domestication. Having constructed nature and culture as distinct domains, the paradigm then elevates culture in significance relative to nature. Both shifted perceptions, then, which might be described as Western (Ingold 2022c), but which might be better defined as post-agrarian, underpin an assumption of human exceptionalism on which the rationale of Ecosystem Services rests. In relation to etic anthropological analysis in which these shifted perceptions are regarded as the standard to which the cultures of forest-dwelling hunters and gatherers should be compared, Ingold (2022b, 92) states,

> This strikes me as profoundly arrogant. It is to accord priority to the Western metaphysics of the alienation of humanity from nature, and to use our disengagement as the standard against which to judge their engagement. Faced with an ecological crisis whose roots lie in this disengagement, in the separation of human agency and social responsibility from the sphere of our direct involvement with the non-human environment, it surely behoves us to reverse this order of priority.

Reflecting the dissonance between epistemology and ontology that undergirds the Anthropocene, a tension remains within the conservation community between scientific and anthropocentric/economistic perceptions and approaches. Recognizing that failure to resolve this tension will lead at best to unsustainable, and at worst catastrophic, solutions, a revolution is under way in economics (Raworth 2017). In an economistic framing of environmentalism such as TEEB, therefore, we should also consider "whose" economics are involved and what are their assumptions. Into these Anthropocene debates, ethno-ornithology is emerging as a field with particular potential, for its framework considers, and seeks to reconcile, ontology with epistemologies. In relation to sustainability and conservation, its attention is focused specifically on the question of whether an anthropocentric perspective has the potential to deliver ecologically sustainable solutions and significantly reduce extinction risk. The essays in this book frame the issue succinctly in terms of "birds are good to – be with, think with, craft with."

In the introduction to this volume, Frédéric Laugrand and Scott Simon reflect on the influence of the ontological turn and ecological turn on the evolution of anthropological insight and the role of bird-human relationships in this. I suggest that the placing of humans at the centre of considerations about the health and viability of the world's ecosystems constitutes an anthropocentric turn in the development of ecology and conservation science. This may have particular significance today because of the "extinction of experience" effect, as the anthropocentric stance now appears to be the default position of people who lack direct experience of being with, and thinking with, wild birds and other animals and plants (Longbottom and Slaughter 2016). My own evidence of this is reflected in the observation that whereas a biologist might ask me, "What species of bird is that?," non-biologists tend to ask, "What breed is it?" Whether or not they know that "breed" implies a form created by humans through selective breeding (pets, crops, and livestock), the use of the word suggests that nature's diversity is somehow dependent on human intervention, as implied by the paradigm of domestication described above.

The sense of separation from reality now experienced by humans is reflected in two further and related considerations. The first is that a distinction is made between ontology and epistemology, between what really is and what we might know about it. Yet, if we believe that knowledge really exists, we must recognize that both the fruits of our epistemological investigations, reflections, and deliberations, and the process of their discovery, expressed and constrained by language, are contained within the realm of the ontological. Similarly, biologists have, until recently, implicitly (if not explicitly) excluded all things human from any definition of biodiversity, which has been taken to mean the diversity of natural, non-domesticated, species, genes, and ecosystems (see MEA 2005, Chapter 4). Reflecting a growing consensus (see Maffi 2001; Sutherland 2003) recognizing the value of Indigenous, hunter-gatherer, or pre-agrarian perceptions of, and relationships within, their environment, however, the UNEP Global Environment Outlook (GEO4) offered a significant revision to this through its landmark statement: "Biodiversity also incorporates human cultural diversity, which can be affected by the same drivers as biodiversity, and which has impacts on the diversity of genes, other species, and ecosystems" (UNEP 2007, 160). In affirming the concept of biocultural diversity, potentially as a preferable concept to biodiversity, this statement affirms the notion of biocultural conservation (Maffi and Woodley 2010), potentially as preferable to that of nature conservation. Driven by a decline in the salience of non-human life and of biocultural diversity, the extinction of experience is a symptom of the Anthropocene. Paradoxically, however, the anthropocentricity that emerges offers a new opportunity, since the paradigm of domestication and its implication that nature is dependent on humans also carries with it a sense of moral responsibility and the potential to reawaken the stewardship ethic (Berry 2006). This ethic occurs ubiquitously in various forms in Indigenous cultures and throughout the world's major religions (Gosler et al. 2013, 2022).

A major criticism of the Ecosystem Services perception of nature as developed from the Millennium Ecosystem Assessment was its unidirectional perception of relationships, in which nature was regarded as serving humanity, with no reciprocal service implied (Ninan 2009). Yet, engagement with Indigenous people has highlighted that this misconception of the ecological role and reality of (forest-dwelling) humans is itself an example of the cognitive dissonance at the heart of the Anthropocene. Anthropological, and especially ethno-biological, studies with Indigenous people have shown frequently that their presence enhanced local biodiversity.[2] Furthermore, their beneficial activities were guided by stewardship ethics embedded within a culture that was contextualized in relation to local biodiversity and ecosystems (Maffi and Woodley 2010; Tidemann and Gosler 2010; Berkes 2017). An outcome of this is the growing recognition that the places where biodiversity best persists on our planet are those managed by Indigenous people (Schuster et al. 2019) and/or those considered sacred by local people (Liljeblad and Verschuuren 2019; Gosler et al. 2022). Such insights, which implicitly challenge the human exceptionalism of Western metaphysics, have influenced the further development of the Ecosystem Services concept so that it recognizes, affirms, and seeks to enhance the reciprocal relationships through which humans serve the ecosystems in which they live (Comberti et al. 2015).

From their ability to fly, to the beauty of plumage and songs, and from the self-sacrificial devotion to their young to their extraordinary ability to navigate and migrate between distant lands, birds challenge many of our assumptions about the true nature of life (Blue 2013). Consequently, since birds are good to think with, ethno-ornithology implicitly challenges the bounded assumptions of academic disciplines founded with the assumptions of the Western or post-agrarian metaphysics and the paradigm of domestication. Of the many ways in which ethno-biology might be framed, no one could dispute that it attempts to define the cognitive space or locus at the intersection between nature, culture, and language, while challenging the existence of their dissociation. When these elements are framed as the academic disciplines of biology, anthropology, and linguistics (Figure 12.1 upper), however, the ontological balance between their essential elements may become distorted by the perceptual bias of practitioners with differing expertise (such as ornithology or linguistics) and differing epistemological cultures. Through a certain epistemological prism, anthropology and linguistics may be perceived as biology. Through another, biology and linguistics might be viewed as anthropology. Through yet a third, since our cognitive space is mediated through language, both biology and anthropology might be subsumed within linguistics (Figure 12.1 lower).

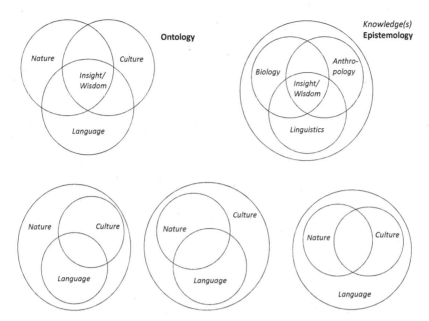

Figure 12.1 A conceptual framework for the relationship between ethno-biological epistemological components (top right) and their ontological equivalents (top left). The three circles at the bottom of the figure suggest how observer-bias due to the differential experience and priorities of practitioners within academic disciplines might distort perceptions of reality. What emerges from a balanced consideration of component disciplines, as for the engagement of ontological domains, is a revealed wisdom in the experienced world (Ingold 2022a).

Ingold (2022c) points out the incoherence of an anthropological framing of nature as a cultural construct, yet it is undeniable that post-agrarian humans perceive bio(cultural)diversity through a certain cultural prism. In seeking to rebalance these perspectives, and in recognizing the unique challenges presented by birds (suggested above), which emphasize uniquely time and space, seasonality and location, ethno-ornithology understands the cognitive locus at the intersection of nature, culture, and language, as ornithologies and knowledges or ecologies of place (Figure 12.2), resonant with Ingold's *ontology of dwelling*.

Ethno-ornithology, therefore, challenges the boundaries of academic disciplines, for although it is recognized as part of ornithology,[3] it is also part of anthropology (Andersson et al. 2011). If this categorization issue defines the challenge of doing ethno-ornithology, its strength lies in the insightful contribution that it can offer its mainstream, component, academic

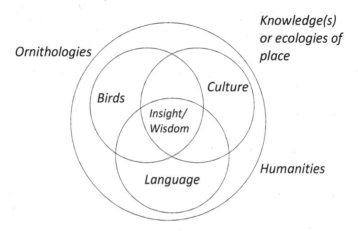

Figure 12.2 An ontological framing of ethno-ornithology defines the emergent property of the engagement between cognitive domains as knowledges or ecologies of place. The insight or wisdom revealed at the heart of this engagement corresponds to the ontology of dwelling described by Ingold (2022c).

disciplines. Whether welcome or not, ethno-ornithology contributes important insights on the nature of ornithological perceptions in areas as diverse as conservation policy (Bonta 2010), the significance of birds to conservation (Gosler and Tilling 2021), and systematics (Gosler 2017). Ethno-ornithology challenges long-held assumptions in linguistics also. Through the onomatopoeic and/or phonaesthetic nature of bird names in many languages (Berlin 2006; Park et al. 2020), ethno-ornithology challenges the presumed arbitrariness of words (Saussure 1983). In anthropology also, however, ethnoornithological analysis offers insight into long-held beliefs about the nature of human relationships with other species. As Laugrand and Simon remark in the introduction to this volume, and reflecting the post-agrarian separation of cognitive worlds into natural and cultural, Claude Lévi-Strauss (1966, 205) noted that Western societies conceived the world of birds as "a metaphorical human society." Drawing on a rather minimal set of examples, however, involving a handful of French names for birds and dogs, he concluded with a general rule: "When the relation between (human and animal) species is socially conceived as metaphorical, the relation between the respective systems of naming takes on a metonymic character; and when the relation between species is conceived as metonymic, the system of naming assumes a metaphorical character." However, a study of more than three thousand English folknames of passerine birds, collected largely during the nineteenth century, challenges this belief. Andrew Gosler and Caroline Jackson-Houlston (2012) and Andrew Gosler (2019) found that birds whose folknames included a human first or Christian name (such as Jenny Wren, Robin Redbreast, Fanny Firetail, Bessy Bluebonnet, Sally Wren, and Polly Dishwasher) were typically associated with the homestead. Their names are terms of endearment, and further analysis suggested that they may have been coined specifically to teach children about common birds. In a deferential culture in which only children or close friends were addressed by their Christian names, the implication was that this taught children to see these birds as members of the family, not metaphorically (see Ingold's remark above), but literally. Furthermore, the suggestion that the birds themselves might also be viewed as children implies a certain dependence and that we should have regard for their welfare. As this is surely a lesson that we need to learn as we travel deeper into the Anthropocene, maybe it also offers an answer to the question, "What are birds for?"

NOTES

1 For information about TEEB, see its homepage at http://teebweb.org/.
2 When this is not the case, we need to research deeply into the anthropology and history and influence of globalization to understand the present nature of entanglement (Awoyemi 2014; Pam, Zeitlyn, and Gosler 2018, 2020; Boakye, Wiafe, and Ziekah 2019).
3 The book *Ethno-ornithology: Birds, Indigenous Peoples, Culture and Society* (Tidemann and Gosler 2010) was conceived at a workshop on the subject at the 2006 International Ornithological Congress in Hamburg.

WORKS CITED

Andersson, Eugene N., Deborah M.Pearsall, Eugene S. Hunn, and Nancy J. Turner. 2011. *Ethnobiology*. Hoboken, New Jersey: Wiley-Blackwell.

Awoyemi, Stephen. 2014. "Vulture Declines in West Africa: Investigating the Scale and (Socioeconomic) Drivers of the Trade in Vulture Parts for Traditional Medicine." Placement Report, MPhil in Conservation Leadership (Examination no. 92), Department of Geography, University of Cambridge.

Berkes, Fikret. 2017. *Sacred Ecology*. 4th ed. London: Routledge.

Berlin, Brent. 2006. "The First Congress of Ethnozoological Nomenclature." *Journal of the Royal Anthropological Institute* 12, S1: S23–S44. https://doi.org/10.1111/j.1467-9655. 2006.00271.x.

Berry, Robert J. 2006. *Environmental Stewardship: Critical Perspectives, Past and Present*. London: T&T Clark.

Bird-David, Nurit. 1990. "The Giving Environment: Another Perspective on the Economic System of Gatherer-Hunters." *Current Anthropology* 31, 2: 189–96.

–. 1992. "Beyond 'the Original Affluent Society': A Culturalist Reformulation." *Current Anthropology* 33, 1: 25–47.

Blue, Debbie. 2013. *Consider the Birds: A Provocative Guide to Birds of the Bible.* Nashville: Abingdon Books.

Boakye, Maxwell K., Edward D. Wiafe, and Meyir Y. Ziekah. 2019. "Ethnomedicinal Use of Vultures by Traditional Medicinal Practitioners in Ghana." *Ostrich* 90, 2: 111–18.

Bonta, Mark. 2010. "Ethno-ornithology and Biological Conservation." In *Ethno-ornithology: Birds, Indigenous Peoples, Culture and Society,* ed. Sonia Tidemann and Andrew Gosler, 13–29. London: Earthscan.

Chivian, Eric, and Aaron Bernstein. 2008. *Sustaining Life: How Human Health Depends on Biodiversity.* New York: Oxford University Press.

Comberti, C., T.F. Thornton, V. Wyllie de Echeverria, and T. Patterson. 2015. "Ecosystem Services or Services to Ecosystems? Valuing Cultivation and Reciprocal Relationships between Humans and Ecosystems." *Global Environmental Change* 34: 247–62.

Darwin, Charles. 1859. *The Origin of Species.* London: John Murray.

Everard, Mark. 2021. *Ecosystem Services: Key Issues,* 2nd ed. New York: Routledge.

Gosler, Andrew G. 2017. "The Human Factor: Ecological Salience in Ornithology and Ethno-ornithology." *Journal of Ethnobiology* 37, 4: 637–62.

–. 2019. "What's in a Name? The Legacy and Lexicon of Birds." *British Wildlife* 30, 8: 391–97.

Gosler, Andrew G., Shonil Bhagwat, Stuart Harrop, Mark Bonta, and Sonia Tidemann. 2013. "Leadership and Listening: Inspiration for Conservation Mission and Advocacy." In *Key Topics in Conservation Biology 2,* ed. David W. Macdonald and Katherine J. Willis, 92–109. Oxford: J. Wiley and Sons.

Gosler, Andrew G., and Caroline Jackson-Houlston. 2012. "A Nightingale by Any Other Name? Relations between Scientific and Vernacular Bird Naming." British Ornithologists' Union Proceedings – Ecosystem Services: Do We Need Birds? http://www.bou.org.uk/bouproc-net/ecosystem-services/gosler&jackson-houlston.pdf.

Gosler, Andrew, Alison Ormsby, Radhika Borde, and Stephen Awoyemi. 2022. "Epilogue." In *Religion and Nature Conservation: Global Case Studies,* ed. Radhika Borde, Alison Ormsby, Stephen Awoyemi, and Andrew Gosler, 292–99. London: Routledge.

Gosler, Andrew G., and Stephen M. Tilling. 2021. "Knowledge of Nature and the Nature of Knowledge: Student Natural History Knowledge and the Significance of Birds." *People and Nature* 4, 1: 127–42. https://doi.org/10.1002/pan3.10265.

Ingold, Tim. 2022a. "Culture, Nature, Environment: Steps to an Ecology of Life." In *The Perception of the Environment: Essays on Livelihood, Dwelling and Skill,* ed. Tim Ingold, 14–30. Abingdon: Routledge.

–. 2022b. "From Trust to Domination: An Alternative History of Human-Animal Relations." In *The Perception of the Environment: Essays on Livelihood, Dwelling and Skill,* ed. Tim Ingold, 73–93. Abingdon: Routledge.

–. 2022c. "Hunting and Gathering as Ways of Perceiving the Environment." In *The Perception of the Environment: Essays on Livelihood, Dwelling and Skill,* ed. Tim Ingold, 47–72. Abingdon: Routledge.

Lévi-Strauss, Claude. 1966. *The Savage Mind,* trans. anonymous. London: Weidenfeld and Nicolson.

Liljeblad, Jonathan, and Bas Verschuuren, eds. 2019. *Indigenous Perspectives on Sacred Natural Sites: Culture, Governance and Conservation.* Abingdon: Earthscan.

Longbottom, Sarah E., and Virginia Slaughter. 2016. "Direct Experience with Nature and the Development of Biological Knowledge." *Early Education and Development* 27, 8: 1145–58. https://doi.org/10.1080/10409289.2016.1169822.

Louv, Richard. 2005. *Last Child in the Woods: Saving Our Children from Nature-Deficit Disorder.* Chapel Hill, NC: Algonquin Books of Chapel Hill.

Maffi, Luisa, ed. 2001. *On Biocultural Diversity: Linking Language, Knowledge and the Environment.* Washington, DC: Smithsonian Books.

Maffi, Luisa, and Ellen Woodley. 2010. *Biocultural Diversity Conservation: A Global Sourcebook.* London: Routledge.

Martín-López, Berta, Carlos Montes, and Javier Benayas. 2008. "Economic Valuation of Biodiversity Conservation· The Meaning of Numbers." *Conservation Biology* 22, 3: 624–35.

MEA. 2005. *Millennium Ecosystem Assessment. Ecosystems and Human Wellbeing: General Synthesis.* Washington, DC: Island Press.

Ninan, Karachepone N. 2009. *Conserving and Valuing Ecosystem Services and Biodiversity: Economic, Institutional and Social Challenges.* London: Earthscan.

Pam, Grace, David Zeitlyn, and Andrew Gosler. 2018. "Ethno-ornithology of the Mushere of Nigeria, Children's Knowledge and Perceptions of Birds." *Ethnobiology Letters* 9, 2: 48–64.

–. 2020. "Ethno-ornithology of the Mushere People of Plateau State, Nigeria: A Comparison of Traditional Bird Knowledge and Perceptions of Adult Urban/Rural Dwellers." *UNILAG Journal of Medicine, Science and Technology 8, 1: 135–59.*

Park, Karen, Felice S. Wyndham, Andrew Gosler, and John Fanshawe. 2020. "Naming, Creating a Meaningful World: Nature in Name, Metaphor and Myth." In *Creative Multilingualism, a Manifesto,* ed. Katrin Kohl, Rajinder Dudrah, Andrew Gosler, Suzanne Graham, Martin Maiden, Wen-chin Ouyang, and Matthew Reynolds, 47–69. Cambridge: Open Book.

Raworth, Kate. 2017. *Doughnut Economics: Seven Ways to Think Like a 21st-Century Economist.* London: Random House.

Rodríguez-Labajos, Beatriz Joan Martínez-Alier. 2013. "The Economics of Ecosystems and Biodiversity: Recent Instances for Debate." *Conservation and Society* 11, 4: 326–42.

Saussure, Ferdinand de. 1983. *Course in General Linguistics.* Edited by Charles Bally and Albert Sechehaye; translated and annotated by R. Harris. London: Duckworth.

Schuster, Richard, Ryan R. Germain, Joseph R. Bennett, Nicolas J. Reo, and Peter Arcese. 2019. "Vertebrate Biodiversity on Indigenous-Managed Lands in Australia, Brazil, and Canada Equals That in Protected Areas." *Environmental Science and Policy* 101: 1–6.

Soga, Masashi, and Kevin J. Gaston. 2016. "Extinction of Experience: The Loss of Human-Nature Interactions." *Frontiers in Ecology and the Environment* 14: 94–101.

Sutherland, William J.R. 2003. "Parallel Extinction Risk and Global Distribution of Languages and Species." *Nature* 423, 6937: 276–79.

Tidemann, Sonia, and Andrew Gosler, eds. 2010. *Ethno-ornithology: Birds, Indigenous Peoples, Culture and Society.* London: Earthscan.

Turnbull, Colin M. 1965. *Wayward Servants: The Two Worlds of the African Pygmies.* London: Eyre and Spottiswoode.

UNEP. 2007. "Biodiversity." In "Global Environment Outlook 4th Report – GEO4 – Environment for Development." United Nations Environment Programme. https://www.unep.org/resources/global-environment-outlook-4.

Wilson, Peter J. 1988. *The Domestication of the Human Species.* New Haven: Yale University Press.

Zalasiewicz, Jan, Mark Williams, Will Steffen, and Paul Crutzen. 2010. "The New World of the Anthropocene." *Environmental Science and Technology* 44, 7: 2228–31.

Contributors

AïKO CAPPE is an anthropologist currently doing her PhD at UCLouvain. Her master's thesis, which focused on wolves in the Yukon, dealt with the concept of animal ethnography. Her PhD project, involving a rainforest ecosystem in Tasmania, attempts to extend the ethnographic approach and tools to a greater community (that of both humans and non-humans). During the first months of her Tasmanian fieldwork, birds became significant actors in her apprehension of the forest and taught her that, from ground to canopy, everyone has a place.

ÉTIENNE DALEMANS is an anthropologist with a keen interest in sonorous environments. His research is articulated around the anthropology of the sensitive, and he is especially interested in how humans use, interpret, and shape their senses to make sense of their world. His master's thesis dealt with the sonorous interactions between birds and men in the context of southern Thailand's Red-whiskered Bulbul contests. His PhD thesis, recently completed at UCLouvain (Belgium), examined Hungarian folk dancing.

GREGORY FORTH, professor emeritus, anthropology, University of Alberta, was educated at Simon Fraser University and the University of Oxford, and is a Fellow of the Royal Society of Canada. Since 1975, he has conducted ethnographic and ethnozoological fieldwork in Indonesia, primarily on the islands of Flores and Sumba. Largely on this basis, he has published several books, including three devoted entirely or partly to local knowledge of birds – *Nage Birds* (2004), *Why the Porcupine Is Not a Bird* (2016), and *A Dog Pissing at the Edge of a Path* (2019). His latest book is *Between Ape and Human: An Anthropologist on the Trail of a Hidden Hominoid* (2022).

ANDREW G. GOSLER is a professor of ethno-ornithology at the University of Oxford. He is also a Fellow in Human Sciences at Mansfield College, teaching courses in ecology, evolution, ethnobiology, and conservation, and is research director of the Ethno-ornithology World Atlas project. A childhood fascination with birds led to degrees in environmental biology, plant taxonomy, and ornithology, and a career in ornithology. Engagement with the Human Sciences at Oxford, of which he is currently director, led to his introduction to ethno-ornithology in 2006, from which emerged the book *Ethno-ornithology: Birds, Indigenous Peoples, Culture and Society,* co-authored with Sonia Tidemann (2010), and a significant career shift.

PERRINE LACHENAL is a French social anthropologist researching in gender studies. She obtained her PhD in 2015 from Aix-Marseille University. Her dissertation addressed the gender and class dimensions of the Egyptian revolution. As a post-doc researcher for Re-Configurations (Philipps Universität Marburg, Germany), she investigated the reshaping of masculinities in the context of revolutions in Tunisia and Egypt. Working as a post-doc at UCLouvain (Belgium), she examined the ways in which birds participate in the making of gender in the Maghreb and the Middle East. She now conducts research for the French National Center for Scientific Research in Marseille.

ANTOINE LAUGRAND obtained his PhD at Laboratoire d'anthropologie prospective, UCLouvain in Belgium. His research focuses on Indigenous cosmologies and relationships with the land and the state in the Philippines. In *Des nomades à l'arrêt* (2021), he used participatory mapping to examine how the Blaan see themselves as occupants of the land. He co-edited a series of bilingual books on Indigenous knowledge in the Philippines, as well as twenty-two books in the Verbatim series (2019–20), and he has co-published articles on human-animal relations among the Blaan, Alangan, and Ibaloy peoples. His monograph *Des voies de l'ombre. Quand les chauves-souris sèment le trouble,* co-authored with F. Laugrand, was published in 2023.

FRÉDÉRIC LAUGRAND is an anthropologist, full professor at UCLouvain, and director of the Laboratoire d'anthropologie prospective, with research expertise on Indigenous cosmologies, rituals, objects, and miniatures, Christianization, and human-animal relationships in the Canadian Arctic and the Philippines. With Jarich Oosten, he co-authored *Inuit Shamanism and Christianity: Transitions and Transformations in the Twentieth Century* (2010) and *Hunters, Predators and Prey: Inuit Perceptions of Animals* (2014). He also edited two series of bilingual books on Indigenous knowledge in the Arctic and the Philippines, focusing on the Ibaloy, the Blaan, the Ayta, and the Alangan (2019). His most recent monograph, co-authored with A. Laugrand, is *Des voies de l'ombre. Quand les chauves-souris sèment le trouble* (2023).

JOHN LEAVITT teaches in the linguistic anthropology section of the Department of Anthropology at the Université de Montréal. He has done field research in the Indian Himalayas and in Ireland, and has worked on oral poetry, divine possession, comparative mythology, and the implications of language diversity (*Linguistic Relativities* 2011). He is the editor of *Poetry and Prophecy: The Anthropology of Inspiration* (1997) and *Le Mythe aujourd'hui* (2005), and is the co-translator of the new English version of Lévi-Strauss, *La Pensée sauvage*, under the title *Wild Thought* (2021). He likes to watch birds.

YI-TZE LEE, who completed his anthropology PhD in Pittsburgh in 2012, teaches in the College of Indigenous Studies at National Dong Hwa University in Taiwan. He specializes in organic farming and science and technology studies, with a focus on the Amis people, the largest Indigenous group in Taiwan. He is involved in a research project on the ritual landscape of the Indigenous peoples of Taiwan, including bird-hunting ceremonies and the use of bird parts in ritual.

GLISERIA MAGAPIN has worked for the Barangay of Loacan in the Philippines. An Ibaloy-speaker and translator, she co-organized workshops that gathered elders and youth from Upper Loacan. She also conducted interviews and recorded life stories from the elders in Tocmo, published in *Lifestories of the Ibaloy from Upper Loacan, Itogon (Philippines)* (2019). She transcribed and edited many texts that were published in the Verbatim series, and she recorded and co-edited a film titled *Késheng ja waray batbat: The Exhumation of Human Bones in an Ibaloi Community*. In 2020, she co-authored a paper titled "Exchanging with the Dead: Exhuming Human Remains among the Ibaloy of Upper Loacan (Philippines)."

ATSUSHI NOBAYASHI completed his PhD at the Graduate University for Advanced Studies in Japan in 2003 and is a professor and researcher at the National Museum of Ethnology in Osaka. An ethno-archaeologist, he specializes in human-animal relations in Indigenous Taiwan in a deep historical context well informed by field-work in contemporary communities. With publications in Japanese, English, and Chinese, he is known for his work on wild boars and on hunting cultures.

SYARUL SAKALIOU is a Mentawaian living in the village of Madobag, which is located in the Rereiket Valley, south of Siberut (Indonesia). He was fascinated by the English language from an early age, when he worked as a missionary's porter. Since then, he has developed a passion and a talent for telling the story of the *arat sabulungan* (the Mentawai way) to anyone who is interested. He contributed intensively to the research that enabled Chapter 10 to be written and is involved in the dissemination of an image of the Mentawaians that highlights the singularity of their being-in-the-world.

COLIN SCHILDHAUER is an artist. To gain a deeper understanding of his craft, he ventured outward from his California roots and ended up in Tasmania, where he acquired a master's degree in fine arts from the University of Tasmania. His master's project documented the clearcut logging that threatens the Tarkine, a rainforest in northwest Tasmania. With brush and paint, his project highlighted the contrast between the unspoiled and the clearcut areas of the Tarkine in hopes of raising awareness about the catastrophe of deforestation. Colin also spent some time in Okinawa, where he became a fascinated birder.

LIONEL SIMON is a scientific collaborator at the F.R.S.-FNRS (Fonds National de la Recherche Scientifique), as well as a lecturer at UCLouvain and the University of Brussels (Belgium). Concentrating on Colombia and Indonesia, his research encompasses Indigenous ontologies/cosmologies; the management of non-filiative dynamics, notably through the movement of goods and animals; human-animal relationships; divination and anticipation; the social, spatial, and cosmological dimensions of daily activities and of shamanic cures, marking of animals, and funerals; and the specificity of ritualized actions. He published *Écouter les résonances du monde: Rapports aux humains et aux non-humains chez Wayùu de Colombie* in 2020 and has written several articles on human-animal relationships.

SCOTT E. SIMON is a full professor at the School of Sociological and Anthropological Studies, University of Ottawa. He is the author of four ethnographies about Taiwan, where he has conducted research since 1996. He has researched human-bird relations in Truku and Seediq Indigenous communities in Taiwan since 2011, and he studied human-bird relations in Japan from 2017 to 2018. His most recent ethnography is *Truly Human: Indigeneity and Indigenous Resurgence on Formosa* (2023).

JAZIL TAMANG is an Ibaloy-speaker and translator, with a bachelor's degree in education from the University of Baguio. She co-organized various workshops in which elders and youth from Upper Loacan were gathered together. She interviewed elders in Tocmo and recorded their life stories (see *Lifestories of the Ibaloy from Upper Loacan, Itogon (Philippines),* 2019). She transcribed and edited many materials that appeared in the Verbatim series of the Presses universitaires de Louvain. She also shot and co-edited a film titled *Késheng ja waray batbat: The Exhumation of Human Bones in an Ibaloi Community.* In 2020, she co-authored "Exchanging with the Dead: Exhuming Human Remains among the Ibaloy of Upper Loacan (Philippines)."

SHUHEI UDA is an associate professor in the Department of Modern Society and Civilization at the National Museum of Ethnology (Minpaku), Osaka. He received his PhD in literature from the Graduate University for Advanced Studies in Japan.

His research focuses on ecological anthropology and environmental folklore, particularly in connection with the relationship between humans and animals in subsistence activities of Asia. Currently, he is interested in cormorant fishing, as practised in China and Japan, analyzing the subsistence strategies of cormorant fishers in the context of social and natural changes.

Index

anthropology and birds: "belief" terminology, 210, 212; birdsong and vocalizations, 9–10, 156; classification systems, 148–52; conventional and conceptual metaphors, 209–10; early studies of, 8; interpretive anthropology, 16; language of science, 120, 139, 140; structured approach, 114–15; types of ontologies, 121–22 (*see also* ontological studies); urban rooftops and the sky, 76–78, 92–93, 93n1. *See also* ethnographies and ethno-ornithologies; ontological studies

Anthus novaeseelandiae (esib bird), 190(t)

archaeology: bird-shaped artifacts, 20 (*see also* bird sculptures, Yayoi period (Japan)); ethnographic, 233–34

Archaeopteryx, 15

architectural adornments, 263–68, 264(f), 265(f); decorations, 259, 261–63, 262(f); forest replication and substitution, 260, 261, 262(f), 267–72, 269(f), 273n13, 274n20; toys for souls, 261, 267, 270

Århem, Kaj, 260

Aristophanes: *The Birds*, 208, 228

Armstrong, Edward A., 7, 15–16; *The Folklore of Birds*, 158

art in ethnography, 100(f), 106(f), 109(f), 110–13, 115–16; sharing, 113–14. *See also* ethnographies and ethno-ornithologies; Tarkine Forest (takayna)

artifacts. *See* bird sculptures *entries*

artists and illustrators of birds (list of), 6

Ashy Tailorbird *(Orthotomus rufi ceps)*, 271; kuliak (Mentawaian), 255–56

Asian Koyal or Koel, 175n17

Asquith, Pamela, 119, 120

'Attar, Farîd-Ud-Dîn, 5; *The Conference of the Birds (Mantiq ut-Tair)*, 155

Aubin-Boltanski, Emma, 85, 92

"Austronesian Worlds," ix, x

avian flu, 135; urban Egypt, 79

Balinese cockfights, 16–17, 80; cockfighting, 54, 57, 67

Baltazar, Marie, 69

bamboo partridges: feathers used, 288, 289, 293

Barbosa, Gustavo, 80

Bare-throated Whistler *(Pachycephala nudigula)*: deza kela (Nagé), 214

Barn Owl *(Tyto* spp.), 215

Bassian Thrush, 107, 108, 109(f), 111, 114, 115

Batchelor, John, 246–47

Bayat, Assef, 77–78

Béchet, Arnaud, 13

Befu, Harumi, 120–21

Bekoff, Marc, 107

Belon, Pierre: *Histoire de la nature des oyseaux*, 5

Berque, Augustin, 119, 122

"Beṛu pāko" (Kumaoni song), 159–60, 162, 175nn18–19

bestiaries, 15

biodiversity definitions, 307; academic boundaries, 210(f), 308–10, 309(f)

"Biodiversity, Local Knowledge and Zoonoses in Austronesia," x

bird banding, 124

bird behaviour: etologists, 6; humans see themselves in, 155. *See also* ethnographies and ethno-ornithologies; ornithology

bird sculptures, Mentawaian (Indonesia): "aesthetic" and "artistic" terminology, 273n17; birds in architectural adornment, 263–68, 264(f), 265(f), 273n18; as generic birds, 268, 271; inauguration ceremonies for houses, 266, 269–70, 269(f)

bird sculptures, Yayoi period (Japan): clay saw-whet owl, 238; compared to continental Asia, 248–49; description of, 235–36, 235(f)–36(f), 237, 239; distribution and morphology, 242–45, 242(f)–44(f); functions of, 20, 239–41, 248–49, 250

bird social life as model for humans, 12–13, 288. *See also* entanglement, humans and birds

bird species: "breed of" vs "species," 306–7; distinguishing species, birdwatching, 148; number of, 234

birdcages: of bulbul breeders in Thailand, 54–55, 54(f)–55(f), 56, 62, 63(f), 68; of Ibaloy, 183; models of, 68

Bird-David, Nurit, 305

birding in Japan, 118–41; animist ontology, 134, 138–39, 141n7; approach to study of, 19, 119–24; commemorating birds (kuyō), 133, 142n7; feeding of wild birds, 132–33, 135, 138; fieldwork and description processes, 118–19, 123–25; hybrids, 135, 141n8;

movement, perception, recognition, and communication, 130, 136–38, 139–41; Osaka and environs, 125–26; social distinctions (birders, non-birders, photographers), 131; speculating on avian minds, 133–34; tanchōkai (seeking birds club), 125–26, 138; Tsurumi Ryokuchi outing, 127, 128–36; Umeda Station and sparrows, 118–19; WBSJ excursions, 126–27, 128, 135–36; wildlife photographers and, 130–31

birdlore. *See* folklore/birdlore

bird-of-paradise or *simorgh*, 15

birdsong and vocalizations: acoustic community, 19, 53, 64, 98; anthropology and, 9, 10, 156; chronological signs, 228–29; disappearance of, 229; good feelings from, 202–3; knowledge and meanings of, 150, 186–87, 193, 194, 195, 196, 197(t), 198–200, 256; listening in the Tarkine, 101–2; non-referential expressive language, 156–58, 174*n*12; poetry and, 156–58; reasons for, 12, 193; regional dialects, 63; singing contests (*see* bulbul finch breeding, southern Thailand); spirits associated with, 246–47; in spiritual or metaphoric representations, 216–19; Swift Parrots of the Tarkine, 99–100, 100(f); system of divination, 150

Blaan (Philippine Indigenous group), x, 184–85, 196, 204, 255

Black Bulbul, 286

Black Drongo, 286

Black Kites (tobi), 131

Black Stork *(Ciconia nigra)*, 13

Black Woodpeckers, 247

blackbirds, 171, 199–200

Black-faced Cuckoo-shrike *(Coracina novaehollandiae)*: cio woza (Nagé), 213–14, 214(f), 219

Black-faced Spoonbills, ix

Black-naped Orioles: oriole python (Nagé), 211, 211(f)

Blainville, Henri Marie Ducrotay de, 6

Blakiston's Fish Owls, 247

boats for fishing with cormorants, 39–44, 39(f), 40(f), 42(f), 45–46. *See also* cormorants

body and embodiment: birds embody culture, 299–301; death and relationship

to birds, 192–202; experiencing the Tarkine Forest, 104, 110–11, 113; harmonies in Thai society, 72; movement, perception, recognition, and communication, 130, 136–38, 139–41, 163–67, 169–72; phenomenological focus on, 121, 126; pigeons and their breeders, 92

bokaw (hawk, Ibaloy), 183, 189, 191, 196, 197(t), 198–99

Boudreault-Fournier, Alexandrine, 204

Boutata, Seham, 84

Bowman, Chellie, 253

Brahminy Kite *(Haliastur indus)*, 221–22, 229

Bramblings (atori), 129–30, 139

British birdlore/folklore, 6–7, 155

Brown Hawk-owl *(Ninox scutulata)*, 215–16

Brown-eared Bulbuls, 118, 130

Brunois, Florence, 108

bulbul finch breeders: Adjaan Chang Pot, 53–54, 67, 72; Pee Stuart, 53, 54

bulbul finch breeding, southern Thailand: bird contest fields (sanaam kaeng nok), 57–58, 59(t)–60(t), 61, 61(f), 65–66, 68, 71(f); bird training, 55, 67–68, 69; birdcages, 54–55, 54(f)–55(f), 56, 62, 63(f), 68; contest rules and types, 58, 59(t)–60(t), 61–62, 64–67, 65(t), 69–71, 69(t), 70(t), 71(f); cost of competitions, 58, 67; entanglement/relationship, 52–54, 68–69, 72–73; gambling, 67–68; judging quality, 62, 64, 65–66, 67, 71; male culture of, 67; origins and tradition, 55–57; prizes, 66–67; sympathetic resonance, 69, 72; Tewadaa, 68, 72

bulbuls, 118, 124–25, 130, 136–37, 286

bullfighting, 54–55, 58, 67

Buryats of Siberia, 10

Camargue flamingo, 13

Canada Goose, 14

Cappe, Aïko, 19, 97–116

Carrion Crows, 129, 133

cassowary, 4, 8

Castellano, Marlene, 298

categorization: Amis bird names, 285–86; human names for typhoons and, 190–91; symbolic knowledge and, 8. *See also* taxonomies of birds

Central Himalayas. *See* Kumaon, Uttarakhand

Chaucer, Geoffrey, 159, 160, 161; *Parlement of Foules*, 155

chickens: in birdlore, 216; bred to eat, 5, 30, 78, 229, 255; cormorant breeding and, 37, 39, 46; humans as "chickens of god," 210, 223–25; omens and predictions from, 205*n*7, 213, 256–57, 257(f), 271; as pets, 205*n*5; in rituals, 184, 283; traps for wild, 205*n*4

China, cormorant fishing locations, 32, 33, 34–35, 36–37, 38, 39–44, 45(f). *See also* cormorants, fishing with

clearcutting: Tarkine Forest, 98, 103, 105–7

Clifford, James, 298

climate change. *See* Anthropocene; development, urbanization, climate change

clockwork duck, 13

cockatoos, 229

cockfighting, 16–17, 54, 57, 67; in Bali, 16–17, 80

collaborations, birds and humans. *See* entanglement, humans and birds

Common Cuckoos *(Cuculus canorus)*, 159

Common Hill Mynahs *(Gracula religiosa)*, 211(f), 218

Common Kingfishers, 130–31

Common Pochards, 135

competition animals, 54–55, 67. *See also* bulbul finch breeding, southern Thailand

condors, 13

conservation: biocultural conservation, 307–8; ethno-ornithology and, 310; "renewing relatives," 17–18, 20–21, 300; role of birding clubs, 138, 141*n*9; winter rice paddies, 137

Corbin, Alain, 71

cormorants: as ancient, 15; city birding, 129; eating of, 245; scent of, 125

cormorants, fishing with, 29–50; overview, 5, 19, 29–30, 49–50; areas studied and methods used, 32–33; autonomy and agency of relationship, 49–50; boats used for, 39–44, 39(f), 40(f), 42(f), 45–46; breeding cormorants, 36–39, 46, 47–49, 50; Chinese and Japanese compared, 30–31, 32, 47–49; cost of domesticated cormorants, 38; feeding cormorants, 37, 37(f), 39, 47, 48; gill nets, 35–36, 38, 41,

44–45, 46–47, 48, 49; map, 45(f); methods used, 33–36, 34(t); three dimensions of, 31, 31(f); throat binding, 42–43; types in China compared, 44–47, 45(f); wing clipping, 43–44, 43(f)

corvids, 151. *See also* crows; ravens

cosmologies: cosmological disorders, 190; humans, animals, and spirits, 208–9, 212–13; involving seasonal and ontological movement, 170–71, 172, 182–83, 203–4, 205 (*see also* seasonal associations); Kumaoni regional, 163–64, 172; metaphors of mythical, magical significance, 213

cowbirds: symbolism of, 155

cranes: ears of rice and, 240; eating of, 246; in Japan, 127, 138, 247; movement of, 119, 129; spring associations, 171

Cree and migratory birds, 13–14

Crested Myna (Sturnidae), 183

crows: in allegories, 155; Amis folktale, 286; bad reputation of, 159, 160–61, 229; city birds, 118, 129, 130, 135, 136, 137, 138; as conveying emotion, 158, 163, 167, 170, 171; eating of, 124, 125, 245; feeding of, 132–33, 169–70, 170–71, 172–73, 176*n*28; Ghughutiyā (festival of dove cookies), 169–70; hunting techniques, 134; Ibaloy birdlore, 205*n*8; multi-species ethics, 18; spiritual birds, 215; symbolism of, 151, 167; Yatagarasu (a giant three-legged crow), 124, 139

Crucian Carp *(Carassius langsdorfii)*, 38

cuckoos: in allegories, 155; Black-faced Cuckoo-shrike *(Coracina novaehollandiae)*, 213–14, 214(f), 219; as conveying emotion, 158, 161, 163, 167, 168; as omen, 158–59, 159–60, 161, 167, 168–69, 171; seasonal associations, 171, 175*n*16, 228–29; witch birds, 246–47. *See also* Kumaon, Uttarakhand

culture and cultures: assume radical difference, 152–53; attributing values and meanings, 130; change and evolution of, 234–35; of cormorant fishing, 32–33, 49–50 (*see also* cormorants, fishing with); cross-cultural studies, 152–54; intersubjectivity, 140–41; Japan in contrast to the West, 120, 133, 137, 138–39, 140, 141*n*2; loss of, 191, 203–4, 229–30;

sharing of thoughts, 139; social and class distinctions, 92, 94*n*5; tradition in bulbul competitions, 55–57, 63, 63(f). *See also* culture and nature; entanglement, humans and birds

culture and nature: assume radical difference, 152–53; biodiversity and biocultural diversity, 307–8; birds carry social rhythms, 204; birds embody culture, 299–301; birds' special place in metaphor, 228–29 (*see also* metaphors); boundary management, 138; "breed" vs "species," 306–7; classification systems, 150–52; knowledge of birds and, 187–88, 229–30; monotheism vs polytheism, 123–24; salience and symbolism, 150, 152, 174*n*6; salience of nature, 154, 304–6. *See also* culture and cultures; entanglement, humans and birds; ontological studies

curlew, 175*n*13

Cuvier, Georges, 6

cynegetic practices. *See* hunting of birds; rituals, hunting activities, and stories

dabaan (hawk, Ibaloy), 197(t), 198

Dalemans, Etienne, 19, 52–73, 84, 87, 114; Ayaraa (Thai name), 53

Darwin, Charles, 305

Datt, Pandit Gangā, 161

Daurian Redstarts (jōbitaki), 129–30

Dave, K.N., 159, 162

Davy, Marie-Madeleine, 12, 14–15, 184

De Tassy, Garcin: *Le langage des oiseaux,* 155

De Troyes, Chrétien: *Perceval,* 157

De Vaucanson, Jacques, 13

death and relationship to birds: goshawks and eagles as metaphoric mourners, 216, 217–20, 222–23, 225–27; in Ibaloy rituals, 192–96, 205; kites in mortuary metaphor, 219, 220–23, 225–26; metaphor and spiritual beliefs, 216–20, 225–28; predictions from movement, 197–202; Yayoi bird figures (Japan), 241

Descola, Philippe: on ontologies, 50, 121–22, 123, 124, 138–40, 141*n*2, 208–9, 267, 272*n*9, 273*n*14

Despret, Vinciane, 12, 93; *Habiter en oiseau,* 204

development, urbanization, climate change: Amis, impact/observations, 284–85, 299–301; biodiversity and biocultural diversity, 307–8; Christian missionaries, 282–83; environmental shifts, 278, 280, 285, 288–89; feather imports, 288–90; hunting of birds, 293–94, 294–97; Ibaloy, impact/observations, 189–91; Mentawaian, impact/observations, 254; Nagé, impact/observations, 229; nature's salience, 304–6; "renewing relatives," 17–18, 20–21, 300

Digard, Jean-Pierre, 80

Digging through Detritus for Insects, Bassian Thrush (Schildhauer), 109(f)

domains: birds as a, 154–55, 174*n*9; birds as guides and agents, 197–202; birds as predictors of weather, 187–91; death and relationship to birds, 192–202 (*see also* death and relationship to birds)

domestication, 305, 307

Doraï, Kamel, 78

doriyan bird (Ibaloy), 193, 197(t), 200, 201

Doupe, Allison, 63

Dove, Michael, 255

dovecotes, 78, 78(f)

doves: in allegories, 155; Amis folktales and symbolism, 286; bad reputation of, 229; as conveying emotion, 158, 161–63, 167; dove cookies (Ghughutiyā), 169–70, 171, 172–73, 176*n*27; feathers used, 289; in symbolism, 15, 102, 213; as valued, 293. *See also* pigeons; Zebra Doves

Downy Woodpeckers, 148

ducks: analogical reasoning about, 186; city ducks, 132, 134–35; eating of, 245–46; in rituals, 184; valued as migratory, 293

eagle porcupine (Nagé), 211

eagle-owl: as a deity, 247

eagles: death and metaphoric mourners, 197(t), 198, 216, 217–20, 225–27; egg symbolism, 155; extirpation of (locally), 293; feathers, 11, 245, 285, 288; kalebis (Amis), 285; as king, 9–10, 172; seasonal and weather associations, 189, 190(t), 191; spiritual birds, 215; tayaw dance (Ibaloy), 184, 191–93, 204

Eastern Spot-billed Ducks, 132, 135

"Ecological and Cultural Approaches to Taiwan and Neighbouring Islands," x

Ecosystem Services framework, 304–5, 307–8

eggs: in bird categorization, 155; Ibaloy rituals and, 193, 194

egrets, 131

emblems, birds as: in Southeast Asia, 184–85

emotions: birds as affectively charged, 158, 161–63, 167–70, 171, 173, 174*n*10, 202–3; birdsong as "emotion sentences," 156; nature of, 175*n*15

entanglement, humans and birds
—general, 20–21: approaches to studies of, 233–34; early history of, 4–5; entanglement concept (yuanfen), ix–xi, 4; ethno-ornithologies, 10; five patterns of, 31; indeterminacy approach, 298–99; studies of, 182–83; threatened and extinct species, 17–18, 97; understandings of culture, 121–23
—specific: attachment and loyalty of pigeons, 87–88; birding excursions, 135–36; bulbul breeders of southern Thailand, 52–54, 68–69, 72–73; collaborations of cormorants and fishers, 30–31; commemorating birds (kuyō), 133; construction of masculinities and, 77; contract of migratory birds, 293, 294–97; environmental shifts, 278, 280–81, 285, 288–89, 298; familiarity, 112–13; of Ibaloy, 183; interdependence/mutual, 253, 305, 307–8; intersubjectivity, birds and humans, 256–58, 257(f), 260–63, 283; learning as mutual, 104–5, 108–9, 112–13, 115–16; learning from birds, 183–84; passion of pigeon-breeders, 83–85, 86, 90; symbiotic relationships, 108; sympathetic resonance, 69, 72–73; typhoons and, 190–92
—*See also* body and embodiment; culture and cultures; culture and nature; movement, human and avian

environmental shifts: about, 278, 280; hunting of birds and, 285, 288–89. *See also* development, urbanization, climate change

ethical considerations: birding, 131; feeding of wild birds, 132–33, 135, 138; owl cafés, 124; stewardship, 307–8, 311

ethnographies and ethno-ornithologies: approaches to, 10, 18–19, 114–16, 119–24; archaeology, 233–34; assumptions and boundaries challenged, 309(f), 310, 310(f); empirical intersubjective experience, 105, 110–11, 136–38, 140–41; ethno-ethology, 108, 124; extinct and threatened species, 306; fieldwork and description processes, 32–33, 72–73, 80–81, 104, 109–13, 116*n*2, 118–19, 123–25, 148, 185, 281–82; human-animal relations, 30, 278; Irish seasonal changes, 171–72; knowledge-transfer workshops, 185–86; multispecies, 278, 283, 298–99; ontology with epistemologies, 306; ornithology, 4–6, 130, 134; painting and text in, 98, 110–16; sonorous ethnography, 19, 52, 53, 56, 64, 69, 69(t), 70–73, 70(t). *See also* anthropology and birds; ontological studies

ethologists, 6, 12

Etruscans, 5

Eucalyptus obliqua, 105, 106(f)

Eurasian Jays, 247

Eurasian Teals, 135

Eurasian Tree Sparrows, 247

Eurasian Widgeons, 135, 141*n*8

extinct and threatened species, 4, 17–18, 97, 234; ethno-ornithology's approach, 306; local extirpation, 287–88, 293, 297

Fabre, Daniel, 14; "La voie des oiseaux," 89

falcons: Falcon God (Amis), 290–92; falconry, 4–5; spiritual birds, 215

feathers: in bird categorization, 154; ceremonial use of, 228; symbolism of, 278, 288; takal headdress (Amis), 280, 285, 287–88, 288(f), 289, 292, 295, 295(f), 297, 298, 300, 301*n*4

feeding birds: cormorants for fishing, 37, 37(f), 39, 47, 48; crows, 132–33, 169–70, 170–71, 172–73, 176*n*28; of wild birds in Japan, 132–33, 135, 138

Feld, Steven, 9, 108, 156, 204; *Sound and Sentiment,* 98

fishing. *See* cormorants, fishing with

flight: aviation imitating birds, 13; in bird categorization, 154, 174*n*9; birds' ability, 102–3; in rituals, 192, 287; symbolism and, 213, 228, 283

Flores Crow *(Corvus florensis),* 215

folklore/birdlore: overview, 4–16, 5, 7, 20; Amis bird names and myths, 285–86; birds as a domain, 155–56, 174n9; categorization and, 8, 154–56; contrasting meanings, 149–52; cuckoos in, 158–60, 167; doves in, 15, 102, 155, 161–63, 167; interconnected web of life, 103; literature and, 6–7, 155–56; owls in, 149; Saim's (when the world stops turning), 165, 167; seasonal changes, 167–72. *See also* rituals, hunting activities, and stories

food, birds as: in bird categorization, 155; categories of animals used for, 30; characteristics passed through, 186; crows, 124, 125; Ibaloy, 183, 186, 189, 192, 202, 203, 204; in Jomon and Yayoi periods, Japan, 236, 245–46, 250; Nagé, 228; reciprocal labour and (Amis), 293–97, 298; shrike, 286. *See also* rituals, hunting activities, and stories

Forth, Gregory, 8, 20, 204, 208–30, 212, 255

France: list of historical ornithologists, 6; wren birdlore/folklore, 7

Frazer, James, 209

Frederick II: *De arte venandi cum avibus*, 5

friarbird: temporal processes and, 204

fūdo concept (Watsuji), 234–35

Fuentes, Agustin, 31

game cuisine, 124–25, 133, 134

Gaozhuang, Huaiyin City, Jiangsu Province, 248

Gaurdā (Kumaoni poet): "Praise of the Rainy Season" *(Cāturmāsya mahimā)*, 168

Geertz, Clifford: cockfight study, 16–17

geese: eating of, 245–46; use of goose quills, 289

Gessner, Conrad, 5

"Ghughuti na bāsa" (Little Dove, Don't Sing), 162–63

Giant Eagles, 293

glass/window collisions, 134

goatsuckers: witch birds, 246–47

goldfinch keeping in Algeria, 84–85

Gopāl Bābū Gosvāmī: "Ghughuti na bāsa" (Little Dove, Don't Sing), 162–63

goshawks: metaphoric mourners, 216, 217–20, 222–23

Gosler, Andrew G., xi, 10, 18, 20, 310–11

Gourou, Pierre, 5

Goushegir, Aladin, 80

Great Cormorants *(Phalacrocorax carbo)*, 36. *See also* cormorants

Great Egrets, 131

Greater Coucal *(Centropus sinensis)*, 271; kemut (Mentawaian), 255–56

Greater Pied Kingfishers, 247

grebe: eating of, 245

Green Rosellas, 103–4, 109, 115

Grey Herons, 131, 132, 136

Grey Wagtail, 186

Grimm fairy tales, 172

gulls, 14; city birding, 129

Hacking, Ian, 69

Hairy Woodpeckers, 148

Handbook of the Birds of the World, 7, 21n3

Hani ethnic group (China), 249

Haraway, Donna, 120

Hat Yai, Thailand, 19, 52–73; bird contest fields (sanaam kaeng nok), 57–58, 59(t)–60(t), 61, 61(f), 65–66, 68, 72; birdcage styles, 68. *See also* bulbul finch breeding, southern Thailand

hawks: bokaw (Ibaloy), 183, 189, 191, 196, 197(t), 198–99; dabaan (Ibaloy), 197(t), 198; feathers for arrows, 245; spiritual birds, 215

heating/cooling idioms (Kumaoni), 164–67, 169–70

Heidegger, Martin, 121

Hermit Thrush: in poetry, 174n12

herons, 129, 131, 132–33, 286, 293

Hertz, Robert, 7, 14

Himalayas. *See* Kumaon, Uttarakhand

Hirayama, Kana, 239–40, 241, 242–43

Hitchcock, Alfred: *The Birds* (film), 14

Hokkaido, Japan: map, 2(f). *See also* Ainu people, Hokkaido, Japan

hoopoes *(Upupa epops)*, 5; in *The Birds* (Aristophanes), 208–9

hornbills, 11, 261

Horned Larks, 150–51

Horstmann, Alexander, 56

horticulture. *See* agricultural and horticultural traditions

Hoshino, Fumihiro: *yamabushi* master, 123, 139, 140

howacuko (wagtail, Amis), 285–86

human exceptionalism, 17–18
human-bird communication: desire for by
humans, 3–4
"Human-Bird Entanglements in the
Pacific Anthropocene," x
Hunt the Wren, 7
hunter-gatherers: nature and culture, 305–
6. *See also* Ainu people, Hokkaido, Japan
hunting of birds: environmental shifts
and, 255, 285, 288–89; Ibaloy techniques,
183; intersubjectivity in hunting practices, 260–63, 270–72, 273n14, 293–97;
resource management and, 258–59, 270;
teker and reintegration ritual, 290–92,
290(f), 292–94, 292(f); traps, types of,
205n4, 290–91, 290(f), 294(f). *See also*
rituals, hunting activities, and stories
hybrids: birding in Japan, 135, 141n8; as
monsters, 173n1; as rare, 148

Ibaloy (Philippine Indigenous group):
overview, 183, 203–5, 205n6; analogical
reasoning of, 186–87; bird sounds, 186,
192, 193, 194, 195, 196, 197(t), 198–200,
202–3; climate change observations,
189–91; death and spirits, 191–94, 196,
197(t), 200–1, 205; eating of birds, 183,
186, 189, 192, 202, 203, 204, 205n4;
fieldwork and description process, x,
19–20, 185; guides and agents, birds as,
194, 197–202; knowledge from birds,
183–84; knowledge-transfer workshops,
185–86; map, 2(f); omens and predictions from birds, 194–96, 197(t), 198–
202, 204–5, 205n7, 255; temporality and
social rhythms, 204–5; value of birds,
203–5; weather predictors, birds as,
187–91, 188(t), 190(t)
Ibaloy elders: Lola Alice, 191, 199–200;
Lola Apolonia (elder from Sabkil),
186–87; Lola Augustina Etop, 188; Lola
Julie, 203; Lola Marcial Monang, 196;
Lola Margarita (elder from Tolibeng),
184, 187, 195–96, 199; Lola Rosita, 195;
Lola Tarcela, 191; Lolo Edward (shaman),
184, 188–89, 190–91, 194–95, 198, 199,
200–2; Lolo Melanio (elder from
Anteg-in), 184, 186, 191–92, 193, 200;
Lolo Nardo (elder from Tolibeng),
183–84, 186, 189, 195, 198, 202–3

Imanishi, Kinji, 119–20
Indian Cuckoos *(Cuculus micropterus)*,
159–60, 175n17
Indian Himalayas. *See* Kumaon,
Uttarakhand
Indian Spot-billed Ducks, 135
Indonesia. *See* Mentawaians of Indonesia;
Nagé of Flores Island, Indonesia
Indo-Pacific: overview, 18; human societies
of, ix; map, 2(f); Yayoi bird carving
sites, 242(f)
Ingold, Tim, 119, 121–23, 138, 140, 305–6,
309
Innes, Michael: *Hare Sitting Up*, 147
integration, birds and humans, 31. *See also*
entanglement, humans and birds
Intermediate Egrets, 131
interpretive anthropology, 16. *See also*
anthropology and birds
Inuit: preservation of birds, 17; rituals,
hunting activities, and stories, 9, 10,
13–14
Ireland: birds and seasons, 171–72
Isle of Man, 7
Izumi Plain, Kyushu, 119

Jabal Hussein (Palestinian refugee camp), 84
Jackson-Houlston, Caroline, 18, 310–11
jadjaran bird (Ibaloy), 188–89, 188(t), 190(t),
191–92, 197(t)
Jakobson, Roman, 209
Japan: aimai (ambiguity or vagueness),
123–24, 135, 139, 140; birds of Hokkaido,
247; in contrast to Western discourses,
120, 133, 137, 138–39, 140, 141n2; cormorant *(ukai)* fishing, 30–31, 32, 47–49,
124 (*see also* cormorants, fishing with);
Descola's ontologies and, 122; expressions of culture of, 140; monotheism
vs polytheism, 123–24; sense of nature,
119–20. *See also* birding in Japan; Jomon
and Yayoi periods (Japan) compared;
Osaka, Japan
Japanese Cormorant *(Phalacrocorax
capillatus)*, 48
Japanese Cranes, 247
Japanese Tits, 128, 132, 136
Japanese White-eyes, 132
Java Sparrow, 142n7
Jerolmack, Colin, 127

Leavitt, John, 19, 147–73, 203
Lee, Yi-tze, x, 20, 277–301
Legrain, Laurent, 69
Lévi-Strauss, Claude, 8, 11, 18–19, 173*n*5, 233, 310; "Entre Marx et Rousseau," 3, 21*n*1; *The Naked Man*, 3; *Totemism*, 151–52; *Wild Thought*, 147, 150–52
Lilienthal, Otto: *Birdflight as the Basis of Aviation*, 13
Linnaeus, Carl, 6, 234
Lloyd, Geoffrey, 208
Long-tailed Shrike, 286, 293
Longtailed Tits, 132
Louv, Richard: *Last Child in the Woods*, 303

Magapin, Gliseria, 19–20, 182–205, 185
Malaysia: birdsong competitions, 66
male culture: adaptation of, 298; of bulbul breeders of Thailand, 67; expressions of affection, 84–85, 86; Falcon God (Amis), 290–92; initiation ceremonies, 281, 283, 287–92, 288(f), 292(f), 299, 301*n*9; kashshāsh (pigeon-breeders) of Middle East, 76–77, 79–80, 85, 88, 92–93; takal headdress (Amis), 280, 285, 287–90, 288(f), 292, 295, 295(f), 297, 298, 300, 301*n*4
Malinowski, Bronislaw, 233
Mallards, 132, 135, 136
Mandarin Ducks (oshidori), 134–35
maps: cormorant fishing, 45(f); Lidlaw and environment (Amis), 282(f); regions discussed, 2(f); Yayoi bird carving sites, 242(f)
Martinez, Dolores P., 120
martinez bird (Ibaloy), 183, 197(t)
Mathevet, Raphaël, 13
Mauss, Marcel, 16, 204
Mentawaians of Indonesia: overview, 20, 254–55; birds in architectural adornment, 263–68, 264(f), 265(f), 273*n*18; chicken and pig intersubjectivity, 256–58, 257(f); forest replication and substitution, 260, 261, 262(f), 267–72, 269(f), 273*n*13, 274*n*20; household well-being, 266–68; hunting practices, 258–63, 260(f), 262(f), 269–72, 272*n*3, 273*n*13; omens and predictions from birds, 255–56; post-hunt adornments, 259, 261–63, 262(f), 269–72, 273*n*16, 274*n*21; toys for souls, 261, 267, 270

—Elders and shamans: Aman Naru, 257(f), 266, 274*n*21; Salomo, 258, 273*n*16; Teorepako, 268
Merleau-Ponty, Maurice: bird observations, 129; *Phenomenology of Perception*, 19, 118, 120, 121, 126, 130, 136–37, 138, 140, 141*n*2
metaphors: in bird naming systems, 216–18; birds' special place in, 228; chronological signs, 228–29; conventional and conceptual, 209–10, 226, 228; eagles as mourners, 216, 217–20, 225–27; kites as soul (mortuary metaphor), 219, 220–23, 225–26; metaphorical naming systems, 11, 216–20, 224, 310–11; number of animal (Nagé), 210–13; owls in, 215–16; prosody and birds' names, 216–20, 222–23, 224, 229–30; sea fowls and mourning, 223–25; spiritual birds in, 213–16, 220. *See also* language and linguistics; symbolism (birds)
Miao people, 248–49
Middle Eastern urban subalternity, 93*n*1; rooftops, 77–79, 92–93. *See also* pigeon breeding in Amman, Jordan
migratory birds: contract made with people, 293–94; in cormorant fishing, 48; cranes, 119, 240; cuckoos, 228–29; East Asian–Australasian Flyway, 18; endangered species, 97; environmental shifts and, 285; hunting societies and, 13–14; rice paddies, 137, 240; through Osaka, Japan, 126
Mizuno, Masayoshi, 241
moorhens, 293
Moss, Charles, 183
Motacilla cinerea (jadjaran bird), 190(t)
Mourning Dove, 161
movement, human and avian, 119, 137–38, 163–67, 169–72, 176*n*24; bird movement and seasons, 188, 188(t); bird movement as omens, 197–202, 197(t), 198, 241; temporality, 204. *See also* entanglement, humans and birds; migratory birds
museum curation, 294–97, 299
music and ethnographic description, 110
musicates ("musiquer"), 69, 72
mynahs, 229
myths. *See* rituals, hunting activities, and stories

orchids, 152

Oriental Greenfinches, 129

oriole python (Nagé), 211, 211(f)

ornithology: in amateur birding excursions, 130; bird minds, 134; historic figures of (list of), 6; history of, 4–6; naturalists and bird specialists (list of), 6. *See also* ethnographies and ethno-ornithologies

ornithophobia, 14

Osaka, Japan: ecology and bird diversity of, 125–26; Ikegamisone excavation site, 237, 240; map, 2(f), 242(f); Umeda Station and sparrows, 118–19; wartime history of, 127–28, 141*n*5. *See also* birding in Japan

ot-ot (Zebra Dove, Ibaloy), 186, 187, 197(t), 200

owls: akop (Ibaloy), 186, 197(t), 199, 200–1; as deities, 247; in folk song, 155; of Hokkaido, 247; Nagé metaphors of, 215–16; owl cafés, 124; in rituals, hunting activities, and stories, 8; saw-whet owl clay figure, 238–39; silent flight of, 13; symbolisms of, 149, 173*n*4; witch birds, 246–47

painting and text in ethnography, 98, 110–13, 115–16; sharing, 113–14

Pale Thrushes, 132

paleontology, 15

Palmatier, Robert, 210

Pant, S.D., 169

Papua New Guinea, 4, 5, 8, 9, 92, 182, 184, 204; Kasua people of, 108

parakeets, 155, 163

parasitic birds: crows in birdlore/folklore, 159; cuckoos, 159

passerines: breeding of, 56–57 (*see also* bulbul finch breeding, southern Thailand)

penguin, 13

Penguin Book of Bird Poetry, 156–57

Persian poetry, 155

Peters, James Lee, 6

petrels: eating of, 245

pheasants: Amis rituals, symbolism, names for, 283, 285, 286, 287; eating of, 245–46; feathers used, 280, 285, 288–89, 301*n*4

Phenomenology of Perception (Merleau-Ponty), 19, 118, 121–22

Philippine Indigenous groups (Alangan Mangyan and Blaan), x, 184–85, 196, 204, 255. *See also* Ibaloy (Philippine Indigenous group)

Philippine quail (ngoweg), 186, 193

phylogeny, 6–8

Picasso, Pablo, 102

Pied Triller, 184, 186–87, 189

Piessat, Marie, 78

pigeon breeding in Amman, Jordan, 76–93; accessories, 85–86, 86(f); attachment and loyalty of pigeons, 87–88; cleanliness, 89–90; entanglement/relationships, 19, 83–85, 86; fieldwork preparation, 80–81; game, war, or sport, 79; knowledge of pigeons, 89; masculine sexualities and, 85; pigeon care, 85–86; reputation of, 79–80, 88–91, 91–92, 94*n*4; rooftop dovecotes, 78, 78(f); rooftop interviews, 82, 82(f); selling of pigeons, 83, 85, 91; women's role, 93

—pigeon-breeders (kashshāsh): Abu Abdullah, 84, 85, 87, 89; Abu Shadi, 78, 78(f), 82(f), 83, 87–89, 91, 93; Lila Abu-Lughod, 84–85; Nasser al-Hindi, 90, 93; Bilal, 84, 88; Hamdi, 84

pigeons: city birds, 128, 134–35, 136, 138; in Nagé mortuary metaphors, 224–25; temporal processes and, 204; as valued, 293. *See also* doves; pigeon breeding in Amman, Jordan

pitpit bird (Ibaloy), 195, 197(t), 201–2

Plum-headed Parakeet (*Psittacula cyano-cephala*), 163

poetry: birdsong and, 156–58; expressions of affection, 84–85

poultry, 5

Poyang Lake, Jiangxi Province: map, 2(f)

Puig, Nicolas, 78

qadis, or Mountain Hawk-eagle (*Nisaetus nipalensis*), 11

quails, 124–25, 293

rainforest. *See* Tarkine Forest (takayna)

Rāmāyaṇa (Vālmīki), 157–58, 175*nn*13–14

Rappaport, Roy, 284–85

raptors, 301*n*2. *See also individual species*

ravens: in rituals, hunting activities, and stories, 10; symbolisms of, 151; winter associations, 171

110–16; sounds while painting, 103, 111–12; Swift Parrots, 97, 99–100, 100(f), 109, 111; watching and being watched, 104–7, 112; Wedge-tailed Eagles, 114
—Aïko Cappe: "I can hear some birds," 101–2; "I met a group of Green Rosellas," 103–4, 115; "ready to reveal ourselves to each other," 112; "when the forest opens doors," 104; "Yellowtailed Black Cockatoo party," 107

Tasmania. See Tarkine Forest (takayna)

Tasmanian tiger (thylacine), 105

taxonomies of birds: Amis bird names, folklore, myths, 285–86; birds as a domain, 154–56, 174n9; classification systems, 138, 148–50; human names for typhoons and, 190–91; radical difference, 152; symbolic knowledge and, 8; Tarkine perspective, 107–8, 114–15

Taylor, E.B., 208–9

TEEB (The Economics of Ecosystems and Biodiversity), 305, 306

Thailand: animals as part of life, 54–55; bird-breeding areas, 57. See also bulbul finch breeding, southern Thailand; Hat Yai, Thailand

thrushes, 155, 174n12, 229

Tidemann, Sonia, 10

tigwi (White-bellied Sea Eagle, Ibaloy), 189, 190(t), 191, 197(t), 198

Tilling, Stephen, 304

tilu (Long-tailed Shrike, Amis), 286

tits, 132

tolatolaw (dove, Amis), 286

tolok (pheasant, Amis), 285

totemism: "animals are good to think," 18–19, 151; barriers between species and, 11; eating birds and, 155; images of totems, 248; metaphoric relations and, 209–10, 211; swan as totem, 10; terminology, 121–22, 267. See also ontological studies

traditional futures, 298. See also environmental shifts

Tremblay, Guy, 255

Tsurumi Ryokuchi Park, 127, 128–36. See also birding in Japan

Tufted Ducks, 135

Turnbull, Colin, 305

Turner, Victor, 226

Turner, William, 5

turtledoves, 155

typhoons, 188–90, 190(t), 191–92, 203–4; with people's names, 190–91

Uda, Shuhei, 5, 19, 87

Umwelt, 115, 116n1, 122, 132

UNEP Global Environment Outlook, 307

Ural Owls, 247

urban anthropology: rooftops and the sky, 76–78, 92–93, 93n1. See also pigeon breeding in Amman, Jordan

urbanization. See development, urbanization, climate change

Uttarāyaṇa (seasonal celebration), 169–70

Vālmīki: Rāmāyaṇa, 157–58

Van Dooren, Thom: Flight Ways, 4, 17–18; The Wake of Crows, 4, 18, 138

Van Gennep, Arnold, 291

Varied Tits, 132

Vedism/Vedicism, 156

Vietnamese Pheasant, 288–89

vocalizations. See birdsong and vocalizations

Von Uexküll, Jakob: Umwelt theory, 115, 116n1, 122–23, 132, 134, 136, 139–40

vultures, 18; egg symbolism, 155

Wada, Kan, 248

Wagner, Wilfried, 265–66

wagtails, 132, 285–86; predictors of weather, 188–89, 188(t)

Watanabe, Makoto, 241

Watsuji, Tetsurō: Climate and Culture (Fūdo), 120; fūdo concept, 234–35

WBSJ. See Wild Bird Society of Japan (WBSJ)

weather predicting, 187–91, 188(t), 190(t). See also seasonal associations

Wedge-tail Vigil (Schildhauer), 106(f)

Wedge-tailed Eagles, 105–7, 108, 114

White-bellied Green Pigeons, 134

White-bellied munia, 183–84

White-bellied Sea Eagle: tigwi (Ibaloy), 189, 190(t), 191, 197(t), 198, 204

White-breasted Sea Eagle (Haliaeetus leucogaster), 220

White-headed Kite (jata ulu bha), 222

Whitman, Walt: "When Lilacs Last in the Dooryard Bloomed," 174n12
"Who Killed Cock Robin?," 155
Whyte, Kyle, 300
Wikipedia: "Beṛu pāko" (song), 160
Wild Bird Society of Japan (WBSJ): birding events, 118, 124, 125, 126–27, 135–36; ethics of birding, 131; tanchōkai (seeking birds club), 125, 138; Tsurumi Ryokuchi Park excursions, 127–36
wilderness, degradation of, 98–99. *See also* development, urbanization, climate change
Wildlife Conservation Act, Taiwan, 293, 297, 301
wildlife photographers, 130–31
Williams, Dai, 247
Willughby, Francis (with John Ray): *Ornithologiae libri tres,* 5–6
woodpeckers, 13, 131, 148; symbolisms of, 151; witch birds, 246–47
working class: Middle Eastern urban subalternity, 77–80 (*see also* pigeon breeding in Amman, Jordan)

wrens: in birdlore/folklore, 7, 155, 177n31; in Hokkaido, 247; midwinter rituals, 171–72
Wyndham, John: *The Midwich Cuckoos,* 159

Xiaotingia zhengi, 15

Yachō (Wild Birds) journal, 125, 141n4
Yamada, Yasuhiro, 241
Yamashina Institute for Ornithology, 125
Yatagarasu (a giant three-legged crow), 124, 139
Yayoi period. *See* Jomon and Yayoi periods (Japan) compared
Y-bird birding (outfitter), 124
Yeats, William Butler: "Cuchulain Comforted," 174n12
Yellowtailed Black Cockatoos, 107, 109
yuanfen (entanglement), ix–xi

Zebra Doves: breeding and competing of, 54, 56, 57, 67; ot-ot (Ibaloy), 186, 187, 197(t), 200

Printed and bound in Canada by Friesens

Set in Myriad and Garamond by Artegraphica Design Co. Ltd.

Copy editor: Deborah Kerr

Proofreader: Caitlin Gordon-Walker

Indexer: Mary Newberry

Cartographer: Eric Leinberger

Cover designer: George Kirkpatrick

Cover image: Artwork by Virginie Gilbert